FIGHTING IRISH

FIGHTING IRISH

The Irish Regiments in the
First World War

GAVIN HUGHES

MERRION
PRESS

First published in 2015 by Merrion Press
8 Chapel Lane
Sallins
Co. Kildare

© 2015 Gavin Hughes

British Library Cataloguing in Publication Data
An entry can be found on request

978-1-78537-022-9 (Paper)
978-1-78537-023-6 (Cloth)
978-1-78537-024-3 (PDF)
978-1-78537-049-6 (Epub)
978-1-78537-050-2 (Mobi)

Library of Congress Cataloging in Publication Data
An entry can be found on request

The...business of a general is to kick away the ladder behind soldiers when they have climbed up a height... he drives his men now in one direction, then in another, like a shepherd with a flock of sheep, and no-one knows where he is going. To assemble the army and throw it into a desperate position is the business of the general.

Sun Tzu, *The Art of War*, 'The Nine Varieties of Ground'

... Colonel Blimp has never lived, yet all the world knows he is dying. He had all the canine virtues. He was honest and brave and steadfast. He never intentionally let a man or woman down. Let this be his epitaph.

'*The Life and Death of Colonel Blimp*' [1943],
Michael Powell and Emeric Pressburger

Contents

List of Plates and Maps

1. 'A Little British Army Goes a D – Long Way', postcard c.1914, Regent Publishing Co. Ltd.
2. 8th King's Royal Irish Hussar captures a valuable prisoner, postcard, G & D London.
3. Unknown Corporal (a musketry instructor and marksman), c. 1914, 4th Royal Irish Dragoon Guards. (Author's Collection)
4. 'The *River Clyde* after the landing taken from V Beach 3 May 1915 Gallipoli'. (Author's Collection)
5. 2nd Royal Irish Fusiliers, Waiting for signal to attack' - a familiar site for Irish regiments from Macedonia, Mesopotamia and Palestine. (Author's Collection)
6. 'The Soldiers' Rendezvous, Dublin No. 3', postcard, Lilywhite Ltd. Halifax.
7. (12th and 5th Royal Irish) Lancers on patrol, Dublin, Easter 1916, Contemporary Print. (Author's Collection)
8. Stretcher Bearers at the Ancre, on the Somme, July 1916. (Author's Collection)
9. View of German lines from 36th (Ulster) Division's lines at Thiepval Wood. (Photo by Gavin Hughes)
10. 10th Royal Inniskilling Fusiliers ('The Derrys') on the Western Front with their battalion mascot 'Billy the Skin' (a goat in a tin hat), *The War Illustrated*, 16 March 1918, No. 187.
11. 2nd Royal Irish Fusiliers, Palestine, 'Wounded being evacuated' - of interest are the troops in the distance wearing steel shell helmets. (Author's Collection)
12. Cpl. Michael O'Leary, VC, Irish Guards, *The War Illustrated*, 28 July 1917 (pp.59-60).
13. Capt. George Averill Read, 7th Leinsters, killed in action, *The War Illustrated*, 5 May 1917 (p.132).
14. Pvt. John Cunningham VC, 2nd Leinsters, *The War Illustrated*, 30 June 1917 (p.133).
15. Capt. Herbert B. Mollman, 7th Leinsters, killed in action, *The War Illustrated*, 5 May 1917 (p.131).

16. Capt. Harry A.V. Harmsworth, MC, Irish Guards, *The War Illustrated*, 2 March 1918 (p.218).
17. Lieut. Eustace E. Hyde, 1st Royal Irish Fusiliers, killed in action, *The War Illustrated*, 5 May 1917 (p.127).
18. Major W. Redmond MP, 6th Royal Irish Regt, killed in action.
19. Pvt. James Duffy, VC, 6th Royal Inniskilling Fusiliers.
20. Lieut. George Haire, 6th Connaught Rangers, killed in action, *The War Illustrated*, 10 March 1917 (p.129).
21. Lieut. James S. Emerson VC, 9th Royal Inniskilling Fusiliers, *The War Illustrated*, 9 March 1918 (p. 149).
22. Lt-Col. A.D. Murphy DSO, MC, killed in action, *The War Illustrated*, 8 December 1917 (p.146).
23. Sgt. James Ockenden, VC, 1st Royal Dublin Fusiliers, *The War Illustrated*, 1 Dec. 1917 (p.143).
24. Plaque on the 16th (Irish) Division Cross, Guillemont. (Photo by Gavin Hughes)
25. The Ulster Tower Memorial, Thiepval. (Photo by Gavin Hughes)
26. Original wooden 16th (Irish) Divisional Cross, c. 1917, War Memorial Gardens, Islandbridge, Dublin. (Photo by Gavin Hughes)
27. Unknown Irish regimental casualty, Connaught Cemetery, Thiepval. (Photo by Gavin Hughes)

Map 1: The Anzac-Suvla Area
Map 2: The Western Front and the Armistice Line
Map 3: Battles of Gaza

Acknowledgements

In autumn 1992, I started my initial Great War research by making copious notes in my study bedroom in Mr and Mrs Davies' attic at 'Tyr Y Fran', Lampeter, Wales. Over the following years, I diverted my attentions to concentrate on the Ulster regiments, but I still couldn't help the notion of attempting my own wider version of the Irish regimental story at some point. The years passed, the research continued and the task remained incomplete. At times, this book has had all the hallmarks of being, in my wife's words, the 'difficult second album'. Yet, it has been none the less rewarding for it. Indeed, it has been a privilege to try and tell the gallant and humbling story of the men who made up the Irish regiments.

Along the way, I have been helped by many colleagues and friends who have given me ample time and generous support; not least Professor Keith Jeffery, Queen's University of Belfast whose scholarship and encouragement is always an inspiration. Similarly, I would like to thank Conor Graham, Lisa Hyde and everyone at Irish Academic Press/Merrion, for their valued experience, suggestions, timely interventions and, above all, patience and good humour.

Equally patient and helpful have been the staff at the National Archives (Kew), PRONI (Belfast), the National Army Museum (Chelsea), the Imperial War Museum and the National Museum (Collins Barracks), Dublin, the Main Libraries at Trinity College Dublin and University College Dublin. My thanks must also be extended to Andrew Dennis, Assistant Curator, RAF Museum (London), Lauren Newell, Mourne Roots (Kilkeel) and my friends at the Military History Society of Ireland (*The Irish Sword*) and the Military Historical Society (London); in particular, Dr Kenneth Fergusson, Colonel Tim Wright and Lieutenant-Colonel Bob Wyatt, who have always provided me with much appreciated interest over the years. Likewise, my appreciation goes to the late Professor Richard Holmes for early inspiration and the late Mr Hugh Rice for his infectious enthusiasm regarding Irish military matters.

In a similar vein, my sincere thanks go to Susan Lovell, Deirdre Devlin and Mike Edgar at BBCNI, for simply having faith in a short mischievous military historian; likewise, for all their friendship and support, David Truesdale, Professor Sarah Alyn Stacey, head of the Centre for Medieval and Renaissance Studies (TCD); Dr Tony Pollard (Glasgow University), Damian Shiels (Rubicon Heritage) and Dr Laura McAtackney. Considerable recognition is also due to Dr David and Mrs. Naina Cheetham, Dr Gerald Morgan (whose championing of Irish soldiers at Gallipoli is long-standing), Kevin Myers (whose determined championing of Irish soldiers in general is equally laudable), Neill and Andrea Scott, Michael Glendinning, Nigel McFadzean, Stanley Wedlock and Dan Steele. Equally, my gratitude goes to Heather Montgomery (QUB/Somme Association), Martin Brown and Jon Price (No Man's Land), John Winterburn (Arab Revolt Project: University of Bristol) and Jonty Trigg for keeping me posted on Great War conflict archaeology with expertise and friendly guidance over the years. In this respect, I'd like to thank Michael Tumelty, Helen Toland and Alison Finch at BBC Radio Ulster, for letting me loose at Warrenpoint and Kilkeel. Similarly, to all at 360 Productions, Sophie Maunter, John Carlin, Chris Nikkel, Brian Martin and Eádoin Heggarty for our poignant Islandbridge excursion; and Ed Hart, Mark McCauley, Eamon McKenna, Matt Gamble, Rod and Jackie Bedford, for helping me to return in one piece from my misadventures on the Somme. I also learnt that hundred-year-old cordite will still ignite wonderfully.

Finally, I am continuously indebted to my family for their unswerving support and help; to Liz, Catherine, Mum and Dad — who also, when reading through the final draft, saved me from a comedy mis-spelling of 'charnel house'; which may have actually added a bit of much needed pace to the text if I'd left it in. To Liz, the cricket bits are for you and, to Catherine, I'm sorry but the bits about pirates may have to wait until next time.

Preface

'From first blood to last man'

On 22 August 1914, on the Soignies road, 'C' Squadron of the 4th (Royal Irish) Dragoon Guards encountered a small German cavalry patrol and attempted to ambush it. The Germans, however, turned back, forcing one British trooper, Corporal Edward Thomas, to open fire on them. These are considered to have been the first British shots of the First World War. Shortly afterwards, Captain Hornby, commanding 'C' Squadron, charged down the lane, sabre drawn. He is believed to have been the first Briton to draw blood in the Great War.

The 4th Dragoon Guards were maintaining an older Irish military tradition of Crown Service and the county regiments from Ireland had a long and proud history in the British Army. In short, the story of the Irish regiments was, and largely still is, interwoven with the story of Britain's wars. When war broke out, the six cavalry regiments, eight infantry regiments and one Guards regiment on the Irish Establishment of the British Army were all scattered throughout the world. Over the course of the following four years they fought in one of the greatest—and most destructive wars—in which humanity has ever engaged. If ever there was a stereotypical image of the First World War, it must surely be that of rain-soaked, mud-clad soldiers in the trenches of the Western Front. Yet, it could equally be an image of the hellish conditions faced by soldiers surrounded by dust, flies, dysentery and shrapnel on the Gallipoli peninsula or the freezing nights in shallow slit trenches across Macedonia or the Holy Land. As the *Daily Telegraph* memorably commented on 18 March 1916 (just before the Dublin Rising and the Somme battles), many of the country's foes had already '...felt Irish steel and fallen under Irish bullets'.

Finally, after years of war and horror, on the morning of 11 November 1918, at around 9.30 am, a cavalry patrol from the 5th Royal Irish Lancers was scouting woods by Mons where, four years earlier, they had been the last British regiment to leave the town. In the last dash to secure the canal, within minutes of the Armistice, one veteran lancer, Private George Ellison, was shot dead. He had cruelly survived most of the Great War, only to become officially the last British soldier killed in action.

In recent years there has been much focus on and research into the role of Irish troops in the Great War and a good deal of excellent academic work has been done. Indeed, much has been revealed about the nature of the Irish military tradition and experience during 1914–1918, which has excited enthusiasm and interest from many quarters. As so many useful books and articles have been written, a certain amount of repetition here regarding the Irish contribution to the war is, regrettably, unavoidable. It is also important to stress that this is a history of Irish regiments in the Great War, not necessarily of Irishmen, and it would be highly problematic to suggest otherwise. Yet, it is the men of these regiments, whether they came from northern or southern Ireland, England, Scotland, Wales or India, that this work concentrates upon. Neither is this book intended to be an exhaustive history of those regiments, but rather, a more condensed consideration of their exploits and achievements as far as I am able. Consequently, any errors or omissions are my own. To the general reader, I hope this work will be enlightening and entertaining; to the student and scholar of the Great War, I hope that it will be of use and kindly received.

Magherally,
Co. Down,
August 2014

Abbreviations

2-i-C	Second in command
ADS	Advance Dressing Station
ANZAC	Australian and New Zealand Army Corps
AOH	Ancient Order of Hibernians
APM	Assistant Provost Marshal
ASC	Army Service Corps
AVC	Army Veterinary Corps
BEF	British Expeditionary Force
Bttn	Battalion
Btty.	Battery
CCS	Casualty Clearing Station
CIGS	Chief of Imperial General Staff
CO	Commanding Officer
Coy	Company
CQMS	Company Quartermaster Sergeant
CR	Connaught Rangers
CSM	Company Sergeant Major
CWGC	Commonwealth War Graves Commission
DCM	Distinguished Conduct Medal
DSO	Distinguished Service Order
GAA	Gaelic Athletic Association
GHQ	General Headquarters
GOC	General Officer Commanding
HQ	Headquarters
ICA	Irish Citizen Army

IG	Irish Guards
INV	Irish National Volunteers
IPP	Irish Parliamentary Party
IRB	Irish Republican Brotherhood
IRA	Irish Republican Army
IV	Irish Volunteers
KRIH	King's Royal Irish Hussars
LTMB	Light Trench Mortar Battery
MC	Military Cross
MID	Mentioned in Despatches
MSM	Meritorious Service Medal
MM	Military Medal
NCO	Non-Commissioned Officer
NIH	North Irish Horse
OTC	Officer Training Corps
RAF	Royal Air Force (1918)
RAP	Regimental Aid Post
RDF	Royal Dublin Fusiliers
RE	Royal Engineers
RFA	Royal Field Artillery
RFC	Royal Flying Corps
Rfn	Rifleman
RHA	Royal Horse Artillery
RIC	Royal Irish Constabulary
RIDG	Royal Irish Dragoon Guards
RIF	Royal Irish Fusiliers
RInnF	Royal Inniskilling Fusiliers
RIL	Royal Irish Lancers
RIR	Royal Irish Regiment or Royal Irish Rifles; throughout this work *Royal Irish* refers to the Royal Irish Regiment and *Irish Rifles* to the Royal Irish Rifles. [see below]

RIRegt	Royal Irish Regiment
RMF	Royal Munster Fusiliers
RSM	Regimental Sergeant Major
RQMS	Regimental Quartermaster Sergeant
SIH	South Irish Horse
UVF	Ulster Volunteer Force
VC	Victoria Cross
YCV	Young Citizen Volunteers

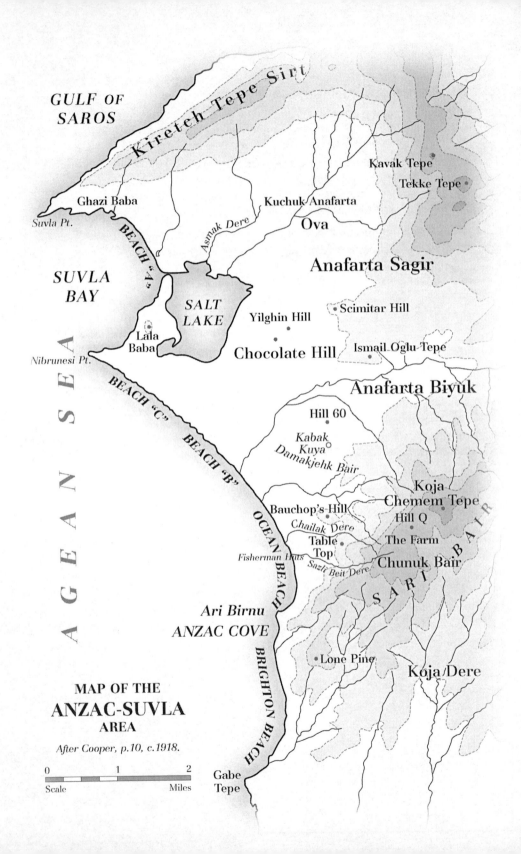

GULF OF
SAROS

Kiretch Tepe Sirt

Kavak Tepe

Tekke Tepe

Ghazi Baba

Suvla Pt.

Kuchuk Anafarta

Asmak Dere

Ova

Anafarta Sagir

SUVLA
BAY

BEACH "A"

SALT
LAKE

Yilghin Hill

Scimitar Hill

Nibrunesi Pt.

Lala
Baba

Chocolate Hill

Ismail Oglu Tepe

A G E A N   S E A

BEACH "C"

BEACH "B"

Anafarta Biyuk

Hill 60

Kabak
Kuya
Damakjehk Bair

Koja
Chemem Tepe

Bauchop's Hill

Hill Q

Chailak Dere

The Farm

OCEAN BEACH

Table
Top

Fisherman Huts

Sazlı Beit Dere

Chunuk Bair

S A R I   B A I R

Ari Birnu
ANZAC COVE

Lone Pine

Koja Dere

MAP OF THE
ANZAC-SUVLA
AREA

After Cooper, p.10, c.1918.

BRIGHTON BEACH

0   1   2

Scale   Miles

Gabe
Tepe

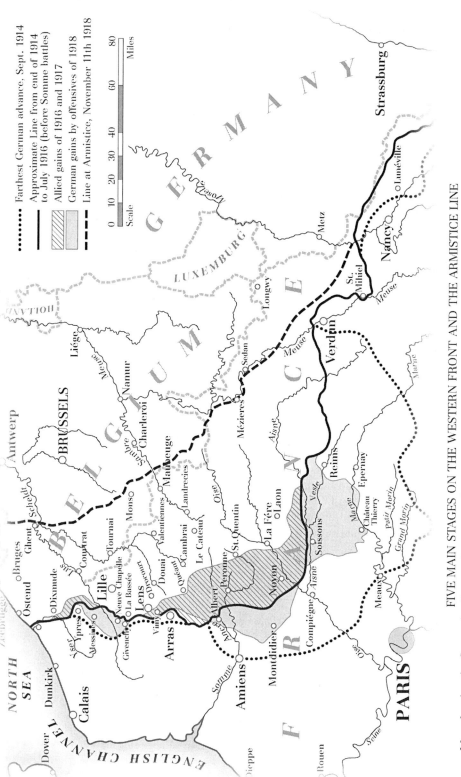

FIVE MAIN STAGES ON THE WESTERN FRONT AND THE ARMISTICE LINE

Map showing the fluctuating line on the western front from 1914 to 1918 and the chief Allied and German gains. The line on the extreme right indicates the limit of the Allied advance known as the Armistice Line, November 11th 1918. *After Hannerton, Vol.5, p.399 (c. 1918).*

Legend:

········· Farthest German advance, Sept. 1914

——— Approximate Line from end of 1914 to July 1916 (before Somme battles)

▨ Allied gains of 1916 and 1917

▨ German gains by offensives of 1918

- - - Line at Armistice, November 11th 1918

Scale
0 10 20 30 40 60 80
Miles

BATTLES OF
GAZA
After Hammerton,
Vol. 4, p.29 c.1918.

MEDITERRANEAN
SEA

Herbie

Beit
Tima

Deir
Sineid

Bureir

Wady el Hesi

To Jerusalem,
Kefr Harris
and Nablus

GAZA

Sheikh
Aasan

Nuj

Jenimameh

Samson Ridge

Sheikh
Abbas

Deir al
Balah

Tel
Sheria

Hareira

Wady es Sheria

Khan Yunis

Shellal

Aba Irgeig

Wells

RAFA

Tel el Fara

El Buggar

BEERSHEBA

Ecani

Wady es Saba

- - - - Railways
——— Roads

0   5   10
Scale   Miles

CHAPTER ONE

'Party feeling could hardly be more strained'[1]

From Ulster Crisis to Great War, 1912–1914

In the opening months of 1914, John Redmond's Irish Parliamentary Party held a seemingly unassailable array of sixty-eight Westminster seats out of an available one hundred and five. However, only four years later, Redmond's brand of moderate Nationalism was, effectively, swept away as the Republican deluge of Sinn Féin celebrated a landslide victory of seventy-three seats. The once great IPP was left with only six seats to its name and, of these, five were held in Ulster.[2] In the 1918 General Election, Irish Unionism stood amazingly firm before Sinn Féin's political *tsunami*, raising its Parliamentary presence to twenty-six seats, but the general electoral trend effectively forced Unionists into a desperate bid for ideological survival. In a depressingly familiar tale, at the end of 1918, the two political polarities in Ireland seemed further apart than ever. Yet, in the years of desperate political turmoil leading up to 1914, such a stark reality was still, arguably, far from certain. Indeed, the concept of Irishmen and Ulstermen being embroiled in a 'world war' that would dwarf any hitherto fought by mankind, was as inconceivable as it was nightmarish.

Since the 1801 Act of Union, Ireland had been an integral part of the United Kingdom and, whilst internal opposition to this certainly existed, by 1900, the country had settled down to a relative period of calm and peaceful co-existence. By the later nineteenth century, many Irish people felt themselves to be both Irish and as 'British' as the concept then existed.[3] Those who saw themselves as both Irish and British were, by and large, more numerous across the two islands and those who professed to be neither were often ambivalent about constitutional affairs. Of course, this does not imply that many Irish people did not want some form of change; rather that the pace and extent varied considerably—usually from individual to individual. In 1912, moderate Nationalists did not call for the Union to be split, preferring to argue for a more devolved and de-centralised version, with more tangible powers removed to Dublin. To Ulster Unionists, however, any transition of power that sidelined the powerhouse of 'Protestant' Belfast in favour of 'Catholic' Dublin was anathema. Furthermore, Unionist resistance to any such transition was driven by their charismatic leader, the Dublin barrister, Sir Edward Carson.

In 1912, Dublin was certainly considered to be the 'second city' of the Empire. It sprawled with genteel Georgian parks and promenades and boasted a robust commercial heart with an increasingly diverse society; but it also hid terrible squalor and urban poverty behind its elegant facade. It had the highest civilian death-rate in the empire and, according to a Government housing report in 1914, nearly 50 per cent of Dublin's working population was living in overcrowded tenements which were described as 'decayed', 'badly-constructed' or even 'ruinous'.[4] In contrast, Belfast, the upstart rival in Ulster, had little of Dublin's grandeur; it did, however, have many of its social problems and surpassed it in sectarian tension. This energetic new city, though, was undeniably the largest on the island, being home to nearly 400,000 people. Belfast was seen as a city of innovation and an acknowledged centre for technological development, especially when, in April 1912, the '… largest vessel afloat…'— the *Titanic*—was launched from the slipways of Harland & Wolff. By 1914, the city was one of the most important industrial and commercial engines of the Empire. Its shipyards and linen mills (joining those in the Bann and Lagan Valleys) guaranteed its place as the undisputed capital of the north and, arguably, the industrial and commercial capital of Ireland. Ulster, despite its reputation for heavy industry, was still largely rural and, by 1912, some 66,618 acres of land were entirely devoted to the production of flax.[5]

Whilst Belfast was the largest city on the island, Cork, down in the south, was the largest county. It had a population of over 300,000 people and, although mainly Catholic in persuasion, it contained a sizable Protestant community. Furthermore, Cork was considered to be one of the most loyal and Unionist areas in Ireland, despite being home to a growing number of Republican sympathisers. Many of Cork's young men were already in the army or navy (with the main Royal Navy base at Cobh) and the city, with its resplendent canals and two famous breweries, vied with Belfast for the title of second city in Ireland. Equally, Londonderry (the 'Maiden City' of Derry) was a busy, thriving centre for north-west Ulster and was seen as the local 'big city' by all communities in Donegal, Monaghan, Cavan, Fermanagh and Tyrone. Another important port-town with a dependent rural hinterland was Waterford; the agricultural communities here eked out a precarious existence, often under the threat of eviction. In the county's two largest conurbations, Dungarvan and Waterford city, commerce preserved its wealth and local prospects.

However, other areas of Ireland were far less fortunate. By 1914, Galway had suffered a steady and substantial drop in population, a fact which is worth noting considering its eligible recruitable population and heroic contribution to the ranks of the Connaught Rangers and Irish Guards. Within the county, only Ballinasloe showed any kind of gain in population—a mere 265 children in 10 years. Equally, in Kerry, rural poverty was endemic and, whilst the county enjoyed a steady stream of tourists, the income generated by them had not lined the pockets of its inhabitants. If anything, the wild, isolated beauty of the Kerry coastline and landscape had contributed to its lack of economic viability. Yet, in spite of the scarcity of many resources in communities all over Ireland, their supply of manpower was plentiful. Many of the homes in the townlands and parishes of Ireland were still built of earth and thatch, but the lads who marched away from these districts were little different from those who did likewise in Galloway, Carmarthenshire or Somerset. Those casual labourers, smiths, or factory workers who could not find employment within the larger Irish centres, always had another route to regular pay, board and food: the army. Many young—and not so young—Irishmen took it. The army was also an exciting escape from the drudgery of everyday existence; it was full of possibilities for daring overseas adventure, and the recruiting sergeants played up to this for all it was worth. In 1900, the strength of the British Army stood at approximately 210,681 Regular troops, with approximately 28,358 believed to be Irishmen, present in every county regiment throughout the United Kingdom.

The Army in Ireland and its Regiments

Irish-associated regiments had served in the British Army almost since its official formation, with the 18th Royal Irish Regiment (raised around 1683–

4) and the 27th Inniskilling Regiment, 6th Inniskilling Dragoons and 5th (Royal Irish) Lancers (all raised in 1689) being the oldest of these. Many more, such as the 35th Sussex Regiment, had actually been raised in Ireland from Irish recruits (and originally had Irish titles—the 35th's being the 'Earl of Donegall's/Belfast' Regiment). Consequently, many Irish regiments had been raised during Britain's wars of the eighteenth century and had seen action throughout the Empire since. It was not only in the rank and file that significant numbers of Irishmen could be found. In spite of popular misconceptions, the British Officer Corps had a notable Irish aspect, especially within its most senior ranks. The list of senior British officers with Irish connections was equally impressive, from the Irish-born First Duke of Wellington to Lord Kitchener. Yet, by 1900, the Irish element in the army had fallen to just over 13 per cent, not least due to the drop in recruitable population.[6]

By 1914, three more Irish regiments had emerged. The Irish Guards had been created as a result of Irish regimental gallantry during the Boer War. A little later, the Haldane Reforms of 1908 had dissolved the Yeomanry regiments but, in Ireland, this had led to the creation of two Special Reserve regiments, the North and South Irish Horse, with headquarters in Victoria Barracks, Belfast and Beggar's Bush, Dublin. This was also indicative of the fact that Ireland was entering a period of unrest when the very presence of the army (and police) was being used as a constant theme by some in their domestic politics. However, by 1914, there were fifteen Irish cavalry and infantry regiments on the Regular Establishment as follows:

> The 4th Royal Irish Dragoon Guards
> The 5th Royal Irish Lancers
> The 6th Inniskilling Dragoons
> The 8th King's Royal Irish Hussars
> The North Irish Horse
> The South Irish Horse
> The Irish Guards
> The Royal Irish Regiment
> The Royal Inniskilling Fusiliers
> The Royal Irish Rifles
> Princess Victoria's Royal Irish Fusiliers
> The Connaught Rangers
> The Prince of Wales' Leinster Regiment

The Royal Munster Fusiliers
The Royal Dublin Fusiliers

Irish Regimental Command: Depots, Barracks and Garrison Towns

The military strength in Ireland ranged between 25,000 and 30,000 men during the late nineteenth and early twentieth centuries. To administer these military resources, the country was treated as an entire command—one of the seven military districts of the British Isles. In charge of Irish Command was Major-General the Right Honourable Sir Arthur Paget, who was renowned for his slightly unpredictable and brusque manner. The Regular British Army battalions and squadrons he commanded were not all from Ireland and, indeed, locally raised Irish units were not all on duty in Ireland from 1912–1914. In the years of the Ulster Crisis and the lead-up to the outbreak of war, military command in Ireland was administered from Parkgate in Dublin and this, in turn, answered directly to the War Office in Whitehall. In practice, Parkgate had immediate control and was responsible for the day-to-day organisation of all aspects of the army in Ireland. Its staff branches dealt with every imaginable administrative duty, from practical recruitment and training to equipment procurement and—when the time came—mobilisation. Acting as a focus for the recruitment and housing of these troops were the regimental depots and barracks throughout the country, the largest concentration of which was in Dublin, the Curragh, then Cork and Ulster. Of all the troops stationed in Ireland, the majority were members of a single cavalry brigade and two infantry divisions of Regulars.

The 3rd Cavalry Brigade was stationed at the Curragh Camp, Co. Kildare, but the divisional artillery trains of the two infantry divisions, the 5th and 6th, were spread throughout the country. The 5th Division's artillery was divided between Dundalk, Kildare and Newbridge, whilst the 6th Division's was spread even further, between Ballincollig, Cahir, Clonmel, Fermoy, Fethard, Kilkenny and Waterford. In the infantry units, however, organisation was more concentrated. The 5th Division had its headquarters and its 14th Brigade at the Curragh, with its 13th Brigade in Dublin and its 15th Brigade in Belfast. The 6th Division had only two of its three brigades in Ireland, with its 16th Brigade in Cork (along with its headquarters) and its 17th Brigade at Fermoy. In addition to the important barracks mentioned above, the country possessed many garrison towns and other such recruitment centres. For example, Kinsale had barracks to house a battalion (Charles Fort) and Macroom had a major military presence. In Ulster, the towns of Omagh, Enniskillen, Armagh and Belfast all possessed significant barracks. In short, any town with a 'fayre day' or where barracks or depots were found became a potential source of manpower for the army.

Yet, there was a wider impending problem regarding these bases in Ireland which was, for obvious reasons, unforeseen in the years prior to the Great War. Barrack accommodation throughout the British Isles was geared for a maximum of 175,000 men but, by the end of 1914, the army had increased in strength by a million men. The shortage of space, even in Ireland, became an acute problem. Short-term measures throughout the UK included removing married quarters (freeing up a further 262,000 spaces), billeting in vacant factories or private homes and temporary tented camps.[7] However, by late summer 1914, plans were already underway for the construction of proper hutted 'wartime camps', the main ones in Ireland being at Finner (Donegal), Clandeboye (Down) Randalstown (Antrim), Renmore (Galway), Kilworth, Aghada (Cork), Ballyvonare (Buttevant) and the Curragh. Indeed, society in Ireland was to become increasingly militarised, with far-reaching repercussions for both soldier and civilian.

In the years leading up to 1914, relations with civilians were, by and large, the same as those in other parts of the United Kingdom with attitudes ranging from cordiality to frustration or resentment. Most Irish garrison towns felt the economic benefit of having troops stationed nearby, and whilst there were regular sectarian incidents and sporadic agrarian violence within the civilian population, these were often highly localised and short-lived. Consequently, many soldiers welcomed a home-posting to Ireland and did not automatically associate it with unrest (frequently the opposite). Whilst it is difficult to say whether or not the experience was typical, the sentiments of one batch of Nottingham recruits to the 12th Lancers, upon being sent to the training depot at Marlborough Barracks in Dublin (alongside the 5th Royal Irish Lancers) demonstrated a potential gulf between English soldier and Irish civilian. Frederick Holmes, who had never before left his county, let alone England, reminisced about how shocked he was to discover that the locals '… were dressed the same way we were'. Perhaps his reaction would have been the same had he been sent to a depot in Glasgow, Swansea or Truro. As it was, this young recruit was assigned a Scot, Lance Corporal Stewart, to keep a watchful eye over his progress. Here was the British Army's practical pluralism in operation.[8]

Who were the Regulars?

In general, Ireland was not unduly hostile to army recruitment or to its practical presence. In fact, Ireland was a huge and obvious recruiting pool for the Regular Army. As in many parts of the United Kingdom, enlistment was attractive for numerous reasons: it offered a route out of poverty and practical ways to fulfil social aspirations, dreams of adventure or simple patriotism. James Somers was born in Belturbet, Co. Cavan, but had moved, with his parents, to live in Cloughjordan, Co. Tipperary, where his father became a parish sexton for the local Church of Ireland (Modreeny). In 1912, he left home and joined the Royal Inniskilling Fusiliers, not out of circumstance or necessity but, perhaps, for some greater cultural affinity. From the isolated rural hamlets in the glens of Donegal, Wicklow or Kerry, to the densely packed streets of Dublin or Cork, young Catholic and Protestant recruits steadily came to the 'Colours'. Similarly, Michael Devine, from Carlow, enlisted in the 8th King's Royal Irish Hussars in May 1902, following in the footsteps of his eldest brother, William, who was also in the 8th Hussars.[9]

The generous 'separation allowance' for families may explain enlistment levels in the poorer areas of Ireland compared to the less pronounced figures in Ulster (with its higher wages and employment opportunities). The Royal Dublin Fusiliers, the 'Blue Caps' or 'Old Toughs',[10] for example, had a large contingent of inner-city Dublin recruits, known for being under-sized and under-nourished but hard, wiry, soldiers. A good number of recruits came from one of the oldest parts of the city—known as the 'Liberties'—where the population lived cheek by jowl in conditions which were barely tolerable. Under such circumstances, where poverty and starvation were ever-present companions, the lure of an army life as a means of escape must have been an attractive one. One such recruit was Private Patrick Emerson, who enlisted in the 5th Royal Irish Lancers and left the 'Liberties' behind to join the ranks of one of the most glamorous arms of military service. Members of the regiment were easily recognisable on ceremonial duties for the dark green plumes on their Lancer caps and by the bamboo, steel-tipped, lance that they were trained to use in battle. Due to the colour of the tunic plastrons on their full dress uniform, the 5th Royal Irish Lancers were fondly known around Dublin as the 'Redbreasts'. Of course, the men in the ranks of the Irish battalions and squadrons were drawn from all over the United Kingdom, although the cavalry regiments seemed to have a slightly higher percentage of non-Irish recruits, probably due to rotational requirements.[11] Men such as George Ellison from

Leeds, for example, had been a former coal miner before joining the 5th Royal Irish Lancers when it was stationed at Catterick in Yorkshire before the war.

Men like William Cosgrove, from Aghada (Co. Cork), enlisted in 1910 with the Royal Munster Fusiliers—the fabled 'Dirty Shirts'[12]—to leave the rural hardships of life on the family farm. Another disenchanted farm labourer from Ardoughaman near Ballina (Co. Mayo), Stephen Kennedy, decided that army life was the only option for him and joined the 'Devil's Own',[13]—the Connaught Rangers, in 1913. Other young men, like Thomas Bacon, born in Carrigmore and living in Tallow, Co. Tipperary, appear to have enlisted on impulse; Bacon joined the 3rd Royal Irish Regiment in 1913 as a Special Reservist, only to be discharged on 26 Jan 1914, when his mother provided the money needed to buy his way out. Of course, a large number of boys, waifs or 'street urchins', also found a protective home in the ranks. Some were orphans, some were disowned and a good many more were reluctantly (or heartily) encouraged to go so that there was one less mouth to feed. In 1909, a young fifteen-year-old lad from New Ross, Martin Doyle, amended his birth details in order to enlist with the 2nd Royal Irish Regiment at Kilkenny; he was soon dispatched on Imperial Service to India. Another boy, Christopher Powell, lived in Loughlin's Lane, Limerick, opposite the malt houses of Thomond's Distillery. His widowed mother was the head of the house and he was the middle brother of a large family in the St Minchin's district. He was exactly the type of young lad who saw the army as a means to better his opportunities and provide a regular income for his family; consequently, he enlisted as a band boy in the Royal Munster Fusiliers. In general, the 2nd Royal Irish Rifles (mainly recruited from Belfast and counties Down and Antrim) was a typical pre-war Irish battalion. Its ranks contained a diverse bunch of Regulars: a former divinity student, perhaps a little too fond of drink, 'decent' sons of farmers, a school teacher, a bank clerk and a loner '... taciturn Sergeant from Waterford...' who had a gift for mathematical theory.[14]

Irish regimental officers naturally tended to come from more privileged backgrounds with military service as part of a family tradition, but not all. The rise of the middle classes had also provided Irish regiments with a new, professional kind of officer. Furthermore, the innovative university Officer Training Corps system, although largely restricted in Ireland to Queen's University Belfast and Trinity College Dublin, opened up the possibility of military advancement still further. Although not exclusively, such officers were generally 'Unionist' in outlook and upbringing. Interestingly, the bond between officers and men was exceptionally strong in Irish regiments and was often noted as being rather unique within the army. As one Fermanagh officer in the Royal Inniskilling Fusiliers commented, the Irish battalions had a sustained '... tradition of "pally-ness"... [like] one large family...' but, like a large family, there was still a definite hierarchy. Many Regular officers and NCOs considered their men to be wards (or even friends) and, whilst this may not have led to wholesale familiarity, as such, there was a considerable degree of flexibility between ranks.[15]

Those in the Irish aristocracy (such as Captain The Honourable Arthur O'Neill, MP for Mid-Antrim who served with the Life Guards) seem to have chosen command posts with the elite Guards or cavalry regiments instead of their local county units. It may seem unsurprising that the majority of Irish peers served in the Irish or Coldstream Guards, whilst those Irish or Ulster officers of lesser social rank commanded companies and battalions throughout the British regimental system. The first Victoria Cross of the war, for example, was awarded to the Royal Fusiliers but it was an Irish officer who won it; Lieutenant Maurice Dease, who came from outside Coole in Co. Westmeath. Equally, Captain Miles Carbery was thirty-seven in 1914 and commanded 'C' Coy, 1st Irish Fusiliers—the 'Faughs'. He had been born in India and was married to Elizabeth Dora Sinclair, the daughter of The Right Honourable Thomas Sinclair, a leading Belfast anti-Home Rule liberal Unionist, businessman and Presbyterian thinker. One of the subalterns of the same battalion, Lieutenant Penrose, recalled in his war diary that, upon meeting an officer from the Cameronians (Scottish Rifles), he discovered he was from Castletownsend, Co. Cork. Another young officer from Co. Cork, Lieutenant Henry Desmond O'Hara from Ballincolig, was a subaltern with the Dublin Fusiliers. He was a nephew of the Bishop of Cashel and his father was a Resident Magistrate; eventually, he was to command the 1st Battalion's 'W' Coy on its way to the Dardanelles.[16]

The Third Home Rule Bill and Ulster Crisis 1912

Within this social setting, the political and security situation throughout Ireland had become steadily worse. The question of Home Rule had, once again, split the country down political and cultural lines. Neither were these stark political stances drawn on a sectarian basis; there were unwavering Catholic Unionists such as Sir Morgan O'Connell and influential Protestant 'Home Rulers' like Lord Pirrie. In fact, by 1912, such was the hostility aroused by the proposal that Ireland seemed to be on the verge of a bloody and unforgiving civil war. In Ulster, a mainly Protestant and Unionist majority saw the imposition of Home Rule as a wider problem and it marshalled the Imperial Grand Orange Council to this effect. Consequently, when the Liberal Prime Minister, Herbert H. Asquith, resurrected the (Third) Home Rule Bill (April 1912), it triggered the first stirrings of the 'Ulster crisis' which was to follow. Using all the modern media means of the age, Irish Unionism set about implementing a concerted propaganda campaign, involving industrial leaders, military heroes, academics, writers and other influential supporters.

In the rest of Ireland, however, many people identified with the moderate persuasive politics of John Redmond's Irish Nationalism. In the three southern provinces, Home Rule was eagerly expected and its prospect was generally welcomed. Indeed, as prominent IPP MP, William Redmond, commented, if Home Rule was reliant on the wider British imperial opinion, then Ireland '…would be immediately emancipated'. Yet, without the support of Ulster, the economic viability of the southern provinces to administer Home Rule became questionable. Fearing the worst, half a million Ulster Unionists signed the Solemn League and Covenant on 28 September 1912, vowing to resist Home Rule with any means at their disposal and effectively threatening Ulster independence. In the ominous words of the RIC Inspector General, it was believed that community relations were at breaking point; a month later, he noted that Catholic Unionists had also signed the Covenant in nearly every part of County Antrim.[17]

The Formation of the Young Citizen Volunteers, Ulster Volunteer Force and Irish Volunteers, 1913

September also saw the formation of the non-sectarian YCV at a rally outside Belfast City Hall. They were initially formed along the lines of the boy scouts but primarily aimed to recruit from amongst middle-class lads from Belfast and its hinterland. Their higher status was shown by their costly—but eye-catching—grey uniforms. Although the YCV were mistakenly seen as the youth wing of the UVF, it purposefully recruited young Belfast Catholics and Protestants, with 'municipal patriotism' as one of its guiding virtues. Even when it was absorbed by the Belfast regiment of the Ulster Volunteers and later, the 14th Royal Irish Rifles, it retained a significant YCV ethos.[18]

It was not until the Ulster Unionist Council meeting in January 1913 that this resistance to Home Rule finally found a cohesive form. At the same time, radical Unionists had already begun limited and strictly legal military training of their own. These 'makeshift' groups, largely meeting in Orange halls throughout Ulster, were forged into one armed body, known as the Ulster Volunteer Force. It was commanded by Lieutenant-General Sir George Richardson, famed for his role in the Boxer Rebellion in 1901 and the capture of the 'Temple of Heaven'. Indeed, a staggering number of former or serving soldiers of the Empire, most with some form of Anglo-Irish extraction, associated themselves with the cause of Unionism. A chief military advisor to the UVF was the venerable Field Marshal Earl Roberts of Khandahar (affectionately known by troops as 'Bobs') and one of their most indispensable allies at the War Office was General Sir Henry Wilson.

The UVF was initially commanded by local gentry and businessmen and was conceived as a 'citizens' army'. It has been estimated that the UVF was largely formed out of the Orange Order (a Protestant loyal order with political affiliations), with as many as 65 per cent of the original UVF being Orange Order members. Furthermore, the initial pre-requisite for admission to the UVF was that recruits had to have signed the Ulster Covenant. At its height, the UVF possessed around 90,000 well-organised men, comprising infantry battalions (based on the British army model), a regiment of cavalry (the Enniskillen Horse), a motor-car corps, ambulance and nursing staff, signallers and despatch riders. The Ulster Special Service Force was also created as a 'special striking force' and was commanded by Francis Percy Crozier, who later became Lieutenant-Colonel of the 9th Irish Rifles. So well-constructed was the UVF that sympathetic former British army officers flocked to its ranks to serve in some capacity. Interestingly, the Royal Irish Constabulary monitored the growth of the UVF, noting that they were created for the communal defence of 'all loyalists' but, equally, to act as 'police' for a Provisional Ulster Government if Home Rule was ever enforced. This also meant that, if necessary, the Ulster Volunteers would very likely have to face both the police and the British Army that it ostensibly identified with. Perhaps unsurprisingly, the mobilisation of Unionist sympathisers was not restricted to Ulster. Some 400 men formed the Loyal Dublin Volunteers in the headquarters of the Orange Order's Dublin district, the Fowler Memorial Hall in Rutland Square. The contingent was commanded by its District Master, Colonel Henry McMaster, and drew its members from the lodges within the city and district. At the height of the unit's strength, it is believed to have had almost 2, 000 men in its ranks.[19]

The Irish Volunteers were formed in direct response to the creation of the UVF but, initially, without the official participation of the IPP or John

Redmond. Indeed, originally, they were raised as the 'Irish Volunteers' (*Óglaigh na hÉireann*) at a public meeting at the Rotunda, Dublin, on 25 November 1913, with Professor Eoin MacNeill as their first president. MacNeill had been heavily influenced by the politics and operations of the UVF and, in his article *'The North Began'* for the journal of the Gaelic League, he actively saw the need for a Nationalist paramilitary force to counterbalance armed Unionism. Military matters were left to Colonel Maurice Moore, a former Connaught Ranger, in his capacity as Inspector-General. Other former British officers with broadly traditional Anglo-Irish backgrounds were also drawn into the organisation; men like Captain Hervey Montmorency (Royal Dublin Fusiliers) and Captain George Berkeley (Worcestershire Regiment), sat alongside respected Nationalist intellectuals such as Professor Tom Kettle. Within a short space of time membership of the Irish (National) Volunteers quickly overshadowed that of the UVF, as they held drill meetings at Ancient Order of Hibernians halls throughout the country, from Limerick to Downpatrick. By mid-1914, RIC Special Branch reports assessed that the UVF had some 80,000 trained men under arms; the INV had 191,000—although arguably they were less well-armed or trained. Like the UVF, they went on route marches in uniform, mostly without rifles, but with growing popular support. The Irish Volunteer Belfast Regiment was estimated to have some 2,100 men and contained all shades of Nationalist opinion, holding drills at venues in North Queen Street and Victoria Street, with '...route marches through their own localities'. Although it was tacitly supported by constitutional Nationalism, it was not until March 1914 that the IPP openly began to lead the organisation. This attracted many more recruits to the Irish Volunteer movement and, although raised as a defensive and protective force (like the UVF), it was expected that they would be used aggressively if necessary. Yet, with the creation of these volunteer private armies, an added, more menacing, spectre fell over the Irish political landscape and this was one from which it never truly escaped.[20]

The 'Incident' at the Curragh, March 1914

With moves well underway to set up a Provisional Government in Ulster, Westminster's options became ever more limited. Unionist resistance to Home Rule was actively supported by the Conservative Party and many others in the British establishment. In an attempt to avert any conflict, the Government still believed that the implementation of the Home Rule Bill was the best way forward. It then began clumsy attempts to persuade the Unionist population in Ireland, and notably Ulster, to accept this decision. With breathtaking mismanagement, Asquith, frustrated beyond measure, put into operation a plan to coerce Unionists by manipulating them to defy the Government openly, so that he could respond swiftly, militarily and decisively. In a pre-emptive strike against the UVF, the British Army was to secure main lines of communication and strategic points of civilian importance in Ulster. The irony was not lost on Irish Nationalists, who saw the move as the potential first sign of eventual British disengagement from Ireland.

Of course, vital to the success of this plan was the co-operation of the army itself. It must be remembered that, in 1914, many of these officers were conservative in mind and Unionist in sympathy. Accordingly, when the GOC Ireland, Sir Arthur Paget, delivered a muddled version of this order on 20 March 1914, it caused consternation. At a special meeting with seven high-ranking officers, Sir Arthur raised the Government's intention to use the army against Ulster and to tackle the Unionists militarily. Paget failed to point out that the army's role was in reestablishing law and order should civil authority break down. Indeed, he seemed to present the plan as a proposed full-scale military campaign. As if to confirm this, officers, uncomfortable with the plan, were given a number of choices. Those living in Ulster could 'make themselves scarce' but would be expected to return to duty when order was resumed. If they felt strongly enough, they could resign their commission but this would not be accepted and a court martial would follow.

At the same time, troop movements went ahead with soldiers arriving in Dundalk and Newry, whilst the garrison at Victoria Barracks in Belfast occupied Holywood. This fitted in with the general aim to erect a military cordon around the city by holding six key towns, which included the ports of Larne and Bangor. As the army manoeuvres continued, the Ulster population braced itself for unrest but, incredibly, there was little animosity (and a great deal of cordial formality) between the watching UVF and deployed battalions. Then the grand plan hit a massive snag. Foremost in the opposition to the scheme was Brigadier-General Hubert Gough, commander of the 3rd Cavalry Brigade at the Curragh Camp (Co. Kildare), whose troops were instrumental to the operation. Gough was a strong Unionist and point-blankly refused to consent to the mission, even at the risk of facing dismissal from the army. However, the Brigadier-General delivered the orders to his subordinate officers along with their options should they choose not to be a part of the plan. At this point, things completely unravelled when the fifty-eight cavalry officers under Gough's command followed his example and resigned their commissions. Eighteen of the 5th Royal Irish Lancers' officers decided to resign their commissions, including Major James Bruce Jardine, Captain J.A. Batten-Pooll, Lieutenant George C. Juler and Lieutenant John Arthur Talbot Rice. Only two officers of the regiment did not respond, since they were away from the regiment at the time, but they too supported their brother officers' stance. Once these officers, at the most important barracks in Ireland, refused to co-operate with the operation, it was effectively dead in the water. The 'Curragh Mutiny' was more symbolic than practical, yet it sent a stark message to Asquith and the Government. It ably demonstrated the depths of sympathy towards the Unionist position in Ulster, not simply from the Opposition parties at Westminster, but right at the heart of the British Army. In fact, General Sir Henry Wilson, 'leaked' developments at the War Office to Unionist supporters and had even considered resigning over the crisis himself.[21]

Operation 'Lion' and Bachelor's Walk

By early 1914, the RIC was increasingly concerned over the number of gun-running incidents, albeit on a small and opportunistic scale. By the very nature of their clandestine activities, details of the exact weaponry held by the paramilitary units in Ireland at this time are frequently sketchy. It is known that, in the earliest days of formation, most groups (including the Ulster Volunteers) often trained with dummy, or non-operational, rifles. Equally, large numbers of sporting or antiquated rifles and shotguns were frequently employed by the various forces. As the Ulster Volunteer Force carefully trained and prepared to take whatever steps may be necessary for open confrontation with Asquith's Government, it soon became clear that proper arms and munitions would be needed. Here, the UVF began actively to seek out conduits of supply, despite being carefully watched by RIC Special Branch. In September 1912, the Inspector General noted from intelligence reports that, as early as 1910, an English arms manufacturer was repeatedly approached by loyalists in Ulster for a quotation on a '... large quantity of modern rifles'. This demonstrates a certain amount of 'gentlemanly' naivety within certain Ulster (and similarly Irish National) Volunteer circles regarding how rifles intended for revolutionary purposes may be obtained by legal and 'above board' means. Despite the fact that such requests were often refused, by 1914, the Ulster Volunteers had already amassed a considerable arsenal. In Belfast, police believed that some 500 Martini-Enfield carbines (about twenty years old) were stashed at Clifton Street Orange Hall. In late 1913, the 3rd (South Antrim) UVF regiment had some 600 rifles to hand. More worryingly, these were no longer dummies or obsolete issue. They were 'point 303' Lee Enfields and state-of-the-art weapons, as used by the army itself. As firms in England predictably refused to handle any orders from Ulster or Ireland, the UVF and INV looked towards Europe for any support they could find. In this, they found a very willing (and mischievous) ally in the form of Germany. Discussions on arms procurement were initiated between the UVF and members of the German High Command, through businessman Bruno Spiro and Major Fred Crawford. Although German support was to be purely at arm's length, its implications were far wider. The testing and subsequent purchase of German supplied rifles led to the almost flawless execution of 'Operation Lion', also known as the 'Larne Gun-Running' on Friday 24 April 1914.[22]

Here, under the cover of darkness, the UVF took over the port of Larne in a carefully planned exercise and landed a huge consignment of guns and ammunition (as much as 2,000,000 rounds) carried on board the ship, the *Clyde Valley*. Once at Larne, the *Clyde Valley* partially unloaded its weapons' consignment onto some 500 waiting motor vehicles and two smaller ships. As these ships sailed on to their destinations of Bangor and Donaghadee, the motor lorries and cars drove through the night to distribute the arms to units across Ulster. The perceived success of the Ulster Volunteers' gun-running operation, combined with the seemingly powerless position of the police, prompted the leadership of the Irish (National) Volunteers to plan a similar exercise.

On 25 May, the Third Home Rule Bill passed all its parliamentary stages, needing only Royal Assent. The impending crisis shattered old allegiances and friendships. It also turned the old cultural assumptions on their head. For example, Captain George Berkeley, a Dublin-born officer in the Worcestershire Regiment, had fought in the Boer War. He was also a famous 'slow left arm bowler' who had played twice for Ireland in the 1890s. Yet, he was friends with Professor Eoin MacNeill and, by 1914, had become a vigorous supporter of Home Rule. Like MacNeill, he decided that the UVF's lead on armaments should be followed and he supplied much of the £1,500 needed by the Irish (National) Volunteers to bring rifles into Ireland. This, as we shall see, was to have dire ramifications for another of his friends, Frank Browning, the celebrated Irish cricket captain, who, contrastingly, threw himself whole-heartedly behind the British war effort.[23]

On 26 July 1914, at Howth, the INV made a daring attempt to bring guns and ammunition into the country on the *Asgard*, a yacht owned by the author

Erskine Childers. The guns were loaded from a German ship anchored off the Scheldt Estuary and, having evaded numerous Royal Navy patrols, the small boat neared the Irish coast in the early hours of 26 July. In an attempt to halt the proceedings, a detachment of King's Own Scottish Borderers had been ordered to secure Bachelor's Walk, at Howth Quay, where the illegal shipment was expected. However, the police and Scottish Borderers were forced to wait on the quayside for most of the day, only to discover that, whilst they stood waiting at Howth, rifles were unloaded at Killcoole further up the coast. The RIC and Scottish Borderers had blocked Bachelor's Walk and were involved in a brief stand-off with an Irish Volunteer unit led by Bulmer Hobson. As they waited, frustrated at their failure to stop the arms getting to the INV, the crowd grew increasingly bold, jeering at them and throwing stones. Eventually, the soldiers were ordered back to barracks, by which time the guns, ammunition and volunteers had successfully melted away, to the delight of the watching crowd. Apparently shots were then fired at the Borderers from some of Hobson's men who had pistols, but, during the confusion, it was not understood from where these had originated. Instead, as the crowd jostled and pushed, the Borderers were ordered to load rifles and seem to have fired a single volley at the largely unarmed crowd. Three civilians were killed and thirty-eight wounded in the process. The entire shipment consisted of only 1,500 guns and roughly 30,000 bullets, at a time when the Irish (National) Volunteers' strength had risen to some 150,000 men.[24]

The Outbreak of War, August 1914

In August 1914, with the world on the brink of war, the crisis surrounding the Third Home Rule Bill seemed as far from resolution as ever. As a result of the mishandling of events at the Curragh, several high-profile resignations occurred, from the Chief of the Imperial General Staff, Field-Marshal Sir John French, to the Secretary of State for War, Colonel John Seeley. However, as the crisis in the Balkans grew, the eyes of the Government turned to more pressing, international concerns. As the political undercurrents bubbled away in Ireland and Ulster, the political situation in the Balkans deteriorated to the point of no return.

On 28 June 1914, Archduke Franz Ferdinand, the Austro-Hungarian heir and Inspector General of the army, and his wife, Countess Sophie, were assassinated by Serb separatists. Ironically, it was the couple's fourteenth wedding anniversary. In response to the murder of the Archduke, a series of bellicose ultimatums zigzagged across Europe. On Sunday 2 August, Germany delivered its final ultimatum to Belgium, demanding unhindered passage through its borders. This was refused. As such, the 1839 treaty with Britain, regarding violation of Belgian territory, suddenly became pressingly relevant. On Monday 3 August, the Germans declared war on France and entered Belgium anyway.

This forced Britain, finally, to deliver its own ultimatum to Germany: they must withdraw from Belgium within twenty-four hours or a state of war would be declared between them. No reply was ever received. Despite the political manoeuvring at Westminster by Redmond and Carson, when push came to shove, both INV and UVF would fight alongside each other. The next day, 4 August, the Regular Irish battalions of the British Army were officially mobilised and its Reservists were called-up to rejoin their regiments. The First World War had begun.

CHAPTER TWO

'Some fella shot Archduke Ferdinand of Austria'[1]

Ireland's Regiments go to War

When it comes to the Great War and the Irish contribution to it, statistics are notoriously capricious. The basic figures (as they have currently been assessed) seem to suggest obvious trends but they are actually far more nuanced. Ireland never had conscription (despite the threat of its implementation) but still as many as 210,000 Irishmen served during the war. This figure includes Ulster recruitment at 62,890 men, with the rest of Ireland contributing some 147,110 men. Of these, 130,000 – 140,000 were direct volunteers with perhaps as many as 65,000 believed to be Catholic; the remainder were Protestant or, at least, non-Catholic. Interestingly, the UVF had approximately 80,600 men, of whom 35,088 enlisted, whilst the INV had a membership of 191,000 men of whom 39,615 enlisted.[2] Yet, all of the above figures run the risk of masking the compelling stories of the men who actually joined the Irish regiments as Reservists or volunteers. If they considered why they had ended up wearing khaki, many Irish soldiers may have wryly agreed with Irish Fusilier Charles McClean's understated observation above on Archduke Ferdinand's assasination.

The Mobilisation and Reserves of the Irish Regimental Establishment

As the crisis on the continent escalated, so did the inevitable preparations for war in Britain and Ireland. On Saturday 1 August 1914, British Naval Reserves were called up, which affected Royal Navy establishments at bases throughout Ireland, such as Londonderry, Lough Swilly and Queenstown (Cobh). By Monday (the August bank holiday), the mobilisation of the Royal Navy was complete and, across the United Kingdom, senior field officers were at their regimental depots. Here they discussed, with necessary urgency, the plans to equip and gather their battalions for active service. This meant that there was an inevitable delay, even for Regular battalions at home on 'stand-by', despite preparations throughout July to ease the mobilisation procedure. On 4 August, Britain declared war on Germany and the mobilisation of the army began in earnest. Within hours, the Irish regiments were on a war-footing.

Notwithstanding the responsibilities of Imperial Service, Britain mobilised more quickly than most nations, with the first British units in France by 9 August. Among the first Regular Irish battalions to leave were the 2nd Leinster Regiment, 2nd Connaught Rangers and 2nd Irish Rifles, based at Fermoy, Aldershot and Tidworth respectively. Joining the Rifles in the 3rd Division was the 2nd Royal Irish Regiment which was stationed at Devonport. The 2nd Dublin Fusiliers and 1st Irish Fusiliers were part of the 4th Division, in the 10th Brigade, the latter being stationed at Shorncliffe before departure. Similarly, the 2nd Royal Inniskilling Fusiliers was the most available battalion of the regiment and was sent to Norfolk to be concentrated with the 12th Brigade of the 4th Division. As such, it was amongst the first British units to be sent to the front. The 2nd Munster Fusiliers were also based in Aldershot and were immediately attached to the 1st (Guards) Brigade in the 1st Division and dispatched to France. The 1st (and only) Irish Guards Battalion was part of the 4th (Guards) Brigade of the 2nd Division; although based at Wellington Barracks in London, they traditionally recruited heavily throughout Ireland, where a good many of their Reservists still lived.[3]

The same process was repeated for the Irish cavalry. The 5th Royal Irish Lancers began their mobilisation process at Marlborough Barracks, Dublin and, by 6 August, it was noted by Lieutenant-Colonel J.B. Jardine that this was 'proceeding without delay'. The next day, a draft of 124 riding horses arrived at the barracks and, by 11 August, mobilisation was complete and the regiment was in full preparation for embarkation for France. They left North Wall Quay in Dublin on the SS Kingstonian on 15 August and arrived at Le Havre (Havre) on 17 August 1914. The 4th Royal Irish Dragoon Guards were also stationed at Tidworth, although they had their regimental depot at Newport in Monmouthshire. On 16 August 1914, they arrived at Boulogne with the 9th (Queen's Royal) Lancers and 18th (Queen Mary's Own) Hussars, serving in the 2nd Cavalry Brigade, as part of the attached BEF Cavalry Division. Meanwhile, the South Irish Horse was enjoying its annual summer camp, as was its sister regiment, the North Irish Horse. Together they supplied a composite force to act as GHQ troops for immediate service with the BEF in France. Consequently, 'B' Squadron from the South Irish Horse and an 'Expeditionary Squadron' made from 'A' and 'C' Squadrons, North Irish Horse were gathered together and appropriate mounts were found for them. In securing horses in Ireland for the war effort, the War Office appears deliberately to have set itself a fairly high standard of conduct. This seems to have been especially welcomed in County Cork with reports of initial high purchase prices for local horses and, it is likely, that this trend continued elsewhere. In the North-West, the War Office purchased fifty-one horses in the opening week of the war, ranging from chargers and pack-ponies to draughts, whilst batches of horses were also bought in Cavan for military use.[4]

Irish Reservists Return to the Colours

Within hours of the declaration of war, the army's Reservists had been issued with their own call-up telegrams and a good number actually presented themselves at barracks and depots that night. One of the first tasks of depot and Reserve battalion officers was to admit, inspect and kit out their returning Reservists and, in some cases, 'reacquaint' them with their Lee Enfield rifles. Within days, Reservists began to arrive steadily at their depots throughout Ireland and almost fifty per cent of the BEF's fighting strength was to be made up of old soldiers returning to the Colours. Of course, men on the Reserve list had no choice but to re-enlist once mobilisation began and such men, if accepted as fit, could add much needed strength to their Regular battalions.

Whilst some of these returning 'old' soldiers had recent experience of military training with the various Volunteers, many others had never expected to be back in khaki, let alone facing the prospect of fighting in a major European war. Fred Vennard, born in Banbridge (Co. Down), had settled down to life working for the Belfast funeral directors, Melville & Company, when the war erupted. He, like many others, had served in the Boer War (with the Inniskilling Dragoons) and was, consequently, called up as one of their Reservists. Of interest is the varying number of Reservists each Irish regiment could draw upon in 1914; for example, the 4th Royal Irish Dragoon Guards had 241, the Dublin Fusiliers had 864 and the Connaught Rangers had 674. The two second largest contingents were both from Ulster, but it was the 'youngest' regiment—the Irish Guards—which had the most Reservists, with some 1,327 men. One of these was Michael O'Leary, born in the rural townland of Inchigeela, outside Macroom (Co. Cork). Like many from the county, he had originally joined up with the Royal Navy but, upon being discharged as unfit for duty, had returned home to work on the land. However, he soon re-enlisted, this time in the Irish Guards, completing his service with them and subsequently being placed on the Reserve list. In 1913, O'Leary was in Canada but returned upon the declaration of war to rejoin his regiment.[5]

Essentially, it was the job of each regiment's Reserve battalion to maintain its strength in the field. In theory, volunteers were initially sent to Reserve and 'Extra Reserve' battalions for training and, when they were up to draft strength, posted to the parent regiment. Within three days, significant drafts had already been collected. The 4th Leinster Regiment, commanded by Lieutenant-Colonel Sir Anthony Weldon, left for Cork and was escorted to the station by the Maryborough National Volunteers and an associated AOH's pipe band. As they stood by the train, the INV cheered the Leinsters and, in a farewell speech, its commander wished them good luck; apparently, Lieutenant-Colonel Weldon had similarly called for three cheers for the INV in the barracks square at Maryborough. In Galway, recruitment to the Connaught Rangers was exceptionally brisk; in the first four days of the war, it was believed that at least 620 men had joined up at Renmore Barracks under Major Henry Jourdain. Yet, there was an added complication in Ireland, where many Reservists, especially those of NCO rank, were actively instructing and drilling the paramilitary units of Irish National, or Ulster, Volunteers. Their sudden disappearance caused considerable disruption to these organisations, something which was noted by many RIC County Inspectors, as local activity in paramilitary units dropped off dramatically.[6]

Heeding Kitchener's Call—the Raising of Ireland's New Armies

Perhaps ominously, a day before the declaration of war, adverts were already in the Ulster press calling for recruits with good physical fitness. If they were aged between nineteen and thirty and were able to ride, they were to contact Sergeant-Major Atkins in Derry and join the North Irish Horse. The adverts seem, in retrospect, eerily timely, although they probably simply coincided with the regiment's annual summer camp in Enniskillen.[7] On 5

August, perhaps the most famous face in recruiting history, Field Marshal Lord Kitchener, became Secretary of State for War. The next day, he made his legendary call for some 500,000 recruits. This extraordinary figure stemmed from Kitchener's realisation that Britain's peacetime army could not possibly endure a prolonged military campaign. Indeed, he demanded of the War Office that 100,000 men needed to be raised immediately. In Ireland, there were already obvious trained manpower resources and, foremost among them, were the members of the UVF. Yet, uncertainty over the suspension of the Home Rule Bill had left Irish politics dangerously unstable. There were now (at least) two armed paramilitary bodies, with thousands of drilled volunteers cautiously eyeing each other to see who would make the next move. Meanwhile, their political leaders talked animatedly in public (and private) about how best to react to the European war.

Kitchener's irritation at Carson's reticence to commit the Ulster Volunteers to overseas' service was only paralleled by his apparent indifference to any initial INV involvement. The War Office went to great lengths to persuade the Unionist leaders to allow the UVF to enlist but this, contrary to some contemporary beliefs, stopped short of any long-term political concessions. A stalling of the Home Rule process was the best that Carson could hope for, with the wholesale incorporation of the UVF into the British Army and the territorial designation of 'Ulster' still intact. Whilst the Irish Volunteer organisation was seen as a natural counter-balance to the UVF, a vicious split came with the outbreak of war. As Redmond (like Carson) discovered, the practical political cost of possessing an armed wing was in being subsumed into the British war effort. Whilst those in the UVF may have been supportive of the war, amongst the ranks of the Irish Volunteers it raised some very uncomfortable issues. It struck at the very heart of the organisation's *raison d'etre*; how was Home Rule to be best achieved—through active service in France or at home?

In this, Tom Kettle and George Berkeley were broadly supportive of the INV being used as a distinctly Irish formation within the British Army on the Western Front. However, there were hints of danger ahead. On 2 September, Denis McCullough proposed a Sinn Féin resolution for the Belfast Volunteers to resist any kind of enlistment, which seems to have been a barometer for a potential split in the organisation's ranks. On 20 September, at Woodenbridge (Co. Wicklow), Redmond urged the Irish Volunteers to offer their services to the army and Allies, to fight anywhere required '... in defence of right, of freedom, and religion'. Many Nationalists, upon hearing Redmond's call for volunteers to enlist in the army, subsequently did so. However, approximately 12,000 dissident Volunteers reacted furiously to this and broke away from the main body. This group continued to use the old title of 'Irish Volunteers', whilst Redmond's volunteers (170,000 strong) remained strongly associated with the IPP. Consequently, as the political posturing died away, preparations were duly made to recruit three Irish divisions: the 10th (Irish), the 16th (Irish) and the 36th (Ulster).[8]

In the meantime, Irish civilians were caught up in the middle of a dizzying recruitment drive. One popular commentator observed that it was in 1914, when the BEF was a small fighting force, dealing with a fluid and often difficult military situation, that the English and Irish proved their mettle, being '… of a romantic temperament, the born adventurers of the world'. Whilst this rather jingoistic epithet may be a flattering exaggeration, it does hint at the atmosphere in the late summer and autumn of 1914. At this stage, the majority of Irishmen viewed the coming war as either an adventure not to be missed, as an escape route from the harshness of industrial or rural life, or as a greater ideal that they were compelled to follow. The heightened recruiting campaign cut through social class and, to a certain extent, political or religious persuasions. Rural areas, such as the Claddagh, appear to have emptied quickly of available men who joined either the navy or the army. Indeed, by Christmas 1914, it was estimated that nearly 200 men from this small community were in the services and the vast majority of them were Catholic IPP supporters.[9]

To many of these young men it may have seemed as if they were embarking upon the greatest adventure of their lives. William Calvert, from Drumbeg, was an apprentice in Britton's Dye Works in Belfast and, although he enjoyed his work there, he immediately joined up when war came. Joseph Caffrey was from a large Catholic family from Tuam in Galway, where his father was a tin smith. He was twenty-four when he enlisted at Renmore Barracks with the Connaught Rangers but, tragically, he died in training (on 12 August) and was buried at Cabra, Co. Dublin. The following day, twenty-year-old Michael Coulter, in training with 'C' Coy, 5th Dublin Fusiliers, died in an accident at Cork as the recruits were working on coastal defences there. He was buried in Aghada Old Cemetery, his gravestone being erected by the officers, NCOs and men of the battalion. Meanwhile, in Co. Antrim, Joseph Watson, from Ballymaconnolly near Rasharkin, was a member of the Orange Order and the UVF but, instead of waiting to be subsumed into the Royal Irish Rifles, he travelled to Glasgow and joined the Highland Light Infantry.[10]

The Honourable Harold Harmsworth was an old Etonian and the eldest son of the Air Minister, Lord Rothermere. Like most of his class, he enlisted within the first week of the war and joined the 1st Irish Guards. Similarly, in September 1914, Terence Verschoyle, from Fermanagh, was offered a commission in his local regiment, the 5th Inniskillings. He subsequently went to war, not out of overt patriotism or outrage over the invasion of Belgium, but simply because '... everybody was doing it'. Equally, Frank Laird, was not in any way warlike, but he certainly felt the emotional weight of the implied moral judgement all around him should he *not* enlist. In these early months, the almost celebratory mood must have been palpable. In Naas, 300 Reservists of the Dublin Fusiliers marched to the station, joined by their regimental pipers and, interestingly, the band of the Naas INV; on the platform, the Dublin Reservists cheered repeatedly and '... waved their hats and rifles in the air'. In this popular spirit of buoyant patriotism or zeal against the alleged atrocities in Belgium, enlisting seemed an obvious thing to do. Mathew Cooper, from Dublin, came from a background with a tradition of military service; his uncle was Major-General Sir Owen Lloyd who had won the VC in Burma in 1893. Yet, it was the plight of Belgium which '... compelled...' him to enlist. He and his friends believed that the call to arms was honourable and righteous and, as if to prove his point, he enlisted as a private in the 8th Inniskillings, much to his barrister father's annoyance. However, the war also presented opportunities for less noble endeavours. At the Ulster Winter Assizes, a man from Ballymoney, called Daniel Kelly, was imprisoned for six months, for obtaining money by pretending to be a Belgian refugee.[11]

Raising the 10th (Irish) Division

The 10th (Irish) Division was authorised on 21 August 1914, forming part of Kitchener's First New Army, with Lieutenant-General Sir Bryan Mahon, KCVO, CB, DSO commanding. It seems to have been a truly 'Irish' division, in as much as any could be, containing all the political and religious creeds and none. This fact was perhaps reflected in its divisional sign which was a simple green stripe. Although considered the 'ugly duckling' in comparison to the 16th (Irish) and 36th (Ulster) Divisions, it was also, arguably, the most representative of Irish society at the time. It included many serving Volunteers from both sides, frustrated at the continual political wrangling, and it had been formed mainly from the first rush of recruits, eager to enlist. Its officers were drawn from the traditional Anglo-Irish and army families, but they

24

also included middle-class Catholics and Protestants. The men under their command came from every city, county and townland in Ireland. All of the 10th's three brigades, the 29th, 30th and 31st (also sometimes referred to as the 'Ulster' Brigade due to its regimental composition) were initially formed from Irish units. This changed slightly when the 10th Hampshire Regiment was attached to the division to replace the 5th Royal Irish Regiment, which had been chosen to be Divisional Pioneers (infantry troops that were also trained to construct trenches, communication saps, roads etc). The 5th was raised in Clonmel, with Lieutenant-Colonel the Right Honourable Earl of Granard as its commander; it left Longford at the end of April 1915 with 749 ranks and 27 officers. Accompanying them was their chaplain, Father Peter Farrell, whose brother, Luke was serving with the Irish Guards.[12]

For 30th Brigade, the 6th and 7th Munster Fusiliers were formed in Tralee, whilst the 6th and 7th Dublin Fusiliers were raised in Naas. Of note was the raising of 'D' Company, 7th Dublins from the city's professional classes, following an address by Mr Frank Browning of the Irish Rugby Football Union to the Dublin rugby clubs. The Company, with typical Dublin wit, became known as the 'Toffs in the Old Toughs' and got an eager response from men like Ernest Julian, Reid Professor of Criminal Law at Trinity College Dublin and young Thomas Summerville Anderson, a nineteen-year-old clerk from Rathgar. Amongst 'D' Company's ranks could also be found the unassuming Assistant Keeper of the Royal Botanic Gardens, Glasnevin, Charles Frederick Ball. Yet, the 7th Dublins—the 'Dublin Pals'—was a diverse battalion. Just as one company may have been seen as a bastion of privilege, another was drawn from the one of the toughest, working-class groups in the city: the Dublin dockers. These men, largely 'Larkinites' (followers of socialist, James Larkin and the Dublin Lock-out of 1913), were equally enthusiastic to enlist; only three days after the division's formation, on 24 August, forty-one-year-old docker, Arthur Allen from Arran Quay, Dublin, enlisted in the 7th Dublins at Naas.[13]

Similarly, John O'Dare, a forty-one year old from Trim, had originally enlisted with the 2nd Leinsters in 1892 and had fought in South Africa. Upon being discharged, he returned home to work as a general labourer and, by 1914, he was married and had a four-year-old daughter. Whether prompted by the prospect of 'separation allowance', wistful for his old career or motivated by other ideals, on 19 August, he was attested into the 6th Leinsters. He was rapidly promoted to corporal the following month and was soon an acting sergeant.[14] The 6th Leinsters had been raised in Dublin in August and, after a period of training at Fermoy, were sent to the Curragh and regimental depot at Birr. In the same 29th Brigade, the 5th Connaughts also spent its formative training months, digging trenches and on the shooting ranges between Kilworth, Dublin and the Curragh. The brigade's last battalion, the 6th Royal Irish Rifles, was commanded by Lieutenant-Colonel Bradford and was raised in both Dublin and Belfast containing a good many of Ulster's first recruits.

At the end of September 1914, it was optimistically reported that recruitment for the 10th (Irish) Division was 'nearly complete' and plans were already underway to form the second Irish division. However, in reality, the recruitment process for the 10th was far slower than expected. In Ulster, it seems as if Ulster Volunteers were deliberately holding back to await the formation of the 36th (Ulster). Additionally, they needed considerable training to make them into a cohesive fighting force. The 5th and 6th Inniskillings were formed at Omagh, whilst the 5th and 6th Irish Fusiliers were raised in Armagh. One of the latter's keen recruits was the unlikely Cecil Barker, a divinity student at Trinity College Dublin, who seemed destined for a career in the church. His brother had already been ordained but, instead, Cecil was one of the first young men to enlist. In September 1914, he received his commission as a second-lieutenant in Lieutenant-Colonel Poole's 6th 'Faughs'. One officer, Terrence Verschoyle, with the 5th 'Skins' (Royal Iniskilling Fusiliers) noted how they trained at platoon, company and battalion level and how eventually they could easily march twenty miles. The recruits trained at musketry at Dollymount, but Verschoyle wryly considered their level to be '…very poor…' throughout the war. The 10th Division left Ireland in May 1915 for final training in Basingstoke, where they were reviewed by King George (in May) and then Lord Kitchener (1 June). However, it was only when they were issued with new khaki 'drill' uniforms a month later that suspicions were aroused about their eventual destination. Worryingly, 'drill' was issued for service in hot climates and the 10th's volunteers had trained to fight on the Western Front. [15]

Raising the 16th (Irish) Division

On 11 September 1914, the 16th (Irish) Division was officially raised by Army Order in Dublin. This Division had two official signs, the first being the monogram 'LP', in honour of the first Divisional Commander, Sir Lawrence Parsons, who oversaw much of the Division's initial recruitment and organisational structuring. The 16th second divisional sign was the one with which it became synonymous—the green shamrock. Whilst recruitment for the battalions of its three brigades (47th, 48th and 49th 'Ulster') was well underway, by September, the expected flood of enlistment by Irish Volunteers was not as impressive as had been hoped. Before the war, a typical INV formation was the Breffni–O'Reilly Regiment, Upper Loughtee Battalion (Co. Cavan). It was commanded by Mr A. M'Carren JP and consisted of around 650 men, split into eight companies and drawn from throughout the locality. These companies were anything from 70 to 200 men strong and enrolled from the Cavan/First Breffni Troop of National Boy Scouts (A, B & C) and the townlands of Drumcrave, Butlersbridge, Castleterra and Crubany (D, E, F, G). It was exactly this type of unit that was expected to join the 16th Division.[16]

Enlistment for the 16th Division proved rather more difficult than had been expected, perhaps largely due to the complexity of the national political situation and the subsequent fractured loyalties. It is difficult to ascertain exactly how many members of the GAA or the AOH enlisted; however, there was a distinct overlap between their members and membership of the INV. A considerable number of Tipperary hurlers had already enrolled in the Volunteers and, by 1914, the IPP stalwart, Joe Devlin MP, was President of the Hibernians. This multiple involvement in Nationalist organisations guaranteed that, when war came, many of their members would support Redmond's call and join the army. The AOH, through their membership, and the Irish National Foresters, by public statement, endorsed the aims of the INV, insofar as it would train Irish youths to secure Ireland's '... rights and the protection of her future interests'. Increasing references to the division as the 'Irish Brigade' seemed to pander to the romantic notions of the 'Wild Geese' (the Irish Catholic soldiers who left Ireland after 1691 to fight as Irish regiments in the armies of France and Spain). Yet, the suspicion that the 'Irish Brigade' would not be a cohesive fighting unit with its own military identity was a powerful deterrent in recruiting those INV men who were already wary about enlisting. Reticence to enlist can also be explained partly by the residual anger still felt in some quarters of Nationalist society over the incidents at the Curragh and Bachelor's Walk. Ironically, in the same newspapers in which patriotic calls were being made supporting Redmond, alongside recruiting adverts for Irish regiments, other views were being voiced. In a debate at Tuam District Council, it was expressed that the Scottish Borderers embodied the worst bigotry in the British Army, largely because they were, in fact, '... the off-shoot of the North of Ireland Unionists'. Perhaps in an attempt to avoid such controversy, it was openly claimed that the 16th Division was to be completely raised from Irishmen, officered by Irishmen and provisioned from exclusively Irish-'... made goods and Irish-grown produce'.[17]

Lawrence Parsons was behind this drive for exclusively Irish recruitment to the 16th Division (due to its political nature) and this, coupled with his own high ideals of what an Irish soldier should be, caused problems. The Division was dogged with recruitment difficulties, despite the huge pool of perceived manpower at its initial disposal. The early unrealistic standards of potential recruits, however, were rapidly dropped in the face of a dearth of men. By the end of the second month of war, adverts were appearing in the press stating that the age limit for service in the 16th (Irish) was extended to fifty-five '... if physically fit'. This was some twenty years older than the normal eligibility, but many volunteers had already joined the 10th Division and Regular Irish regiments. The case of Bernard Beggan, a twenty-four-year-old labourer from Clinaroo, Newtownbutler, is a fascinating example of this contorted enlistment process. Beggan had originally signed up in Enniskillen on 27 November 1914 for service with the largely INV 6th Connaught Rangers. He was then transferred to the 8th Inniskillings but, finally, sent to the 10th (Irish) Division (in June 1916), to reinforce the 6th Dublins.[18]

Enlistment became such a headache that battalion commanders were forced to go further afield to make up unit strengths. In political terms, the Nationalist units attracted other politically and religiously affiliated groups, most notably from Scotland and the large English cities. Yet, the growing split caused significant notes of discord across the entire volunteer movement. Many believed that Home Rule had already been legitimately secured and that the IPP was now actively assisting the Unionists to destroy the only mechanism Nationalists had to guarantee its future implementation. Despite all of these hurdles, steady bursts of INV enlistment occurred. In mid-August, the Cashel Volunteers were commanded by Colonel Thomas Cahill and assisted in drill by Captain Gibson, Durham Light Infantry; by December, a hundred had joined the army. In Sligo, the local INV committee held a public meeting in the Town Hall, fully supporting Redmond's Woodenbridge speech. Interestingly, the parish priest of Collooney, Father Doyle, issued a bald statement telling the audience that the rival Volunteers had never done '... a decent day's work for God or country'. In despair at the impasse, Hervey de Montmorency resigned as Inspector of the Wicklow Volunteers, to continue his captaincy in the Dublin Fusiliers, believing the split to be disastrous for Irish Nationalism. Montmorency resolved that being an ordinary captain in the British Army was better than being a '...Field Marshal in the Irish

Volunteers'. His friend, Captain George Berkeley, former INV Inspector for Belfast, also left the National Volunteers soon afterwards and joined the 3rd Cavalry Reserve regiment as Brigade Musketry Officer.[19]

The loss, or lack, of experienced officers was also a pressing concern. The INV officer corps, largely due to the lack of OTCs in Irish Catholic schools or universities, was woefully under-trained. Colonel Cox, commander of the 'Fighting Seventh' Inniskillings, discovered that his INV battalion had a cadre of enthusiastic but militarily naïve officers. Some preferred to invent their own orders and formations, while others were continually confused by basic squad drill. Indeed, one officer was baffled by his veteran NCO bawling out: 'When I says "fix", you don't fix; but when I says "bayonets", you fix!' This is, perhaps, why Parsons insisted, reasonably enough, that his divisional officers should possess some vestige of military experience. Many INV officers who had been to school in England did have this, though; Gordon Shaw had been in the OTC at Marlborough and was 2-i-C of the Limerick Volunteers. In contrast, Cecil William Chandler, born in Lee, Kent, was a marine insurance broker with Lloyds and came from a stockbroker family. As if to show the lottery of officer material in the 16th Division, upon gaining his commission on 28 September 1914, 2nd Lieutenant Chandler was posted to where the need was greatest— the 8th Munster Fusiliers. Yet, to make up the local deficit, Parsons created an officer cadet battalion, the 7th Leinsters, at Fermoy in October 1914. Due to its over-subscription (and initial lukewarm reception by those Volunteer officers who did not wish to enlist as privates), Colonel Moore eventually persuaded Parsons that any INV subalterns who wished to have immediate commissions should be sent to Irish units in Great Britain. Equally, basic tactical training was rudimentary, with little or no guidance in preparation for entrenchments or the use of modern musketry. In England, the 16th (Irish) Division came under the control of a distinctly unimpressed Lieutenant-General Sir Henry Wilson. Yet, his assessment that the 16th Division needed further intense training was shared by its popular new commander, Major-General Sir William Hickie. Both men realised that, despite almost a year of training, the Division would not be battle-ready until spring 1916. As it was, the better trained medical, engineer and artillery wings of the 16th (Irish) ended up being transferred to other divisions far sooner than their infantry colleagues.[20]

On 6 September, the 6th Royal Irish was raised at Clonmel as part of the 47th Brigade under Lieutenant-Colonel Curzon. Captain William Redmond, John Redmond's brother, was amongst its officers, and one company consisted of men of the 'Royal Guernsey Militia', whilst another was from the Derry

Volunteers. This contingent arrived at Amiens Street station in November, led by Captain McManus, and the men were given free cigarettes as they embarked for battalion training at Fermoy.[21] Another part of the brigade consisted of the 6th Connaughts, raised in September 1914 and mostly comprised of the Belfast Regiment of National Volunteers. On 20 November, they paraded from Victoria Barracks to the Great Northern railway station for the journey to Fermoy. As they marched through the city in greatcoats (only one officer was in uniform, possibly Lieutenant Telford of the Connaughts), they were led by Hibernian banners and associated bands. As they passed along Royal Avenue, the Clann Uladh Pipers, the O'Neill Pipers, the Mandeville Flute Band and National Volunteer Bugle Band played the Nationalist anthems, 'O'Donnell Abu' and 'Clare's Dragoons'.[22] Captain Wray's Enniskillen Volunteers was another large INV unit within the 6th Connaughts but, interestingly, the battalion commander, Lieutenant-Colonel Lenox-Conygham, was a veteran UVF officer who had been prominent in 'Operation Lion'. In addition to the 7th Leinsters, the final unit in the brigade was the 8th Munster Fusiliers, raised at Fermoy and commanded by Lieutenant-Colonel O'Meagher (one of the few Catholic battalion commanders in the division).

In 48th Brigade, the 9th Munsters were the last 'Service' battalion to be formed from the regiment and recruited heavily throughout the south of Ireland during September and October. Alongside them were the Dublin-raised 8th and 9th Dublin Fusiliers; the latter became known as the 'Scholar's Battalion' due to its reputation of having highly educated recruits from more affluent or university backgrounds. Amongst its officers was the leading Nationalist academic and poet, Professor Tom Kettle. The last battalion in 48th Brigade was the 7th Irish Rifles, mostly raised from INV units within Belfast and County Antrim. As the battalion was under-strength before it departed for training in England (September 1915) it received a contingent of men from the Royal Jersey Militia; this contingent of 6 officers and 224 men formed 'D' Company. Battalions from the brigade were sent for initial training at Kilworth, Ballyvonare and Fermoy before their final months of training at Blackdown in England and departure for the Western Front in the last days of 1915. Indeed, the majority of the 16th (Irish) arrived in France in late December, proudly displaying their green shamrock 'flashes' in recognition of the Division's origins.

However, 49th (Ulster) Brigade had the most severe problems in recruitment and training of all the 16th Division's brigades. Indeed, the general lack of appropriate experience or military training can be shown by the amount of time spent at home before they were sent to France. The 7th and 8th Irish Fusiliers were formally established at Armagh, with the 7th and 8th Inniskillings raised in Omagh and trained at Finner Camp (Co. Donegal). The 7th 'Faughs' had a core of INV Tyrone Volunteers, many of whom came from Strabane and were in Tipperary for almost a year before being sent for further training at Pirbright in September 1915. Similarly, the 8th Irish Fusiliers were sent to Newry in July 1915 and, like the rest of the brigade, neither battalion arrived in France until February 1916, well behind other battalions of Volunteers in either the 16th or 36th Divisions.

Raising the 36th (Ulster) Division

In contrast, recruitment for the 36th (Ulster) Division was comparatively straightforward. There were still concerns over Ulster's loyalty to the Crown (the *Times* correspondent privately commented that if the King signed the Home Rule Bill he would not be able to 'show himself' in Ulster ever again) but the country's need proved greater. The GOC, upon authorisation, was Major-General Sir Herbert Powell and, whilst recruitment for an Ulster Division effectively began on 3 September, it was officially raised as the '36th' Division on 28 October. Its headquarters were in Belfast city centre, at No.29 Wellington Place, and its three brigades were, at first, numbered 1st, 2nd and 3rd; although these numbers were changed to 107th, 108th and 109th Brigades in November. The backbone of each battalion was to come from the intensely local UVF regiments, already organised along the lines of the territorial structure and fairly ready for incorporation into the army. It seems that, by the end of 1914, most eligible Ulster Volunteers had volunteered in some capacity. William McConnell was a UVF man and, with his friend, he enlisted in the army following Carson's call. William was posted to the 11th Irish Rifles whilst his friend ended up in the 12th Rifles; another friend, Gordon Paisley, deliberately enlisted in the Black Watch. However, not all of these volunteers were fit and able for active service. For example, Private William Gregg, 8th Irish Rifles, was a thirty-four-year-old labourer from Ballylesson (Co. Antrim), who enlisted in September 1914 but was discharged as unfit for duty on 10 December 1914. Conversely, George McBride, who was in the UVF and worked in Mackie & Sons, was still accepted into the 15th (North Belfast) Irish Rifles despite being underage.[23]

As with the INV, a number of 36th Division recruits appear to have been members of two organisations. It is estimated that 100,000 Orangemen served during the Great War, not necessarily all on active service. Of interest is that many lodges were directly affected by army recruitment and nearly every lodge saw a reduction in its membership. Of the brethren in Ardstraw LOL 502, 50 per cent volunteered and some lodges effectively closed for the duration of the war; one such was King William's Defenders LOL 127 in Portadown, which held no meetings from November 1914 until July 1918. In Dublin, it was thought that around eighty Loyal Dublin Volunteers enlisted in the 'Dublin Pals' Battalion, directly from men of the Trinity College Dublin LOL.[24] Whilst the rush to enlist for the Ulster Division was notable, there were some in the Ulster Volunteers who did not join up immediately. Indeed, in Nationalist circles, the UVF was coming under some scrutiny regarding its enlistment figures. Redmond had already declared the 10th (Irish) Division was the first such formation to represent Nationalist Ireland in the field (slightly mischievously perhaps, as the 5th and 6th Inniskillings had large units of Ulster Volunteers). In a speech at Tuam, Redmond declared that over 16,000 INV had joined the army, whilst only 10,000 UVF had done so. This brought a furious response from Major-General Richardson. Redmond may have been exercised by the fact that his own brother was about to enlist. Yet, it also came at a point, December 1914, when Nationalist recruitment was faltering and, it was largely due to this, that Willie Redmond had taken dramatic action. Addressing a crowd in front of the Imperial Hotel, Cork, the fifty-year-old former Wexford Militia officer famously told his audience: 'Don't go, but come with me.' He received his captaincy in the 6th Irish Regiment in February 1915.[25]

Many of the Belfast Ulster Volunteers were formed into the distinct 107th Brigade, which contained the 8th (East Belfast), 9th (West Belfast), 10th (South Belfast) and 15th (North Belfast) Irish Rifles. Although the 8th Rifles was raised in September 1914 from the UVF's 'East Belfast Volunteers', locally, the men were simply called 'Ballymacarrett's Own'. Similarly, the 9th Rifles became known as the 'Shankill Boys' and were initially commanded by Lieutenant-Colonel George S. Ormerod, a veteran Munster Fusilier officer with thirty years' service. It seems that, within the ranks of Ulster paramilitarism, the war was seen as an opportunity to transform the unworthy or ignoble into the heroic. As Major Frank Crozier commented, the war regenerated '...orange-blooded revolutionaries...' into reputable soldiers of the Royal Irish Rifles.[26]

Equally, Sir James Craig's brother, Captain Charles Craig, MP for South Antrim, had been commissioned into the 11th Irish Rifles in early September 1914. It was one of the four battalions in 108th Brigade which comprised three units of Irish rifles and the 9th Irish Fusiliers. The 9th 'Faughs', known as 'Blacker's Boys' (after their commander, Lieutenant-Colonel Stewart W. Blacker), were mostly raised from the Armagh, Cavan and Monaghan Volunteers and contained large numbers of men from Portadown, Armagh and Lurgan. The other rifle battalions were equally recruited from rural Ulster, with the 11th (South Antrim), 12th (Central Antrim) and 13th (1st Co. Down) Irish Rifles. Indeed, the intensely local 'pals' nature of the division can be shown by looking at the geographical origins of the 13th Irish Rifles: its 'A' Coy recruited from Holywood, Bangor, Donaghadee and Ards; 'B' Coy was from Ballygowan, Comber, Newtownards and Ards; 'C' Coy came from Killyleagh, Downpatrick, Ballynahinch, Dromore, Hillsborough, Castlewellan and Newcastle; and 'D' Coy's recruits came from Banbridge, Rathfriland, Gilford, Newry and Kilkeel. John Gregg, of 'C' Company, 13th Irish Rifles, lived outside the village of Hillsborough (Co. Down). He was a farmer by occupation and Moravian by religion but, when war came, he joined his friends and enlisted in the local unit. By this time, he was the man of the family and had to leave his mother and sisters to cope with the running of the farm by themselves.[27]

The old UVF regiments of the west of Ulster also, effectively, maintained the core of 109th Brigade, with the 9th (Tyrone), 10th (Co. Londonderry) and 11th (Donegal and Fermanagh) Inniskillings. The 'Tyrones', 'Derrys' and 'Donegals' were all officially raised at Omagh and, in a reverse situation to that faced by the Belfast INV and 6th Connaughts, a contingent of Loyal Dublin Volunteers formed a platoon in the 9th 'Skins'. The men's backgrounds were varied but the majority came from Dublin with William Long and Vivien McKenzie Meyers both born and enlisted in the city. Frederick Carter, born in St Paul's, Dublin, travelled to Donegal to enlist at Finner Camp, whilst Daniel Griffith had grown up around St James' Gate, Dublin, and worked as a fitter's helper in the engineering department of Guinness. The last battalion in 109th Brigade was the 14th Irish Rifles (YCV), which boasted that it had an 'Old Public School Boy's Company'. Indeed, the battalion was sometimes cheekily referred to by other units in the Ulster Division as the 'Chocolate Soldiers' because of their generally privileged backgrounds. The last divisional unit raised, effectively as a 'special battalion' attached directly to the GHQ, was the pioneer battalion, the 16th (2nd Co. Down) Irish Rifles. It was formed in Lurgan (Co. Armagh) and was known as 'The Terrors' due to their adoption of the 'South Down Militia' as their marching song.[28]

The four training camps for the Division were at Ballykinler, Donard Lodge, Clandeboye and Finner, in Co. Donegal. However, conditions at this last camp were notoriously poor. With the onset of winter, the men were housed in tents which caused much sickness and even fatalities, especially amongst the YCVs and Inniskillings of 109th Brigade. By mid-December 1914, it was stated that roughly 1,600 more men were needed to complete the Division but, whilst it was considered to be much better trained than their equivalents elsewhere, it was still far from ready for active service.[29] In July 1915, the Division arrived at Seaford Camp in Sussex, ready for review by Field-Marshal Earl Kitchener on 20 July. During September, it was moved to undergo final training at Bordon Camp and Bramshott, before arriving in France in early October, under the new command of Major-General Sir Oliver Nugent from Cavan. As the men arrived in France, the divisional sign, the Red Hand of Ulster, was to become an increasingly common sight.

Miscellaneous Irish Units in British Service 1914–1918

It may be useful to pause, at this point, and briefly consider those units or contingents within regiments from Great Britain who had their own overtly Irish military identity. Throughout the great industrial English, Scottish and Welsh cities, large enclaves of Irish communities lived and thrived, and many in these communities rushed to create deliberately Irish units, from London and Liverpool to Newcastle-Upon-Tyne and the cities of Scotland.

The vast majority of soldiers in the 1/18th and 2/18th London Regiment ('The London Irish Rifles') were, unsurprisingly, Londoners but with a sprinkling of first-generation Irishmen. The famous poet and author, Patrick McGill, came from Glenties (Co. Donegal) and served with the London Irish as a stretcher-bearer. Another London Irishman, Edward Casey, actually enlisted with the Dublin Fusiliers. Casey grew up in the slums of Kerry Street, in the East End of London and came from an Irish Catholic family. He was very proud of his Irish roots but extremely aware of his British and Londoner status too. Whilst on training in Ireland, he visited his Sinn Féin cousin in Kilmallock in Limerick, where he was bluntly told that he was not an 'Englishman' but an Irishman born in the 'wrong place'. To this Casey angrily replied that he couldn't understand why there was so much hostility towards the English. Despite his heritage, he did not 'feel Irish'; indeed, in his words, he was a born and bred cockney, from Canning Town, in '… the biggest city in the whole bleeding world'. Such a city raised two battalions of the London Irish Rifles.[30]

Equally, in Newcastle-upon-Tyne, on 12 September 1914, influential Irish businessmen and community leaders combined to issue a plea in the local press for the creation of an Irish 'regiment' of Tynesiders. The ensuing recruitment frenzy throughout Northumberland and Durham began a fierce rivalry between the Tyneside Scottish and Irish as to who could provide the most recruits. The winner, if 'winner' was ever the correct term, was hotly disputed by both sides. An impressive five battalions each were raised for the war. By early November 1914, enough men had already volunteered to fill the ranks of the first two designated 'Tyneside Irish' battalions, now officially known as the 24th and 25th Northumberland Fusiliers. The 'Tyneside Irish' even adopted a cap badge which was based on the Connaught Rangers' crowned 'Maid of Erin' above a scroll which bore their unit title. The volunteers came from throughout northern England, with the four 'Service' battalions (24th – 27th Battalions, 30th 'Reserve') drawing men from Yorkshire, Cumberland, Northumberland and beyond. One such eager recruit was Private Benjamin Garrett of the '1st Tyneside Irish', born and raised in Newcastle-upon-Tyne and enlisted in South Shields. By August 1915, all four Tyneside Irish battalions were in training on Salisbury Plain and, before long, many of these men would find themselves in the chalk-trenches of Picardy.

Similarly, Liverpool had a long tradition of immigrants from Ireland. Like Newcastle, the rivalry between the Scots and Irish communities in the city developed into a competition to see who could raise a battalion first. As it turned out, each nationality raised two battalions. On 4 August, the 1st 'Liverpool Irish' was raised at 75 Shaw Street before being initially placed in the Liverpool Brigade of the 55th West Lancashire Division. Recruits for the 1/8th and 2/8th (Irish) TF King's (Liverpool) Regiment were plentiful, with the majority of men coming from Liverpool but with strong contingents from Manchester, Oldham, Lancashire, Cheshire and North Wales.

Contingents of Irishmen, mostly from Ulster, could also be found throughout the Scottish regiments, with many making the conscious decision to join for cultural and social reasons. The 42nd Royal Highland Regiment, the 'Black Watch' held a particular attraction for Irish recruits, and it came as little surprise when the regiment actively sought recruits from Belfast. These men were attested into the 1/6th (Perthshire Territorial Force), making up roughly 3 per cent of the unit (4 per cent of men in the unit came from the whole of Ireland). A group of Belfast men served in the 1st (Queen's Own) Cameron Highlanders and yet another small number of Belfast men found themselves serving with the 4th (Angus and Dundee) Black Watch. Indeed, as if to reinforce this close Scots' link, the 1/4th (Ross Highland Territorial Force) Seaforth Highlanders actually had a recruiting office in Belfast for the duration of the war. It is estimated that 2.5 per cent of the 4th Seaforth's recruits came from Belfast with nearly 4 per cent of them being born, or living, in Ireland when war broke out. One of those men was Private Charles McMullen who was born in Belfast and living in Antrim with his mother and eldest brother in 1914. Whilst his eldest brother was a colour-printer in the print works there, Charles was a general labourer in Boal's linen factory. He duly enlisted in the Seaforths and became part of the esteemed 51st (Highland) Division, serving with its 154th Brigade.

Finally, whilst not actual Irish formations, the Hampshire Regiment had very strong links with both of the Irish divisions, with their 10th and 11th Battalions serving in the 10th and 16th respectively. Both units were raised at Winchester in August–September 1914 and moved to Ireland that month. The brilliant young English classicist, George Leonard Cheesman, had just published 'Auxilia of the Roman Army' but, within months, he had been commissioned and posted to the 10th Hampshires. They arrived in Dublin with a strength of around 1,070 men and, on their first parade before Brigadier-General Hill at Beggar's Bush Barracks, he was clearly impressed by their soldierly appearance telling them that they had '…the mark of class about you'. Shortly after this, they were posted to Mullingar, where they were joined by their brother battalion, the 11th Hampshires, the new pioneer battalion for the 16th (Irish) Division. Both units were so warmly received by the townsfolk (especially the local ladies' committee, led by Mrs Patrick) that they never forgot their welcome. Indeed, when the Hampshires left Mullingar in March 1915 (the 10th for the Curragh, the 11th for Kilworth) they were given a public vote of thanks by the town commissioners who wished them a genuinely safe return from the war.[31]

The Irish Regiments on Imperial Service

Meanwhile, for those Irish regiments on duties throughout the Empire, the process of practical mobilisation took longer. The 1st Munster Fusiliers were actually in Burma, whilst the 1st Irish Rifles were on duties in Aden and only arrived at Liverpool at the end of October 1914. In early November 1914, the Rifles arrived at Le Havre and were put into reserve trenches in preparation for their use in the new-year offensives. Another battalion, the 2nd Irish Fusiliers had been stationed in Quetta on the North-West Frontier and had also only arrived back in Britain in late November. Within a fortnight, they were organised into the 27th Division and hurriedly sent to France on

19 December. The 1st Inniskillings were stationed at Trimulgherry in India and sailed for Britain in early December. By the time they arrived at Avonmouth, in January 1915, the war's fronts had been extended and, instead of service in France, they were sent to Gallipoli. On 4 August, the 6th Inniskilling Dragoons were also on service in India, at Muttra, as part of the fabled Mhow Cavalry Brigade. The 6th Dragoons sailed from Bombay in November and arrived at Marseilles a few weeks before Christmas 1914. They were not alone. The 8th King's Royal Irish Hussars and 1st Battalions of the Royal Irish, Dublin Fusiliers, Leinsters and Connaughts were all stationed in India when war broke out.

Indeed, the 1st Connaught Rangers may have the dubious honour of being the first unit with a sustained number of casualties in the war. On 17 August, the battalion entrained from Gough Barracks, Ferozepore, for Karachi. The summer heat was overbearing and some ten men collapsed from heat stroke and had to be left behind. Despite treatment by their medical officer, Captain John Errol Boyd RAMC, three men died before even leaving for the Western Front: Private Jeremiah Cronin from Cork, Private Christopher Fitzgibbon from Kilkeel (Co. Down) and Private Michael Lapparth from Castlebar (Co. Mayo). All were buried at Mombai (Bombay). Another soldier, Private Martin Keeley from Ballinasloe (Co. Galway), died of severe heat stroke whilst actually on board the train to Karachi (where he was subsequently buried).[32] It was a faint indicator of the unfathomable extent of casualties which were to visit the Irish regiments over the next four years.

CHAPTER THREE

'There's going to be a row on here!'[1]

Mons to First Ypres, August 1914–December 1914

In August 1914, the strength of the British Regular Army stood at approximately 125,000 officers and other ranks, formed into six infantry divisions and one cavalry division. From these limited resources were drawn the men that made up Britain's BEF and in its ranks were many Reservists who, in all honesty, had never expected to fire a rifle in anger again. During the opening weeks of the war, the British public anticipated that the BEF would stem the German advance in Flanders and defeat the Kaiser's army almost single-handedly. Yet, the opening weeks of the war brought a swift shock to British society. From August 1914 to September 1915, the very life-blood of the British Army, its stalwart Regular battalions, seeped away into the fields, ditches and trenches of France and Flanders.

The First Irish Regiments Arrive in France

At the outbreak of war, the initial British base in France was to be at Maubeuge (against Kitchener's wishes that it should remain further south at Amiens) where it was planned that Field Marshal French would cross the river Sambre and co-ordinate with his allies around Mons. Within ten days of the declaration of war, the first Irish battalions were on French soil. Among the first to land in France were the 2nd Connaught Rangers, who disembarked only nine days after the declaration of war. It was as the khaki-clad ranks passed through the streets of Boulogne that George Curnock, journalist with the *Daily Mail*, observed the various British troops singing 'Dolly Grey' and 'Soldiers of the Queen'. Then he heard an unfamiliar tune, being sung lustily by the very enthusiastic voices of the Connaughts. Florrie Forde had sung the ditty in the music-halls of Britain in 1912 and it was rumoured to have been written for a bet, but it had also been taken up by a travelling accordion player in the streets of Galway in early 1913. It was here that Captain Dryden of the Connaught Rangers had heard it—as had many of his men. They adopted it on route marches and, as they marched through the streets of Boulogne, their song quickly became synonymous with the war itself. It was, of course, 'Tipperary'. Ironically, Irish regiments, as a rule, were not known for singing on the march but, as the strains of 'It's a long way to go' faded away, they inadvertently created a legend.[2]

On the same day, the Irish Guards landed at Le Havre and, almost immediately, were soaked in a violent thunderstorm as they embarked on trains for the front. Amongst them were Privates Richard Daughton from Killenaule (Co. Tipperary), Edward Daly from Ballycannan (Co. Kilkenny) and Luke Farrell from Longford, whose brother was a parish priest there. They were part of the steady stream of troops now arriving daily in France, fresh from their barracks and depots in the UK. The non-Regular troopers of the two regiments of Irish Horse had also been pressed into service as part of Sir John French's 70,000-strong BEF. The day after war broke out, the officers, NCOs and men of Enniskillen, Londonderry, Dundalk and Belfast Troops of 'A' squadron, North Irish Horse, were quickly mobilised. By 7 August, they were in Dublin to form a Special Service Squadron and, over the course of the week that followed, intensive training was carried out and campaign equipment was drawn. Twelve days previously the men had been on their summer camp in Enniskillen. Now, the 'part-timers' of 'A' Squadron were deemed ready for active service and left North Wall Quay, Dublin, on *SS Architect* bound for Le Havre. Two days later, the first active service unit of the South Irish Horse, 'B' Squadron, duly arrived before entraining the following day for, as their war diary stated, an '… unknown destination'. The troops of South Irish Horse 'C' Squadron arrived on 20 August and both the North and South Irish Horse were posted for use as divisional cavalry, employed as GHQ troops and scouts. Indeed, these Ulster and Irish troopers had the official honour of being the first non-Regular British troops to enter the war. Their ranks ranged from the North Irish Horse's squadron commander, the aristocratic Major Lord Cole, to one of the South Irish Horse's troopers, Leo Le Bas, a recently graduated dentist from Rathmines and prominent officer in the local Boy's Brigade.[3]

By 21 August, the BEF concentration in France was almost complete and, as more and more units arrived, the spirit of optimism seemed to increase. The following day, the 2nd Royal Inniskilling Fusiliers landed in France, whilst back in Southampton, the 1st Irish Fusiliers were on their troopship, *SS Lake Michigan,* accompanied by the Seaforth Highlanders. Lieutenant Penrose noted that, as they pulled away from the dock, the Highlanders and Fusiliers clambered onto the rigging and booms, raucously singing 'Tipperary' to the precious few quayside observers. Their enthusiasm was clearly infectious, as he happily concluded: 'We are "for it" at last.' Perhaps it was just as well that the eager and experienced Regular soldiers did not know what lay ahead of them. On the same day as the 'Faughs' and Seaforths were crossing the English Channel, the Second German Army under von Bulow smashed through the French Fifth Army along the Sambre. It threw the French into a sublime, if unexpected, panic. General Lanrezac was so dismayed that he ordered a full-scale retreat the next day. It was to be a fateful decision and one which would have a huge impact on the newly arrived BEF. From his 'Royal and Imperial Headquarters' at Aix-la-Chapelle, the Kaiser purportedly issued his infamous order that his troops should concentrate on 'exterminating' General French's '... contemptible little army'. By 22 August, British troops were hurriedly deployed in a position along a line from Condé, through Mons, to Binche; the men serving with 8th Brigade of the 3rd Division were right at the heart of the BEF. Those men included the 2nd Irish Rifles and 2nd Royal Irish, followed a day later by the 2nd Connaught Rangers.[4]

First Contact on the Soignies Road

Like most military commanders, Field Marshal Sir John French, had fully intended to begin his campaign with a glorious advance. However, as the Germans 'rolled up' the French Army, meeting fierce pockets of Belgian resistance, the British, instead, found themselves in a hurried retreat. General Lanrezac and the French had been fought to a deadlock around Charleroi but, instead of pushing against the right flank of the opposing Germans, Field-Marshal French decided to hold his position—for twenty-four hours—at Mons. The French army command had informed the BEF that the German forces against them consisted of two army corps, with a possible cavalry division at its head. These reports were confirmed by aerial reconnaissance and British cavalry scouts, who had penetrated along the Brussels road and reached the town of Soignies.

In the early hours of 22 August, 'C' Squadron of the 4th (Royal Irish) Dragoon Guards, led by Major George 'Tom' Bridges, was advancing along the Soignies road as 'contact squadron' for the cavalry division. The main squadron halted at the village of Casteau, where Major Bridges sent out a scouting party to ride further along the road. Shortly afterwards, these scouts reported seeing an enemy mounted patrol approaching them. In response, 'C' Squadron split into four troops: two dismounted to prepare an ambush, whilst the other two remained saddled up and ready to pursue. Just before the trap could be sprung, however, the party of six German Kurassiers turned and began to trot away. It was at this point that Corporal Edward Thomas, from Nenagh (Co. Tipperary), fired after them—and ensured his fame as the first British soldier on the Western Front to shoot at the enemy.

As the patrol from the 4th Kurassier (Prussian Household) Regiment hastily galloped away, Captain Hornby, with two mounted troops, charged after the fleeing patrol, only to find the main German squadron blocking their path. However, this larger unit, seeing their comrades fleeing down the road, turned about and did likewise. Captain Hornby and his men rode onwards, chasing the larger fleeing German cavalry force for one and a half miles before catching them at the foot of a hill and charging them at sabre point. The resultant skirmish was decided in Captain Hornby's favour (the first officer to 'draw blood' in the war) and consolidated by Major Tom Bridges, with prisoners taken and much information gathered, namely that the 4th Royal Irish Dragoon Guards had just engaged, and beaten off, the spearhead of the German cavalry division.[5]

The Battle of Mons

On 23 August, some 80,000 British had established themselves along the twenty-one mile line of the Mons-Condé canal, but in front of them in opposition were over 160,000 Germans and nearly 60,000 Germans, with 230 guns, threatened their left flank. The main weight of the German thrust was to concentrate on the bustling mining town of Mons, held by the British 3rd Division. It was not an ideal position to hold. Some eighteen bridges crossed the canal, with numerous lock-gates, all of which could easily be crossed on foot. Furthermore, the town was a confusing labyrinth of narrow cobbled lanes and streets, jumbled with miner's cottages, railway and tram lines, and dominated by slag heaps. The canal was a natural barrier, however, and the British troops soon set about fortifying it as best they could. Barricades were hastily formed from beds, tables, wardrobes or anything else they could find and these makeshift fortifications sprang up all along the embankment. Preparations, however, were all too brief and within hours the German artillery bombardment began with field-guns and heavy howitzers. From behind their barricades, the British defenders, including the 2nd Irish Rifles, braced themselves for the inevitable attack.

Meanwhile, Lieutenant-Colonel St J.A. Cox, 2nd Royal Irish, found himself stranded at Brigade HQ and command passed to Major St Leger in his absence. The Royal Irish were posted behind the Irish Rifles and the Middlesex Regiment which were defending the Obourg Bridge and the area to Bois la Haut. As a dangerous gap opened up between the two battalions, the 2nd Royal Irish were ordered up in support, all the time under heavy fire. Athough they were supposed to be in reserve, they ended up plugging the gap between the 8th and 9th Brigades and actively stemming the massed German advance at Petit Nimy and the Obourg Bridge. At around lunchtime, the Germans crossed the bridge and, for three hours, the two battalions doggedly refused to yield any further territory. As German cavalry was sighted coming out of the wood of Bois d'Havre, the 2nd Royal Irish's battalion machine-guns (all two of them) opened fire and cut them down in swathes. Just as it appeared that the 2nd Royal Irish were holding their own, enemy artillery knocked out both machine-guns and began to inflict heavy casualties. Although one gun was repaired, by quarter-past-three, the Germans were only 600 yards away from the makeshift British defences. A series of bitter push-backs followed until the 4th Middlesex and 2nd Royal Irish eventually fell back to Bois La Haut, where they attempted to make a stand. The pressure on them was only released at around four o'clock by the covering fire from the battalions on their right flank, namely the Gordon Highlanders, Royal Scots and 2nd Irish Rifles, commanded by Lieutenant-Colonel Bird. Two companies of the Rifles were ordered to 'double-time' to a position next to the Royal Scots, dodging shell fire as they ran to their new positions. Belfast and Dublin accents could be heard laughing and jeering at the misses, as one rifleman allegedly shouted out mockingly, 'Send for the police, there's going to be a row on here!'[6]

The British 3rd Division doggedly held its position despite increasingly desperate German assaults to break the British II Corps. At 7.00 pm exactly, the Germans launched a mass attack against the positions on the Condé canal. Their artillery stopped and the massed German infantry advanced to within 300 yards of the British lines before the Regulars opened fire. For the Irish Rifles, the legendary fifteen aimed rounds a minute that followed was dreadful, with the ranks of advancing Germans hit repeatedly as '… field grey human targets'. The German advance effectively halted where it was. Just over a mile south from Mons, the 2nd Connaught Rangers had 'dug in' by a crossroads high on a ridge and could see the battle unfolding. From their position they watched the shelling of the town below and cheered when they saw the massed battalions of field-grey sent reeling back by the single, stretched line of khaki. The remnants of the German assault melted back into the twilight, as the groans of dying and wounded men filled the evening air. However, the British had sustained some 1,642 dead and wounded in return, with 2nd Royal Irish casualties alone standing at around 300 men.[7]

The Retreat from Mons and Le Cateau

Whilst the battle of Mons had undoubtedly shaken the Germans, it was at a terrible price. Furthermore, the actions of General Lanrezac in continuing his retreat forced the British to do the same, rendering the gallantry on all sides at Mons utterly redundant. As night fell on the smouldering town, a cease-fire was allowed so that the Germans could remove their casualties. Corporal Lucy of the 2nd Irish Rifles could see the enemy collecting their dead and injured by the eerie lamp-light of the lanterns they carried. The British silently withdrew the next morning and destroyed as many crossing points over the canal as they could.[8]

As part of the Guards Brigade, in the early hours of 23 August, the Irish Guards had been ordered to Bois La Haut in the Mons suburbs but they were eventually re-posted southwards to take up positions on a chalk ridge at Harveng. The Guards came under shellfire and were forced to 'dig in' for the first time but, by the following morning, they were also marching south towards Etreux. It was here that their drill sergeant, CSM Michael Moran, from Rosturk (Co. Mayo), rejoined the battalion from home, only to find it marching in the wrong direction. His subsequent outburst—'Fwat's all this about a retreat?'—caused a ripple of laughter among the Irish Guards which had to be quickly stifled. For the 2nd Connaughts, the ominous order to withdraw on the morning of 24 August signalled the reality of the situation, as did their instructions to act as rear-guard. At midday, the German shelling of the ridge began, as they observed unit after unit pouring through their position as they left Mons. The Connaughts noted that the men of the Irish Rifles and 4th Middlesex who, despite bearing the brunt of the previous day's fighting, had still marched off smartly as if on the drill ground.[9]

As General Fergusson's 5th Infantry Division was heading down the
Cambrai road, it was caught by murderous shellfire from eleven German guns
which overlooked their position. These were entrenched on a hillside, by the
edge of a wood, at Andregines which was between Mons and Valenciennes.
The 2nd Cavalry Brigade was ordered to silence them and a disastrous charge,
notably by the 9th (Queen's Royal) Lancers and 4th Royal Irish Dragoon
Guards, followed. It was officially known as the 'Flank Guard Action at Elouges'.
The 4th Dragoon Guards and 9th Lancers galloped down an old Roman
road towards an abandoned sugar-beet factory. As they charged forward, under
heavy shellfire, their horses stumbled directly into a set of wire entanglements
and the 9th Lancers were cut to pieces. One corporal recalled that, as he
rode across the fields, at about 200 yards from the guns, he could only see
three troopers and an officer alongside him. Then, at 150 yards from the gun
position, twenty concealed machine-guns opened fire. The result was utter
carnage. As the 4th Dragoon Guards wheeled to the right and obliquely onto
their objective, the Lancers ploughed into the guns and the wire defending
them. Although the guns were eventually neutralised, at the rallying point
(a nearby railway embankment), only seventy-two Lancers formed up. Up
to 500 Lancers had been involved in the charge. Major Bridges of the 4th
Dragoon Guards had two horses killed under him before he was rescued by
the Brigade signals officer and, rather bizarrely, whisked away in a blue and
silver Rolls Royce. Whilst the car driver's identity may never be confirmed,
soon afterwards, it was noted that the Duke of Westminster personally drove
his friend (the gravely wounded Captain Francis Grenfell of the 9th Lancers)
away from the action in a Rolls Royce. The news of the Lancers' massacre
soon spread throughout II Corps, with the Royal Irish Fusiliers hearing about
it three days later. Lieutenant Penrose commented that the 9th Lancers had
fallen into '… a trap like Bannockburn…' with only sixty-seven survivors.[10]

General Sir Horace Smith-Dorrien's II Corps retreated west of Mormal
Forest (with I Corps, under General Haig, dividing eastwards) with the aim
of reuniting south of the forest, at Le Cateau. Although Smith-Dorrien's
II Corps had successfully retired to Le Cateau, he was ordered by Sir
John French to make a further withdrawal. Yet, by now the 3rd Division,
and particularly the 7th Brigade, was utterly worn out. The newly arrived
(but tired and incomplete) 4th Division, consisting of the 1st Irish Fusiliers,
2nd Dublin Fusiliers and 2nd Inniskillings, was hastily deployed. Lieutenant
Penrose, 1st 'Faughs', recalled that the enemy shellfire was '… damnable…'
and that he helped carry his men's rifles to help them along. As the retreating

British troops were already vulnerable, General Allenby's Cavalry Division continuously attempted to protect their flanks, shepherding them southwards. Acting Squadron Quartermaster Sergeant, W. Clenshaw, 5th Irish Lancers, was in command of the rear troop of the rear guard and controlled it admirably against superior enemy numbers, enabling infantry—and a battery—to withdraw in good order. The situation worsened, however, when Allenby warned Smith-Dorrien that his cavalry may not have the strength or numbers to be able to continue to protect the withdrawal. Additionally, II Corps' own rearguards were coming into Le Cateau shattered with weariness and with news that the Germans were close behind. If the British could leave the town before the enemy's arrival and delay their progress further, then II Corps might be saved. Consequently, Smith-Dorrien made a monumental decision. He would fight a holding action, which might buy enough time for the majority of II Corps to retreat in good order. On 26 August, in an effort to slow down the powerful advance by General von Kluck's German First Army, a desperate rearguard battle began.[11]

The resultant clash lasted for eleven punishing hours. von Kluck's assault included intense shelling and determined massed infantry attacks which threatened to turn the British flank. As at Mons, the British held their ground, supported by the impressive efforts of their divisional artillery. All along II Corps' position, pockets of battalions were fighting for their very survival. The 2nd Irish Rifles, having lost nearly 300 men in the two days prior to the action, stood firm at Caudry, whilst Lieutenant-Colonel Cox, 2nd Royal Irish, having missed Mons, was wounded whilst directing the defence of their slit trenches near Audencourt. He continued to command the battalion from his stretcher. When the Germans finally made a determined effort to clear the ground around Le Cateau, shattering the British slit-trenches with high explosive shells, the order to retire was finally issued. Sadly, the 'runners' who were dispatched had extreme difficulty getting through the shellfire and some battalions never received their orders. They were subsequently overwhelmed, slaughtered or captured. Despite nearly 8,000 British casualties, the German pursuit was considerably delayed and II Corps escaped. The strongest testimony of the courage and resilience of British troops during the battle is General von Kluck's assessment that he had pushed back nine enemy divisions. The British had only three.[12]

Meanwhile, without cavalry protection, I Corps (which was thought to have been less vulnerable) suffered numerous surprise attacks on its own beleaguered rearguards. One such attack came at the village of Le Grand-Fayt where Lieutenant-Colonel A.W. Abercrombie's 2nd Connaught Rangers were defending the nearby ridge. They had already become divided when covering the brigade's withdrawal; the constant flow of British, French troops and civilians added to the confusion. Communications were virtually impossible and, without any new orders or, indeed, contact with brigade headquarters, Lieutenant-Colonel Abercrombie discovered that the Germans were advancing with machine-guns towards the village. Having also been told by a French civilian that there were no Germans in the village, the remaining three companies of 2nd Connaughts entered Le Grand-Fayt, only to find it occupied by German Guard Cavalry and, more worryingly, expert marksmen in the form of Guard Jagers. The engagement at Le Grand-Fayt was as instantaneous as it was a surprise for all parties. In a desperate attempt to try and force southwards through the village, the Connaughts were actually squeezed northwards, eventually ending up in the village of Maroilles. However, the Germans soon occupied here too and, utterly exhausted, the survivors of 'C' and 'D' Companies were captured, along with Lieutenant-Colonel Abercrombie. The 2nd Connaughts had lost their Commanding Officer, 5 officers and some 284 Rangers, killed or captured. The remnants of the battalion were to reunite with the straggling survivors of the fight at Le Grand-Fayt at Guise on 27-28 August. By then, Major W. Sarsfield had reorganised them into a cohesive fighting unit and the 2nd Connaughts returned to the Retreat.[13]

The 2nd Royal Munster Fusiliers, having recaptured two guns from German cavalrymen—at the point of a bayonet—had continued to fight their way southwards. On 27 August, they found themselves acting as rearguard to the Guards' Brigade which was covering Haig's I Corps. The 2nd Munsters were commanded by Major Charrier, a highly respected officer, and were deployed three miles north of Etreux. It was here that the Munsters were repeatedly attacked, at first tentatively and then, in overwhelming strength as elements from the German X Reserve Army Corps advanced. Charrier's men fought gallantly, delaying the advance again and again. For nearly twelve hours, the Munsters fought off six battalions before they were eventually forced to surrender. When they did, some 500 Munsters were dead or wounded. At one point, Father Frank Gleeson found himself the sole remaining unwounded officer and did something that was quite remarkable for any chaplain; he removed his insignia of clerical rank (indicating his non-combatant status) and briefly commanded the Munsters until he was relieved.[14]

It was only a matter of days into the Retreat and already many battalions had seen their companies become detached, with small groups of foot-sore, hungry, men struggling to maintain their formations. It was obvious that any straggling units would be enveloped by the enemy and the tension in battalions became palpable. With an ever-pressing enemy close at hand, there was nothing left for the British to do but stumble onwards. On the hot afternoon of 27 August, Major Bridges' 4th Dragoon Guards were ordered to protect the northern route into St Quentin. Many exhausted and demoralised men from shattered regiments had poured into the town's square. The soldiers who reached St Quentin were at their lowest ebb. Indeed, Lieutenant-Colonel Mainwaring commanding the 2nd Dublins had made what now seems to be a strange offer to his men (along with Lieutenant-Colonel Elkington of the 1st Royal Warwickshires)—to surrender should the Germans occupy St Quentin. On closer analysis, it becomes apparent that these men had fought unswervingly since their arrival but were now almost dead with weariness and fatigue. Among their ranks was the recently transferred New Ross man, Martin Doyle; an underage recruit who had already spent five years with the Royal Irish Regiment soldiering in India. It was at this point that Major Bridges entered a small toy shop and bought a number of penny whistles and drums. He gathered the stragglers together and 'miraculously' recovered their spirits, parading them out of the town, led by a little toy band. However, there were also darker mutterings that troopers of the 4th Irish Dragoon Guards had reinforced any failing morale by threatening to shoot the stragglers.[15]

Yet, during the Retreat, the pressure on the British had been enormous. They had marched and fought near-constant rear-guard actions for 13 days and nights and sustained some 15,000 casualties. The Irish Fusiliers having been either marching or fighting solidly for four days were also on the point of exhaustion. In the early hours of 27 August, they were anxiously awaiting the arrival of the 2nd Dublins and 2nd Inniskillings. As Captain O'Donovan recalled, the Fusiliers waited as long as they could but, with no sign of the Dublins or Inniskillings, they were forced to move off as the Germans had already established outposts behind them. In these circumstances, battalions tried desperately to stay together, fearing the vulnerability of separation, yet for the men of the 2nd Dublin Fusiliers, separation from each other is exactly what happened; the battalion became divided and some soldiers actually broke through to Boulogne. One of the men left behind was Private Thomas Donohoe of the 2nd Dublins, who was captured and taken to the infamous Sennelager camp, Paderborn, Germany, where conditions were terrible.[16]

At Villers-Cotterets, on 1 September, the Irish Guards, under Lieutenant-Colonel Morris, were ordered to delay the German advance through the forest of Compiègne, which the enemy was then shelling. This incident is often cited as a worthy example of the Guard's exploits during 1914 and it is easy to see why. As the Germans fiercely pressed home their advantage, the Irish Guards seemed contemptuously languid in their response. During one particularly heavy barrage, the Colonel is alleged to have gestured to the blasting explosions all around them and shouted out that the Germans were only trying to frighten them. At this, one soldier called back that they might as well stop now, as they had already succeeded in doing that to him '… long ago'. The Guards also, famously, picked berries under fire and one private even managed literally to stir up a hornet's nest with his bayonet before the men stolidly marched to Betz that night.[17]

However, the continual delays were putting German plans further and further into jeopardy, confusing and complicating the overall German strategy. The Schlieffen Plan, which determined Germany's over-arching strategy, dictated a lightning 'knock-out' blow against France, in order to allow German troops to counter-act the military threat from Russia. The British fighting-retreat simply prevented this from happening. General von Kluck was pushing the British back towards the river Marne but they, along with the French, were fighting every inch of the way. At Nery, after a furious bombardment, the one remaining gun of 'L' Battery, Royal Horse Artillery, successfully held up the approach of six German cavalry regiments and fought off three German four-gun horse artillery batteries. The 'Action at Nery' and scattering of the German 4th Cavalry Division effectively robbed von Kluck of intelligence regarding the existence of the French 6th Army on his right flank. Consequently, he misjudged the French forces opposing him on the Marne and, from the 5–9 September, Generals Gallièni (veteran military Governor of Paris) and Maunoury stopped the German First Army and started to push it back. The struggle opened up a dangerous gap between it and von Bulow's Second Army, into which slammed an increasingly buoyant BEF. The Germans, similarly fatigued after a month's hard fighting and marching, were forced to retreat, re-group and re-think the Schlieffen Plan.

The Aisne Offensive and the 'Race to the Sea'

Following the victory at the Marne, the German withdrawal towards the river Aisne was swift. This time, it was the Germans who were forced to fight a series of desperate holding battles. At Sablonniere, on 9 September, the 4th Royal Irish Dragoon Guards successfully charged a defended German bridgehead, capturing the crossing at Petit Morin. It was also here that a

German Jager machine-gun unit was dug into a position in the nearby wood guarding the village of Boitron. The German position in the village and the wood dominated Petit Morin but, a combined attack by the 3rd Coldstreams and forward companies of Irish Guards led to the capture of the village. Under further fierce enemy bombardment and in miserably wet weather, the remaining companies of the Irish Guards charged through the wood and silenced the machine-guns. Additionally, the Guards captured ninety-three men, including two officers. In a rather disarming display, characteristic of the early war, these officers were invited to 'mess' with the officers of the battalion at a dinner of chicken and wine. From 10-12 September, the 5th Irish Lancers were acting as advance-guard and, as such, they were engaged against German infantry at Chézy, taking sixty-one Germans prisoner. They found themselves in the same position again at Chassemy where they captured 101 of the enemy. At St Cyr, they managed to catch a retreating German column and oust them from the village. It was only when the Germans counter-attacked in force, supported by heavy artillery, that the 5th Irish Lancers were forced to withdraw. By 12 September, the Germans had re-organised themselves behind the Aisne and, the following day, the British crossed the river.[18]

One of the first units to cross was the advance company of the 2nd Connaught Rangers, who carefully traversed the blown girder bridge at Pont Arcy, before the Royal Engineers came to repair it. Elsewhere, the 1st Irish Fusiliers crossed at Bucy de Long, using an iron girder bridge that had only been partially split by German shells. The battalion was able to cross two-deep but all artillery pieces had to be transported across the river by pontoon. The 2nd Inniskillings crossed the Aisne at Venizel, also under intense fire, and continued to hold their position throughout the battle. Meanwhile, the 2nd Connaughts and 4th Guards Brigade had continued on to the Aisne valley. On 14 September, the Connaughts had made new positions above the wooded river line and dug themselves in around the heavily tree-covered hills of Cour de Soupir. The Germans attacked through the morning mist and, following a ferocious battle, were stopped at a distance of only a hundred yards. As German reinforcements were brought up, the 2nd Connaughts were bolstered by companies from the Coldstream Guards. Rather bizarrely, after their attack had been repelled, large numbers of the Germans simply raised their hands and surrendered, with some 250 captured. However, the battle for the ridge continued and, as the Germans still held the heights of the surrounding rolling valleys, the Irish Guards were ordered to attack the forested high ground on the left flank of Cour de Soupir. It was finally secured as dusk fell but, during the battle, 150 Germans were seen sitting on haystacks and waving a white flag. Lieutenant Fitzgerald led No.8 Platoon, accompanied by Lieutenant Cotteral-Dormer and a section of Coldstreams, to parley their surrender and good treatment. At a range of only thirty yards, the Germans suddenly opened fire. It was a harsh lesson about the nature of this new and desperate type of warfare.[19]

As the Germans clung to their positions, Allied plans were made to outflank them in Flanders and drive them back further. On 14 September, the Germans gained a new impetus and direction when General Erich von Falkenhayn was appointed chief of the General Staff. The Aisne advance had effectively ended and, with it, the era of fluid warfare, so characteristic of the early weeks of the war. Instead, the trench stalemate began, although almost imperceptibly at first. On 16 September, the 2nd Leinsters reached the Aisne as part of the newly arrived 6th Division, eager and impatient to get to grips with the enemy. Portentously, on the same day they arrived at the Aisne, Sir John French gave the legendary order for 'strong entrenchments' to be dug and, three days later, the Leinsters crossed at Pont Arcy and relieved the 43rd/52nd Light Infantry at Cour de Soupir. By then, the attempts by the British and French to capture the Chemin Des Dames ridge had proved ineffective and a series of outflanking manoeuvres only succeeded in drawing the enemy nations nearer to the north coast. This became known as the 'Race for the Sea'. Although German attempts to break the mighty fortress of Verdun were futile, they did oust the French from the St Mihiel Salient, which stayed in German hands for most of the war.[20]

First Ypres: the Fight for Flanders

By early October, the fighting had developed into embryonic trench warfare. The remains of the Belgian Army were evacuated from Antwerp on 8 October, with the city quickly falling afterwards. Indeed, the veteran, 'old sweats' in the 2nd Leinsters mumbled amongst themselves that they would soon be off to Belgium, to much good-natured leg-pulling from their officers; only to find that their men had got it right all along, in Colonel's Whitton's wry phrase '...not for the first time'.[21] When the 'Race for the Sea' had finished, the trenches extended deep into Flanders. The four-week-long battle of First Ypres, fought day and night, hinted at the savagery to come in the tortuously stalemated battles that would become synonymous with the Western Front. Yet, even during this clawing campaign, the change was not as immediate as may have been expected. Trenches were still often shallow and urgent battles for towns or villages to be used as strong-points in the ravenous trench-lines were still important. At the start of the campaign, British trenches in the Ypres sector were not strengthened nor, indeed, were they intended to be constructed as a permanent line of defence. This was to change by the end of October, although some sectors retained these shallow trench-lines well into the New Year. First Ypres was also notable for the terrible conditions in the trenches, which soon became endemic. The newly created trench systems were deepening as the weather worsened. As a result, other hardships began to appear around the waterlogged Ypres sector at the onset of winter. The war diary for the Irish Fusiliers stated flatly that the men's feet were badly affected by the miserable wet conditions and exacerbated by three days of snow-covered ground. 'Trench-foot', as it became known, was only one of the distressing experiences of the winter campaign of 1914-1915.[22]

As the need for men on the front line increased, cavalrymen were also flung into dismounted action. On 11 October, as III Corps massed around Hazebrouck, the forested heights above them needed to be secured and it was essential to drive the enemy out, urgently. Consequently, on a misty Sunday morning, cavalry regiments in dismounted order worked their way around the Hazebrouck heights with supporting machine-gun teams. As part of this operation, the 5th Irish Lancers and 16th (Queen's Own) Lancers crept their way slowly upwards through the woods and then launched a furious assault on the monastery of Mont des Cats (Katsberg, overlooking Godewaersvelde) with 'D' Battery of the Royal Horse Artillery in support. After a brisk engagement, the Irish Lancers then occupied the monastery for the night and whilst there, the 5th Irish Lancers' medical officer, Captain Charles Paget O'Brien-Butler, tended to the wounded on both sides. This included the young Prince Maximilian of Hesse-Kassel, Kaiser Wilhem's cousin, who was mortally wounded but was made as comfortable as possible. Before dying, he gave Captain O'Brien-Butler his gold watch as a token of his gratitude for trying to save his life. Less than fortnight later, on 30 October, the 5th Irish Lancers relieved the 125th Baluchis (Napier's Rifles) in the trench lines around Hollebeke but were extremely heavily shelled for almost five hours. The Lancers had no option but to evacuate their position and they fell back to St Eloi where the extent of their casualties became clear. Two men had been killed and twenty-five were missing or wounded. Tragically, one of these men was Captain O'Brien-Butler, mortally hit by shrapnel whilst trying to reach an injured comrade.[23]

Since the start of the war, constant drafts of fresh troops had been needed to maintain the battalions on the battlefield. The 2nd Irish Rifles had lost hundreds of men, including their Commanding Officer, Lieutenant-Colonel Bird DSO, severely wounded before the crossing of the Aisne. They were constantly reinforced with fresh drafts from the Special Reserve (3rd, 4th and 5th Battalions) and regimental depot at Belfast. After Eteaux, the 2nd Munsters had been brought up to fighting strength in the same manner, although its companies had been divided amongst the BEF's Corps' headquarters. Similarly, in mid-October, a fresh draft of soldiers from Ireland, over 350 men and 6 officers, arrived to reinforce the depleted ranks of the 2nd Royal Irish; it was notable that this was the seventh such draft to the battalion since Le Cateau.[24]

On 17 October, the 1st Irish Fusiliers fought a bitter engagement to secure Armentierres, which was taken at noon. Yet, as they moved out of the town, resistance increased, until they came across a small farmhouse called Phillipeaux. A number of German snipers were picking the Fusiliers off as they tried to advance, so Lieutenant Penrose's platoon was ordered by the Acting Commanding Officer, Captain Miles Carbery from Belfast to clear the farm. As soon as they entered the yard, they came under very accurate sniper fire from a loft, which hit several men, before they could take cover behind the walls of the house itself. With Lieutenant Penrose pinned down, Captain Carbery, seeing the danger, dashed across with Corporal Shields to support him, as the snipers continued firing from their position. In spite of Penrose's urgent entreaties to go back, a flurry of snipers' bullets brought both men down. Seeing his friend and superior officer lying in the mud by the wall, Lieutenant Penrose called out to him to see if he'd been hit, to which Miles Carbery replied '…yes – badly'. In fact, within minutes, he was dead. Undoubtedly aware of this, Lieutenant Penrose stopped his men, in particular, Lance Corporal Hurst, from trying to rescue either Carbery or Shields. By now, the surviving Fusiliers determined that the snipers were hiding in the corner of a room with only one door, but all attempts to break through the wall were pointless. As darkness fell, Captain Kentish ran forward armed with a rifle, leading an assault party to bomb the farmhouse and fire at point blank range into the room where the snipers were thought to be. Very soon the house was ablaze, with wounded Fusiliers lying by the entrance whilst tiles and burning debris fell around them. Seeing this, Sergeant David Jones (from Cloverhill in Cavan) volunteered to rescue them, recovering one injured man but being mortally hit in the process. Again, Lance Corporal Hurst volunteered to gather the wounded in but was directly ordered not to. Instead, he helped cut off Sergeant Jones' equipment where he lay. As the smoke hung around the ruins of the farmhouse, Lieutenant Penrose and the Fusiliers buried Captain Carbery in a nearby garden without any ceremony.[25]

Over the weeks which followed, the entire trench line would pulsate with intense fighting, with four battlefields—Arras, Yser, Ypres and La Bassée—linked together to form one long and horrifying battle front. Around La Basée, following the capture of Fromelles, the reinforced 2nd Royal Irish was ordered to take the German-held village of Le Pilly. In the early afternoon of 19 October, the Royal Irish (now commanded by Major Daniell) charged the German positions and, by late afternoon, secured the main part of the village. However, they had also suffered 163 casualties in the attempt to oust the German defenders and consolidate the position. A flank attack by the French on nearby Fournes had not succeeded and instead had left the 2nd Royal Irish dangerously exposed. Predictably, when the enemy bombardment drove the battered remains of the 4th Middlesex Regiment from their position on the other flank (at La Riez), the Royal Irish were left 'up in the air'. Even when they were cut off from the main British line, Major Daniell refused to yield Le Pilly. Surrender may have lost all that they, and accompanying battalions, had gained during the previous days' fighting. In the hope that they could be relieved when the British counter-attack was delivered, the battalion clung on. Even though they were now hemmed in by both German artillery and sporadic but fierce infantry assaults, Major Daniell and the 2nd Royal Irish made a determined last stand. However, no British counter-attack was forthcoming. The Germans had, in fact, totally surrounded them. A concerted attack duly came from all sides, with dominating fire from machine-gunners which raked the defenders mercilessly. Major Daniell was killed whilst trying to rush to the aid of one of his companies. His last order is alleged to have been to fix bayonets and fight to the last man. By the end of 20 October, the fight at Le Pilly was over. In all, some 340 Royal Irish were left dead or severely wounded with 302 captured, most of whom were also injured. Militarily, the 2nd Royal Irish Regiment had, once again, practically ceased to exist.[26]

Meanwhile, the 2nd Leinsters had fought for three gruelling days during which the Premésques trench line outside Lille had been taken and then lost again. It had felt the full force of a sustained and extremely brave assault by the 179th Saxon Regiment which tore the battalion to pieces; over 400 men became casualties, including 5 officers, and some 150 men had been killed. During the battle, the contribution of Lance Corporal Maher is worth noting—he repeatedly carried several messages despite coming under direct fire. He had previously been noted for similar bravery at Cour de Soupir when he volunteered to bring up rations to the trench line under heavy shelling. Just a few days later, at Neuve Chapelle, the 2nd Leinsters were again embroiled in fierce fighting, wrestling repeatedly with the enemy alongside the 2nd Irish Rifles, and 2nd Inniskillings for possession of the sector. Trenches were captured, lost and recaptured. The 2nd Irish Rifles were part of the counter-attack by 7th Brigade at Neuve Chapelle, where they stood like a rock before the continual German onslaughts, apparently firing and swearing their heads off at the enemy. Indeed, one Dublin rifleman, utterly exasperated by their offensive blasphemy even in the face of death itself, is said to have reprimanded them in the name of '... the sufferin' Saviour'; to which, a low Belfast voice simply muttered: 'Listen to yon.'[27]

Yet, the spirit of the Irish Regulars could have been epitomised by Lord Roberts, the hero of Khandahar. Although in his eighties, he travelled to the Ypres Front on a morale-boosting visit, but died at St Omer on 1 November from pneumonia. On the same day, the 2nd 'Skins' were ordered to retire from Douve Farm, south of Ypres, near the town of Messines, in the face of a massive German assault. In the confusion, two Inniskilling companies did not receive the order and, instead, delayed the advance of an entire German Corp's which included elite Guard cavalry. Everywhere along the Western Front, the valuable experience and ranks of the Irish regiments were whittled away. At Heronthage Chateau, the remnants of the 2nd Irish Rifles stopped an advance by the West Prussians and Pomeranians, displaying the same steady fire that aided them at Mons. The Irish Guards' heaviest action of First Ypres came when they were sent to plug a hole in the defence line of the Zillebeke sector. By this time Privates Daughton and Daly, who had arrived in Le Havre in the violent thunderstorm just months before, were already dead, killed within days of each other. From 1 to 9 November, the 1st Irish Guards resolutely defended their stretch of trench-line. They lost NCOs, officers and men on a daily basis, some of whom, such as Private George Griffith, from Finglas, were killed on the first day of the defence. The Irish Guards refused to yield any ground and, even when relieved, they only used the opportunity to re-organise their front line. After nine days of fighting, the remnants of the battalion were commanded by Captain N. Orr-Ewing, on attachment from the Scots Guards. The cost to the battalion was almost unimaginable—even considering the rising casualties of the war—with 613 amongst all ranks wounded or dead in just one week.[28] To this depressing background, Captain Harold Harmsworth arrived at Meteren (along with a draft of 6 officers and 288 NCOs and men) on 28 November, before they too were flung into the fires of First Ypres.

As the year ended, the Irish battalions on Foreign Service were finally being gathered together. Lieutenant-Colonel Lauries' 1st Irish Rifles had left Aden and only arrived in Liverpool at the end of October. They were hurriedly sent to Winchester, as part of the 8th Division and, by early November, had arrived at Le Havre. The 1st Rifles occupied reserve trenches at Rue Tilleloy and, even though these were not front-line, from the 15–21 November they suffered forty-one shell casualties. Most battalions, however, came directly from service in India. The 8th King's Royal Irish Hussars arrived in France in November 1914, direct from Bombay as part of the 1st Indian Cavalry Division, accompanied in their Brigade by Hodson's Horse and the 30th Lancers. As with most cavalry, the 8th Irish Hussars served in a mounted and dismounted role, their first engagement coming at Givenchy, on the extreme of the line held by II Corps. The 1st Connaught Rangers, like the Rifles, found itself at once engaged in near-constant trench fighting. By the end of their first month on the Western Front, their initial strength of up to 1,000 men (though probably significantly fewer) had been slashed to just over 350 including officers. Their second battalion had, again, been decimated a few weeks previously in the woods of Nonne Boschen but, this time, it could not be resurrected. Instead, on 5 December, its survivors were collected together and reorganised into the senior battalion.[29]

The close of 1914 brought little relief to the men of the BEF. When First Ypres finished, the ranks of the Irish regiments were thinner still; the 2nd Irish Rifles had suffered nearly 350 dead since the start of the war, with estimates of double this figure in wounded. As the battalion marched out of the Ypres salient and arrived at Westoutre, it had a fighting strength of exactly forty men. As Captain Cyril Falls memorably recorded, they had been devastated by one battle, then been inadequately reinforced, only to be flung into a greater battle, where they were '… again cut to pieces'. The same could have been said for the Royal Irish Regiment, the Connaught Rangers, Irish Guards, Dublins or Munster Fusiliers. Indeed, it is estimated that by the end of 1914, approximately 10,000 soldiers from the Irish regiments had been killed or wounded. Yet, the resolve and resilience of the Irish Regulars was truly astounding. When things looked bleak, by and large, they simply got on with the job in hand. The 2nd Leinsters proudly considered this to be an aspect of their Irishness—never to cheer unnecessarily, except when things were deemed particularly difficult '… such as shellfire and rain'. Whether the Kaiser's order to 'walk over' the 'contemptible little army' was genuine or not, it soon spread like wildfire through the British and Irish consciousness. By Christmas, the men who had been 'out since Mons' now proudly called themselves the 'Old Contemptibles'. By the end of the year, there was even a popular postcard rebuttal, drawing upon 'Tipperary' and the Kaiser's words, which simply stated: 'A little British Army goes a d--- long way!' Yet, for men like Private James Somers, 2nd Inniskillings, they had indeed come a long way, both literally and psychologically. Private Somers had been badly wounded during the Retreat from Mons and was eventually sent home to Cloughjordan, in Tipperary, in time for Christmas. Within weeks, he was well enough to rejoin his regiment and was soon posted to the 1st Inniskillings. As the war on the Western Front continued, 1915 was to see it widen even further into new horrors and dashed hopes, as James Somers was soon to discover.[30]

CHAPTER FOUR

'Victory in sight'[1]

Ireland's Regiments at Stalemate—Western Front, 1915

After the first year of war, the strength of the Regulars had been spent. When the war began, the British Army had a fighting strength of 125,000 officers and other ranks yet, by the end of 1914, the BEF had suffered almost 90,000 casualties. Captain Miles Carbery's wife, Elizabeth, had been informed of his death at Armentierres only weeks before, when she returned as a young widow to her parents' home at Hopefield House in Belfast. In Tuam, the local papers were replete with the deeds of the Connaught Rangers and, although already out of date, many of the readers would have been more concerned about the accompanying casualty lists. The merger of both of the Connaught battalions after First Ypres had been masked by the news that they had '... lost 450 but gained the position'. Consequently, for thousands at home, Christmas 1914 was a time of heartbreak, and throughout the country, families dreaded the official telegrams notifying them of a loved one's death. Yet, the winter of 1914–1915 was to bring little solace as the war dragged on and, unbelievably, intensified.[2]

The need for troops guaranteed that the Irish Regimental Depots, from Armagh to Tralee, were to be very busy indeed. The last Irish battalions on Imperial duties had returned to the UK and, after a brief reorganisation, were ready for war. The 6th Inniskilling Dragoons had left Bombay under Lieutenant-Colonel Neil Wolseley Haig on 19 November, with a regimental strength of 26 officers and 514 other ranks. They arrived in Marseilles a few weeks before Christmas and here they received their additional Reservists, one of whom was former funeral parlour employee, Frank Vennard. Meanwhile, the 1st Dublin Fusiliers arrived in England from India in December and were introduced to their new chaplain, Father William Joseph Finn, just before Christmas. Father Finn was born in Hull and educated at Durham, but his parents came from Aghamore, Ballyhaunis (Co. Mayo).[3]

The Christmas Truce, 1914

As December wore on and Christmas came upon the miserable trenches and blasted 'No Man's Land' that had developed in between, an Old World courtesy and a certain 'kindred' feeling briefly emerged. On Christmas Day 1914, in some sectors of the Western Front, the guns fell unusually silent. It seems as if the truce was an organic and sporadic event, although it was clearly seen by the opposing High Commands as a serious breach of army discipline. What began as a ceasefire to collect the dead grew into a mutual exchange of greetings which, in turn, made way for wider fraternisation. Before long, Christmas carols were being sung, games being played and cigarettes and chocolate being swapped between 'Tommy' and 'Fritz'.

Some Irish regiments such as the 2nd Leinsters, 2nd Dublin Fusiliers and 1st Irish Rifles seem to have been a part of this truce; others were half-hearted participants. Some, such as the 2nd Irish Rifles, Irish Guards and Connaught Rangers stubbornly refused to have anything to do with it. Even when Irish troops did decide to hold a brief 'non-aggression' pact for Christmas Day itself, it was rarely extended. Lieutenant-Colonel Laurie of the 1st Irish Rifles noted that he had to post sentries to keep his men from fraternising, as they were genuinely keen to talk to the Germans. He was reasonably worried but, having convinced himself that it was to be an honest twenty-four hour ceasefire for Christmas Day only, he went over the top himself and led the 'official' fraternisation. They chatted with the Germans about developments in the war and, naturally enough, the horrible state of their trenches. Then with no shots being fired all day, a single shot from each side above each other's heads at midnight signalled the end of this festive truce.[4]

The tales of the Christmas truce are almost universally positive; however, it appears that there was a certain inconsistency and ambivalence within battalions over the whole thing, with individual companies, such as those of the 2nd Leinsters, both supporting—and ignoring—the truce. Charles McClean, an Irish Fusilier from Banbridge, Co. Down, simply said that he had heard about the truce but that it never happened in his part of the line.

The Fusiliers were in billets in La Creche on Christmas Day 1914; it was recorded as a 'fine, frosty morning' and noted that they held a Catholic service in the local chapel with a Protestant service in the nearby school-house. Afterwards, the King and Queen's Christmas cards were distributed, along with Princess Mary's chocolate boxes and numerous gifts from home. To round things off, the men had a Christmas dinner and the Regimental Sergeant Major led a group of 'carol singers' around the village. Another Sergeant-Major, J.H. Leahy, of the 2nd Munster Fusiliers, wrote to a friend in West Passage, Cork, and dryly told him that the war had turned them all into 'saints' regarding their spiritual devotion over the Christmas period. The Sergeant-Major had even served mass on Christmas Eve and Christmas Day to over 200 men, with bullets '...whizzing over us'. Their devotion was actively nurtured by their popular, harmonica-playing, chaplain from Tipperary, Father Francis Gleeson. The 'Old Contemptible' spirit, with its strong regimental identity, persisted into the New Year, but only just. The battles of 1915 would see newly raised battalions of Irish soldiers placed in the same old stalemate. There followed the grim deadlocks at St Eloi, Neuve Chapelle, Second Ypres (which included St Julien, Mouse-Trap Farm and Aubers Ridge), and the blood-letting seemed relentless.[5]

Cuinchy to Neuve Chapelle

Early in 1915, at Cuinchy, near Bethune, the Irish Guards were holding a particularly bleak and flat area of line, filled with culverts and railway embankments. The trench lines (on either side) needed to be 'straightened' by continual raids and attacks. One such German assault was on a post held by the Coldstream Guards which lay in a slight hollow; on 1 February, they surprised the defenders by rushing a communication sap and a bloody battle ensued. Lieutenant Robert Blacker-Douglass led a party of Irish Guards to support the Coldstreams but, as he reached the Germans' improvised barricade, he was blown over by a grenade. He picked himself up, only to be shot through the head. As the Irish Guards tried to enter the post, more guardsmen were hit in the struggle and Lieutenant Lee was killed instantly by a bullet through the heart. Two more officers, including the Company Commander, Captain Long-Innes, were wounded and command fell to Company Quartermaster Sergeant Carton who, despite verbal orders to retire, refused to move. Instead, he set up his own barricades and held the trench until artillery ranged on the Germans the next morning. When the barrage lifted, the Irish Guards attacked again and the Cork Reservist, Lance Corporal Michael O'Leary, dashed across the embankment in full view of the enemy, killing eight Germans, three of whom were working a machine-gun. O'Leary then captured a couple of prisoners and, because of his breathtaking coolness under fire, he was awarded the Victoria Cross. The resultant struggle had left a heap of dead in the hollow, Coldstreams, Germans and some fifteen Irish Guards. It was a small but necessary engagement and one in which more valuable 'old sweats' died, including Private Luke Farrell from Longford. His brother, now a chaplain with the 5th Royal Irish Regiment, would soon be heading for a very different theatre of war. [6]

The transition to war for the 1st Royal Irish was slightly slower. It had been stationed at Nasirabad when war broke out and by the time it reached England (in November 1914) it was earmarked for the 82nd Brigade of the 27th Division. As such, the battalion found itself on the Western Front and in operations during the Ypres sector. On 14 March, Lieutenant-Colonel George F.R. Forbes led the 1st Royal Irish into action at St Eloi to recover the town and the nearby domineering 'Mound of Death'. A month earlier, the 1st Royal Irish and 1st Leinsters had recaptured this position in a bitter night assault, during which Private Collins, of the 1st Leinsters, won the DCM by cheering his friends on as he stood conspicuously on top of the parapet, under fire and only ten yards from the enemy. Now supposedly in reserve, the 1st Leinsters were ordered to stem a very heavy German offensive in the sector. Exaggerated reports heralded a collapse of the British line and of a German breakthrough, but small pockets had held firm and were merely awaiting support. This was to come in the form of the 1st Leinsters and 1st Royal Irish who, now seriously under-strength and with little supporting fire, made their first attack with vigour and secured the village of St Eloi. The follow-on attack on the 'Mound', however, confounded them and, with three German machine-guns sweeping the mud around it, the 1st Royal Irish were cut to pieces in their attempts to dislodge them. During the battle, the Royal Irish were given another 'fight to the death' order by Brigade Command and, again, the regiment fought with exceptional determination to keep St Eloi from falling into enemy hands. Lieutenant-Colonel Forbes was badly wounded in the action and died of his wounds on St Patrick's Day. When the smoke had cleared, the main street of St Eloi was littered with British and German wounded and dead. One of these was Captain Robert McGregor Bowen-Colthurst, 1st Leinsters; he was thirty-one and formerly from Dripsey Castle, Co. Cork. He left a widow, Winifred, and his brother, John, who had been wounded at the Aisne as a Regular Officer with the 2nd Irish Rifles. [7]

For the 1st Irish Rifles, the opening assault at Neuve Chapelle on 10 March was to be truly testing. Lieutenant-Colonel George Laurie had written to his family the day before, sending his son and daughter his regimental badges from the old coat he had worn throughout the South African war and on the Western Front. He commented on how nice his new coat was and, ominously, that the only leave he was due would come should he be wounded. This, he felt, was an increasing certainty. In the opening attack, the Rifles advanced in waves towards the village of Neuve Chapelle under shell and machine-gun fire, adopting scattered artillery formation. As they moved towards their right, onto the Armentierres road, their undefended flank was hit mercilessly by shells and machine-guns and 'D' Company, in particular, led by Lieutenants Burgess and Barrington, was mown down. Somehow they still surged forward to the second Germen trench line, then onto the third and into the outskirts of the village itself. It was said that Lieutenant-Colonel Laurie was the first man into the outskirts of Neuve Chapelle and the Rifles secured their position and 'dug in' at the chateau's garden. However, as they did so, they made a gruesome discovery. Corpses were soon unearthed and discovered to be the remains of their 2nd Battalion, identified by their cap badges and buttons. The Rifles consolidated their trenches, under heavy enemy bombardment, and awaited further orders.

On 11 March, Lieutenant-Colonel Laurie wrote again in a few snatched moments between heavy fighting, shelling and alarms. This time, he told his wife of the recent loss of officers and men and recorded that the Rifles were due to attack Neuve Chapelle proper. It was the last message he sent. The next morning they renewed their advance but, disastrously, further orders were received which delayed their attack. The subsequent assault, with utterly exhausted men against superior enfilading fire, was a bloodbath. George Laurie led his men over the top once more but, this time, every Rifleman must have known that their task was virtually unattainable. As soon as men left the parapets, they were swept off by German fire; Captain Arthur Colles, from Dublin, dashed out to cut the wire entanglements in front of them and died in the attempt. Reports differ as to when Lieutenant-Colonel Laurie was killed but most say it was from a single shot to the head sometime later in the day and, after this, the Rifles' advance ground to a halt. This was unsurprising as, in addition to the death of Lieutenant-Colonel Laurie, 8 other officers were killed (including the adjutant), another 7 officers were wounded and 391 other ranks killed, wounded or missing. Indeed, Sergeant Leaney recalled that most of the Battalion's Orange Lodge, the 'Rising Sons of India LOL 703' had been

'… wiped out'. The losses of the 1st Rifles had been for absolutely nothing. The small gains at Neuve Chapelle were quickly lost in the German counter-attack of 12 March which soon re-established their hold over the sector. The focus of the war returned to the quagmire and salient around Ypres.[8]

Second Ypres: St Julien and Aubers Ridge

By early spring 1915, the 1st Leinsters and 2nd Irish Fusiliers were in trenches along the Menin Road, at Ypres. Behind them, in various reserves, were the 1st Royal Irish, 1st Irish Fusiliers, 2nd Dublins and 1st Connaughts. These units were mainly being held in readiness or were in training for the planned great assaults, not least the attempts to take and hold Hill 60 which had been retaken by the British in April 1915 and subsequently lost. Whilst in the Douve sector at Messines on 12 April, the 1st Irish Fusiliers were extremely heavily shelled and Private Robert Morrow, from New Mills, Co. Tyrone, repeatedly risked his own life to rescue wounded men who had been buried in the explosions. All the time, Private Morrow worked calmly under direct fire but, as Lieutenant-Colonel Burrowes noted, this quiet unassuming young man was well-known for his gallantry. On one prior occasion, the Colonel met Morrow with a huge tear in his trousers and upon asking how he had come by it, Morrow replied that it was only a '… bit of shell'. Indeed, some of the extreme conditions Morrow faced at Douve can be guessed at by the stories of fellow soldiers; on the same day, Private Frank Alderman, from Winchester, was hit in the eye by a bullet which slammed though the wood of his rifle. The doctor 'double-timed' to reach him but he died just before he got there.[9]

As if to demonstrate how Regular regiments were decimated by April 1915, Captain Burgoyne of the 2nd Irish Rifles bitterly noted that his battalion was now effectively an Irish militia regiment and was filled with men who would never originally have been passed fit for service. In preparation for the upcoming Ypres offensives, men were trained in grenade tactics and trench storming, learning how to become either good 'bombers' or 'bayonet men'. At Givenchy, on 16 April, 2nd-Lieutenant Harold Marion Crawford, 1st Irish Guards, was accidentally killed in an explosion whilst instructing officers and men of the 4th Guards' Brigade in bombing. One of his brother officers commented that he was admired for volunteering for this 'dangerous' duty, whilst another simply stated that he was a great loss to the Irish Guards being a popular and '… great-hearted…' officer. On 22 April 1915, the furious battle of Second Ypres began. A massive breach in the Allied front was torn open from St Julien to the Ypres Canal, some five miles, and into this swarmed a determined German enemy. Although the Canadians had gallantly stemmed much of this onslaught, they were, by 24 April, forced to pull back from St Julien and the 1st Royal Irish were sent to plug the gap. The battalion only just managed to reach the heights above the village before the Germans. The 1st Royal Irish held the position above the Fortuin crossroads until reinforcements came in the form of the 4th East Yorkshire Regiment and the 4th Green Howards. Although a concerted attack pushed the Germans back to St Julien, all attempts to oust the enemy from the village were futile.[10]

All of the engaged units were briefly withdrawn and, in the early hours of 25 April, a massed battalion assault was enacted. As part of this 'grand attack', Lieutenant-Colonel Burrowes 1st Irish Fusiliers and Lieutenant-Colonel Loveband's 2nd Dublins were force-marched towards St Julien. Captain Penrose, 1st Irish Fusiliers, recalled that his fellow officers wryly called the imminent assault the 'high jump' and that Major Kentish had jokingly ordered bugles so that their musicians could sound the appropriate 'charge'. They were to run, in full pack, 250 yards without halt or cover, to the German first line trenches. It was an enormous task. At this stage, they still thought they were being used against St Eloi, the 'Mound of Death' or Hill 60. In the early hours of Sunday 25 April, the Dublins and Fusiliers marched up in complete silence but could hear the pipes of the Argyll and Sutherland Highlanders drifting through the night. At dawn, they attacked, with the officers of the Fusiliers each being issued with a rifle and bayonet. The attackers quickly deployed from column into extended line and then the companies began their headlong dash. They reached a point within 100 yards of St Julien when the enemy opened fire with everything they had. There were 4 Regular battalions which hurled themselves at the village and some 73 officers and 2,026 other ranks fell. Two of those Irish Fusiliers killed were Captain Penrose and Private Robert Morrow, VC, but some of the Fusiliers and 2nd Dublins did claw their way into the ruins of St Julien. Elsewhere, a disorientated party of the Dublins pulled back, only to be rallied by Lieutenant-Colonel Arthur Loveband, who was famed for simply carrying a stout blackthorn stick. He calmly motioned for his men to 'dig in' and they did so. Even when the German shells began to tear their improvised slit trenches apart, the Dubliners' spirits were given full voice as they allegedly shouted out a defiant cheer for the Trade Unionist, Jim Larkin.[11]

The following day, the 1st Connaughts were sent against Mauser Ridge, as part of the Lahore Division's attack, nearly taking the German front line trenches, despite being hit by a murderous artillery bombardment and the release of chlorine gas. At this stage in the war, without proper gas respirators, the usual practice was to hold or tie a moist handkerchief around the nose and mouth; as water was scarce, the most common liquid to use was urine. With men dying horribly around them, the Connaughts scraped their way into a position a mere eighty yards from the Germans, supported by a company from the 1st Manchesters. They held this patch of ground until relieved in the early hours of 27 April by the 1st Highland Light Infantry. By the end of the battle, the Connaughts had suffered approximately 369 casualties, including over 60 killed outright; one of these men was Sergeant James Mynes from Kilkenny.[12] He had been a typical career soldier, enlisting as an eighteen-year-old in 1902 (gaining a tattoo of a girl on his forearm in the process) and, as Corporal, had signed on for another twelve years' service in April 1914.

Indeed, the battles of May were particularly bloody for the Irish regiments. On the left and right flanks of Aubers Ridge, from 6–9 May, the British launched a series of mostly unsuccessful assaults against well-prepared and reinforced German defences. Due to their recent losses, the 1st Connaughts were in support on the opening day but, on 8 May, the 2nd Munsters, who were recently up to strength, led by Lieutenant-Colonel Victor Rickard, were sent to attack Rue de Bois. As they marched towards the front line, Lieutenant-Colonel Rickard famously halted the battalion at a road-side shrine, where Father Francis Gleeson gave the men a general absolution. The Munsters formed a hollow square before him, carrying their green company flags (of dark green, with a golden harp in the centre and with 'Munster' in gold underneath) and silently bowed their heads as the din of the battle for Aubers Ridge raged in the distance. They then resumed their march and, the next morning, attacked the German trenches at Rue de Bois. As the British pre-offensive bombardment had not cut the wire as planned, the leading waves of the assault were easy targets for the German machine-gunners. Despite this, some advance companies did get into the enemy front line before the subsequent counter-barrage and defensive fire. The 2nd Munsters had charged over the top with only about fifty making it to the enemy front line. Among the first Munsters killed in the mad dash towards the German lines was Lieutenant-Colonel Victor Rickard, who was struck down soon after he clambered over the parapet. The leading waves of 2nd Munsters soon found themselves utterly stranded. Those that made it into the German trenches had to fight for their lives; those out in the open were caught on the wire and gunned down. Then, to make matters worse, the British artillery opened up on No Man's Land, in an appalling effort to 'soften up' the enemy for further assaults. The casualties sustained by the 2nd Munsters for the sake of a few hours of attack amounted to nearly 390 officers and other ranks.[13]

On the left flank of Aubers Ridge, in the fighting at Fromelles, the battalions fared little better. The 1st Irish Rifles faced exactly the same difficulties as the 2nd Munsters and found that the wire in front of them was effectively unbroken. About thirty men of the 2nd Northamptonshire Regiment, under Lieutenant Parker, ploughed through the few gaps in the wire that could be found only to be cut off in the enemy trenches. Equally, the Irish Rifles still managed to squeeze their way through but in painfully few numbers. Upon hearing that his 25th Brigade had successfully stormed the German front line, Brigadier-General Lowry-Cole, from Fermanagh, at once advanced to direct the further assaults. He found the attack stalled and most of his men now hanging on the wire; in full view of the enemy, Lowry-Cole made it to the German parapet and was killed urging his men onwards. Although the 1st Irish Rifles clung on, they lost over 470 men with their gains—and Lowry-Cole's personal leadership—squandered. All their officers were killed or died of wounds, including a Belfast Lieutenant, twenty-year-old Arthur McLaughlin, son of Henry McLaughlin, the recently appointed Chairman for Recruitment in Ireland. Captain Falls later commented that nothing was won at Fromelles, with men simply mown down, making its memory '…entirely evil'.[14]

Festubert—Attrition and Atrophy in the Trenches

By 12 May, the 2nd Leinsters had been billeted in a lunatic asylum near Armentierres but, just after midday, as the men were milling back and forth about the canteen, five shells exploded amongst them, causing eleven casualties. Two men, Patrick Penders from Drogheda (Co. Louth) and Terence Quinn, from Virginia (Co. Cavan) were killed instantly. On 15 May, the battle of Festubert started, after two days of British artillery bombardment. There was no pretence of strategy or tactics; the battle's aim was simply to wear the Germans down through eventual sheer loss of numbers. For any initial battalions involved it was to be almost certain death. One of the Ulster Regular battalions present was the 2nd Inniskillings, which met with chequered success in its attack. The right wing succeeded in capturing two enemy trenches but, on the left, the forward companies could make very little ground against severe opposition. Without any advance on the left flank, the 2nd 'Skins' were pulled back. They had lost 649 men in a few short hours, for virtually nothing. Over the next two days, the Irish Guards were to lose 430 men (including 15 officers) in less than 100 yards. In the light of such madness, Brigadier-General Lord Cavan, commanding 4th Guards' Brigade, stopped any further assaults and was told bluntly by his divisional headquarters to 'dig in' and hold what ground they could. Festubert was to be the first true 'attritional' battle of the Great War, as if the ones prior to it had merely been opening gambits to butchery.[15]

Just over a fortnight later, on 24 May, there followed the German assault on Mouse Trap Farm, also known as Shell Trap Farm by the 2nd Dublins who held it. This was one of a number of old 'moated farms' in the sector, which gave the position an ancient, fortified, appearance. In the early hours of 24 May, heavy shelling and gas were used to break British resistance in the sector. As the farm was a mere thirty yards from the German lines, when the order to 'stand to' was shouted—along with the dreaded gas alarm—the Dubliners had little time to defend themselves. The Germans successfully gained entry into the trenches, where the battle for the farm raged all day, changing possession twice; the Dublins retook it and held their defences with a meagre collection of battalion headquarters and transport troops. The rest had been wounded or killed with approximately 640 men listed as casualties. Lieutenant-Colonel Arthur Loveband had been killed during the first few minutes of fighting and it says something of the enormity of the battalion's losses that the 2nd Dublins were pulled out of Mouse Trap only twenty men and a single lieutenant strong. They did not see action as a unit again for the remainder of the year.[16]

As the battle of Festubert continued, 'D' squadron North Irish Horse found itself more directly involved in the fighting, although by now it was surely clear to any cavalryman that their role in the war was not at all how it had at first been envisaged. The stark monotony of trench life in comparison to the idealised notion of battle was noted by a veteran officer, T. H. Gore-Brown, when he commented that his newly arrived squadron of North Irish Horse was thoroughly fed up with the style of warfare being conducted. He wrote, exasperatedly, that he presumed these troopers were expecting an '…orgy of shooting and stabbing'. Instead, from 14–16 June, Captain King-King was sent with two troops to a farm at Le Touret to act as prisoner escorts. However, no German prisoners filtered in. On 16 June, Major Hamilton Russell arrived with his two troops to relieve him. On the hundredth anniversary of Waterloo, the Major returned with his men to Carvin, empty-handed. In the stark words of their war diary, heavy with loaded implications of failure, the NIH had not received any prisoners in the entire four days they were bivouacked at Le Touret.[17]

A few weeks later, the 6th Inniskilling Dragoons were manning the trenches by Ypres when, on 26 June, the Reservist and Boer War veteran, Frederick (Frank) Vennard, was killed in a period of 'holding the line'. Similarly, Sergeant Joseph Cole, from St Finbarr's, Cork, was killed on 15 July along with five other 2nd Munsters when a shell exploded directly above their trench. Writing to Sergeant Cole's mother, Sergeant-Major O'Leary seemed to reinforce the religious devotion that Father Gleeson instilled in this battalion, assuring her that Joseph had recently received Communion and that he was buried with his rosary and hymn book in his pocket. There was a poignantly human note too—Sergeant-Major O'Leary confirmed that he had buried members of the party with a wooden cross over their graves and interred Sergeant Cole with a little dog by his feet, as it was his '... great favourite and died with him'. Such tragedies were happening on a daily basis and regardless of religious persuasion or political affinity. A few days later, the former Ulster Volunteer, Joseph Watson from outside Rasharkin (Co, Antrim) was killed on 19 July, serving with the 11th Highland Light Infantry. The battalion had a significant number of Ulstermen within its ranks and Private Watson was killed during a supposedly 'quiet day' of routine trench duties repairing and levelling a captured German trench, not far from Rue de Bois.[18]

Loos 25 September–10 October

On 25 September, the 47th London Territorial Division was ordered to secure the trench-lines between the German-held positions of Lens and Loos. As the British released deadly clouds of gas, the 1/18th London Irish Rifles led the attack, with their forward waves famously kicking a football out in front of their advance. Every time they kicked the ball into a German trench, the shout of 'goal!' allegedly went up as the London Irish surged onwards. However, Patrick McGill stated that no such cries were shouted (or at least in the confusion of the battle he heard none) although he later saw the leather ball, riddled with bullet holes and impaled on a length of barbed wire entanglement. When the London Irish had succeeded in capturing three German lines, they continued their advance into Loos itself. Throughout the sector, the weary assailants of the London Territorial Division then consolidated the German third line, reversing parapets and fire-steps as they waited for relief. Incredibly, they had to withstand a further three days of shelling and furious counter-attacks before they were pulled out of the front line.[19]

In the associated attack, the British gas was found to have rolled back onto their own lines, affecting the assaulting brigades. The 2nd Munsters, under Major Gorham and now pitifully few in number, were sent into the carnage, supported by the 2nd Welch Regiment, against Bois Carré. They struggled to make it up the heavily shelled trenches, filled as they already were with men choking for air and heading towards aid posts. In desperation, Major Gorham ordered the Munsters to scramble out of the protective trenches and attempt to cross the open ground to the British front line. In the confusion, two companies heard the order and did so. As they crossed the British front line and scrambled into the bursting hell of No Man's Land they were cheered onwards by the watching men. The Munsters were slaughtered, with hardly a man getting past the uncut wire. A mere handful returned to the British lines, with absolutely nothing gained. It typified the shameful, needless waste of manpower and, among the thousands lying dead, was the Irish cricket International, James Ryan, who had played for Northamptonshire.[20]

Following the severe losses at Ypres, a new Irish Guards' Battalion, the 2nd, had been formed at Warley Barracks in July. Within the month, they too were sent to France but their baptism of fire truly came at Loos when they were ordered to relieve what remained of the 21st and 24th Divisions from the initial offensive. As such, on 27 October, the 2nd Irish Guards attacked Chalk-Pit Wood and a position of an old colliery head and buildings. The Guards worked their way forward under fire but only suffered a small number of casualties before they reached the northern edge of the wood. However, digging into the hard chalk ground proved difficult work. As they did so, the 1st Scots Guards under Captain Cuthbert moved through them to attack the heavily defended colliery pits and a party of Irish Guardsmen (who had been trained by the Captain at Warley Barracks) followed them. Amongst this party were 2nd-Lieutenants Clifford and Kipling (Rudyard Kipling's son, John) who, along with the Scots Guardsmen, were caught in the flank by German machine-gunners and killed. The survivors reeled back to the wood and, under the same direct machine-gun fire and shelling, the Irish Guards released their hold of Chalk-Pit Wood. At least, most of them did. Captain Harold Alexander's men were still holding on north of the wood and he urgently sent a runner back saying that he would be 'obliged' if they could send reinforcements as soon as possible, although his actual words were believed to have been '...somewhat crisper'.[21] The battle of Loos constituted yet another failed offensive. It had cost some 50,000 British lives and was the depressing backdrop to the arrival of new hopes on the Western Front: Kitchener's New Armies.

Kitchener's Ulster and Irish New Armies Arrive in France, Winter 1915

In October, the 36th (Ulster) Division arrived in France and was quickly sent to the Somme sector, via Boulogne and then Amiens. The crossing was not without its own misadventures; when the 9th (West Belfast) Royal Irish Rifles landed, Major Crozier discovered that someone had gained entry through a port-hole to the ship's bar and consumed several bottles of wine. To all intents and purposes, it looked like the Rifles were the culprits. Crozier immediately told Lieutenant-Colonel Ormerod and the two noted that, although no sign of the bottles could be found, it might be best to show willing and pay for the wine. Crozier knew that his men were not showing outward signs of drunkenness but, equally, all fingers pointed to them. Consequently, he had the 9th Rifles parade by the quayside at Boulogne, asking the battalion if anyone present would confess. When no-one did, he docked the pay of the Riflemen who were posted nearest the bar on the journey across.[22]

In contrast to the Catholic ethos of the 2nd Munsters, the men of the largely Protestant Ulster Division found themselves in a potentially unsettlingly environment once in France. Indeed, there was concern among some officers that their men would be deeply antagonistic towards their allies' religious practices. In fact, the 11th (South Antrim) Irish Rifles were deliberately briefed before they left England on how to behave in France. They were solemnly told to uphold the good name of the Division and to respect any emblems or displays of faith. In fact, relations appear to have been naturally quite friendly and, where they were strained at all, it was probably due more to the imposition of soldiers impressed upon a civilian population. As the Ulster battalions were rotated with front-line troops to gain trench experience and then placed in reserve billets, they soon grew accustomed to trench warfare. At Beaumont Hamel on 21 November, the Division won its first gallantry awards when 2nd-Lieutenant J.H. Harpur and Company Sergeant-Major W.D. Magookin of the 15th (North Belfast) Irish Rifles carried a wounded man to safety under heavy shrapnel and machine-gun fire. Harpur, a member of Rostrevor Company, South Down UVF, was awarded the Military Cross whilst Sergeant-Major Magookin won the Distinguished Conduct Medal.[23]

Consolidation and Christmas 1915

So, the winter of 1915 ended as it started, in miserably harsh conditions. For the Ulster Division, it was their first hard experience of trench life and it proved to be stark. They were sent into trenches previously occupied by the French, which had no proper supports, dugouts, communication saps or fire-steps; these trenches were prone to collapse and, when they did, they frequently spewed forth battlefield debris and hastily buried dead. With the onset of winter, the weather worsened considerably and the Ulstermen found that ration supplies stopped. They were forced to wade through icy, foetid, water that came up to their waists and the trenches became so waterlogged that it was said that even the rats started to drown. Shortly afterwards, in December, Lieutenant-Colonel George Ormerod, over sixty years of age, became a victim of these terrible conditions; he was hospitalised with pneumonia. Although he made a full recovery and was intent on returning to active service, Major-General Nugent intervened and gave him a home posting. By this time, the 16th (Irish) Division had also finished final training in England and left Southampton on 17 December, landing at Le Havre the following day. On 19 December, as Lieutenant-Colonel 'Jack' Lenox-Conyngham's 6th Connaught Rangers stood at Béthune railway station, the men all heard the distant but chilling noise of artillery barrages along the front line. One of these recruits was Belfast National Volunteer, Joseph Crowley, from My Lady's Road, Belfast and former carman in the city. Miles away, that same morning, 'C' Squadron North Irish Horse was suddenly 'stood to' due to a gas attack on 3rd Division's front line.[24]

By mid-December, the men of Kitchener's New Armies had settled into life on the Western Front. The second Christmas of the war did not end, as the first had, with a brief truce and the optimistic hope that the conflict would surely soon be over. Instead, Christmas was celebrated quietly at home, almost hesitantly, as the thousands of civilian soldiers, the eager recruits of mid-summer and autumn 1914, found themselves amidst mud, filth, rats and lice. There were also constant casualties, surely whittling away at unit strengths and morale. In the days before Christmas, troopers from 'A' Squadron, South Irish Horse, were training to operate a trench catapult battery. It was whilst they were preparing this weapon on the evening of 22 December, that Privates Frank Larkin, William Sadlier and the Rathmines dentist, Leopold Le Bas, were killed by a direct hit from a German high explosive shell on their position. Back home, Jennie Adams, sister of Sergeant John Adams of the Irish Fusiliers, wrote that it would be a '...lonely Xmas for us all this time'.[25]

On the last day of 1915, it was reported back home that Rifleman Samuel Lemon, from Ballymacarrett, serving with the 10th (South Belfast) Irish Rifles, had been killed in action. On 14 December, he had accompanied Captain Edward W.C. Griffith into No Man's Land where the former was hit by a sniper; in an attempt to bring the officer back, Lemon was killed by the same sniper. His body was later recovered and buried a couple of days later by a party of South Belfast Ulster Volunteers. Samuel Lemon had lived just off Sandy Row and, like most in the 10th Irish Rifles, had signed the Ulster Covenant in 1912. No-one could have foreseen that it would have brought him—and thousands of his fellow Ulstermen—to their deaths in the chalk trenches of the Somme or the ragged bluffs of the Mediterranean.[26]

CHAPTER FIVE

'The whole show was a washout...'[1]

The Gamble at Gallipoli, 1915

As the trench lines on the Western Front ossified, daring new ideas to break the deadlock began to be formed. The one which proved to have most traction may not have been new as such, although it was certainly daring in both imagination and prospects. By 1914, Germany had secured the Ottoman Empire's support and Turkey's control of the passage to the Black Sea resurrected Russia's old fears regarding access to the Mediterranean. Consequently, hostilities between Turkey and the Entente Powers officially began on 31 October 1914 and, in the Caucasus, the Russians became bitterly engaged in active campaigns against the Turks.

In Britain, a plan to 'knock-out' Turkey with a lightning strike against Constantinople (by forcing the Dardanelles Strait) had been regularly considered by War Office strategists in the past. Yet, pivotally, in all scenarios it was believed that without the element of surprise any such undertaking was impractical. Equally, to Lord Kitchener, preparations for the upcoming struggle in France and Flanders were paramount, as his 'New Armies' were still under-trained. However, when it became apparent that the main thrust of the campaign would not come from Greece, the grand design to humble Constantinople took new form; naval supremacy was the proposed means by which the Turks would be tamed. Accordingly, for any naval plan to succeed, Kitchener realised that infantry must naturally follow. Although Australian and New Zealand troops were waiting in Egypt to be posted to the Western Front and could be diverted to Gallipoli, only one British division, the 29th, was available as a standby in case of emergencies. As it transpired, Gallipoli was to be exactly that emergency.[2]

From Avonmouth to Alexandria

Theoretically, the odds were just in the Allies' favour. The Ottoman Army was still ineffectively-supplied and poorly equipped, although the Turks had also recently been re-organised and retrained. They made up for any deficiencies with raw courage and tenacity and also had two immense assets in their commanders in the region: German General, Liman von Sanders and the energetic Mustafa Kemal. Although considerably junior, Kemal's bravery and strategic prowess forged an inspirational leader for the Turks. Similarly, von Sanders was decisive and thoroughly aware of events on the ground. His style of command was in complete contrast to Sir Ian Hamilton, the intelligent but ineffectual Corfu-born Scottish Commander of the Mediterranean Expeditionary Force.

To this uninspiring background, the Irish regiments of the 29th Division left Avonmouth for the Greek islands and Gallipoli in mid-March 1915. Companies and transport from the 1st Munster Fusiliers departed in three ships (*Ansonia, Alaunia* and *Haverford*) whilst the 1st Dublin Fusiliers left on the *Ausonia*. The battalion's first casualty came as they neared Alexandria, when Private Peter Kavanagh, from Dublin, died aboard ship from pneumonia. A twenty-seven-year-old drummer with the 1st Munsters, Christopher Powell, wrote to his brother that the Regiment was sad to leave England before St Patrick's Day and that it celebrated on the 'high seas' instead. On the morning of St Patrick's Day, the 1st Inniskillings set sail on the *Andania*. No sooner were these troops in transit than a significant naval engagement occurred in the Dardanelles Strait that was to have disastrous ramifications for them all. On 18 March, the British Naval Commander, Vice-Admiral Sir John de Robeck, attempted to force a way through the straits with eighteen battleships. However, in the push towards the Narrows, six vessels were hit by Turkish guns and floating mines. Accordingly, de Robeck was persuaded that the Narrows could not be broken without military intervention.[3]

This intervention took over a month to appear, by which time any chance of surprise had long since gone. Hamilton had concentrated his entire force upon Alexandria, as the nearest most practical base to provide acclimatisation and reorganisation. This gave Liman von Sanders ample time to overhaul the Turkish positions and fortify those areas where landings may take place. In this,

his task was made easier by Gallipoli itself. The geography of the peninsula has often been referred to as a natural series of strong-points and fortresses, with topographical barriers and bluffs, ramparts and easily defendable high ground. Despite this, Sir Ian Hamilton fervently believed that he did have the factor of tactical surprise, in that naval dominance could move his forces at will across the campaign theatre. The 29th Division was to land on three beaches on the southern tip of the peninsula (Cape Helles) as the Royal Naval Division and a supporting French division (including the French Foreign Legion) was to make diversionary attacks at Bulair and Kum Kale respectively. The job of the main landings fell to Lieutenant-General Sir William Birdwood's Australian and New Zealand Army Corps (the ANZACs), who were to assault the spacious western shores of Gallipoli. Once ashore, Hamilton put his considerable faith in the calibre, gallantry and initiative of the men under his command. For the Inniskilling, Dublin and Munster Fusiliers, the landings at Cape Helles were to test these qualities to the full.

The Landings Begin, 25 April 1915

The battle for the beachheads of Gallipoli began in the dark early hours of 25 April, when General Birdwood's ANZACs landed with as much surprise as possible and without any preliminary naval bombardment. Birdwood's hope was simply to get his men ashore quickly and intact, before they stormed the heights of the Sari Bair ridge. Unfortunately, as dawn broke, the ANZACs discovered that the tides had taken their landing boats northwards and deposited them on the wrong beach. They gained their foothold there but, seeing the danger, Mustafa Kemal ordered his division up to hold the dominant spine of Sari Bair ridge and Chunuk Bair mount. This effectively stopped any further ANZAC advance and, arguably, determined the fate of the entire campaign.

Ironically, the diversionary assaults at Kum Kale were a complete success, with the French succeeding in storming the position and capturing nearly 600 Turkish prisoners. However, any prospect of a straightforward lodgement on the five beaches at Cape Helles was unrealistic. This was largely due to the fact that nearly every unit was conveyed to their landing point in a different manner and that these landing points were all very different in their terrain and in terms of opposition forces. Most battalions had to be ferried in lighters or small boats which were lowered from the battleships and then either rowed or towed ashore; others were in transports specially adapted for the purpose. At three of the beaches ('X', 'Y' and 'S'), troops were able to wade ashore, climb the cliff-faces and dig in relatively unchecked. The 1st Inniskillings, under the command of Lieutenant-Colonel F.G. Jones, had left Mudros harbour (on Lemnos) the evening before with a fighting strength of 26 officers and 929 other ranks. They landed on 'X' Beach at 9 am, in support of the 2nd Royal Fusiliers and the 1st Border Regiment, and made their way across the 200 yard strip of beach and up the 40 foot high bluff before 'digging in'. Interestingly, Lieutenant-Colonel Jones had made it clear to his men beforehand that, should they be wounded, they were to empty their ammunition pouches; this tends to suggest that he, at least, was unconvinced that his unit would be adequately re-supplied.[4]

'V' Beach and the *River Clyde*

In ghastly contrast, the landings on 'V' Beach became a murderous killing ground. The outnumbered Turks controlled numerous high vantage points (including the old fort at Sedd-el-Bahr) overlooking the beach-heads. It was intended that nearly 2,000 troops would be landed from the former collier ship, SS *River Clyde,* which would be deliberately run aground. Second-Lieutenant Reginald Bousfield Gillet, 2nd Hampshire Regiment, was involved directly in the landings on 'V' Beach and repeated the popular assertion that the *River Clyde* was seen by contemporaries as a new 'Trojan horse'.[5] Hatchways were cut in the ship's reinforced, armour-plated sides and the men inside were to use these to run onto a series of lighters, lashed together, to form a bridge to the beach. The remaining 1st Dublins, under Lieutenant-Colonel Richard Alexander Rooth, were to be landed by picket-boats, rowed by Royal Naval crew.

Inside, men of the Royal Engineers, two companies from the 2nd Hampshires, the entire 1st Munsters (commanded by Lieutenant-Colonel H.E. Tizard) and Lieutenant Henry O'Hara's 'W' Coy, 1st Dublins, were nervously waiting for the assault. The night before was extremely cold and, as the *River Clyde* neared its destination, it was noted that few of the soldiers in the crowded and uncomfortable holds slept. Inside the hull, the Fusiliers and Hampshires were told to brace themselves for a hard impact with the shore but, as it transpired, the *River Clyde* came to rest more or less smoothly. As the collier beached at 6.25 am, the naval parties aboard (aided by men of the Munsters) attempted to tow and tie the lighters together as a make-shift pontoon whilst under fire. Then, the first men of the Royal Munster Fusiliers stormed out of the 'sally-ports' on the ship. On either side of the *River Clyde*'s hull, Royal Navy crews rowed feverishly towards the beach in four tow-boats, containing the three companies of the Dublins. Eerily, the enemy guns and rifles were silent. One anonymous Dublin Fusiliers' officer recalled that he could see the Turks running for cover during the initial bombardment and that he genuinely believed that their landing may actually be unopposed.[6]

It was at roughly this point that the Turks let loose everything they had. They were able to hit the Dublins' unprotected boats easily and sweep the decks and gangplanks of the *River Clyde* with sustained fire without any serious check. The result was utter carnage. Hundreds were killed within the first few minutes and, in the slaughter that followed, only small handfuls of men managed to reach the beach. To add to the confusion, many of the skilled 'blue jackets' rowing the assault boats were hit in the maelstrom of deadly bullets and shrapnel. Without their essential skill, some of the Dubliners did their best to take over the oars. It seems that most of the Dublins' casualties were hit in the boats, or as they tried to wade ashore; more were drowned by the weight of their packs or, worse still, burnt alive when the boats caught fire. One NCO, Sergeant J. McColgan, was with thirty-two Dublin Fusiliers in a piquet-boat but, of these, only six made it off the boat relatively unscathed. Sergeant J. McColgan famously recollected that, as he was shouting to his men to just dive into the sea, the brains of the man beside him were shot into his mouth.[7]

As they splashed towards the shallows, many men found that the Turks had anticipated such an assault and placed wire entanglements in the water. Lieutenant-Colonel Rooth was killed as he neared the shore, whilst his Second-in-Command, Major Edwyn Fetherstonhaugh, was mortally wounded in one of the overcrowded boats. Although he was not supposed to go into the battle, Father William Finn, the Dublins' chaplain, determined that he should administer the last rites to his men and was in the first landing barge. Within minutes, Father Finn was struck in the chest and seems to have gallantly made it to the shore before dying there. Given the nature of the deathtrap which 'V' Beach had become, Father Finn may have been wounded in the leg and arm whilst scrambling from the boat in the first wave. It was reported that, shortly before his death, he gave the last rites to those around him whilst holding up his own wounded hand. Myth or not, he was the first member of the Royal Army Chaplain's Department (of any denomination) to be killed in action.[8]

At the same time as the Dublins were being cut down, similarly, the Munster's first wave of 'Z' and 'X' Companies, commanded by Captains Henderson and Geddes, were struck in a deadly flurry of bullets. Then, as the second wave of men followed, the lighter-bridge it was crossing broke away in the current; again, many men were drowned or simply cut down in the water. Of the first wave of 200 men dashing out of the *River Clyde*, it was thought that some 149 died almost immediately, whilst around 30 were wounded and knocked out of action. One officer, however, had decided to take a more direct approach to save his men and get ashore. In the midst of the gunfire, the Boer War veteran, Captain Guy Geddes, turned to his men and urged them to simply 'fall' into the water as best they could. He then promptly flung himself into the sea and swam for the shore. However, those of his men who were able to follow him, had to wrestle with the weight of their equipment from the moment they entered the water and braved the constant peppering of bullets. A rallied detachment of Munsters under Sergeant Patrick Ryan (the first Munster Fusilier to hit the shore), were taking refuge behind a sand bluff when Geddes' meagre band scrambled towards them. One of the Munsters with Captain Geddes, Private William Flynn, recollected that the small group of combined Dublins and Munsters then tried to work their way around to a safe position by the undercliff. As they did so, Geddes was hit in the shoulder, two more Fusiliers were wounded and another killed. In spite of this, they briefly forced their way into Sedd-el-Bahr fort before having to retreat from there to a position by its foot, where they dug themselves in and established a suitable 'jumping off' point.[9]

The only surviving intact Dublin company was 'W', led by Lieutenant O'Hara; it had been on *River Clyde* but the majority could not get off due to the nature of its grounding. It was a chance of fate which saved them from the slaughter below; they were left with nothing to do but grimly observe. Among the hundreds of Dublin Fusiliers already lying dead or floating in the water were twenty-four-year-old Francis Deegan of 'D' Coy, Lower Dorset Street, Dublin and thirty-eight-year-old Sergeant William Thomas Covill from Shrubbery Road, Lewisham. The Dublin born and bred Sergeant, Christopher Cooney had successfully splashed ashore and, despite being less than seventy yards from the Turks, continued to conspicuously rally the Dublins forward, assisting his men and coolly organising them in the chaos of the landings. As the situation worsened, one section of 'W' Coy was able to advance and, led by Sergeant C. McCann, was ordered ashore to support the remnants of the battalion. As they ran down onto the corpse-strewn barges, the Turks opened fire yet again. As the Dublins flung themselves down as best they could, Sergeant McCann asked one of the Munster Fusiliers beside him if he could bunch up to make some room. A little annoyed at the lack of response,

McCann pushed him with his hand only to find that the man's head was partly missing. Amongst the other Munster dead on the barges and beach, was twenty-four-year-old John Long from Glanworth (Co. Cork), twenty-five-year-old Lance Corporal William Morrison from Carlisle and one of the battalion's drummers, Christopher Powell from Limerick. As a bandsman, his duties ashore included tending to the wounded. His last letter home had simply asked his brother to look after everyone and commented that it was only a '...Goodbye for a while I hope!'[10]

At approximately 9.00 am, Lieutenant-Colonel Tizard knew that the landings at 'V' Beach, as originally conceived, were at an end. Somehow, combined knots of Dublins and Munsters had succeeded in clawing themselves onto the beach and lodging in small clusters. Without reinforcement, however, even this pitifully small foothold would be crushed. Equally, remaining onboard ship seemed a bleak prospect. Within the *River Clyde*, the remainder of the battalions of Hampshires, Dublins and Munsters were effectively pinned down and unable to move anywhere, as the decks and bridge were a deathtrap. For those inside the hold of the old collier, the deafening rattle of bullets striking its hull and the sounds of explosions from the Turkish battery at Kum Kale shredded the nerves still further. Consequently, Tizard ordered a limited advance (with platoons from 'Y' Coy, under Major Jarrett) to work their way slowly ashore and bolster the beleaguered forces there.[11]

By 9.30 am, less than 200 men had managed to lodge themselves on the enemy's shoreline. With the commander of 29th Division, Major-General Hunter-Weston, utterly oblivious of the horror on 'V' Beach, it was left to subordinate senior officers to see for themselves how they could overcome the Turkish resistance. When Lieutenant-Colonel Tizard (now effectively 86th Brigade's commander) urgently requested Hunter-Weston to outflank the Turks at 'V' Beach, the response was lethargic. Only Brigadier-General Napier, commanding 88th Brigade, seemed to grasp the urgency of the situation and he had arrived aboard *River Clyde* to assess what was happening. Whilst there, a direct order from 29th Division HQ materialised to continue the landings at all costs. Tizard was forced reluctantly to comply and sent a company of the Hampshires forward. Predictably, it was met by accurate Turkish fire as it stumbled across the barges towards the beach. Resolutely, Napier decided that this was the best place for him and his Brigade Major, Captain Costeker, to give some direction to the assault. When he was told that it would be impossible to land, in a somewhat heated conversation, Napier responded hotly that he would give it a '...damned good try'. The redoubtable Napier and Costeker did indeed make it to the shore but were there for less than fifteen minutes before both were killed. One eye-witness recollected that Napier was hit by a tornado of bullets, whilst another claimed he was struck by shrapnel in the stomach that left him dying in the blistering sun. At the height of this carnage, one Dublin Fusilier, Private P. Loftus, won the DCM for volunteering to advance to a forward position under heavy fire; he established himself there and ensured further progress up the beach.[12]

For the remainder of the day, the men on the beach did their best to survive. Huddling together behind isolated sand dunes and bluffs, the only meagre protection from the withering hail of gunfire and shrapnel, they waited for nightfall. At dusk, Major Jarrett gathered less than fifty unwounded men and established a thin outpost line with sentry posts a little further up the beach. As he was inspecting these, he was killed by a bullet to the throat. The tragic irony was, when darkness came, the remaining troops on board the *River Clyde* were able to disembark without further casualties. When the rest of the Hampshires finally made it down the gangplanks later that evening, they saw the barges piled high with, in one eye-witness account, disfigured human remains with a '…pier formed by dead men'. He also chillingly recollected that the water '…around the cove was red with blood', an image which recurs again and again. The littered corpses of the Dublin and Munster Fusiliers lay thick on the snared boats, lighters and shoreline, or floating in the shallows. In the memorable words of the war correspondent, Henry Nevinson, the '… ripple of tormented sea broke red against the sand'. Out of a thousand men, the 1st Munsters lost around 600, with 17 officer casualties; similarly, the 1st Dublins were just under 1,000 strong before the landings and, by the end, had only 1 officer and 374 men remaining.[13]

Hill 141, Battles of Sedd-el-Bahr and Krithia

The following morning, the survivors of the combined force of Dublins, Munsters and Hampshires pushed inland and against the dominating scrubland heights. With the loss of Brigadier-General Napier and so many senior officers, leadership for the operation fell to a staff officer, Lieutenant-Colonel Charles Hotham Montagu Doughty-Wylie of the Royal Welsh Fusiliers. Aided by Captain Stoney (King's Own Scottish Borderers), Captain Walford, Royal Field Artillery and Lieutenants Nightingale and O'Hara, he organised the attack on the fortified village and fort of Sedd-el-Bahr. This was to be a highly tactical pincer assault, with the British forces making their way around either side of the hill, though again, under very heavy fire and hampered by wire. Indeed, the Turks had three lines of wire so thick that the men were unable to cut it with their cutters, as Munster Private, William Cosgrove from Aghada, recalled; their attempts were like cutting the '...round tower at Cloyne with a pair of lady's scissors'.[14] Finally, in utter despair, Cosgrove started heaving at the pickets which held the entanglements in place and managed to break enough down that a sufficient gap was made. The Munsters surged through led by Sergeant-Major Bennett who was soon felled by enemy fire; again, Private Cosgrove instinctively took over and led the charge up the hill.

On the other flank, Doughty-Wylie, armed only with a cane stick, had led his men upwards towards the village and Hill 141 and was killed urging them on in the first few moments of the attack. As the men ploughed into Sedd-el-Bahr, it was noted that the Irish units appeared to welcome the opportunity of getting to grips with the enemy at last. Private Thomas Cullen of the 1st Dublins, from Old Kilmainham, was officially the first man to force his way into the old fort, and he won the DCM for his courage. The Turks put up a solid resistance, mounting counter-attack after counter-attack, before the hilltop defences of Sedd-el-Bahr fell. By the evening of 26 April, the beaches on the peninsula were consolidated, but the Turks were now well aware of the Allies' strategic intentions. Eventually, another ragged trench line was to be established, cutting off the tip of the peninsula from the enemy but, instead of the swift push to Krithia and onward to capture Constantinople, another stalemate emerged. In the dusk of 26 April, Lieutenant-Colonel Doughty-Wylie was buried by the Munsters where he fell, in an isolated grave, overlooking the spot where the *River Clyde* came aground. The casualties inflicted upon the Dublin and Munster Fusiliers meant that these 2 Regular units were briefly formed, on 29 April, into a composite battalion of just 8 officers and 400 men; they were known simply as the 'Dubsters'.[15]

On 1 May, the Turks mounted a furious night attack on the Inniskilling lines, apparently accompanying it with the battle-cry 'Eeneeskeeling, Eeneeskeeling, do not fire!' As the enemy's leading waves were bombers, loaded with grenades, the 'Skins' obliged but, instead, went in with bayonets. When the following waves of Turks came to within twenty or thirty yards' range, they were duly hit by the Inniskillings' rapid fire which broke the assault and, in its aftermath, over a hundred prisoners were captured. Sadly, the next day, Lieutenant-Colonel Jones was fatally wounded by shellfire. The 1st 'Skins' had already seen violent action at Achi Baba (the overall name for the landings at

Cape Helles, 25–27 April) and supported the vulnerable left flank of the New Zealand Brigade during its continued attack on Krithia (28 April). Here, on 1-2 July, Captain Gerald O'Sullivan and Corporal James Somers both received the Victoria Cross for conspicuously leading parties of Inniskillings forward to recapture a trench. Corporal Somers, recently rejoined from injuries received at Mons, virtually retook a section of trench single-handed from the Turks, bombing them until defences could be established. He recalled in a letter to his father that the Turks had 'swarmed' in upon him from all sides but that he had given them '… a rough time of it'. [16]

The 10th (Irish) Division at Anzac Cove and Suvla Bay

By the time the 10th (Irish) Division had left Ireland for final training in Basingstoke, in May 1915, it was clear that the Gallipoli venture was a failure. The Suvla Bay operation was to be Hamilton's final gamble to shift the odds in his favour. The following month, the Division left the UK in various transports, the first fully operational Irish division ever to take to the battlefield. Suvla was a deep crescent-shaped bay to the north of Anzac Cove. Inland from these landing beaches was a salt lake (or marsh) which led directly onto a plain (Anafarta) and the northern coastal high ground of Kiretch Tepe, a large ridge, with a series of southern hills ('Chocolate', 'Green' and 'Scimitar'). These were overlooked by the Sari Bair ridge, the Gallipoli peninsula's spine, dominated by 'Rhododendron Spur', 'Hill 60', Chunuk Bair and Koja Chemen Tepe.

The Corps Commander, General Stopford, knew that the original plan of attack, such as it was, was to use Lieutenant-General Sir Bryan Mahon's 10th (Irish) Division in a swift massed attack to secure the high ground of Kiretch Tepe Sirt; if this ridge was taken quickly, then the vulnerable Turkish ammunition depot at Ak Bashi could be overrun. However, by the time of the landings, the Division had already been fatally split up; the 29th Brigade came under urgent orders to land at Anzac, whilst the other brigades, the 30th and 31st, were destined to continue the landings at Suvla. The dismembering of the 10th (Irish) Division prior to its immediate engagement seems an idiosyncratic military decision at best, but was perhaps unsurprising in light of Hamilton's general mishandling of the campaign. Furthermore, Lieutenant-General Mahon (along with his staff and three battalions) was delayed in getting ashore due to the unsuitability of 'A' Beach. Consequently, things went incredibly wrong, incredibly quickly.

The 29th Brigade at Anzac—Chunuk Bair and Sari Bair Ridge

The 29th Brigade, temporarily attached to General Birdwood's Australian and New Zealand Corps (the ANZACs), landed at 'Z' Beach, Anzac Cove, on 6 August. As the Brigade came ashore, Ivor Powell, serving with the 6th Leinsters, recalled that there was '... nothing very special...' about Anzac, except the plague of flies and the utterly breathtaking scenery.[17] Inland, the Anzacs were fighting a bloody engagement to secure 'Lone Pine', but their accompanying assault on Sari Bair had stalled. As the battle raged ashore, the four battalions in 29th Brigade, the 6th Leinsters, 6th Irish Rifles, 5th Connaught Rangers and 10th Hampshires, disembarked and assembled in a dried up riverbed, known as 'Shrapnel Gully'. As Turkish shells burst in the distance and overhead, the men halted and awaited further orders.

Whilst there, they were told to rest in preparation for an imminent attack which never came; the battalions were marched in darkness up towards Russell's Top but, in the early hours of 7 August, they were marched back down again.[18] Only the 6th Leinsters remained, and the Rifles, Rangers and Hampshires could see the steady flow of Anzac stretcher-bearers bringing down their wounded and dying from the gully top. At this stage, the Irish battalions had no idea of the battle for Lone Pine and, as Major Bryan Cooper commented, had not yet heard of the Sari Bair ridge. Any eager questions directed at the passing Anzacs about what was happening was met, if it was met at all, by the standard reply of 'Pretty tough up there.'[19]

Indeed, the fury of the fight for Sari Bair had exhausted the Australians, New Zealanders and Gurkhas sent to capture it. By midday, yet another futile and costly attack was repulsed by the Turks on Chunuk Bair and soon it was the turn of the Irish regiments. Lieutenant-Colonel Bradford's 6th Royal Irish Rifles were sent up to advance upon the Sari Bair Ridge and suffered casualties from intense shellfire almost at once. Having only advanced 400 or so yards, they halted and dug in before renewing their advance in the darkness. The Rifles eventually got under cover, holding positions at 'The Farm', and remained there until the general advance on Sari Bair was resumed on 10 August. The Rifles held their position, despite escalating casualties, before they were finally given a point-blank order to fall back. This was an order which the 6th Irish Rifles were apparently furious with and only grudgingly obeyed. Accordingly, the Rifles sustained 372 missing, wounded and killed during the battle until they were finally relieved in line by Lieutenant-Colonel Jourdain's

5th Connaughts. By the end of 10 August, Irish Rifleman and Staff Captain, Gerald Nugent, had been killed at the head of his men, service revolver in his hand, whilst Lieutenant-Colonel Bradford and Brigadier-General Cooper had both been wounded. Indeed, command of the brigade temporarily fell to Lieutenant-Colonel Jourdain, whilst his 5th Connaughts were heavily committed to the action at Aghyl Dere.[20]

Similarly, Lieutenant-Colonel John Craske's 6th Leinsters were very heavily shelled whilst relieving troops from the New Zealand infantry brigade at Rhododendron Ridge on 9 August, sustaining forty-seven casualties. At dawn on 10 August, the Turks launched a surprise counter-attack. The Leinsters not only fought off this counter-attack but went on to counter-charge up the hill. Apparently they were alerted to this Turkish attack by a New Zealander who was seen running down the hill, frantically shouting out, 'Fix bayonets, boys, they're coming!' Throughout the day-long battle, the Turks continued to attack the Leinster lines, over-running them in places though they were aggressively beaten off by the bayonet and frantic rifle fire in others. The assault continued into the night when the last Turkish waves came to be met by another desperate counter-charge which drove the Turks back. The courage displayed by the 6th Leinsters from 9–11 August was exemplary. Lieutenant-Colonel Craske was shot through the arm, as was Captain J.C. Parke, one of the most famous British tennis players of his day. Two officers, Captain Charles William D'Arcy-Irvine from Castle Irvine (Co. Fermanagh) and 2nd-Lieutenant. James Vernon Yates Willington, aged twenty, from St Kieran's in Birr (Co. Offaly), were last seen charging into the Turkish ranks. Alongside the 6th Leinsters, the 10th Hampshires had only one officer remaining by nightfall, Lieutenant Quartermaster W.J. Saunders. Among the men lost was the distinguished Roman military scholar, Lieutenant George Cheesman. Perhaps typically, for a man steeped in the history of the previous battles in this Homeric landscape, Cheesman had written shortly before his death in praise of the military qualities of the Turks. Among the 10th (Irish) Division, classicists and scholars of all kinds found themselves fighting and dying in this historic setting, replete with its imagery of heroism, sacrifice and tragic loss.[21]

Suvla Bay landings—'Chocolate', 'Kidney' and 'Scimitar' Hills

Meanwhile, the main landings at Suvla Bay saw Irish battalions from the 30th and 31st Brigades put ashore at 'A' (Ghazi Baba) and 'C' Beaches (just south of Nibrunesi Point). However, the assaulting brigades were unexpectedly redeployed from their planned landing zone on 'A' Beach, near their objective, and were disembarked, instead on 'C' Beach, miles away on the southern tip of the bay. Consequently, Brigadier-General Hill (as Lieutenant-General Mahon had not yet arrived), disembarked with five active battalions but without any clear orders of how his men should reach their objective. Unfortunately, many Battalion Commanders were kept equally ill-informed and Lieutenant-Colonel F.A. Greer, 6th Irish Fusiliers, complained that his immediate orders or battle-plans were shrouded in secrecy.[22]

The 6th Inniskillings landed on 'C Beach' in the early hours of 7 August and, almost immediately, came under enemy shrapnel fire and were ordered up to positions at Lala Baba, from where they were to assault the Turkish held 'Chocolate Hill'. The 6th 'Skins' were by far the stronger numerically of the two Inniskilling battalions in the division, with Lieutenant-Colonel H.M. Cliffe's force standing at 967 officers and other ranks. They launched a courageous attack upon 'Chocolate Hill', although none of the officers had been given any prior indication of either the terrain or scale of opposition before them. As they advanced under direct fire, they discovered that the dried-up 'Salt Lake' which had to be traversed before reaching the hill was covered with scrub and hidden Turkish snipers. Having cleared their way through these and, having arrived at the base of the hill, they then found that the Turks were in a defended gully which commanded the approaches to 'Chocolate Hill'. After a brutal hand-to-hand battle, 'A' Company secured the trench (with bombs and bayonet) whilst 'C' Company passed through them and onwards up the hill. The 6th Inniskillings continued to consolidate the gains made and, with other battalions, continued to defend them until ordered back to Lala Baba on 10 August. Lieutenant-Colonel Cliffe was wounded in the assault and his Second-in-Command, Major Frazer, found himself with the very difficult task of coordinating the continuing attack of the supporting companies. This was compounded by the fact the Major had no knowledge of his commanding officer's intentions, largely because Cliffe probably had no such orders himself. However, once the lower trenches were secured, the 'Skins' regrouped as darkness fell and brought up their support companies, who had withdrawn to the northern side of 'Salt Lake'. The battle at 'Chocolate Hill' had cost the 6th 'Skins' some 100 casualties in killed, missing or wounded. One of the latter was twenty-six-year-old Lieutenant Archibald Douglas, from Dalkey, who had attended Tipperary Grammar School and Trinity College Dublin.[23]

As they landed on 'C' Beach, the 7th Royal Dublin Fusiliers (the 'Dublin Pals') could see the intense shellfire inland and many recalled how similar the coastline seemed to Dublin Bay. Indeed, it was even noted that a certain 'picnic' atmosphere had developed among the 'Pals' as their 'beetles' (landing-craft) ran ashore, their ramps were lowered and men casually strode onto the beach. However, they came under accurate shrapnel fire as they did so, with one boat claiming sixteen casualties alone. On their first day of landing, they joined the assault on 'Chocolate Hill', being temporarily attached to the 31st Brigade, and took part in the successful storming of the Turkish position. Similarly, Lieutenant-Colonel Pike's 5th Irish Fusiliers had also advanced towards Lala Baba and been sent into the assault on 'Chocolate Hill'. As they crossed 'Salt Lake', the Turks trained their artillery on them and they were obliged to change direction and sweep through the Anafarta Plain instead. Whilst attempting this, they discovered enemy snipers concealed in positions in the scrub; once again their progress was hampered. By roughly 8 pm, the 5th 'Faughs' had reached 'Chocolate Hill', ousting the enemy from its trenches, before being ordered to relieve the troops on nearby 'Green Hill', which they did on 9 August. As the slit trenches in this position were not very deep, the 5th Irish Fusiliers could not move safely along them, and many casualties were caused by constant Turkish sniping. Furthermore, two Turkish counter-attacks were fought off and there was a spirited mission undertaken by the 5th 'Faughs' to remove enemy snipers from the frontage of their firing line. The 6th Irish Fusiliers were in support of the 5th Irish Fusiliers' assault on 'Chocolate Hill' and were raked by shrapnel fire as they progressed up the beach. As they pushed onwards, they met with comparatively little opposition and were finally able to consolidate the gains made and secure the hill. Even with little opposition, they still lost eighty-nine men before their major assault (on 9 August) on 'Scimitar Hill', during which they lost a further 249 men. Among the dead was 2nd-Lieutenant Hugh Maurice MacDermot, eldest son of The MacDermot, Coolavin (Co. Sligo), killed at the age of just eighteen.[24]

The Landing at 'A' West and Kiretch Tepe Sirt

By mid-morning, 7 August, Lieutenant-General Mahon and his staff, including the 5th Royal Irish, with the 6th and 7th Munsters, had landed at a new site, nearer Kiretch Tepe, hurriedly termed "A' Beach West'. When the 5th Inniskillings had tried to land at 'C' Beach earlier that morning, intense shelling had forced them to withdraw and instead they were landed at 'A West'. Yet even here, their 'beetle' landing-craft boats were caught on submerged rocks and they found themselves isolated from the rest of their brigade. As one officer recalled, by the time they reached the shore, '...chaos had already set in'.[25]

The allied ignorance of coastal waters was a recurring theme. Some of the lighters transporting the 6th Munsters had already run aground in the rocky shallows, forcing the men to wade to the beach. When they got there, they found the shore booby-trapped with landmines but continued forward along Kiretch Tepe Sirt until they reached the British advance line, 800 yards from the Turkish entrenchments. From here the 6th Munsters attacked the Turkish defences and got to within 100 yards of them, digging in and renewing the assault the following morning. It was here that 'A' Company, led by Major John N. Jephson, stormed and captured the summit, thereafter ensuring its name as 'Jephson's Post'. Among the numerous 6th Munsters lying dead on the knoll was volunteer, Patrick Cullinane, from St Finbarr's, Cork. The 7th Munster Fusiliers, proudly wearing green shamrock badges stitched onto the arms of their tunics, followed their 6th Battalion inland, moving cautiously up the eastern slopes of Kiretch Tepe Sirt. As they made their way steadily upwards, passing the fly-blown corpses of the 11th Manchesters, they were checked by heavy Turkish fire which caused seventy-six casualties. The next morning, the 7th Munsters attacked again along the line facing 'Kidney Hill' and 'Beacon Hill' but, once more, due to the determined resistance against them, all but one company was forced to retire. The casualty list for the day's action had increased to a further 127 killed, wounded or missing; among those killed in the desperate fighting for the rocky outcrops was Acting-Sergeant Andrew Joyce, from St Michael's, Limerick.[26]

The 5th Royal Irish, under Lieutenant-Colonel the Right Honourable the Earl of Granard, had duties to build Corps Headquarters, working on trench lines by Ghazi Baba but, as a pioneer unit, it was also expected to man the trenches. On 9 August they unexpectedly saw General Sir Ian Hamilton as they were filling their water-bottles from the well at Charak Chesme, whilst under Turkish fire. By now, the Suvla operation was entering its second phase to secure the northern high ground and, on 12 August, the 5th Inniskillings were finally reunited with the 31st Brigade for another massed attack on Kiretch Tepe. The next day they were ordered to assault 'Kidney Hill' and the full battalion strength of 775 men (including 25 officers) slowly advanced in the crucifying heat of a midday sun, all the time under heavy Turkish shellfire. Their difficulties were increased significantly by viciously accurate rifle fire from Turkish positions which held back any movement the 5th 'Skins' attempted to make. At approximately 3 pm, Lieutenant-Colonel A.S. Vanrenen was hit and fatally wounded, and this incident seems to have heralded the high-water mark of their attack, with remaining companies ordered to retire to their original position. The combined cost to the 5th 'Skins' was scarcely thought possible: 356 killed, wounded or missing in just one assault. One of those killed was Corporal Richard Coldwell, from Rose Cottages, Lavender Hill, London. Corporal Coldwell had originally enlisted in St Pancras and had formerly served with the Duke of Cornwall's Light Infantry.[27]

However, the battle for dominance of Kiretch Tepe Sirt only increased in desperation. From 15-16 August, the 7th Munster Fusiliers sustained another 158 casualties on its slopes, where Privates Bellamy and Carbutt, caught and hurled back the enemy's grenades during the attack.[28] The 6th Dublins also attacked the ridge (with less than 500 men), assisting the Munsters in the capture of the summit. At 'Green Knoll', the 7th Dublins were in support against the Turkish line and took over captured trenches that evening. They entered these lines with 532 men and 21 officers but, following sustained counter-attacks by the enemy throughout the night, upon their relief the next morning the 7th Dublins had only 10 officers and 375 men remaining.

The 6th Irish Fusiliers received little respite and were engaged in rotational duties in reserve lines at Lala Baba and Karakol Dagh before being committed to the defence of 'The Pimple' from 15-16 August. It was here that the battalion lost over 200 men and where erstwhile divinity student, 2nd-Lieutenant Cecil Barker, was killed in action at only twenty years of age.[29] Their senior battalion, the 5th Irish Fusiliers, also fought desperately at 'The Pimple', where they took over forward firing lines and were heavily engaged by the enemy. As they clung to their position, the 5th 'Faughs' were hit by shell and shrapnel fire on one flank and by machine-guns on the other, whilst the Turks launched themselves upon them again and again. Despite this, they held their ground until ordered to withdraw. Along the battered Irish regimental lines the story was repeated. The battle for Kiretch Tepe had left hundreds dead and wounded in two days of fierce combat; among those killed were Major Jephson, 6th Munsters, fatally injured during a further advance on 15 August, and Lieutenant Kevin Emmet O'Duffy, 7th Munsters, killed in action on the same day.[30] Also lying dead was Pioneer Officer, Lieutenant John Rowswell Duggan, 5th Royal Irish Regiment, whose Cavan-born father was Manager of the Provincial Bank of Ireland in College Green Dublin. With many of his officers hit, Private J. O'Keefe, 5th Royal Irish, noticed part of the line was giving way under pressure and led a party to plug the gap; when his rifle was blown to bits by a grenade, he calmly turned around and '...asked for another one'. O'Keefe was subsequently awarded the DCM.[31]

As August wore on, the misery continued, with units rotated between front-line duty and the rear, but difficulties in supply often led to troops being left without food and, more worryingly, water. In fact, conditions at Gallipoli were, by now, nauseating, with flies, disease and, as on the Western Front, the problem of unburied dead. Generally speaking, troops tried to dispose of as many corpses as best they could whenever the opportunity arose. The 5th Irish Fusiliers sent a unit out beyond their wire to examine the bodies of a Turkish raiding party that had been killed in the brushwood near to them but they could not tell how long they had lain there ('... around four days...') because the corpses had only been accidentally discovered in the scrub.[32] The smell of death became one of the features of Gallipoli. As Corporal James Somers of the 1st Inniskillings recalled, the stench of corpses in the heat of the Mediterranean became overpowering.[33]

On 20 August, the 1st Inniskillings were redeployed to Suvla Bay being transported by sea and fighting at 'Scimitar Hill' the very next day, in a battle which became almost legendary. At first, their advance was unchecked but, after only 400 yards, the front ranks virtually disappeared under a hail of bullets and grenades. Despite this, the first trench was captured and the attack pressed onward. The leading Inniskilling waves scrambled up the slopes of the hill but were sent reeling back by the Turkish defenders at only 150 yards from the summit. Here, the battalion could plainly see the Turks standing on the parapets, shooting and bombing down onto them as they approached. As the supporting battalions advanced (from the King's Own Scottish Borderers and South Wales Borderers), another charge was made. Sometime after 7 pm, Captain Gerald O'Sullivan VC reputedly led the last charge against the top of 'Scimitar Hill', where he was killed. It is telling that, at the commencement of the Suvla Bay operations, the 1st 'Skins' had a fighting strength of 839 in all ranks but, after 'Scimitar Hill', it had a mere 234 officers and men.[34] The next day, the 5th Connaughts ferociously attacked 'Hill 60', where they courageously bayonet-charged the Turkish lines near the wells of Kabuk Kayu, capturing them. The remnants of the Connaughts were cut down by machine-gun fire as they attempted to take the other trenches on the hill. Eventually they did so, despite abysmal casualties. The Connaughts were again in action on 'Hill 60' on 27 August in another bloody assault on Turkish positions, in which they were further depleted by shrapnel, rifle, machine-gun and shell fire. Despite this, the Connaughts captured their objective, with the enemy dead being noted as 'six deep' in the northern trench alone. The Turks, equally determinedly, counter-attacked with extreme ferocity and a hand-to-hand battle ensued until well past midnight. The 5th Connaughts were finally relieved the next morning, but the Turkish counter-attack had overcome them and left their ranks incredibly thin.[35]

Around this time, a most extraordinary event occurred within Hamilton's chain of command and one which had a direct effect on the 10th (Irish) Division. The failure to take Kiretch Tepe Sirt was understood to lie in either Lieutenant-General Mahon's handling of the assault or in the calibre of the volunteers themselves. Neither understanding was reasonable. It is likely that, had it been a sudden *full* 10th Divisional attack as originally planned, Kiretch Tepe Sirt would have fallen. Yet, Mahon was seemingly undermined by Hamilton and his division was repeatedly diminished as a fighting force; firstly by the re-allocation of the 29th Brigade and then the chaos over the landing beaches. When Hamilton sacked General Stopford, the natural replacement in seniority was Lieutenant-General Mahon, but instead, he appointed Major-General De Lisle, commander of 29th Division. In response, Mahon refused point blank to serve under De Lisle and, from 19-25 August, he peevishly resigned his command and left for Mudros. Although Hamilton gave him permission to go, it is hard not to see this act as effective desertion. Indeed, other men were already being shot for similar offences throughout the other campaign theatres.[36] It was only on Kitchener's intervention that Mahon returned to his post and, interestingly, the 10th (Irish) Division was shortly redeployed to Salonika, with Mahon promoted to command there. Ultimately, whatever the support, provocation or injustice which Mahon had received, his actions appear to have been petulant, especially given the circumstances with his men dying in the scrub of the gullies and slopes ashore.

Evacuation of Gallipoli and Move to Serbia

The 10th Division was finally evacuated from Gallipoli in late September, this time bound for the campaign in Macedonia. By now, some of the most eager Irish volunteer battalions of autumn 1914 had lost almost 75 per cent of their initial strength. In the context of the Western Front, Gallipoli promised persuasive bounties if it actually proved successful; it was the quick-silver, ever-illusory, 'swift, conclusive victory' that became so narcotic to the combatant High Commands. Furthermore, of those 10th Divisional Battalion Commanding Officers, no less than eight became casualties;

Lieutenant-Colonel A. Vanrenen (5th Inniskillings) had been killed, whilst Lieutenant-Colonels E. Bradford (6th Irish Rifles), F. Greer (6th Irish Fusiliers), W. Bewsher (10th Hampshires), H. Cliffe (6th Inniskillings), J. Craske (6th Leinsters), V.T. Worship (6th Munsters) and G. Downing (7th Dublins) were all wounded in just over a month's fighting.

The evacuation of Gallipoli was largely heralded as a great success by the popular press back home. Undoubtedly, some saw it as such, but it exposed a very painful reality. The 10th Division had lost over 2,000 casualties with the Regular Irish battalions losing over 1,500 men in the Dardanelles. Indeed, one of those who survived was 6th Leinster Sergeant, John O'Dare, from Trim. He had been poisoned by explosive fumes whilst on the peninsular and, although described as '... smart, intelligent and hard working... ', Gallipoli broke him. In September, he developed dysentery and then tuberculosis. He was invalided back to England and discharged in January 1916 at Birr (the Regimental Depot) as unfit for further service. In January, Sergeant O'Dare's medical board felt he was '... likely to improve...' and he was duly admitted to the workhouse hospital at Trim where he died in March 1916. [37]

Gallipoli has been seen variously as a bold strike in a bid to secure a quick way to end the war or as a disastrous charnel house. The blunt cost of the operation stood at almost 200,000 British Imperial casualties, wounded, killed or missing. However, soon even the Irish regimental casualties of 'V' Beach, Anzac and Suvla were to be eclipsed by a rebellion at home and the unimaginable carnage of the long battle of the Somme.

CHAPTER SIX

'Ypres on the Liffey...'[1]

Emergency at Home—the Easter Rising, 1916

Meanwhile back in Ireland, trouble was slowly but surely brewing. To many at home, recruitment became the most pressing issue, focusing on those who had already committed to the war effort and those, tellingly, who had not. To them, the arguments of Sinn Féin and the dissident Irish Volunteers seemed attractive but, for the time being, a steady trickle of recruits still entered the training, Reserve and Garrison units of the Irish regiments.

Dublin, with its plentiful barracks and high military profile, was still not a hostile place for soldiers in 1916. There was a widespread regimental family support system and, especially with separation allowances, the army was a strong economic provider in the city.[2] There were also many new venues established throughout the metropolis where wartime soldiers could relax off-duty. Numerous cafes and social clubs flourished across Dublin and all of these reinforced the wartime presence of the military, from the *Soldiers' Home* (Parkgate St), *Soldiers' Recreation Rooms* (Rathmines Road), *Garrison Buffet* (Dawson St) and the *Khaki Club* (Aungier St), to the *Soldiers' Social Club* (College St) and the *Soldiers' Rendezvous* (Lower Abbey St). The latter is particularly interesting, as its aim was to provide soldiers in Dublin with the opportunity to relax, buy cheap meals and have entertainment provided for them. It was maintained on the premises of the Methodist church and there were writing materials provided, with tea for a penny and an associated 'Temperance Bar'. Like the others, it was sanctioned by the military authorities and seems to have been a genuinely popular spot with all 'classes and creeds'.[3]

Irish Regimental Reserve, Garrison Battalions and Volunteer Training Corps

Irish troops on the Reserve and Garrison list have sometimes been overlooked in favour of the Service or Regular battalions, but their contribution to Ireland's war experience deserves note. Whilst the stories of these battalions can sometimes seem like a complicated list of changes in personnel, or mundane postings, there was an urgency behind them. Once a recruit's eligibility for service was assessed, he was posted to a draft-finding, Training Reserve or Garrison Battalion, depending on his suitability. Ireland did not possess an official Training Reserve as such, although the Ulster Division did have 'Local Reserve' battalions serving in the 15th Reserve Brigade. Instead, many of the Irish Reserve battalions had duties which went beyond normal draft-finding or recruit training. [4]

For example, the Royal Irish Rifles had an impressive number of twenty-one battalions, with the 17th–20th battalions formed out of depot companies from the Ulster divisional surplus. During the first days of the war, the 4th Irish Rifles had been raised in Newtownards, whilst the 5th had been created at Downpatrick and both were eventually transferred to the Irish Reserve Brigade at Larkhill. Interestingly, the 3rd Irish Rifles was formed in Belfast but saw considerable military service at home during the Easter Rising (as did the 18th) when it was stationed in Dublin (from August 1914 to May 1916). It was later moved back up to Belfast (and later still to Larkhill) where, in April 1918, it merged with the 17th, 18th, 19th and 20th Reserve Battalions as part of the Irish Reserve Brigade. The 21st Irish Rifles Battalion was the 1st Garrison Battalion, RIR, raised in Dublin in November 1915 and sent to India for the duration of the war in February 1916. Also present in Dublin during Easter 1916 was a contingent from the 12th Inniskillings on musketry training at Dollymount.

It is important to note here that general Reserve units were not expected to contain the highest calibre of troops, except for those 'passing through' to parent battalions. Some battalions, such as the 3rd Royal Irish, enticed middle-class recruits by appearing to have some form of Officer Training Company. John Frederich Eberli, from Islington, was a clerk at Hammond & Company Ltd, Lloyd's brokers; he had been in the Inns of Court Officer Training Corps and found himself commissioned into the 3rd Royal Irish on 22 April 1916. All too soon he found himself involved in the rebellion in Dublin. Equally, some senior and junior Reserve officers ranged from inadequate disciplinarians with little practical military experience, to 'dug-outs' (those recalled from retirement for service). Colonel Lyle was removed by Major-General Nugent as Commanding Officer of the 8th Irish Rifles as he was considered to be unsuitable to command an active service battalion. He was sent to take over the Reserve 17th Irish Rifles instead. The 3rd Reserve Inniskillings (based in Londonderry) was commanded by the fifty-six-year-old Lieutenant-Colonel J.K. McClintock from Seskinore (Co. Tyrone). It is ironic that he still saw action in Dublin during Easter Week and was Mentioned in Despatches.[5]

In some cases, an Irish regiment could even raise a new service battalion from this surplus of its volunteers. In late 1915, a meeting was held at 85–86 Grafton Street to review the current status of the 'Commercial Pals Company' of the 5th Dublin Fusiliers. Brigadier-General Hammond informed those present that the Company was ready to be moved for training to the Curragh but that its recruitment had been so successful that a new 'Tenth' battalion of the Dublins could be formed. Interestingly, General Hammond felt that the men should be asked about whether they would be willing to form the nucleus of this new battalion or whether they would prefer to remain as 5th Dublin Fusiliers. The 'Commercials' overwhelmingly agreed to form the core of the new 10th Dublins and consequently remained at Royal Barracks whilst the battalion was officially formed there in February 1916.[6]

Among these Reservists and home defence forces was Frank Henry 'Chicken' Browning, a renowned wicketkeeper/batsman who had captained Ireland twelve times. He was the first Irish cricketer to achieve over a thousand runs and was the first to be elected as President of both the Irish Cricket Union and the Irish Rugby Football Union. Browning was also in command of the Dublin contingent of the IVTC formed at Lansdowne Road from professional men who were not of military service age. By early 1916, Browning regularly took his men on local route marches and the unit was a well-known (and well-liked) sight across Dublin. Whilst these men were never intended to be part of a combat unit, they still openly drilled and were easily distinguished by their 'GR' armbands and, later, belt-buckles. These initials were a constant source of amusement for Dubliners; the initials stood for 'Georgius Rex' but the unit soon became known as the 'Gorgeous Wrecks'. There certainly seemed little animosity towards these men, many of whom were doctors, accountants or civil servants and well past any active service duties. However, they, along with the 10th 'Commercial Pals' were to find themselves fighting in the streets of their own capital city a few months later.[7]

Countdown to Rebellion

In effect, there was a section of Irish society that felt disaffected with society itself: those who were well-enough educated to understand, and be stimulated by, the raging intellectual debates of Republicanism.[8] These debates were reflected in the pages of *The Irish Volunteer*, which firmly believed that the cause of the Irish Volunteers was to secure Home Rule with immediate effect and through the threat of violence. It witheringly pointed out that, had Redmond not prompted so many Irish Volunteers to enlist, they would have had over 200,000 armed men who '...mean business...' and could implement Home Rule through force. Equally, the *Connaught Tribune* published patriotic recruitment adverts which declared:

'You must join an Irish Regiment and learn to sing "God save Ireland" with a gun in your hands.'

On 7 July 1915, as part of this potentially skewed policy, an 'All-Ireland' War Demonstration was held at Warrenpoint (Co. Down), with the sole intention of promoting mass recruitment at a time when enlistment was falling throughout Britain and Ireland. The optimism surrounding the event was, perhaps, unjustified. Furthermore, as recruitment in Ireland began to stutter, certain solutions were sought to attract those sections of the Irish community which refused to enlist. To cater for both the rise of Irish patriotism and the need for a perceived 'higher status' regiment, Dublin Castle and the War Office agreed, in principle, to raise the saffron-kilted 'Irish Light Infantry'. The proposal was probably too whimsical and unrealistic to be of any practical use and the notion was quietly dropped. Consequently, the Irish Light Infantry became a little-known footnote to the Irish regiments of the Great War. At the same time, there were worrying concerns regarding floods of young men emigrating to escape any move towards conscription. This was to become an issue which was to haunt moderate Nationalist politicians for the remainder of the war. As recruitment in Ireland was so entirely wedded to its political situation, any disturbance in one had a knock-on effect on the other.[9]

Support was found when Cardinal Bourne asked his followers to pray for a 'speedy victory' for those fighting against Germany and for those who had died for King, Country '... and the Pope'. Yet, as the wider Irish Catholic Church seemed to turn against the war, Redmond's traditional ally seemed to slip away. On the streets, the warning signs of potential conflict were already showing. In the early hours of 15 August 1915, a number of men stole four wooden crates from the L&NW Railway Stores on North Wall Quay, Dublin. Yet this was no ordinary robbery, as the boxes were addressed to 'Mr John Redmond MP' and contained twenty-five Martini-Metford rifles in each crate. The men made off with the rifles until they were picked up by a waiting motor car which sped off, 'destination unknown' with the haul. As if to confirm the deteriorating situation, at Liverpool docks in November, approximately 800 men ('chiefly Irishmen of military age' and mostly, it would seem, from Connaught) attempted to embark on the *Saxonia* for the United States. The liner's crew threatened to strike and, when the crowd was physically stopped by Cunard stewards, disturbances ensued as the men tried to board the ship. To observers in Great Britain and Ireland, these men of eligible age seemed to be trying to evade military service. Whilst the National Register (and limited conscription) was introduced in October 1915 in Great Britain, the associated Lord Lieutenant's appeal for fresh volunteers in Ireland was unsuccessful. Ironically, so was the National Register, as it was replaced by full conscription under the Military Service Act of January 1916.[10]

The Irish Volunteers and Irish Citizen Army—Invasion, Espionage and Intrigue

With this unstable background, the separatist 'Irish Volunteers' had re-organised with a core of approximately 12,000 dissidents and Professor Eoin MacNeill as its nominal leader. With committed leaders such as Patrick Pearse, their Director of Organisation, it soon became clear that there were two very distinct—and rival—sets of Volunteers. The Irish Volunteers soon became the prime choice for young Nationalists who feared conscription or who actively sought a more militant approach to independence. This militancy was reflected by that fact that Pearse was also leader of the Irish Republican Brotherhood's 'Military Council', established to undertake military operations in Ireland. Although training and equipment were very inferior to that of the INV or UVF, the organisation had enthusiasm and youth on their side. Contingents, detachments and sections were often commanded by local GAA or IRB men, who energetically threw themselves into plans for future rebellion. Similarly, the Irish Citizen Army had been formed in November 1913 as a militant socialist force to counter the Dublin Metropolitan Police, although it soon became linked with wider radical groupings such as Sinn Féin and the IRB. Whilst the ICA originally viewed the Irish Volunteers with (in Sean O'Casey's words) 'passive sympathy', under James Connolly's leadership this became 'active unity'. In turn, the IRB saw the obvious potential in the ICA and, in January 1916, Connolly was appointed to its 'Military Council'. At the same time, a date for the insurrection was set for Easter and the ICA was to become a vital element in it.

In many quarters, there was the very real fear of a German invasion of Ireland and the threat of espionage. It was exacerbated by visions of German plots and conspiracies throughout the Empire, from German-instigated unrest in India to their more visible recent efforts in Ireland and Ulster.[11] This fear was not helped by the public defection to Germany of former British Consul-General to Rio-de-Janeiro, Sir Roger Casement. Although there may not have been the same depth of anti-German sentiment in Ireland as was displayed in Great Britain, the RIC and Irish public were increasingly on the look-out for suspicious activity. In early 1915, the RIC in Wexford even issued posters asking the public to destroy their own property should the Germans invade. Shortly afterwards, four handwritten notices appeared in the county and urged citizens to actively assist the Germans 'when' they invaded. The notices declared that the Germans would be in Ireland '... as friends to put an end to English rule...' and, tellingly, that they would explicitly pay for any stores or forage they took. This, of course, was completely contrary to what had already happened in occupied France and Belgium.[12]

In late May 1915, a German sailor was arrested in Dundalk, having been discovered lurking at the artillery barracks in the town. Another German, was arrested at Cleggan (Co. Galway) for possessing maps and illustrations of the coastline. Interestingly, at Whitespots (Co. Antrim), the men of the Reserve 10th Irish Fusiliers trained at the old lead mines in the hills by Conlig. Whilst there, members of the Non-Combatant Corps (conscientious objectors) were attached to them and, as Private William Allen noted, these educated intellectuals were made to do degrading work, such as emptying the base latrines. It was clear that the loyalties of these men were also under scrutiny. As a consequence of this widespread suspicion, Germans in Ireland were rounded up from Hans Heinsmen of Skidoo House, Swords (Co. Dublin), who possessed undeclared firearms, to German workmen in Ulster who were placed on a train for Dublin. All were housed in Templemore Jail for the duration of the war.[13]

For Irish prisoners of war in German prison camps, life was frequently hard, with conditions and treatment harsh. Private Tom Donohoe, 2nd Dublin Fusiliers, had been captured in late August 1914 and was sent to Sennelager camp where he claimed the food was rotten, latrines open and the men effectively worked to death. If men slacked, they were beaten; if they grew weak, they were beaten; if they became ill they were taken to hospital. There, one German orderly oversaw fifty patients without the benefit of any medicines, with the exception of morphia. As Private Donohoe noted, some men never woke up from their 'morphia treatment', administered in drops by this one orderly who was not '... very particular about the dose'.[14]

The Rebellion Begins

Consequently, it was unsurprising that men tried to find ways of escaping their predicament. One option came in the guise of Sir Roger Casement's invasion plan of Ireland, using an 'Irish brigade' recruited as part of the Imperial German Army. To secure enlistment, Casement had decided to approach British PoWs from Irish regiments. His recruitment drive lasted from mid-1915 to early 1916 but appears to have produced fairly unimpressive results. Instead, it seems that many Irish soldiers refused to have anything to do with him and he was '... hounded out of the camp'. Casement made some progress in enlisting a small cadre of troops, some fifty-six men in total. Casement and his comrades would come to see this brigade as a tangible demonstration of German intervention in Irish affairs. Meanwhile, he continued with his operation of supplying arms for the imminent uprising and made plans accordingly.

In early April, a Portuguese-registered ship called the *Aud* secretly sailed from Lubeck in Germany with a consignment of some 20,000 rifles, ammunition and ten machine-guns, bound for Tralee Bay. A few days later, as the Irish Brigade languished in Limburg, Sir Roger Casement left on the submarine U-19 with Robert Monteith (from the IRB) and Daniel Bailey (a Royal Irish Rifleman), to meet up with the *Aud* at Tralee. On 21 April, U-19 surfaced at Banna Strand, just off Tralee from where Casement swam ashore. The difficult swim left him utterly drained. As he lay exhausted on the beach, he told his two companions, Monteith and Bailey, to fetch help. It arrived in the form of the dark-green uniforms of a detachment of the RIC, who duly placed Casement under immediate arrest. Similarly, the *Aud* was surrounded by Royal Navy ships which compelled it to sail into Cork bay under escort. Once there, and before it could be boarded, the *Aud* hoisted the Imperial German flag and scuttled itself.[15]

Despite this news, the Irish Volunteers were still fully prepared for rebellion when Pearse issued the order for 'manoeuvres' to begin on Easter Sunday.

However, confusion spread throughout the Volunteers when Professor MacNeill countermanded the initial order, which effectively derailed any mass uprising. At a meeting of the Military Council at Liberty Hall (the headquarters of the Irish Trade and General Workers Union) Pearse re-issued orders to fully mobilise on Easter Monday. The four Dublin battalions mobilised as intended, albeit seriously under-strength, and assembled at their various locations. However, smaller numbers of volunteers turned up at the rendezvous points than expected and, outside Dublin, the rebellion's impact was extremely limited. Instead of a widespread insurrection, the fate of the rebellion seemed to rest upon the outcome of the battle for Dublin.

Early on Easter Monday morning, Frank Browning led his veteran detachment of 'Gorgeous Wrecks', the Volunteer Training Corps, out of Dublin on a pre-scheduled route march. A matter of only a few hours later, around 1,800 Irish Volunteers along with the Irish Citizen Army seized the General Post Office and other significant objectives across the city. The 1st Battalion Irish Volunteers, under Commandant Daly, planned to capture the Four Courts, whilst the 2nd Battalion, commanded by Commandant McDonagh, was to take and hold Jacob's biscuit factory. The 3rd Dublin Battalion, led by Commandant De Valera, was to block the roads from Kingston Harbour and stop British reinforcements from aiding any siege of Dublin. Finally, the 4th Battalion had a similar task and, under Commandant Kent, it was to occupy the South Dublin Union Workhouse and halt any British advance from Kingsbridge Station. Ironically, the first British soldier officially killed in the Easter Rising was Captain Guy Vickery Pinfield, 8th Irish Hussars, who was shot during Sean Connolly's assault on Dublin Castle. As Pinfield lay dying on the pavement by the castle gate, the noted Nationalist sympathiser and pacifist, Francis Sheehy-Skeffington, persuaded a nearby chemist to join him in running the gauntlet of fire to try and help the wounded officer. By this time, Captain Pinfield had already been dragged into the Castle and died soon afterwards, aged twenty-one; he had been educated at Marlborough and Cambridge, obtaining his commission in the Irish Hussars on 15 August 1914, just eleven days after the declaration of war.[16]

Meanwhile, Pearse and the other remaining Irish Volunteers (with the ICA) were to occupy and hold the GPO which they did, hoisting the Irish flag from its roof. Many telephone lines were successfully cut and, across Dublin, a number of railway stations were occupied with bridges or lines blocked, effectively cutting the capital off from the rest of the country. Yet, the capture of the GPO was intended more as a symbolic military objective.

It was an impressive and famous landmark, opposite Nelson's Pillar, and its capture, very publicly, symbolised the Rising as well as being a place from where the rebels could mount a very public defense. The ICA divided into three contingents; seventy-five under James Connolly joined Pearse in the GPO, whilst a smaller section of twenty-five (under Sean Connolly) were sent against Dublin Castle and the largest group, under Michael Mallin and Countess Markievicz, was to hold St Stephen's Green. Here, they significantly failed to secure the overlooking buildings around the Green, which were soon occupied by the army, who brought troops up to the roof-tops. The Volunteers attempted to dig trenches which were then raked by sniper and machine-gun fire, compelling them to retreat the next day to the Royal College of Surgeons' building. The fate of other rebel units was similar; Sean Connolly was killed in street fighting around Dublin Castle and the objective never secured, whilst the remnants of the garrison in the GPO were eventually forced to attempt a breakout following artillery shelling of their position.[17]

The Battle of Dublin

During Easter week, numerous bitter and hotly contested battles erupted on street corners and hastily built barricades across the city. Against the rebels, there were around 5,000 British troops in and around Dublin; these were mostly untried soldiers on the Reserves, those on leave or veterans recuperating from wounds received at the front. The majority of these troops were Irishmen and there appears to be relatively little contemporary evidence to suggest that the Irish regiments on duty in Dublin had sympathy with the insurgents. Indeed, when the Rising occurred, the Reservists of the Irish regiments found themselves on the front line. On Easter Monday morning, the number of troops on piquet duty was approximately company strength (a hundred men) across the barracks at Portobello (3rd Royal Irish Rifles), Richmond (3rd Royal Irish Regiment), Royal (10th Royal Dublin Fusiliers) and Marlborough (6th Cavalry Reserve Regiment, including the 5th Royal Irish Lancers). The 3rd Royal Irish Rifles at Portobello barracks was mostly made up of recruits in training for active service with the regiment's 2nd Battalion, but they were also hurriedly thrown into the chaos of the rebellion. The news of the fighting reached them just after midday, when 2nd-Lieutenant C.R.W. McCammond, 19th Irish Rifles, galloped into barracks, having just been fired upon by rebels stationed in Davy's Public House overlooking Portobello Bridge. With just twenty-five men, led by 2nd-Lieutenant J. Kearns, they quickly garrisoned and held the strategically crucial Telephone Exchange, whilst a hurried detachment of seven men under Sergeant Morris held the Bank of Ireland.[18]

Sometime shortly after the capture of the GPO, the Dublin Metropolitan Police asked the military in Marlborough barracks to send as many troops as possible to Sackville Street on account of a 'disturbance' there. The depot squadron of the 5th Royal Irish Lancers, based in Marlborough barracks as part of the training cadre of the 6th Reserve Cavalry Regiment was dispatched, along with a party of 12th Prince of Wales' Royal Lancers. Ironically, the 6th Reserve Cavalry's commander, Colonel Kirk, along with its adjutant and RSM, were among those many officers away at the Easter Monday races at Fairyhouse. Accordingly, a small sortie of 5th Royal Irish and 12th Lancers trotted down Sackville Street to see exactly what was happening. As the small mounted party of 5th Royal Irish and 12th Lancers made their way towards the GPO, rifles from inside and on the roof opened fire, catching the lancers completely by surprise. Four Lancers were killed, whilst the others escaped. Following the Dublin Police's call for assistance, the 10th Dublin Fusiliers left Royal Barracks and quickly went into action. Among them was Arthur Allen, a twenty-five-year-old bank clerk with the Bank of Ireland in Tipperary; he had only enlisted in January but was soon promoted to corporal. He and the 10th 'Commercial Pals' assaulted the Mendicity Institution and, as they dashed along Usher's Quay, snipers opened up on them.[19]

In the late afternoon of 24 April, the 'Gorgeous Wrecks' were returning from their manoeuvres when they heard the news that Dublin had been occupied by rebels. Frank Browning then made a fateful decision. As a Volunteer Reserve force, it must be stressed that his men had no ammunition and many of their rifles were dummies for training purposes. This body of men were, to all intents and purposes, unarmed and militarily ineffective. It would not have been dishonourable for Browning to allow his men to 'dismiss' and return home, nor for them to do so. However, it appears that their general feeling was that, in their effective role as 'special constables' to the DMP, their duty was to support the civil authorities. Accordingly, Browning formed two columns, the larger of these under Major G.A. Harris (TCD OTC). He then marched his men back to their depot at Beggar's Bush. At the corner of Northumberland and Haddington Roads, the Volunteer Training Corps column under Browning walked into a rebel ambush. Fourteen men were hit, five of them fatally. One of these casualties was none other than Frank Browning, mortally wounded whilst marching at the column's head. Browning was rushed to Beggar's Bush barracks, where Major Harris' column had arrived to find it garrisoned by twenty-seven men of the Catering Corps. Browning later died of his wounds, whilst Harris took over effective defence of Beggar's Bush; his hundred or so men bluffed the rebels with only thirteen active rifles until they were relieved the next day.[20]

Although the army could draw upon its troops already posted in and around Dublin, 1,000 more were immediately dispatched from Belfast to be followed by more contingents from the Curragh, Athlone and England. This response demonstrated the government's belief that the Rising was not 'home-grown' but German influenced and, as such, a potential attempt to open up another war front. Early on 25 April, fresh battalions arrived by train in Dublin from the Curragh Camp; the 5th Leinsters (Royal Meath Militia, Extra Reserve) and 5th Dublins were all in the middle of training and still fairly raw recruits. An officer in the 5th Leinsters recollected that hardly any men in his company could accurately fire their rifles and that, during fire-fights, they were prone to 'rattle-up', a term used to describe ammunition being fired off in a panic. Although troops also fought in mixed units in the general disorder of the following days, the 5th Dublins took part in the battle for the City Hall and the Daily Express offices. Equally, the 4th Dublin Fusiliers arrived from Templemore and soon engaged rebel forces to secure the railway line from Cabra Bridge to Broadstone Station, in between the rear of the GPO and east of Grangegorman. Colonel R.G. Sharman Crawford's 18th Irish Rifles were also involved in the capture of Liberty Hall from a determined contingent of the Citizen Army.[21]

Irish Regimental Reaction to the Rising

The Dublin Rising at Easter 1916 is naturally thought to have had an important effect upon Irish troops serving during the Great War. Yet, it would appear that the practical reaction was extremely varied and ranged from muted frustration and dismay to downright hostility. Indeed, the reaction to the rebellion from Irish regimental officers and other ranks has been expertly examined elsewhere and it appears that it had little practical effect on regimental morale, loyalty or breaches of discipline. There were, however, serious breaches of military discipline in quelling the rebellion, notably when Captain John Bowen-Colthurst (3rd RIR) and Company Quartermaster Sergeant Robert Flood (5th RDF) both summarily executed innocent men. In Flood's case, he killed two Guinness nightwatchmen and two Canadian officers from the King Edward's Horse. Captain Bowen-Colthurst became infamous when he executed Francis Sheehy-Skeffington and two Unionist newspaper editors, being convinced they were all rebels.[22]

Yet, many shades of opinion existed within the ranks of the Irish regiments and it would be misleading to contend that a lack of outward support hinted at British allegiance. As John Lucy, 2nd Irish Rifles, recalled, there was little initial conflict of loyalty; he was a British soldier, an Irishman and a Catholic. The rebellion was an injury to his Irishness and it was only when the leaders were executed that the Rifles had a twinge of sympathy and Lucy felt a form of cold anger. As such, the military authorities were clearly worried that the rebellion in Dublin might become a crippling mutiny within its Irish regiments at the front. The War Office made attempts to clamp down on news of the rebellion and seems to have attempted to stop all news or letters from home filtering across to France or elsewhere. Even Regular battalions, such as the 1st Munsters, were briefly 'quarantined' due to concerns over their loyalty. The 1st Munsters seem to have been actually withdrawn from the front line and placed into the reserve during the period of the Rising. Equally, the Commanding Officer of the 1st Irish Guards was recalled to the War Office to advise London on the potential repercussions of the rebellion on his and other Irish front-line troops. Notable entries for the period in the war diary of 'D' squadron, North Irish Horse, merely comment on gifts that had been sent to them by Queen Alexandria at the start of the month and that the French battle of Verdun had been 'terminated' by 28 April. Ominously, however, even they noted that the 'Sinn Féin rebellion started in Dublin on 24 April 1916 is still continuing.'[23]

For Unionist troops, little sympathy for the rebels could be expected. The trench newspaper of the 14th (YCV) Royal Irish Rifles, *The Incinerator*, produced a predictably damning editorial regarding the 'insurgent dogs' in Dublin. Even amongst Nationalists—such as the 8th Munsters—their disdain at seeing German placards revelling in the rebellion could not be ignored. In trenches opposite the 16th (Irish) Division, a German placard went up declaring that Ireland was in 'heavy uproar' at home with the 'English' shooting down their families. According to Lieutenant-Colonel McCance, the Munsters apparently captured one such placard in a raid specifically designed to give the Germans a practical demonstration of their loyalty. Other sources, including their war diary, seem to suggest that the placards were discovered in an unoccupied trench during a routine patrol. Other units, such as the 7th Leinsters, were also deliberately taunted by these placards and they treated the baiting with equal contempt; intriguingly, they played *Rule Britannia* and

Irish tunes on a melodeon for an hour or so in response. They then raised their own placard requesting that, should the Germans wish to desert, could they please do so in ones and twos, as the Leinsters had mistaken the last lot for a patrol and fired upon them. This sign was apparently not greeted well. Either way, as one Irish Guards officer recalled, there was little political or ideological debate regarding the rebellion. Instead, the practicalities of staying alive had more relevance and the '... news from home [seemed] unreal and irrelevant'. It is probable that these sentiments were true for most within Irish regiments, and only contributed to widening the gap between serving soldier and civilian.[24]

The Rebellion Ends

On the afternoon of 28 April, a cavalry patrol of 5th Irish Lancers, which had been pinned down at North Wall whilst carrying ammunition, was relieved by a detachment of motor lorries supplied by Guinness and hurriedly armoured with boiler plates by the Inchicore Railway Company. Throughout the city, the fighting was unremitting and casualties severe. Sergeant Frederick Burke, 10th Dublin Fusiliers, was shot in the head by a sniper and taken to Dublin Castle Red Cross Hospital, where he died. Twenty-one-year-old Sergeant Burke had been born in Quetta on the North West frontier, where his father, John Burke from Lisburn, was serving with the Dublin Fusiliers. Frederick Burke initially joined the Corps of Army Schoolmasters but, by 1916, had transferred home to his father's regiment. Tragically, whilst Sergeant Burke was killed in Dublin, his father was a serving officer with the 2nd Dublins on the Western Front.[25]

By 28 April, James Connolly had been wounded twice and the rebellion throughout the city was on the verge of collapse. Heavy artillery was pounding the rebel positions and troops were tightening their stranglehold on the city. A determined rebel contingent had established itself in Moore Street but was contained by an increasing military presence. Nearby, a composite battalion of Inniskillings, which had been sent from Ulster as reinforcements, was with the 3rd Royal Irish and 5th Leinsters manning the cordon around the GPO and Sackville Street.[26] On Friday, these Irish and Ulster troops were preparing to assault the building when the ceasefire was declared. By evening, the rebellion had officially ended. When the surviving insurgents surrendered, they marched out of their positions, shouldering their weapons and, when they reached the statue of Parnell at the end of Sackville Street, they solemnly dumped them. As the evening and days wore on, the small pile of weapons and equipment grew as, bit by bit, rebel contingents from all over the city wearily capitulated. Perhaps fittingly, the British officer who took the surrender at the Royal College of Surgeons was Co. Kildare man, Captain Henry de Courcey-Wheeler of the Royal Dublin Fusiliers.

Post-Rebellion Recruitment and Politics

As Professor Keith Jeffery has noted, the casualties of Easter week (around 500 people killed, 2,500 people wounded) when compared to those of the 16th (Irish) Division's casualties for the same week at Hulluch (570 men killed, 1,400 wounded) were stark. After a week of bitter fighting, the rebellion failed utterly but its legacy, and the reaction to it, was to have a profound effect on Irish and Ulster society. At a time of war, General Maxwell's response was predictable but perhaps counter-productive. Pearse, Connolly and thirteen others were executed, including three of the four Dublin Battalion Commandants (Daly, McDonagh and Kent) and all the members of the IRB Military Council. Newspapers, such as the *Kerryman* and *Kilkenny People,* unfavourably compared the stance of Redmond's Volunteers still at home to those Irish Volunteers who had fought and died in Dublin. Although, they suggested the rebels were misguided, they were certainly '... not afraid to die. Some fellows should be ashamed to live'. The final act of the rebellion came on 3 August, following a scandal-ridden trial, when Sir Roger Casement was taken out into the cobbled courtyard at Pentonville Prison and hanged.[27]

In fact, the Battle of Dublin (or 'Ypres on Liffey' as it became known by Dublin wits) had become just as attritional as any Great War campaign and, as ever, it was mainly the civilian population that suffered. There was a strong element of truth in the words of Lieutenant Monk Gibbon (educated at St Columba's College, Rathfarnham, Co. Dublin) when he wrote that there were '...too many Dubliners fighting with Irish regiments...' for an insurrection to have popular support. Certainly, at the annual prize-giving ceremony at St Columba's College two months later, 289 names of those who had enlisted since 1914 were read out; of these, fifty-one had either been killed or wounded. In subsequent months, the *Soldiers' Rendezvous* still seemed a popular city venue and was apparently handling approximately 800 letters in just one week in July 1916.[28] For many of the opposing sides in Dublin 1916, this was to be their first taste of warfare for it must be remembered that the majority of British troops employed were from Reserve battalions and were, themselves, still in training. To most Irish regimental troops, the sight of

Dublin's ruined streets and the destruction that the Rising had caused seemed unforgivable. More so, it was perceived as a breaking of the 'unspoken truce' between Nationalist and Unionist for the duration of the war. However, a few months later, as the focus shifted back to the Western Front, many in Irish and Ulster regiments were determined to demonstrate their own collective form of 'blood sacrifice' in one of the most infamous offensives of the war: the long battle of the Somme.

CHAPTER SEVEN

'Human cornstalks falling before the reaper'[1]

The Long Battle of the Somme, 1916

By 1916, the strain of the war was showing among all of the fighting nations, but none seemed more besieged and embattled than the French. The immense bloodbaths of the previous two years had taken their toll. As a result of the Chantilly Conference, in December 1915, it was decided that the British should relieve the pressure by opening a new offensive in Picardy. By late February, many French fortresses had already fallen, placing intolerable pressure on the defence of Verdun. Here, Falkenhayn intended to fix the French firmly to the salient, forcing them to pour ever more men into its defence. Consequently, the military focus shifted to the famously quiet sector of the Somme. That quiet, however, was about to be literally torn apart. From 1 July to 18 November 1916, 616 British infantry battalions were engaged in one of the most horrendous battles of the war; of these, thirty-eight were Irish and twenty-one of these Irish battalions fought there in the first week.[2]

The 36th (Ulster) Division had arrived in France in early October 1915, under the active command of Major-General Sir Oliver Nugent while initial problems in recruiting for the 16th (Irish) had led to continual delays in its deployment. Due to these difficulties, the 16th Division did not 'officially' arrive in France until December 1915 and, even then, the Division had no artillery support and was lacking its 49th Brigade. Both of these eventually arrived in February 1916, by which time the Division had been sent to the Loos Salient.

106

On 7 February, the Ulster Division took over its first front line, with its HQ at Acheux and a daily routine typical of the British front line. An hour before dawn, 'Stand To' would be called, when every soldier was expected to man the trench line with bayonets fixed, in readiness for any possible German assault. When light came, sentry pickets were posted and the majority of men stood down; they spent their time cleaning rifles and maintaining equipment, sleeping, heating food or 'brewing up' in their 'billy-cans'. The following months were noted by the official 36th Divisional historian as being of 'little interest' but men were still being wounded or killed on a daily basis. Thomas Devlin, a forty-one-year-old former linen bleacher from Knocknagor, Tullylish (Co. Down), served with the 13th (1st County Down) Irish Rifles when he was killed on St Valentine's Day during 'routine' trench duty. Elsewhere on the Western Front, it is clear that some Irish cavalry officers believed that their routine guard, fatigue or escort duties were diminishing their role as soldiers. It was noted that, by mid-February 1916, whilst at Steenwerck, 'E' squadron of the North Irish Horse had been so diminished by working and bridge-guarding duties that it had 'ceased to exist' as an effective unit. Ever mindful of military practicality, Captain Ian Finlay lamented that if there was a '…sudden emergency…' his squadron could only muster twenty-six officers and men for the firing line. Indeed, on 27 February, in response to these daily lists of men drafted to working parties, Finlay's sense of humour shone through when he wrote simply: 'No fatigue!'[3]

Yet, for the soldiers on rotational front-line duty, their tours were not without incident; the night-time brought a cloak of darkness to cover all manner of military activities. In March, Rifleman R. Wilson, 2nd Irish Rifles, had just captured four Germans in a raid, when one turned and threw a grenade, allowing the others to run away. Wilson bayoneted one, shot two and captured the fourth—all single-handedly. Such acts may have been untypical (he was subsequently awarded the DCM) but, generally speaking, routine war work continued no matter the occasion. On 17 March, it was noted by 'A' Squadron, South Irish Horse, that it was officially St Patrick's Day holiday. Sixteen troopers returned to the squadron from the 'catapult battery' but thirty men ended up on 'police' duties. Likewise, between 26 and 27 March, three troops of 'C' Squadron, North Irish Horse, proceeded under Major Holt Waring to Dickebushe to escort German prisoners. The following day, the men were employed in clearing the recently captured communication trenches and the area still known as the 'Mound'. For a further three days the troops formed working parties for the grim task of burial details and salvaging what weapons and equipment they could. Back in France, the men of the 13th and 11th Irish Rifles were rotationally manning the front line at Mesnil and casualties were constant. On 8 April, Sergeant Alexander Devlin, 13th (1st Co. Down) Irish Rifles died of wounds received; he was twenty-six and had been a 'Bootling Engine Man' in the linen mills of the Bann. As an Ulster Volunteer, he had enlisted in 'D' Coy of the 13th Rifles with his cousin, Thomas who had been killed only two months before.[4]

The 16th (Irish) Division at Loos and Hulluch, Easter 1916

At Loos, Irish casualties from shellfire, sniping and raiding continued to mount up. At the end of March, the 6th Royal Irish received a fresh draft of thirty men from their 4th (Kilkenny Militia) Battalion but, within days, their billets were shelled and eight casualties sustained. At around the same time, Major-General Hickie had gathered prior intelligence that an enemy gas attack was planned and precautions were duly taken. Despite this, a few weeks later, the 16th Division suffered terrible casualties, some 570 men killed and 1,400 wounded, from gas attacks at Hulluch from 27–29 April. On 27 April, that attack had been two-fold. At 5 am, intense shelling began, followed by the dropping of lachrymatory shells ('tear-gas') on the Division's reserve and support lines. Ten minutes later, smothering screens of chlorine gas rolled towards the Irish front line. The brunt of the first gas attack fell upon the men of the 8th Dublins, 8th Irish Fusiliers and the 'Fighting Seventh' Inniskillings at 5.40 am; it was so dense that objects beyond two or three yards were completely masked. As men scrambled to pull on their canvas 'sack' gas helmets, Lieutenant H.W. Ruddock saw that Private Cassidy of 'A' Coy, in reserve lines, had been caught by the attack as he tried to change his socks. He was ordered to put his gas helmet on and, in the panic, Cassidy put it on the wrong way round; he then spent frantic minutes bumping about the trench in his bare feet until he finally blurted out: 'I wish I could find the bloody windows!'[5]

All along the 16th Irish's front, the Bavarian troops stormed the trenches but were doggedly beaten back by rifles and machine-guns. As the war diary of the 6th Royal Irish recorded, the Germans attacked the division's entire line, '...under cover of gas and smoke...' but were unable to break through completely. It was only in the subsequent, second attack, with the front line smashed by shellfire and gas, that the Germans did enter the lines and capture prisoners in some sections. Their gain was only brief; one source stated that they were lodged for only a '…matter of minutes…' before the Inniskillings dashed up from the support and drove the enemy out at bayonet-point. However, Lieutenant-Colonel Young's 7th Inniskillings also observed that the German gas had blown back against them slightly, forcing their withdrawal. Yet, the Irish division's own battered front line was filled with the stench of chlorine fumes, debris, craters and dead, whilst wounded men slowly made their way back to the aid posts. The 'Fighting Seventh' had lost 10 officers and 253 other ranks in the three days. Among the dead, from the first attack on the 27 April, was Private Tom Cassidy, from Irvinestown, Co. Fermanagh.[6]

Over the next few hours and days, shells repeatedly landed on the division's lines, obliterating parapets and duckboards, smashing the Irish trenches to smithereens. The 6th Royal Irish Regiment noted that in the last German assault on 29 April, the gas attack was again blown back into the enemy trenches but, this time, they had the full effect. This seems to have halted any further German attempts. Indeed, although the majority of Irish casualties were as a result of shellfire, the gas had a horror all of its own. Lieutenant Wallace Lyon, 7th Leinsters, was on burial detail after the attack and made the grim discovery of dead men, lying grotesquely in varying horrific poses with some simply '…holding hands like children in the dark'. It was an unbearable sight. On the same day, the 6th Royal Irish relieved the 9th Royal Dublin Fusiliers and began to set to work repairing communication trenches which had been damaged over the course of the battle of the previous days. Yet, the shelling continued and a dugout in the 6th Connaught's line was hit directly by a German shell; Privates J. Gaffney and P. Reilly worked desperately for three quarters of an hour, under fire and '… in view of the enemy…' digging out three wounded comrades.[7]

Background to the Somme Campaign

Meanwhile, the British plan for the Somme was taking shape. It was to be the New Armies' first major engagement (as it was Sir Douglas Haig's as Commander in Chief) and it was imperative that it should be a noted victory. To 'soften up' the German defences, Haig intended a firestorm artillery bombardment to cut the wire to ribbons, smash any strong-points and, presumably, kill large numbers of the enemy in the process. The unremitting barrage was to last for three days and nights and the first phase was to be implemented strictly to timetable for the success of the second. 'Zero Hour' was originally scheduled for 4.30 am, 25 June, but Sir Henry Rawlinson, commander of Fourth Army (which was to lead the assault) delayed it until 29 June to allow for a more comprehensive artillery barrage of the German lines. Then, 125,000 British soldiers were to storm the German front-line trenches, capture thirteen fortified villages and redoubts and, aided by the Reserves, press on and take the second line. Having broken through, the cavalry in reserve would consolidate the gains by riding hell for leather to exploit the gap and rout the fleeing Germans. An atmosphere of optimism seemed to permeate British High Command, to such an extent that it appears largely to have filtered down the ranks. This optimism, perhaps even delusion, had infected them all. As the war diary of the 14th (YCV) Irish Rifles stated, '*Everyone* [author's emphasis] is looking forward to the Great Day.'[8]

However, everything that High Command depended upon for success was to dissolve around them, either due to mismanagement, ill-judgement or plain bad luck. The reasons seem inconsequential when compared to the effects; the advance which was to take a day took nearly five months to complete.

Preparations, April, May and June

By early summer 1916, the Ulster Division was in a pivotal position with its objectives straddling north and south of the river Ancre. Their northern target was Hamel Railway line and Beacourt Station whilst, to the south, 108 and 107 Brigades were ordered against the 'Schwaben Redoubt'. It was variously known as 'Hell Corner' and the 'Devil's Dwelling', being a parallelogram of trenches with sixteen rows of barbed wire and concealed machine-gun nests. The Division's objectives were also to secure St Pierre Divion and the final German fifth line just outside Grandcourt. To focus the troops' determination, the objectives had local names such as 'Dungannon' or 'Portadown', which was a practice repeated throughout the British line. Worryingly, all of these German trenches overlooked the British lines and, even if the 36th Division reached their objectives, if the neighbouring divisions on either side failed to achieve theirs, the 36th would be left stranded and surrounded.

As 'Zero Day' approached, British raids intensified in an attempt to cause as much confusion in the German trenches as possible and capture prisoners for intelligence purposes. One such raid by the 12th (Central Antrim) Irish Rifles, on the night of 5 June, was against a trench parallel to a railway line, on the extreme left of 108 Brigade's flank. The raiding party discovered that the Germans had been mining the area, with two tunnels leading directly to the Ulster Division's lines. These were duly exploded. Yet, the indication that the Germans were still very much active in the area and had made serious preparations to go 'underground' during the bombardment appears to have been lost on High Command.

On 24 June, the unremitting artillery bombardment began. Using the heaviest shells they had at their disposal (15" and 18"), the divisional artillery pounded the German lines night and day in an effort to silence the defenders. It was certainly the most vicious artillery attack the British had ever launched and it was genuinely believed that nothing could survive the barrage, which made the reality even more difficult to grasp; about 50 per cent of the shells were found to be 'duds'. Additionally, the shells used were not 'High Explosive' (HE) but shrapnel. The decision to use shrapnel is almost unfathomable, given that the French Army had successfully used HE shells to tear apart enemy entanglements. Indeed, since shrapnel bursts several feet above the ground, it was useless for the job of cutting wire. Subsequently, areas of wire were only sufficiently cut in parts of the line where HE had been used (basically the French sector) or where the skill of the gunners had been close to perfection. Instead, the only available routes through the wire were via precarious paths. German machine-guns were patiently trained on them.

Furthermore, preparatory work undertaken in British trenches had to be done furtively and surreptitiously, to avoid enemy observation. Everything had to be done under German artillery fire and, for those in trenches in Thiepval Wood around the Ancre, there was an additional risk of splinters from the shattered trees. On 'Y' Day (28 June), No. 11 Platoon, 13th (1st Co. Down) Irish Rifles was on the way up the line to relieve the 11th (South Antrim) Rifles in Thiepval Wood when a shell landed amongst them. The effect was catastrophic. Fourteen men were killed outright and nearly sixty men were wounded, including the Second-in-Command, Major Maxwell and his adjutant, Captain Wright. Men from both the 13th and 11th Irish Rifles rushed to the stricken men's aid but, in the darkness, confusion reigned. One Rifleman, Tommy Russell, of the South Antrim Volunteers, recalled that when morning dawned on the scene of the explosion it was a sight filled with horror, with blood and entrails spattered over the statues and walls of the already ruined chapel of Martinsart.[9]

By 'Y.2' Day (30 June), final preparations were well underway. To maintain unit cohesion, New Army battalion commanders were under explicit orders not to accompany their men the next morning. However, a good many disobeyed this order. Commanding Officers such as Crozier and Bernard (9th West Belfast and 10th South Belfast Irish Rifles respectively) decided to advance with their battalions the night before. Their decision was not merely an empty gesture of solidarity. If the flanking troops on either side of the Ulster Division were unable to capture or hold their objectives, then it was vital to have a senior officer on the spot to direct the men as tactically required. Whilst battalion commanders such as Bernard and Crozier were not entirely uncommon, the pact that both men made that evening is rather surprising. Both agreed that if they saw Thiepval village still in German hands by the time they marched through Thiepval Wood, then they would meet up in No Man's Land and '…alter our plans'. Indeed, Lieutenant-Colonel Bernard of the 10th Rifles was concerned that the attack here by the 32nd Division would fail and, if it did, he told Crozier bluntly that it would leave the Ulster Division defenceless. Throughout the night the barrage and counter-barrage continued, with the ferocity of the explosions increasing as 'Zero Day' approached. The war diarist of the YCV complained that during the shelling he had '…great trouble keeping the candle alight' in their dugout. However, somewhat in keeping with their more refined image, he also, rather disarmingly, recorded that they could hear a water hen calling to its mate and the singing of a nightingale.[10]

'Zero Day'

In the early hours of 1 July, men up and down the British line were busy with the small rituals of life, anything to distract or calm them for the ordeal to come. It may have been the need to write letters home or, more ominously, make their wills. Handily, a 'pro forma' for this was printed in the back of every man's pay-book. Others took comfort in religion and yet others, particularly in the Ulster Division, took solace from their Orange traditions. In the moments before 'Zero Hour', the Worshipful Master of LOL 862, John Crumlin, folded up the lodge's warrant and put it in his tunic pocket with his Orange sash placed safely in his back-pack. For some, it was just the simple—but essentially cultured—act of shaving that seemed to steady the nerves; as Lieutenant-Colonel Crozier recalled, sometime around 5–6 am, the officers of the 9th Irish Rifles were all busy shaving, so his batman, Corporal David Starret, brought him some water so he could do likewise.[11]

When the attack began on the fifteen-mile front, High Command was in high expectation of a breakthrough, although most subordinate soldiers suspected it would be at a high cost; Major-General Nugent, writing shortly before the offensive to his old comrade, Lieutenant-General Sir George

Richardson, merely said that it made him '…very sad to think what the price may be'.[12] However, even senior officers like Nugent could not have foreseen the appalling fact that, by the evening of the first day, some 60,000 British soldiers were dead, wounded or missing. The day of the assault was famously bright and sunny, with a clear and cloudless blue sky. They were almost idyllic conditions for a warm summer's day in Picardy, were it not for the business of killing and carnage that utterly overshadowed them. At 7.30 am, the men of the Irish regiments rose from their assembly trenches across the Somme front and advanced into No Man's Land. For those involved in the initial assault, Irish regimental objectives seemed straightforward: the 1st Irish Rifles and Tyneside Irish had Ovillers, La Boiselle and Contalmaison; the 36th Ulster Division was to take Beaucourt, Schwaben Redoubt and secure all the way to Grandcourt; the 2nd Royal Irish was sent against Fricourt and Memetz; whilst the 1st Inniskillings, 1st Dublin Fusiliers, 1st Irish Fusiliers and 2nd Royal Dublin Fusiliers had to secure Beaumont Hamel and the Hawthorne Redoubt.

Beaumont Hamel, Hawthorn Ridge and Ovillers-Pozières

At the extreme north of the Somme sector, as part of the 4th Division, both the 2nd Royal Dublin Fusiliers and 1st Irish Fusiliers were in action at Redan Ridge and the 'Quadrilateral' near Beaumont Hamel. As the 2nd Dublins left their trenches, in diamond formation, they discovered that the enemy's wire had not been cut properly and they were badly cut up. The order to advance in 'extended sections' was given by company officers whilst still in No Man's Land, to avoid machine-gun casualties. Even with this precaution, only a handful of Dublins made it to the German front line, one of these being Major John Burke, from Tullynacross, Lisburn, who rallied his men despite being wounded and was subsequently awarded the Military Cross.[13] At 9.10 am, the 1st Irish Fusiliers were sent to relieve the 2nd Seaforth Highlanders at the 'Quadrilateral' but, again, intense fire stalled their advance. Despite mounting casualties, one company managed to reach it by nightfall, only to be ordered to retire the next morning.

During 29th Division's assault on Beaumont Hamel, the 1st Dublin Fusiliers were behind the 2nd Royal Fusiliers in the advance towards Hawthorn Ridge; the mine here had been exploded prematurely at 7.20 am, giving the Germans time to gather their defences. The front waves of the 1st Dublins struggled to get beyond their own wire, as enemy machine-gunners targeted the channels through the broken entanglements and cut down swathes of men. By midday, when their advance was halted, almost 300 men were casualties. Likewise, the 1st Inniskillings launched themselves against Beaumont Hamel and the Hawthorn Redoubt—a German strongpoint bristling with defences, entanglements and sited on a dangerous slope which provided absolutely no cover. As the Inniskillings attacked, they were subject to heavy enfilading fire on both flanks and murderous fire to their front. When they got stuck at the uncut German wire, they were effectively wiped out, with 549 officers and other ranks becoming casualties.

To the south of this attack, at 7.30 am, the 1st Irish Rifles were thrown into the savage and ultimately doomed attack on the Ovillers-Pozières Line. Many Riflemen were swept away as they rose from their trenches and many more were killed or wounded as they negotiated their way to their own wire. The remaining few that managed to get across No Man's Land slammed into the first and second German lines and secured them to make their way onwards to their last objective—an oblique thrust against the Pozières line. However, the supporting battalions from the 2nd Royal Berkshire and 2nd Lincolnshire Regiments were brutally cut down only minutes after leaving their trenches. Consequently, the Irish Rifles, despite making progress, had to withdraw in order to balance the positions of troops on their flanks. In the centre, 'C' Coy, commanded by 2nd-Lieutenant H.M. Glastonbury, was believed to have ensconced itself in the German first line, although this was unconfirmed at the time '… owing to the severe machine-gun fire'. Only 'D' Coy, led by 2nd-Lieutenant S.D.I. Smith, was known to have established itself in the German second line but, alone and unsupported, it was obliged to retreat. It was only 10 am but the assault on Ovillers had caused the 1st Rifles some 446 casualties. Among the dead, wounded and dying was their acting Colonel, Charles Macnamara; despite being severely wounded in the leg and having lost an eye, he refused to leave his men until he passed over command to Major Fitzmaurice. Colonel Macnamara died a fortnight later.[14]

The 36th (Ulster) Division and the 'Breakthrough' to Grandcourt

The first casualties for the Ulster Division came even before the men had climbed their assault ladders and left their parapets. As the minutes ticked away, their trenches were undergoing ferocious German shelling in response to the heavy pounding of the enemy front-lines by the British. An hour before the attack, the barrage was at a crescendo, with Captain Stewart-Moore of the 12th Irish Rifles remembering that the ever-present buzzing noise was like a multitude of hornets. At the crowded assembly trenches in Aveluy Wood, bombers of the 14th Irish Rifles were preparing boxes of grenades when a box slipped into the trench and two grenade pins fell out. In an instant, Private William McFadzean threw himself on the grenades to shield his comrades from the explosion. As a result, only two other soldiers were wounded and, for this truly selfless act, he was posthumously awarded the Victoria Cross. As his remains were borne away on a stretcher down along the line, despite the whirlwind of shells all around them, the shocked men instinctively removed their helmets in respect. They then resumed their positions and waited grimly for the whistles and bugles to blow.[15]

At 7.30 am, the leading battalions of 109 Brigade, the 9th and 10th Royal Inniskilling Fusiliers (the 'Tyrones' and 'Derrys') slowly made their way forward at a steady walking pace. Lieutenant-Colonel Ambrose Ricardo of the Tyrones had wished his men 'good luck' by shouting through his megaphone as they strode towards the German lines. The 'Derrys' were subject to very heavy fire and lost most of 'A' Company as they emerged from the British front line but, within an hour, they had established themselves at the Schwaben Redoubt ('B') and Mouquet Switch ('C'). The 'Skins' fought off numerous counter-attacks and Captain Eric Bell, (9th Inniskillings, but attached to 109 Brigade Trench Mortar Battery) posthumously won the VC for standing on the parapet, in full view of the enemy, picking the Germans off with his rifle and grenades. Another of the 'Tyrones' killed was the former Loyal Dublin Volunteer, William John Long; he was just one of the battalion's 477 casualties. As the 36th Division advanced, one Ulsterman was reputed to have shouted out defiantly above the rattling machine-guns, 'Let her rip, ye devils!' to which his company officer responded that the enemy '...let her rip all right'. Following on behind, the successive waves of the 11th (Donegal and Fermanagh) Inniskillings and 14th (YCV) Irish Rifles were cut down as they left the protection of Thiepval Wood. For the survivors, their experience of the Somme was mostly made up of the struggle in and around the Schwaben Redoubt.[16]

The troops of 108th Brigade advanced from No Man's Land at 7.30 am but had mixed success. The 11th (South Antrim) Irish Rifles arrived at the German front line five minutes later and, by 7.50 am, they were crossing the second line trenches; however, they were caught by their own artillery barrage whilst securing the third line trenches at 8.46 am. They consolidated these until a determined German counter-attack at 3.30 pm forced many Ulstermen to withdraw to the second line, until this line too was counter-attacked from Thiepval just after 8 pm. Although they withdrew to the German first line again, by 11.45 pm, the defenders evacuated their captured trench sections and pulled back across No Man's Land. The attack left over 130 South Antrim men dead and almost twice that number wounded; among the latter were two Lisburn brothers, James and Thomas Abbott. Tragically, their other brother, William, had transferred from the 11th Rifles to 108 Machine-Gun Coy and had been killed in the same attack. One of those captured was Captain Charles Craig, MP, who had been wounded in the leg during the battle and was unceremoniously transported into German captivity in an old wheelbarrow. Meanwhile, the 12th (Central Antrim) Rifles had been split to assist the 9th 'Faughs' in their assault on Beaucourt Station and both units were hit by devastatingly accurate machine-gun fire from St Pierre Divion as they crossed No Man's Land. Just one of the 500 casualties sustained by the 12th Rifles was former 'dealer' James Davidson from Pound Street, Larne, killed in action aged twenty-three.[17]

Similarly, the 9th 'Faughs' had actually started their advance early, at 7.28 am, but were virtually massacred before they even got to the enemy's wire. As they tried to charge over 300 yards of open ground, Lance Corporal Burnett heard many of the Fusiliers shouting 'No Surrender!' and '… other Orange phrases…' as the machine guns cut them down; then he too was hit, just 50 yards from the German first trench. With a badly shattered leg, Lance Corporal Burnett crawled into a shell-hole and could see 'Blacker's Boys' reach the second line; he shouted himself hoarse cheering them on before he saw the German counter-attack overwhelm them. As the 9th 'Faughs' stated, they simply could not progress '…without support…' as the attack stalled and was soon halted altogether. The battalion was withdrawn to the start line but, by this time, it had already suffered horrendous casualties at just under 700 men. Also caught by this deadly hail of bullets was the 13th (1st County Down) Irish Rifles, which had actually moved off a little before 'Zero Hour' and advanced upon the Schwaben Redoubt. These men fought for most of the day but they had infrequent information on the rest of the attack and little direction, due to their early loss of officers. One of these was thirty-seven-year-old Captain William Haughton Smyth, from Milltown House outside Banbridge—an Oxford and Cambridge graduate and keen golfer (who had helped set up Banbridge Golf Club). He was killed leading his men of 'C' Company. The gunfire from St Pierre Divion also ripped the men of the

15th (North Belfast) Irish Rifles apart as they struggled to their objectives, eventually reaching the German second and third lines but, without support, they subsequently had to fall back. In these circumstances, the pioneers of the 16th Rifles were sent to repair the St Divion road at Hamel urgently, but found it in enemy hands. They were ordered to dig a trench to the German first line—under heavy fire—and eventually had to abandon the work. These men of the 2nd County Down, who delighted in their battalion anthem of the South Down Militia, simply noted how the entire Thiepval Wood was shelled '...beyond description'.[18]

It was at 7.45–8.00 am when 107th Brigade made their way across No Man's Land. By this time, the Germans were well aware of the advance and the 107 Brigade sustained hundreds of casualties from machine guns at Thiepval village. The South Belfast Volunteers had already lost their commanding officer, Lieutenant-Colonel Bernard, who was killed by a shell as the 10th Rifles formed up in Aveluy Wood but, by 8 am, many of their officers and senior NCOs had also been hit. Lieutenant-Colonel Crozier, true to his pact with Bernard to reassess their battalions' plans in No Man's Land, was watching their leading companies through his binoculars as bullets whined all around him. According to David Starret, he then '...went off at the deep end...' as he saw men mown down before his eyes. For a man of his somewhat stout appearance, it was noted that he 'doubled' across to the men in between shell and gunfire bursts in a very agile manner. He roared out to them that the 10th Rifles had been decimated and encouraged the bugler to sound the advance. However, the bugler had been wounded, hit through the lungs and, although he tried valiantly to signal to the men, he died in the effort.

Nevertheless, the men of the 8th, 9th and 10th Irish Rifles somehow managed to lodge themselves in the Schwaben Redoubt, where intense and bitter hand-to-hand fighting ensued. Again, Crozier conspicuously encouraged his men forward to the objectives beyond the Redoubt, dodging explosions, stumbling into craters and with his uniform '...torn with bullets'. After the Redoubt's capture, remnants of the battalions reorganised themselves to take and hold the 'Crucifix'. According to Private Edward Taylor, Major George Gaffikin, 9th Rifles, had previously taken out an orange handkerchief and waved it above his head, exhorting them forward with the words that it was glorious First of July. At this, Taylor said that some of the 'Shankill Boys' cried 'No Surrender!' as they surged forward. Although this event is subject to considerable debate, at the 'Crucifix', Gaffikin repeatedly rallied the men there until he too was killed, command falling to Major Warren Peacocke of the 9th

Inniskillings. It is perhaps less well-known that George 'Skipper' Gaffikin had been a notable cricketer before the war, playing for Holywood, Co. Down.[19]

As darkness fell, small parties still controlled the Schwaben and German front line but these too were gradually ordered to retire to the British front line. Yet, they had performed the most successful and sustained attack of the day, captured over 600 prisoners and, of the nine Victoria Crosses awarded that day, four were awarded to the division. During the advance of the 12th Irish Rifles, Lieutenant Sir Harry Macnaghten, Baronet, was killed and his batman, Private Robert Quigg from Bushmills, went out repeatedly under heavy fire to find him. Private Quigg made no less than seven attempts on the 2 July and, on every trip, he brought back another wounded man. Although Lieutenant Macnaghten's body was never recovered, Robert Quigg was later awarded the VC for his bravery. Similarly, Lieutenant Geoffrey St George Shillington Cather, the adjutant of the 9th Irish Fusiliers, spent the night of 1 July trying to rescue wounded men from No Man's Land, until he too was killed on the morning of 2 July; he was posthumously awarded the Victoria Cross.[20]

The casualty list for the Ulster Division's first attack stood at some 5,500 men for 1-2 July; almost a third of the division's initial total strength. Whilst there remained a divisional 'battle surplus' of Reserves, these were pitifully small. Indeed, the remains of the Ulster Battalions were pulled away from the front line late on 2 July and sent to Martinsart to rest. On 11 July, the Division was moved to Flanders, where yet another ordeal awaited them. The next day, although celebrations for the Twelfth of July had been cancelled back home, the Ulster Division still defiantly wore marigolds in their caps as bands played *King William's March* in '… honour of the day'. However, the struggle on the Somme was to continue.[21]

Aftermath and Midsummer Battles

The 2nd Royal Irish Regiment, as part of the brigade Reserve, was moved against Mametz in the last desperate stages of 1 July, although their role was to reinforce the 22nd Manchester Regiment. From 4–6 July, the 2nd Royal Irish made continuous attacks against enemy trenches to the front of Mametz Wood and even their casualty rate, for a unit not involved in opening assault on the First Day, stood at 227 killed and wounded for the first twelve days of July. The chaotic nature of the Somme is clearly illustrated even in its aftermath. In the evenings following the 1 July, troops of the 2nd North Irish Horse, among many, were given the disagreeable job of clearing the battlefield. To carry out these duties, the troops of the 2nd North Irish Horse were divided between Toutencourt, Acheux, Forceville and Senlis. Their orders here were tragically simple—to recover what weapons and equipment they could and to bury the dead if possible. On the morning of 5 July, two troops of 'A' Squadron (Inniskilling Dragoons) had been on salvage duty in Aveluy Wood and had brought in rifles and scattered paraphernalia from the area. At around 1 pm, they had just finished eating their dinner when Lieutenant Seymour and his men were ordered to return to regimental HQ. They were in the process of saddling up when a furious bombardment erupted all around Aveluy Wood, with high explosives, shrapnel and concentrated bursts of machine-gun fire peppering their position. As the trees shattered, sending razor-sharp splinters flying throughout the British position, Lieutenant Seymour quickly ordered the cavalrymen to dash for whatever cover they could find in the nearby dugouts and trenches. However, the horses had to be left in their lines during the attack, which lasted for three-quarters of an hour, leaving one horse killed and four others wounded. Eventually, there was a lull in the shelling and the men quickly mounted up and tried to lead their horses through the wood back to the main road. There the bombardment began again and, if anything, it was more intense than before. The horses, having endured the terrifying shelling in Aveluy Wood were becoming '...almost unmanageable...' and Lieutenant Seymour believed the best course of action was to get them away as quickly as possible. Yet, not all of his men had left the wood, so he posted 2nd-Lieutenant Mathews and Sergeant McEvoy to direct any stragglers. In the meantime, he, Sergeant Quinn and the majority of the troop continued down the road until they came to a quieter lane which seemed a perfect place to steady the horses. Unfortunately, this lane became the new target for the German artillery and, as Sergeant Quinn was wounded by shellfire, the horses stampeded in every direction (even back to the wood), utterly out of control. By the time the horses had been recovered frantically by Lieutenant Seymour and his party, they had all sustained a number of casualties; no less than sixteen horses were killed or wounded with two missing. In addition to Sergeant Quinn's injury, 2nd-Lieutenant Mathews had been badly wounded by high explosive fragments which tore into his knee, three troopers were hospitalised and six men slightly wounded.[22]

On 14 July, the 2nd Royal Irish again attacked Bazentin-le-Petit, successfully holding the village and capturing over 200 German prisoners, but at a further cost of 326 casualties. Around the same time, the 2nd Irish Rifles were fighting at Ovillers, from 7–16 July, where they captured and maintained

119

a number of vital positions, each at the cost of over a hundred men a time. This included Bazentin Ridge which signaled an end to a very prolonged and exhausting period of fighting for the Riflemen, many of whom collapsed in the captured trench almost dead with weariness. The 2nd Munsters took over positions before Contalmaison in mid-July but they discovered the village clouded in thick poison gas. Despite this, during their night assault on 16 July, they swept all before them quickly over-running their initial objectives of the German first and second lines before swarming into the enemy's third line. The fighting here was desperate and hand-to-hand. From this point, the 2nd Munsters were almost able to attack Pozières which, for the first time in the campaign, seemed extremely vulnerable. However, the Munsters were halted beyond Contalmaison and, by the time they were relieved, they had suffered over 200 casualties, mostly from German gas shells.[23]

Eighteen days after the battle, troopers of the 2nd North Irish Horse were still clearing the battlefield, a duty which grew steadily worse as the days passed. Tellingly, on 20 July, the regiment was allowed to issue rum to its burial parties. The previous day, they had reburied a further sixty-three British and thirty-six Germans from around the Albert area but it was noted how much ammunition was still present. In fact, it was recorded, rather pointedly, that there were 'numerous' bombs lying about, as if they were intended for use in the front line but had never reached their destination. This seems to have been confirmed a few days later when two dug-outs were discovered full of bombs and munitions which had apparently been overlooked since 1 July. The last North Irish Horse burial party appeared to have been active on the evening of 21 July, when three British officers and forty-eight other ranks were recovered; two Germans were also reburied. That such great numbers of men were still being discovered some twenty days after the Somme assault bears sickening testimony to the number of casualties sustained.

Yet, even in the midst of war, the technical competencies of the parade ground were valued—at least to Company Commanders, Squadron Leaders or Regimental Sergeant-Majors. At Chateau de la Haye, a large parade ground had been established and the 2nd North Irish Horse decided to use it at the first opportunity. Although individual squadron parade grounds were already in use, this larger area enabled the precise drill of 'Cavalry Training 1914' to be carried out, or so it was assumed. On the first morning, 'A' Squadron (Inniskilling Dragoons) performed their drill as laid out in the drill book. However, as the regimental adjutant noted somewhat caustically,

'B' Squadron (North Irish Horse) performed theirs '…under some different arrangement'. There followed a period of intense drilling by both the adjutant and Regimental Sergeant-Major who each worked with one troop and attempted to show them how it was supposed to be done. After this, an instruction to all squadron and section leaders was issued ordering them to learn the proper cavalry drill thoroughly since regular inspections would be carried out at future parades. However, as if to demonstrate the changing roles of cavalrymen, shortly after this, on 4 August 1916, Major Holt Waring was transferred from the North Irish Horse to the 13th (1st Co. Down) Royal Irish Rifles.[24]

Michaelmas on the Somme

By August, the British had advanced beyond Pozières, through the line of Martinpuich and Bazentin-le-Petit, made gains at High Wood and pressurised west of Guillemont. Whilst the 1/8th King's Regiment ('Liverpool Irish') saw considerable action throughout France and Flanders, one of their heaviest engagements here came on 8 August. Whilst many of his fellow Belfast men had been flung into the First Day of the Somme with the 36th (Ulster) Division, ironically Sergeant John Cameron, from the Shankill, was to die at Guillemont a few weeks later with the Liverpool Irish. Indeed, similar attacks on the shattered fortress-village of Guillemont were to continue for another month. The 2nd Leinster Regiment had arrived in 'Happy Valley' from Ypres at the end of July and worked on communication trenches between Bernafay Wood and Trônes. Their new objective was yet another infamous name on the Somme front—a simple shattered village which, as two Leinster officers observed, was the famed '… Guillemont, seven times attacked'. On 18 August, it was the turn of the 2nd Leinsters to try and wrestle the village from German defenders, the men of the 73rd Hanoverian Fusiliers who, ironically, bore the battle-honour 'Gibraltar' on their shoulder titles. Initially, the Leinsters were to support the leading waves but, held in the British front line, they were slaughtered before they even went over the top, cut down by machine-guns located in a sunken road. By the start of September, they had lost 584 casualties.[25]

By this time, the 16th (Irish) Division had also been moved to the Somme and it was to be their first major offensive action. Although this was supposed to be 'secret', every French civilian they met seemed to know their destination. To many in the Division, it seemed an inevitable posting. When the 7th

Inniskillings made the tiring march from the Loos Salient to Lapugnoy, it was bitterly noted that the only thing they left behind was the small cemetery at Philosophe, where so many of them were buried after the Hulluch gas attacks. Yet, the 16th Division had come a long way since then. At Loos, it had spent three months in near constant raiding and taken over 2,600 casualties in the process. It had consequently built up a considerable reputation for 'offensive spirit', especially in Brigadier-General George Pereira's 47th Brigade. Here, the 8th Munsters, 7th Leinsters, 6th Connaught Rangers and 6th Royal Irish, had all become known as 'hard-fighting' units, who carried out their orders to control No Man's Land through continuous and aggressive raiding. By the time of its move, the 6th Connaught Rangers had already suffered 417 casualties, around half of its initial strength. Now, as it moved to the Somme, its task was to be part of Haig's co-ordinated operation with the French to capture the stubbornly-held fortified villages of Guillemont and Ginchy.[26]

Guillemont, 3 September 1916

The assault on Guillemont was hampered from the very beginning by the fact that a heavy thunderstorm on 29 August prompted the French to ask the British to delay the combined attack until 3 September. Furthermore, the Irish Division's battalions had been ordered into the line bit by bit and its brigades were scattered amongst the 5th and 20th Divisions to consolidate the sector. On top of this, 47th Brigade was only given orders to attack Guillemont the afternoon before the assault. In the hours before the attack, the men received absolution and took Communion. A little later the pipers of the Leinsters, Munsters and Connaughts played traditional battle tunes, finishing with *The Wearin' o' the Green* and *A Nation Once Again*.[27] As 'Zero Hour' was scheduled for midday, there was considerable shelling of the sodden British front lines beforehand, churning up the already repellent battlefield and its ghastly contents even further. Lieutenant-Colonel Lenox-Conyngham's officers were gathered for a final briefing in the fetidly cramped 6th Connaughts' HQ dugout when a shell exploded violently at the doorway, spraying a fine '…jet of wet dust…' over all inside. Twenty-four-year-old Private Joseph Crowley, from Belfast, had been standing by the entrance and had caught the full blast; his upper torso and head were atomised.[28] By the time the 6th Connaughts attacked, just before midday, they had already suffered nearly 200 casualties from shellfire, including several of their own heavy mortar shells which had 'fallen short'.

By most accounts, the charge of the 47th Brigade was daring, gallant and extremely brutal. With regimental pipers accompanying them into battle, the 6th Connaughts, 6th Royal Irish and 7th Leinsters smashed their way across the broken landscape and, when the Germans appeared from their shattered trenches, they were engaged with the bayonet, rifle butt or anything that came to hand. In the advance, Lieutenant-Colonel 'Jack' Lenox-Conyngham of the 6th Connaughts was killed. The death of this ex-Ulster Volunteer veteran so enraged his mostly National Volunteer Rangers that they allegedly gave no quarter when their unremitting charge finally hit the German lines. The 7th Leinsters' attack on the first German line was fierce and often hand-to-hand before they swept onwards to capture the second line. It was here that Lieutenant John Vincent Holland (from Athy, Co. Kildare) of the 7th Leinsters and Private Thomas Hughes (from Coravoo outside Castleblaney, Co. Monaghan) of the 6th Connaughts each won the Victoria Cross. Lieutenant Holland led his party of bombers through the initial barrage, clearing German trenches with grenades and capturing some fifty prisoners. Meanwhile, Private Hughes had already been wounded four times in the attack before he charged a German machine-gun, killed its gunners, captured their gun and took four prisoners back to the British lines.[29]

Indeed, crossing the cratered battlefield under fire was immensely difficult and, according to one 8th Munster Fusilier, the ground was simply a net with '...all holes tied together'. Furthermore, everywhere was littered with dead and decaying soldiers from this and previous assaults. The 6th Royal Irish had advanced steadily and grimly fought their way into their objective by mid-afternoon, continuing to hold it until they were relieved almost twelve hours later, in the early hours of the following morning. The battle of Guillemont had cost the battalion some 311 dead, wounded and missing. The following day, the victorious 7th Leinsters, dressed in captured German greatcoats and helmets, were also relieved, having lost 231 men. Among their dead was John Breen from Belfast; in the soldier's will at the back of his pay-book, he had made the deliberate handwritten addition that he wished to leave all his worldly possessions to his '...beloved wife'.[30]

Although perhaps allegorical, as the smoke settled around the ruined village, one Irish soldier, standing amidst the rubble, apparently called out asking where their objective was. At this, an anonymous and bemused 8th Munster Captain calmly replied, 'We're in it, boys', as he placed a small green flag with a yellow harp on a mound of wreckage that, according to his map, had once signified the centre of Guillemont.[31]

123

Ginchy, 9 September 1916

By 5 September, Major-General Hickie had the majority of his division at his disposal once again with its objective to secure the fortified village of Ginchy. On the same day, the 7th Irish Fusiliers had dug in at Falfemont Farm before advancing upon the enemy-held Combles Trench. As the battalion struggled through a waist-high cornfield and dense weeds, they encountered wire entanglements hidden within it and, as they laboured forwards, German machine-guns cut them apart. They made another attempt later that evening, only to be further decimated with their final casualty figures resting at around 273 men. On the left of this assault, the 8th Irish Fusiliers moved across the Combles-Ginchy road to dig in at Bouleaux Wood and, the following morning, at 'Arrow Head Copse'. Even though they had met comparatively little opposition, they too lost 182 men.[32] The depletion of the Irish Division's strength was all too apparent to its senior officers, who knew it had been in almost incessant combat for nearly a week. Meanwhile, the approaches to Ginchy were being hammered by sustained shelling in preparation for the task ahead. It was highly unusual to use such a weakened division as the spearhead in such a major—and difficult—assault.

On 'Zero Day', 9 September, the 16th Division's front line was garrisoned by 47th and 48th Brigades, with 49th Brigade holding the reserve. As part of 47th Brigade, the 6th Connaughts, 8th Munsters (now only around 200 men strong) and 6th Royal Irish were in the leading waves but found the German front line well-fortified and undamaged by the British bombardment. Consequently, these battalions were quickly hurled back by withering machine-gun fire from the enemy front line. The newly arrived Commanding Officer of the 6th Connaughts, Lieutenant-Colonel Rowland Fielding (a former Coldstream Guardsman), bitterly noted that this devastating fire came from a position previously '...hidden and believed innocuous'.[33] The 8th Munsters got little further than 100 yards or so. The Commanding Officer of the 6th Royal Irish, Lieutenant-Colonel Fitzroy Edmund Penn Curzon, was killed only minutes into the attack. Soon, the entire brigade stuttered as the dead, dying and wounded clogged the assembly trenches; when the 7th Leinsters tried to scramble forward they discovered their parapet effectively blocked by '...disembodied bodies'.[34]

In 48th Brigade, the 7th Irish Rifles had dug assembly trenches (200 yards or so in front of the British front line) the night before, which were accidentally shelled by British gunners prior to the assault. However, at 4.45 pm, the 7th

Rifles advanced with the 7th 'Faughs' on their left flank and the 1st Munsters on their right, with all three battalions quickly capturing the German front line. Sweeping onwards into the village itself, were the 8th Dublin Fusiliers with the 8th Inniskillings on their right. Yet the deaths or wounding of so many battalion commanders was staggering. As Captain Cooper recorded, the 8th 'Skins' lost their 'inspirational' Commanding Officer, Lieutenant-Colonel Hubert Pultenay Dalzell-Walton who, at fifty years old, was determined to fight in the front line. Equally, Colonel Francis of the 7th Irish Rifles was knocked down and stunned by an explosion; Lieutenant-Colonel Sir Edward Bellingham of the 8th Dublin Fusiliers, took over practical command of this battalion and personally captured fourteen of the enemy.[35]

The 7th Rifles, with the 9th Dublins behind, secured the German front line on the outskirts of the village and, when a party of forty or so Germans attempted to organise a resistance, the Stokes mortars of 48th Brigade Light Trench Mortar Battery quickly forced their surrender. At exactly 5.25 pm, the 'Scholar's Battalion' of the 9th Dublins passed through and fought their way into the shattered remnants of the western end of Ginchy. It was here, whilst leading his men of 'B' Coy, that Lieutenant Tom Kettle was killed by a bullet which hit him above a steel vest which he wore; the incident was witnessed by his friend, Lieutenant James Emmet Dalton, who was leading the company directly behind. As the attack pushed on, there were many exuberant Irish Riflemen with the Dublins who, now officer-less, had decided to continue their own private advance against the Germans. These troops soon captured and continued beyond their second objective, which they also cleared of the enemy.

The disorganised knots of Irishmen from various regiments were quickly pulled together, largely by Lieutenant-Colonel Sir Edward Bellingham, and they were sent to work consolidating their gains. As the Irish Division had effectively punched a hole in the German line, it was inevitable that the enemy would attempt to retake Ginchy. Somehow, despite casualties and utterly exhausted troops, the surviving Irish units repelled the German counter-attack later that evening and held on until relieved by 3rd Guards Brigade. When the 1st Munsters were relieved by the 1st Welsh Guards at 10.30 pm, they had only five unwounded officers left.[36]

Father Willie Doyle, chaplain to 48th Brigade was, along with Fathers O'Connell and Wrafter, noted for his heroism that day. It was Doyle's first experience of a full-scale battle and, for his unstinting efforts to bring comfort to the wounded and dying he was awarded the Military Cross. So was the eighteen-year-old Emmet Dalton, 9th Royal Dublin Fusiliers, for taking personal command of leaderless troops and consolidating their hold on Ginchy against enemy attacks. Others, such as Tom Kettle or Lance-Corporal Joseph Corrigan, who lived just off Dame Street, were to be counted amongst the 9th Dublins' numerous dead.[37] Indeed, the 16th (Irish) Division, just like the 36th (Ulster), had been wrecked by its experience of the Somme battle; it had absorbed 4, 230 casualties in 10 days of fighting. The experiences of many Irish battalions at Guillemont and Ginchy were painfully revealing. The 6th Connaughts lost 23 officers, including its Commanding Officer, and 407 men; by 10 September, the 7th Leinsters could only muster 15 officers and 289 men. Ominously, as the Leinsters passed Trônes Wood on their way back from Ginchy, they witnessed a strange new 'armoured machine' advancing into position. It was the first time these Irish troops had seen a tank preparing for action but it would certainly not be the last.[38]

Winter on the Somme, 1916

The 16th Division's success at Ginchy, whilst it may have been epitomised by the ragged lines of troops returning with weary smiles and captured German equipment, did not mark an end to the agony of the Somme. On 15 September, the 1st and 2nd Irish Guards were flung into battle as part of the Guards Division sent against Lesboeufs in a desperate, gruelling slaughter. The 1st Irish Guards had received absolution from their stalwart padre, Father Francis Browne from Cork, a distinguished amateur photographer who had famously taken the last pictures of the Titanic at sea. The men moved off in support of the 2nd and 3rd Coldstream Guards as they advanced through the German counter-barrage and witnessed one of their leading platoons being completely annihilated in a single explosion. In their battle for these positions near Lesboeufs, the Guards were supported by the tanks which had been seen advancing through Trônes Wood. As the leading waves crept forward under intense shelling and machine-gun fire, they found themselves fighting desperately to consolidate the captured trench lines.[39]

The 2nd Irish Guards eventually clawed their way into the German trenches, crater by crater, under the direction of Captain Harold Alexander, who won an immediate DSO for being the '…life and soul of the attack'. By the end of 15 September, he was commanding men of all the Guard Regiments and leading their defence of the captured trenches. Only 166 2nd Irish Guards returned unwounded from the assault; many others, like the 'Old

Contemptible' Private John Dyra, from Crossmalina (Co. Mayo) or twenty-year-old Tom Connor, from Cootehill (Co. Roscommon), fell in the fighting. In the confusion of the battle, many of the Guards Regiments became mixed up and CSM Moran conspicuously led the defence of the captured trenches until he was wounded. Michael Moran, from Rosturk (Co. Mayo), was highly regarded in the 1st Irish Guards and was the drill sergeant who infamously uttered the 'what retreat' line after Mons. Although he won the DCM for his gallantry at Lesboeufs, by the time notification of the award was made known, CSM Moran had already died from wounds he received during the battle. Equally, Private J. Boyd, 1st Irish Guards, advanced single-handedly against an enemy machine-gun post, shooting one of the crew, bayoneting another and then punching the officer with his fist. Although the officer managed to scramble away, Private Boyd brought the gun back and was also awarded the DCM for his actions.[40]

On 16 September, Thiepval was finally captured but only through the concentrated efforts of five divisions. The pressure continued and, from 9–14 October, the 1st Royal Irish Fusiliers were shelled in trenches at Trônes Wood and Lesboeufs, from which they launched an attack on Rainy and Dewdrop Trenches. In these 5 days, another 385 men became casualties, including the young Lieutenant Eustace Emil Hyde. Just over ten days later, at Le Transloy, the 2nd Dublins took a series of heavily defended German gun-pits near Lesboeufs and secured a nearby enemy strongpoint. During the battle, the Germans had managed to stem the advance of the Dublins' who had lost most of their officers as casualties. At this point, Sergeant Robert Downie, a veteran Dublin Fusilier from Glasgow, rushed forward alone, urging his company onwards to the German line. Despite being wounded, Sergeant Downie took effective command of the company, captured an enemy machine-gun and killed its crew in a bitter engagement; he was awarded the Victoria Cross.[41]

There was one final Irish volunteer battalion on the Somme as the great battle drew to a close. The 'Commercial Pals', 10th Dublin Fusiliers, had not been sent to the 16th (Irish) Division upon completion of their training and arrival in France, after all. Perhaps this was due to their battle experience in Dublin during the Rising, although it appears that the decision to place them elsewhere caused some resentment within Irish Nationalist circles. Indeed, John Redmond believed the 10th Dublins were of exceptional quality and implored the government to send them (and all Irish troops in non-Irish regiments, along with the Tyneside Irish) to reinforce the 16th (Irish) Division. On 15 October, the 7th and 8th Irish Fusiliers had merged, as the combined losses in these already fragile and vulnerable battalions forced their amalgamation. Equally, the 2nd Royal Irish Regiment was posted to 49th Brigade to replace losses there amongst the original volunteers. The 8th Munsters was disbanded in November and all of its 467 officers and men transferred to the 1st Battalion. Consequently, it seems likely that an operational gap had appeared within the 63rd Naval Division; the 10th Dublins were duly sent there. As such, they fought at the battle of the Ancre on 13 November 1916 and assaulted German trenches at Beacourt in a snowstorm, capturing some 400 prisoners and clearing the associated strong-points the following day. The 'Commercial Pals' sustained some 50 per cent casualties, with 81 men killed in action. One of these men was Private William O'Riordan from Ballyporeen (Co. Tipperary), who had survived the Easter Rising only to be killed on the Somme. He left everything to his mother, who lived in Kilcoleman, Enniskean (Co. Cork). William O'Riordan was believed to be seventeen at the time of his death.[42]

So another year of the war came and went on the Western Front. On 25 December, a fresh draft of troops arrived from Base Depot to bolster the 2nd North Irish Horse and it was noted, rather cheerily, that their Christmas Day was '…very enjoyable'. The 'Fighting Seventh' Inniskillings spent their day in front-line trenches but the lack of activity was noted as being distinctly '… uncanny'. Major-General Hickie visited them, as he did with all his units in the 16th (Irish) Division that day and his visit seems to have been genuinely well received. By this time, the 16th and 36th Divisions were side by side in trenches at Ypres, opposite the infamous Messines Ridge. The year had seen the slaughter of these volunteers on an unimaginable scale and the divisive events in Dublin threatened to poison relations further. Yet, whilst individual political convictions remained, there was also something of a 'brotherhood of the damned' being formed. On New Year's Eve, 1916, General Sir Alex Godley, commanding the ANZACs near to the two divisions, invited a number of friends to dinner. Among them were Captain Stephen Gwynn and Major Willie Redmond MP from the 16th Division along with Major-General Sir Oliver Nugent and Major Somerset Saunderson MP of the 36th (Ulster). The talk at the table turned hotly political as each side goaded the other regarding Home Rule but, as Godley stressed, they seemed '… in reality, the best of friends'.[43] As the old year slipped into 1917, the relationship between the Irish and Ulster Divisions was finally to be put to the test.

CHAPTER EIGHT

'Quiet day. Heavy shelling on our right...'[1]

Messines, Third Ypres and Cambrai, 1917

At approximately 5 am on 1 January, a furious British bombardment began from batteries close to the camp of the 6th Royal Irish at 'Derry Huts'. The Germans duly replied with gas shells and there was an urgent order for the 6th Royal Irish to 'stand to' in case an attack was imminent. Whilst the shelling continued all morning, no further activity occurred and, the next day, the battalion relieved the 6th Connaughts who were garrisoning a new subsection of trench, grandiosely called 'Fort Victoria'. Indeed, the bombardment and activity had begun in earnest many months before. As 1917 began, the strength of the BEF on the Western Front now stood at an incredible fifty-six divisions. For the 2nd Irish Rifles, the New Year had begun with a full inspection by Lieutenant-Colonel H.R. Goodman, who found them with a fighting strength of 498 officers and men, looking '... fit and clean'. The following day, they manned the trenches at Ploegsteert ('Plugstreet') and, by 4 January, had already lost two officers, Captain Ernest W.V. Leach and 2nd-Lieutenant Patrick A.D. Jackson, killed in action. Nearby, in General Sir Herbert 'Daddy' Plumer's Second Army, the two Volunteer armies from Ireland, the 16th (Irish) and 36th (Ulster) were poised to attack Messines Ridge.[2] Here, on 7 January, a young Sligo-born officer of the 6th Connaughts, Lieutenant George Haire, died of wounds; he was the son of the Reverend Canon Haire of Lewes, Sussex.

Field Marshal Haig launched diversionary attacks on the Somme sector in January and it seemed, briefly, as if a new offensive would open up there once more. In parts of the line, with trenches less than 250 yards from the enemy in some places and with prolonged icy weather, an 'understanding' if not an actual truce had developed. When the 2nd Irish Guards were manning trenches at Rancourt, facing the woods of St Pierre Vast, the Germans and British openly walked and worked above ground without any interference from either side. When orders came from Brigade HQ to restore the fighting spirit in the zone, the Guards were supplied with warning notices—in English—that any German seen in daylight from 19 January would be shot. The Irish Guards, who were slightly further away from the German trenches, duly went out to place the signs upon the German wire. One party, led by Private King, who had been a colonial policeman, saw a German watching them from his parapet and, in a constabulary fashion, beckoned him over. Eventually a small group gathered warily by the wire and, although neither side could speak the other's language, Private King gave the German the notice and asked him to hand it to his officer. The Irish Guards then returned to their lines without incident, but Private King later commented that the enemy troops, as far as he could make out were all '…oldish men, over yonder, and thoroughly fed up'.[3]

Elsewhere on the Somme, the 8th Irish Hussars were in line at Gamaches sending out sniping parties and busy with squadron exercises. As these cavalrymen trained in the bitingly cold weather, casualties related to the cold and sickness increased. Yet, as if to show the increased activity on the Somme, in mid-February, the Irish Hussars handed over twenty-two riding mounts to the Canadian artillery and Machine-Gun Corps and, the following month, twenty-three men were posted to the Ambala Pioneer Battalion.[4] Yet, in reality, operations were afoot elsewhere. Haig's plan was for an almighty 'Somme-like' offensive in Flanders to push the Germans back but, for this to work, the 'bulge' of the Messines Ridge needed to be 'straightened out'. By the end of March, the Germans had actually tactically straightened their own front line, effectively falling back upon the formidable Hindenburg Line. The ground they released, as the Allies pushed forward, was filled with minefields and deliberate contamination of water supplies. In fact, the desolated landscape around the Ypres plain, with its heavily water-logged ground, would become a nightmarish slaughter-field.

Since their operations on the Somme, the 16th and 36th Divisions had needed considerable re-organisation and reinforcement. Immediately after their losses on 1 July, the 36th Division was sent 193 officers and 2,182 men which, according to Captain Cyril Falls, still left it '...considerably...' under-strength. Despite this, it was manning front-line trenches by the end of the month, relieving battalions from the 20th and 41st Divisions. The 16th (Irish) had arrived in the sector in mid-September and both Divisions found the area a distinct change from recent experiences. Although the Germans in this sector were not as bellicose as those on the Somme, the trench conditions were almost unbearable. Indeed, the term 'trench', as it is commonly understood, hardly referred to those before Messines; the fighting line was made up primarily of a high wall comprised of clay-filled sandbagged parapets. The high water table meant that attempts to construct deeper trench lines were pointless. Dugouts were simple wooden shelves placed in the parapet or corrugated iron-arched shelters piled high with sandbags which gave some protection from the elements, if not most forms of shellfire. Equally, communication trenches in this sector were long and, due to the water level, no deeper than a foot or so, with all defences being built above ground. Consequently, the trench lines opposite Messines were miserable. The various unit war diaries all note the driving, almost freezing, rain of January turning to depressingly regular bitterly hard frosts, snow and sub-zero temperatures. In these '...arctic...' conditions, Lieutenant-Colonel Rowland Fielding noted that his 6th Connaught Rangers had to 'stand to' for hours, numbed and paralysed with the penetrating cold. This description was echoed by the 9th Inniskillings—the 'Tyrones'—who stated that, due to the '...prevailing hard frost...', work in the trenches was limited, whilst the 7th Leinsters, working out in their front line, simply found it in a '... very bad state'.[5]

Bearing in mind the offensive spirit fostered within the Irish Division's 47th Brigade, the men of the 7th Leinsters lost eight men killed in action during a raid on 1 February; their dead included the Swiss-born Acting Captain, Herbert Bernard Mollman, aged twenty-four. On 19 February, a large-scale raid was carried out by the 6th Connaughts, with 9 officers and 190 men. Under the veil of a thick freezing fog, some advanced '...cheerfully tucking miniature Irish flags into their caps...' but the optimism was disastrously misplaced. In the chill night air, not one Connaught made it over the German wire; they were easily picked off by the Germans who were— at times casually—watching them. As they went forward, 2nd Lieutenant William Bradshaw, from Ballymoney (Co. Antrim), was wounded and, as he tried to get back to the British line, killed. Captain I.M. Garvey was then fatally hit and brought back by Lieutenant T. Hughes and Lieutenant Fenton

K. Cummins, helped by Privates M. Healy and P. King, the latter being 'Mentioned in Despatches'. In total, forty-four Rangers became casualties and ten were killed in the raid, including Dublin-born Sergeant Augustine Hackett, who had enlisted in Belfast a year before. As part of these grinding raids, on 8 March, the 7th Leinsters lost eleven men, including thirty-year-old Captain George Averill Read, from Dungar, Roscrae (Co. Tipperary). Although raids had their uses, they were universally disliked by men in the 16th and 36th Divisions alike. Some months previously, two officers in the 9th Inniskillings were out in No Man's Land, preparing to lead their men in a raid, when they got lost in the darkness. The opposing trenches were only fifty yards apart and, unsure whether the bit of wire they were facing was friendly or not, they tossed a coin to settle the matter. As the leading officer approached the wire he was fired at repeatedly—and missed—by a sentry, whose exasperated colleagues finally blurted out, 'Jasus, what are ye shootin' at?' The two Tyrone officers quickly replied and safely came in to the 16th's line, to successfully continue their raid later that night. The following month, the Germans launched a highly successful raid of their own which, following intense shelling, successfully smashed into the trenches held by the 7th Irish Rifles, capturing twenty-five prisoners and inflicting some seventy-one casualties.[6]

Behind these ragged front lines, headquarters and strong-points were built into the cellars of ruined farms and buildings. Within this landscape, the presence of the Irish and Ulster Divisions was easily distinguished by the local naming of trenches and features. Throughout the area, there were indications of where the troops came from. In addition to 'Derry Huts', there were: Birr Barracks, Kingston Junction, Clandeboye Range, Curragh, Baldoyle, Fairyhouse, Fermoy, Lurgan, Shankill and Magilligan Camps; Larne, Antrim and Crumlin Lines and, naturally, the more sarcastic or comical titles of 'Stinking Farm', 'Rat Alley' and 'Un-named Wood' were all familiarly-named features for allied soldiers in this unfamiliar place; even 'Un-named Wood' was later re-titled 'Inniskilling Wood'. One dugout, built near the Ulster Division, had originally been made in August some twenty feet deep but, by November, the water had reached the top of its stairs. With typical black humour, it soon had a notice placed at its entrance: 'The R.E. Swimming Baths'.[7] Indeed, it was due to the sodden nature of the ground that the Germans believed that any tunneling operations were doomed to failure. Yet, for some considerable time, British mining operations had been underway under the dominating feature at Ypres, control of which would determine the fate of the Salient.

Arras, April–May 1917

Throughout the spring, horrific bombardment and counter-bombardment dominated the battlefield as the great guns on either side slogged it out. Beneath the ground, the British tunnelling companies continued their urgent work, carefully ploughing deeper and deeper under the German trenches. Above ground, the infamous battle of Arras began in a snowstorm in the early hours of 9 April and, although the Canadians captured the vital Vimy Ridge, the offensive became bogged down on the wire before Bullecourt. On 12 April, a furious engagement was fought at Bois-en-Hache, a wood between Givenchy and Souchez, on the northern edge of Vimy. Here, the 2nd Leinsters had set up a forward post, when twenty German stormtroopers descended upon them. At this point, twenty-six-year-old Corporal John Cunningham, from Thurles, Co. Tipperary, took his Lewis Gun and, single-handedly, held the post until all his ammunition was gone. He then jumped onto the top of the parapet and hurled grenades at his attackers. It was only when these ran out that Corporal Cunningham reluctantly fell back to British lines, by which time he had multiple bullet and shrapnel injuries, including a shattered arm. He later died of his wounds and was posthumously awarded the Victoria Cross. Similarly, Private Kieran Phelan, from Dunkerrin (Co. Tipperary), was also mortally wounded that day. He had enlisted in Birr with the Leinsters and fought in Salonika before being transferred to their 2nd Battalion. He left everything to his mother and wrote, rather sadly, on the last page of his pay book that, should he have the '… misfortune…' to be killed, could whoever found his book '…kindly give it to the Company Quarter Master Sergeant, C Company'.[8]

Whilst the Germans had sometimes developed an indifference towards aggressive raiding, on 9 April, such a raid recovered clay from a spoil-heap and confirmed suspicions of British mining activity. However, due to the belief that sustained tunnelling could not be successful in the area, no action was taken. Yet, many Germans must have been uneasy. At twilight on 18 April, whilst at Spanbroek, the 10th Inniskillings saw a German running across No Man's Land, dashing from crater to crater. It was believed that he was trying to surrender but, before he made it to the 'Skin's' position, a Trench Mortar NCO shot and wounded him. The German turned and tried to get back to his own lines and, as he did so, some of the 'Derrys' opened fire and brought him down.[9] It was seen as a sign that German morale was fracturing, coming at a time when severe mutinies had already occurred within the French armies.

The Battle of Wytschaete *(Wijtschate)*, 7 June 1917

By June, the vital operation to straighten the British front line before Messines was well in hand. The impending assault on the ridge was to fall to the 'Cinderella' Second Army, commanded by General Sir Herbert Plumer. He was a rather plump, white 'walrus moustached' general and the inspiration for David Low's infamous 1930s cartoon character, 'Colonel Blimp'.[10] Yet, General Plumer was very far from the stereotypical British general. He was genuinely held in affection by the men he commanded, who recognised that he was imaginative, diligent, compassionate and intelligent. He made supreme efforts to save their lives and, accordingly, made meticulous preparations to the smallest detail in order to make the upcoming attack a success. Some seventy-four 'Mark IV' tanks were to support the attacks on enemy strong-points and concrete fortifications and vital German intelligence on the ridge's strategic defence had been intercepted. Extraordinary efforts were also made to ensure the quick evacuation and treatment of the wounded. In the rear, a scale model of the enemy trenches was made at Kemmel, with no attempt at subterfuge, and visits by staff and attacking battalions were regularly encouraged. This, combined with copious orders and briefing notes to every officer from brigade to company level, ensured a thorough knowledge of what lay ahead. As Lieutenant-Colonel Fielding, 6th Connaughts, observed, the preparations for the attack on Wytschaete ('Whitesheet') were impressive. Reams of papers and operational orders streamed into the battalion HQs and led to the popular, if disparaging, saying that, if '…ink will win this war then we shall certainly win it'.[11] As such, it was intended that the numerous mines dug deep under the German trench system would be exploded at the same time as the attack on the ridge (3.10 am, 7 June), the aim being to save as many lives as possible. In front of the 16th and 36th Divisions were seven giant mines: three before the Irish at Petit Bois and Maedelstede and four facing the Ulsters at Kruisstraat Caberet, Spanbroekmolen and Peckham. The Germans opposing the attack here were drawn from the 4th (Grenadier) and 104th Regiments (40th Saxon Division), whilst those defending the lines opposite the 16th (Irish) were with the 33rd Regiment (2nd East Prussian Division).

In the midst of the final preparations on 4 June, the temporary acting CO of the 7th Leinsters, Major T.R.A. Stannus, presided over a 'battalion dinner' which was given at Locre Hospice. Among the forty-five guests were recently returned Battalion CO, Lieutenant-Colonel G.A.M. Buckley, the Brigade's Belgian interpreter, Mr. Vanderbutt, the chaplains Captain Father

Wrafter and Captain Reverend J. Swinhoe and Lieutenant Francis Jourdain of the 6th Connaughts. The guest of honour was undoubtedly Major Willie Redmond of the 6th Royal Irish, whose health was toasted, along with that of the 16th (Irish) Division. According to Captain Farrell of the 7th Leinsters, he responded with '...deep sincerity and emotion...' regarding the hope that the two traditions would somehow unite by serving together in France and Flanders. However, the underlying joviality of the evening was also indicated by the addition of three names on the neatly typed list of guests: 'Mack of the 'orses, 7th Leinsters', 'Spud Always. 7th Leinsters' and 'J.M. Roche, Vagrant, a C.O. to-morrow probably or 2/Lieut'. This last possibly refers to Captain James Roche who is variously (and perhaps aptly considering the above) described elsewhere as serving with the 7th Leinsters and also attached to the 47th Trench Mortar Battery. Many of these names were to feature on the casualty lists a few days later. At roughly the same time as this celebratory 'last supper', the 6th Connaughts again raided the German line south of Petit Bois in an attempt to glean any last-minute intelligence; they gained forty-four casualties but estimated they had killed some sixty of the enemy. Only that afternoon, another party of eighty-five men from the 9th Irish Fusiliers had, in daylight, raided the German line south of Spanbroekmolen at a point known to them as 'Clogher Head'. Amongst the dead from these raids were Ballinderry man, Private Patrick Gawley, with the 6th Connaughts and Private George Cave, a former 'Sherwood Forester' from Plymouth, who had found himself re-allocated to the ranks of the 9th Irish Fusiliers.[12]

At precisely 3.10 am on 7 June, nineteen of the ammonal mines were fired. What happened next became legendary. The ground before the attacking divisions simply erupted to the skies and the scene was variously described as '...towers of crimson flame...' or, even more eerily, like '... hell... let loose...'. In the forefront of the 16th's assault on Wytschaete was 47th Brigade. The 6 Royal Irish and 7th Leinsters, led by Major Stannus, stumbled through the smoke. Major Willie Redmond was one of the first casualties, hit in the wrist, then the leg, which knocked him down. As his men ran past, he tried to cheer them onwards. Soon, Major (Acting Lieutenant-Colonel) Stannus also lay dead, killed in an explosion that had ripped through the Battalion HQ. Battalion command fell to Captain J. Farrell. Some units were held up by the deep craters now left before them. As previously planned, officers were able to circumvent these new obstacles through the use of compasses which had been issued prior to the attack, and the front line was quickly consolidated to allow the following waves to push on to Wytschaete. At Spanbroekmolen, the explosion was delayed by a mere fifteen seconds but, true to their orders, the men of the Young Citizen Volunteers rose from their trenches and started forward. As they did so, the huge mine went up and many of the 14th Irish Riflemen were hurled to the ground. Amazingly, there were no casualties reported and the leading waves continued their advance. The 8th Inniskillings also experienced this massive explosion to their right, with one officer noting that the shockwave caused one man to fall to the ground, '…shivering and babbling…' until he had to be taken away, their first casualty of the attack.[13]

Reeling in the confused dust and smoke and, undoubtedly shaken by the eruptions all around them, many Germans surrendered. The 'Fighting Seventh' Inniskillings took their objectives in a mere twenty minutes as the enemy's 'Nail Switch' trench had simply ceased to exist. The 6th Connaughts had been designated as sector 'moppers up' and Lieutenant Francis Jourdain noted how, by 8.00 am, German prisoners were streaming through their lines; some of his signallers had purloined a rum jar and were busy drinking away. It was then that Lieutenant Jourdain did the '…bravest thing I have ever done…', emptying the rum onto the ground in front of fifty to sixty disgruntled Rangers. Meanwhile, their Commanding Officer, Lieutenant-Colonel Fielding, noted that, when the Irish and Ulster Divisions reached Wytschaete, the Germans surrendered en masse, running towards their attackers with hands or handkerchiefs in the air. Just one example, perhaps, demonstrates why German resolve initially evaporated. A raiding party of around 300 Germans was above ground just before the Spanbroekmolen mine exploded. These men from the 40th (Saxon) Division did not stand a chance. According to Sergeant Bob Grange, 12th Irish Rifles, he had never seen a scene of such carnage in all his life. It was a grotesque spectacle of body-parts and blood, with the crater left by the explosion some 430 feet in diameter.[14]

Despite this, the German front line was deliberately thinly held, with far more numerous forces manning the strong-points, bunkers and lines behind. Evidence for this practice had been recovered by the recent raids and it was hoped that the detonation of the tunnels underneath them would silence any remaining opposition. By and large it worked, although as the Ulster Division's leading waves neared Steenbeke, the resistance hardened with enemy machine-guns delaying the advance. The 15th Irish Rifles got to within 100 yards or so of the Messines–Wytschaete Road when German machine guns opened up on them. A fierce battle developed, during which Lieutenant Falkiner grappled with a German officer who had tackled him around the waist; the Irish Rifles' officer broke an arm free and shot his opponent dead. At 'Skip Point', two

BRITISH INFANTRY MARCHING TO THE FRONT

A LITTLE BRITISH ARMY GOES A D —— LONG WAY

1. 'A Little British Army Goes a D —— Long Way', postcard c.1914, Regent Publishing Co. Ltd.

2. 8th King's Royal Irish Hussar captures a valuable prisoner, postcard, G & D London.

3. Unknown Corporal (a musketry instructor and marksman), c. 1914, 4th Royal Irish Dragoon Guards. (Author's collection)

4. 'The *River Clyde* after the landing taken from V Beach 3 May 1915 Gallipoli'. (Author's collection)

5. 2nd Royal Irish Fusiliers, Waiting for signal to attack' – a familiar site for Irish regiments from Macedonia, Mesopotamia and Palestine. (Author's collection)

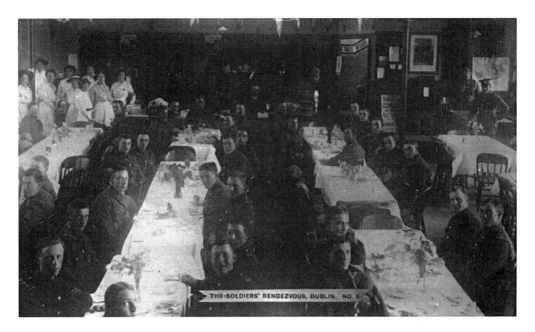

6. 'The Soldiers' Rendezvous, Dublin No. 3', postcard, Lilywhite Ltd. Halifax.

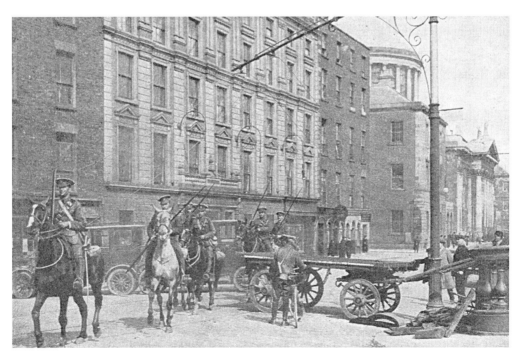

7. (12th and 5th Royal Irish) Lancers on patrol, Dublin, Easter 1916, Contemporary Print. (Author's collection)

8. Stretcher Bearers at the Ancre, on the Somme, July 1916. (Author's collection)

9. View of German lines from 36th (Ulster) Division's lines at Thiepval Wood. (Photo by Gavin Hughes)

10. 10th Royal Inniskilling Fusiliers ('The Derrys') on the Western Front with their battalion mascot 'Billy the Skin' (a goat in a tin hat), *The War Illustrated*, 16 March 1918, No. 187.

11. 2nd Royal Irish Fusiliers, Palestine, 'Wounded being evacuated' – of interest are the troops in the distance wearing steel shell helmets. (Author's collection)

12. Cpl. Michael O'Leary, VC, Irish Guards, *The War Illustrated*, 28 July 1917 (pp.59–60).

13. Capt. George Averill Read, 7th Leinsters, killed in action, *The War Illustrated*, 5 May 1917 (p.132).

14. Pvt. John Cunningham VC, 2nd Leinsters, *The War Illustrated*, 30 June 1917 (p.133).

15. Capt. Herbert B. Mollman, 7th Leinsters, killed in action, *The War Illustrated*, 5 May 1917 (p.131).

16. Capt. Harry A.V. Harmsworth, MC, Irish Guards, *The War Illustrated*, 2 March 1918 (p.218).

17. Lieut. Eustace E. Hyde, 1st Royal Irish Fusiliers, killed in action, *The War Illustrated*, 5 May 1917 (p.127).

18. Major W. Redmond MP, 6th Royal Irish Regt, killed in action.

19. Pvt. James Duffy, VC, 6th Royal Inniskilling Fusiliers.

20. Lieut. George Haire, 6th Connaught Rangers, killed in action, *The War Illustrated*, 10 March 1917 (p.129).

21. Lieut. James S. Emerson VC, 9th Royal Inniskilling Fusiliers, *The War Illustrated*, 9 March 1918 (p. 149).

22. Lt-Col. A.D. Murphy DSO, MC, killed in action, *The War Illustrated*, 8 December 1917 (p.146).

23. Sgt. James Ockenden, VC, 1st Royal Dublin Fusiliers, *The War Illustrated*, 1 Dec. 1917 (p.143).

24. Plaque on the 16th (Irish) Division Cross, Guillemont. (Photo by Gavin Hughes)

25. The Ulster Tower Memorial, Thiepval. (Photo by Gavin Hughes)

26. Original wooden 16th (Irish) Divisional Cross, c. 1917, War Memorial Gardens, Islandbridge, Dublin. (Photo by Gavin Hughes)

27. Unknown Irish regimental casualty, Connaught Cemetery, Thiepval. (Photo by Gavin Hughes)

machine-gun nests were rushed and the defences overwhelmed by the 9th Irish Rifles (with bombers from the YCV) and 150 prisoners were captured. Similarly, on the edge of Wytschaete Wood, a machine-gun nest pinned the advancing 7/8th Irish Fusiliers down until it was rushed and put out of action. They then engaged another machine-gun at Leg Copse by Sonnen Farm and, by the end of the day, had captured over seventy prisoners and many vital supplies. They had also received the heaviest casualties of any battalion in the 16th Division; some 193 men were killed or wounded.[15]

As the YCVs secured their objective ('Jump Point'), an intelligence officer attached to 109th Brigade HQ allegedly informed Brigadier-General Ricardo that he had seen a yellow flag in the forward trenches. In response to this, Ricardo apparently snapped, 'Yellow be damned!' and slammed the phone down. According to the battalion's war diary, 'yellow' flags were issued to the YCV as markers. In personal communication with Captain Falls, however, General Ricardo took issue with this and stated that the flags were '… *orange* [sic] a far more significant shade'.[16] The 6th Royal Irish and 7th Leinsters reached their objective at the 'Blue Line', consolidated the area and dug in as the other advancing units passed through their position and continued the assault. The 1st Munster Fusiliers followed on behind as a tank rumbled into the shattered southern ruins of the village, and it was here that they linked up with Inniskillings from the Ulster Division. The leading waves of the 2nd Royal Irish Regiment leapfrogged the Munsters and took the fortified strongpoint of L'Hospice; they suffered some 149 casualties but secured their objectives and captured 300 prisoners. Behind the assault, the men of the 2nd North Irish Horse were held in readiness at Boeschepe, although each squadron was dispersed across the Corps' front. Only 'B' Squadron was recorded as being prepared for mounted action for a push through if it got the chance, but the Regiment's war diarist seemed hugely relieved—and a little surprised—when he wrote that they 'Got through the day without any casualties.'[17]

The Death of Major Redmond, MP

According to most sources, Major Willie Redmond, MP was hit in the wrist and leg as he went forward in the leading waves. The fifty-six-year-old had been assigned to 16th Divisional Staff and had only been allowed to go into the assault on the explicit orders that he return to lines as soon as the front line was consolidated. With supreme poignancy, Major Redmond, who so persuasively argued for the merits of Ulster Unionist and Irish Nationalist serving together, was brought back to British trenches by stretcher bearers from the 36th (Ulster) Division.

Indeed, Private John Meeke, from outside Ballymoney, Co. Antrim, discovered the wounded Major as his own unit, the 11th Inniskillings, advanced. Meeke tried to carry Redmond on his shoulders but was soon wounded himself; both men were taken by stretcher-bearers to the 36th Advanced Dressing Station at Lindenhoek Crossroads before being taken by ambulance to the main dressing station operated by 108th Field Ambulance. Major Redmond died here at 6.30 pm from his wounds. John Meeke of the 'Donegals' was awarded the Military Medal for his attempts to save Major Redmond whose death, arguably, became the most famous of any Irish Parliamentarian during the war. Yet, his death was certainly not unique. The Nationalist MP for North Tipperary, Dr John Esmonde RAMC, died whilst on service in France during April 1915 and, the very first Parliamentarian casualty was the death of the Unionist MP for Mid-Antrim, Captain Honourable Arthur O'Neill who was also killed at Ypres, serving with the Life Guards on Klein Zillebeke Ridge in November 1914. Redmond's death cast a long shadow over the 16th (Irish) Division and, it could be argued, its repercussions are still felt today in any study of Ireland's contribution to the First World War. It is perhaps unsurprising that many contemporary observers, and those since, saw the exploits of the Irish and Ulster Divisions fighting side by side as a beacon of hope for cultural traditions on the island. Major Redmond was widely mourned by both sides and, indeed, soldiers from the 16th and 36th Divisions presented Honour Guards at his funeral at Locre (Loker) Convent, exactly twenty-four hours after he had died at Dranouter. It is perhaps important to stress that these men still held diametrically opposed viewpoints. However, they had cast aside their differences for the duration of the war, each side expecting favourable—but conflicting—rewards for their loyalty. The acid test of cooperation was yet to come.[18]

The Battle for Guillemont Farm, 22 June 1917

Back on the Somme, the troopers of the 8th Irish Hussars were employed in the thankless task of 'fetching and carrying', road mending and the hated duty of acting as wiring parties at Somerville Wood. Yet, the fighting of 1917 was also about to demonstrate that the role of cavalry in mounted action was not a thing of the past. By mid-June, the 5th Irish Lancers had relieved the 2nd Dragoons at 'Guillemont Farm', near Lempire and Ronssoy and, once there, they soon came under sustained enemy bombardment. The situation intensified until 22 June when, at 1.30 am, the German barrage lifted and their infantry swarmed against the lancer's post from the east, north and south. Captain John Rice, seeing that the Germans were trying to encircle them, reconsolidated his position by taking his men into a nearby communications trench. Supporting troops from 'A' Squadron, under Lieutenant A.C. Nugent, were immediately sent up from the reserve to assist Captain Rice's men.

Both squadrons fought with considerable daring on either side of Guillemont Farm and re-established their defences there. It was 'believed' that a good number of Germans had been killed by the British counter-barrage, with at least twelve enemy dead recovered at the post itself. However, Lancer casualties seemed far greater. In Captain Rice's 'D' Squadron, thirteen had been killed outright and these were men from varied backgrounds: Jack Black from Croughton, Northamptonshire, Lance Corporal Charles Burnham from Hackney, Corporal David Cassells from Newtownhamilton (Co. Armagh) and Patrick Fitzpatrick from Carlow. Fourteen lancers were also wounded, including four officers, John Rice being one of them. Tragically, the British counter-barrage had also accidentally caught troopers from the Oxford Hussars, inflicting heavy casualties as a result.[19]

Third Ypres and Langemarck, 31 July–16 August

By 14 June, Messines was in Allied hands and, just over a month later, the artillery bombardment against German lines at Pilckem Ridge started. For ten days the guns pulverised the already water-logged battlefield and, with constant rainfall, the ground turned into a murderous bog. In charge of offensive operations in the Salient was General Sir Hubert Gough, commander of the Fifth Army, who deliberately asked for the 16th and 36th Divisions to be transferred to him. Haig, possibly swayed by the notion that Gough would be more dynamic in attack than the methodical Plumer, opted for the former.[20]

On 31 July, the opening day of Third Ypres and the battle of Pilckem Ridge, Gough's objective was to strike 6,000 yards into German territory. On 31 July, the 2nd Irish Guards were sent against German positions along the Yser Canal, with their first objectives being the German front-line 'Cariboo' and 'Canon' trenches. Having gained these with minimal loss and pushing onwards gallantly to achieve the final objectives by the next morning, their success was sadly tainted. In addition to the loss of the battalion's Padre, Father Knapp, acting Lieutenant Colonel Eric Greer (who had been Battalion Machine-Gun

Officer with the 1st Irish Guards in 1914) was killed either by flying shrapnel or a bullet whilst in the first line objective. He had been known as an affable and humorous man who was able to make '... hard life a thing delightful'.[21] Certainly, this was a much-needed quality on the Western Front. On the same day, the 1st Irish Rifles attacked Westhoek Ridge with 20 officers and 620 ranks but, by 4 August, they had lost 13 officers and 175 ranks. Losses included Colonel Reid, who was killed in the first few hours of the assault. Similarly, the 2nd Leinsters were sent against the Gheluvelt Plateau and were mercilessly cut down by machine-guns as they crossed a little valley; they found ways around and pushed on. They clawed their way towards a series of loop-holed concrete bunkers and, taking them in a series of dogged flank attacks, they dug in. Like the 1st Rifles, by the end of the fighting, the 2nd Leinsters counted 17 officers and 230 other ranks among their casualties.[22]

Among the dead of the 1st Inniskillings, in the reserve near 'Hell-Fire Corner', was the 'peasant poet', Francis Ledwidge from Slane, Co. Meath who was atomised by a shell whilst drinking tea with his pals. The difficult offensive at Pilckem Ridge halted at the German second line, after only 3,000 yards and at a terrifying cost of almost 31,000 casualties. To make up these horrific losses, in early August, the practice of partially dismounting cavalry regiments and retraining squadrons as infantry was well underway. Troops from the 1st North Irish Horse were detached to the 16th and 36th Divisions and, by 14 August, horses belonging to the 2nd North Irish Horse were also replaced or sent to new homes. Lieutenant Leader was in charge of taking 265 horses by train from Beaurainville to Marseilles and, the next day, their saddlery was handed into the stores and the officers were ominously examined for fitness for infantry duties.[23]

During the long and wasteful battle of Third Ypres, the rain intensified and the ground conditions got worse. On 10 August, the 2nd Irish Rifles attacked the 'village' of Westhoek, although it was more accurately a warren of pill-boxes and concrete dug-outs, bristling with machine-gun posts. It was noted that the enemy only put up pockets of determined resistance and that many were already broken by the barrage, offering little resistance as '...our waves were upon him'. Even with relatively little resistance, the battalion's casualties, from 5 August to their relief in the captured line on the night of 11 August, stood at 350 all ranks. As Gheluvelt Plateau remained untaken, the planned offensive for 14 August was postponed again. However, the assaulting 16th and 36th 'spearhead' Divisions remained in the front line, enduring miserable conditions at Frezenberg and Wieltje respectively. For twelve days they were shelled, gassed and machine-gunned from the dominating German heights. The assaulting divisions had their fighting strength cut by a third before they even entered No Man's Land. Father William Doyle, Jesuit chaplain to 48th Brigade, regularly went out into No Man's Land to give the last rites to dying men or to perform what acts of kindness or duty he could. He was idolised by the men of both divisions for his humanity and compassion but also deeply respected for the numerous acts of raw courage he displayed. To him, these Irish regimental soldiers, of whatever religion, were his 'children' and it devastated him personally when he discovered their corpses in craters, where they had miserably '...crept to die'.[24] In the coming days, Father Doyle's grim work would intensify.

The subsequent assault at Langemarck by Gough's Fifth Army was mismanaged and, in contrast to Wytschaete, became an absolute disaster. When British battalions advanced at 3.10am on 16 August, they again found fortified machine-gun emplacements which were still intact and which their artillery barrage was expected to have eliminated. The difference between brigade, battalion and company commanders could not have been starker. On the right flank, towards Zonnebeke, the men struggled up the slopes, through mud and under murderous fire, supposedly covered by the British barrage—which quickly overtook their tortuous progress. The units in 108th Brigade, 11th, 12th and 13th Irish Rifles along with the 9th Irish Fusiliers, flung themselves against the strong-point, rather prophetically known as Somme, and were slaughtered. Lieutenant-Colonel Maxwell, commanding the 13th '1st County Downs' finally led the Battalion HQ and 'battle reserve' in a desperate attempt to reach their objective; he fell wounded as the 9th 'Faughs' held on to their gains atop Hill 35 for as long as they could.[25]

Colonel McCarthy-O'Leary's 1st Irish Rifles scrambled up the ridge past Hanebeke Wood and, after bitter fighting at a bunker called 'Anzac Farm', secured it. The 1st Rifles even managed to reach their final objective (at 6.20 am) but, as they had lost so many men in the initial attack, they could not consolidate it. Indeed, at 7.50am, the Germans nearly swamped the Rifles' defences, forcing them to pull their line back by 200 yards. At this point, Colonel McCarthy-O'Leary fell wounded with command passing to Captain Whitfeld and, as they returned to Hanebeke Wood, the Germans proceeded to shell it violently. As the surviving Rifles suspected, it was the opening phase to an immediate counter-attack (*eingreif*), a strategy used to take back any sudden gains. Consequently, six battalions of stormtroopers emerged from the bombardment and fought the depleted 1st Irish Rifles almost back to their original position. At 9 pm, the 1st Rifles eventually received orders to retire but, by then, two-thirds of the battalion had become casualties and Captain Whitfeld was the only surviving officer.[26]

Following a sustained period of shelling, one company of the 2nd Royal Irish was sent against the redoubtable Borry Farm strongpoint to very little effect. By this time, a number of 49th Brigade battalions (the 8th 'Skins' and 7/8th Irish Fusiliers) had already attempted to capture it, but the position had proved too well defended. The insurance clerk from Islington, 2nd-Lieutenant John Eberli, 2nd Royal Irish, was attached to 49th Trench Mortar Battery and mortally wounded in the fight for Borry. He died from loss of blood and the effects of shock on his way to the Casualty Clearing Station. On their flank, the 'Fighting Seventh' Inniskillings had captured Hill 37 with Delva Farm and determinedly fought their way into the final Langemarck–Gheluvelt line. However, they soon discovered that the 8th Inniskillings were having difficulties advancing at Borry Farm, now garrisoned by over a hundred Germans, supported by heavy machine-guns. At 6.25 am, Captain Parr reported that the forward units of the 7th Inniskillings had already become enveloped as the 'mopping up' operation disintegrated, allowing '...a number of enemy in our Rear'. Under such circumstances, the 'Fighting Seventh' could not hold on, although they tried for nearly three hours. Eventually, they withdrew to their own lines, all the time under persistent fire. This, indeed, was the story of Langemarck. When the German *eingreif* suddenly came, many already shattered units were simply overwhelmed. The 9th Dublin Fusiliers, 7th Irish Rifles and 8th Inniskillings all attempted to stand their ground and many were killed doing so. The 7th Rifles were caught on 'Fortress Potsdam', which maintained its machine-gun fire throughout the British barrage. A few managed to cross Hanebeke stream and reach their objective, only to be obliterated by their own artillery. The 9th Irish Fusiliers mounted an equally spirited, but doomed, defence on Hill 35 as their battalion strength could not resist any further counter-attack. Like other units in the 16th and 36th Divisions, the survivors limped back through the mud to the British lines.[27]

To the Ulster and Irish Divisions, the disastrous battle of Langemarck was a terrible blow to their respective national prides. Major-General Nugent wrote to his wife that evening, '...heartbroken over it...' believing that his Ulster Division had failed to support their flanking divisions and had been slaughtered for nothing. As it transpired, soon after the opening waves had assaulted, the 7th Inniskillings reported that the Ulster Division had '... heard a rumour...' that one of their flanking divisions, the 48th, had already retreated.

In fact, the 48th (South Midland Territorial Force) Division had been virtually destroyed in its advance, just like the 36th, 16th and 8th Divisions. They had all experienced the same dreadful mauling. Yet, there was a direct inference that Ulstermen and Irishmen had shown cowardice during the attack. Indeed, High Command initially felt that both divisions had failed to hold their gains because the German shelling had unnerved them. Gough's criticism following the failed assault appears to have been particularly unjustified and was something he appears to have almost instantly regretted. Both divisions, desperately under-strength and fatigued, were, in the words of Philip Gibbs, deliberately '…broken to bits and their Brigadiers called it murder'. In his report after the battle, Lieutenant-Colonel A.J. Walkey, 8th Inniskillings, determined that its failure was due to the German garrisons at strong-points remaining intact, the immediate loss of officers and NCOs in the initial attack and inadequate communication with the front or staff in the rear. Given the circumstances, the result was unsurprising. Gough had effectively whittled away the fighting capability of both divisions by squandering them on trench duties under continuous shellfire.[28]

During the miserable mess of Langemarck, the evacuation of the wounded was especially arduous. The Reverend Frank Johnson Halahan, from Berehaven, Cork, was noted for his gallantry in assisting bearers with their work whilst under fire. Serving with the 36th (Ulster) Division, Reverend Halahan was Church of Ireland rector of Drumcree in Co. Armagh and had been a signatory of the Ulster Covenant; he ended the war having been awarded the MC and Bar. One stretcher bearer in particular, from the 2nd Royal Irish, Lance Corporal Frederick George Room, from St Georges in Bristol, was singled out for his bravery. Even in a battle noted for the stretcher-bearers' extreme lack of regard for their own personal safety, Lance Corporal Room's continued efforts to rescue wounded comrades (many from battalions who had fought in the early part of the day) won him the Victoria Cross. His efforts in bringing the wounded back to the Regimental Aid Post at Frezenberg were a faint spark in an otherwise dismal day for the Irish regiments. Among the staggering 7,800 casualties, was the legendary Father Doyle MC, killed by a shell whilst at the same Aid Post to which Lance Corporal Room was bringing the wounded; Major-General Hickie simply stated that he was the '… most wonderful character I have ever known'.[29]

As if to prove these heavy losses, on 23 August, the two Inniskilling Battalions of the 16th Division had so few men left that they were amalgamated to form a new 7/8th Battalion. In the desperate need for men, cavalry units dissolved and, on 28 August, it was sadly stated by the 2nd NIH that three squadrons were transferred to the infantry at the 36th Divisional base depot at Le Havre. For many men like Robert Hall, a former clerk from the Limestone Road in Belfast, serving with the 6th Inniskillings, their termination of duty with their regiments was abrupt and the terminology stark. He was simply '…compulsorily transferred…' to the 9th (NIH) Royal Irish Fusiliers under Army Order 204 at his '…last rate of pay'. With this, the men of 'A' Squadron (Inniskilling Dragoons) and 'B' and 'C' Squadrons (North Irish Horse) began their war again—this time on foot. Similarly, on 1 September, the 1st and 2nd South Irish Horse were dismounted and merged to form the 7th (SIH) Royal Irish Regiment and posted to 49th Brigade of the 16th (Irish) Division. It was a transition period for its former South Irish Horse troopers, as they trained for their upcoming role as infantrymen. Until mid-October, they were vigorously instructed in the infantry methods of drill and musketry, along with the necessary tactics relating to Lewis Guns, wiring, bombing and bayonet fighting. All of this was to become vitally important in mid-October when they took over 'Belfast Camp' from the 7th Irish Rifles at Boisleux au Mont. Interestingly, the remnants of the Nationalist 7th Irish Rifles were soon absorbed by the 2nd Irish Rifles, also generally Nationalist in opinion, when it was transferred to the 36th Division later that winter.[30]

The Final Phase at Passchendaele, September–November 1917

By the time of the final push towards Passchendaele itself, Haig had reverted to using Plumer's Second Army and successes again followed, firstly at Menin Road, then Polygon Wood. In mid-September, Sergeant John Milligan of the Irish Guards was granted leave to go home to Portadown but, before he returned to the front, Corcrain Orange band formed up outside his house one evening and began to play '…a number of lively airs…' to honour him. Meanwhile, the 2nd Irish Guards were out of line around Elverdinghe, when their CO '…took exception to the hang of their kilts' during a planned piper's inspection. The matter was finally resolved by getting the Gordon Highlanders' Pipe-Major to advise them, whereupon the kilts were re-pleated by the Master Tailor and gas-helmets used as sporrans. Weeks later, at Ney Copse, Lance Sergeant John Moyney (from Rathdowney, Co. Laoise) and his fifteen-man section held an advance post for almost ninety-six hours without support against German attacks; until he and Private Thomas Woodcock (from Wigan,

Lancashire) covered its withdrawal with Lewis Gun fire. For this action, both Moyney and Woodcock were awarded the Victoria Cross. On 9 October, in an attempt to strengthen the six mile front from the north of Langemarck to east of Zonnebeke, the Irish Guards were involved in the assault across the Broembeek. This was a 'stagnant ditch' within a flood plain, effectively a shell-pocked bog, with steep sides. Under persistent rainfall, the Guards were in the second wave of the assault and made an uncomfortable advance through to the second line objectives (taken by the Grenadier Guards) ready for their attack on the ultimate objective—the edge of Broembeek Forest. Before this, however, lay concrete strong-points and numerous entanglements and machine-gun posts. They secured their objective and clung onto it until relief came on the following evening; by then they had been subjected to vicious sniping, protracted shelling and every company commander had become a casualty. Indeed, a total of 228 officers and other ranks were wounded, killed or missing.[31]

Before their despatch to boost the strength of the 16th (Irish) Division, the last act of the 1st Dublin Fusiliers in the 29th Division was to go into action at Broodsiende in mid-October. It was during this attack that Sergeant James Ockendon discovered that a German machine gun was successfully keeping the Dublins' advance at bay and so, as acting CSM, Ockendon charged the position, killing two of the gun crew. The third German gunner tried to escape across No Man's Land but Sergeant Ockendon ran after him and shot him down. He then led the 1st Dublins' attack on an enemy held 'farm', running ahead of his company to kill a further four Germans. Seeing his advance, sixteen of the enemy duly surrendered to him and, for his actions, Sergeant Ockendon was awarded the Victoria Cross. Following the costly battles around Third Ypres, the 9th Dublins were formally amalgamated with their 8th Battalion on 25 October. On 29 October, troopers from the newly formed 7th (SIH) Royal Irish were working in a sector of line when a German shell hit one of their Lewis Gun emplacements, killing two men. Later on in the day, the 7/8th Inniskilling Fusiliers launched a successful raid against the German lines and, in retaliation, the enemy began to shell the British trenches opposite. It was during this bombardment that the South Irish Horse had another three men injured and a portion of their trenches slightly damaged.[32]

When the Canadians finally entered Passchendaele on 6 November, it heralded the final phases of the battle of Third Ypres. Yet, the war in the Flanders' mire continued, as did the casualties. In the push to consolidate the ridge further, the 2nd Munster Fusiliers got cut off while attacking the heights at Goudberg and were surrounded by a rapid German counter-attack, resulting in 413 casualties. On 16 November, the very popular twenty-seven-year-old CO of the 2nd Leinsters, Lieutenant-Colonel A.D. Murphy, DSO, MC, was killed when a stray shell hit the Regimental Aid Post he was visiting.[33]

The 'Half-Breakthrough' at Cambrai, 20 November 1917

With Passchendaele secured, the focus of Haig's planned offensives shifted to Cambrai, a German-held railhead which was originally intended to be the target of a 'tank raid in force'. If captured, this would silence German artillery and strong-points, whilst also causing confusion and sapping enemy morale further. However, by November, the plan had spiralled, as ever, into an ambitious breakthrough strategy with 378 tanks and 6 infantry divisions, supported by 5 cavalry divisions.

The battle began on 20 November in a thick fog, with the massed tanks rumbling towards the Hindenberg Line and the infantry advancing behind. However, the Ulster Division had advanced without the tanks and had launched an attack upon the Canal du Nord, using trench mortars, bombing teams and bayonet men. The combined assault of the 'Tyrones', 'Derrys' and 'Donegals' in 109th Brigade forced its way through the German defences and onwards to the heights overlooking the canal. Using the divisional engineers, mostly experienced men from the Belfast shipyards, a temporary bridge was constructed and the infantry advance continued. By the afternoon, some 4,000 yards of enemy territory was in the 36th's hands; elsewhere, the 1st Inniskillings, led by Lieutenant-Colonel John Sherwood-Kelly, were supporting the attack of the 29th Division. Finding that the enemy fire was halting any attempts to cross the Marcoing Canal, Lieutenant-Colonel Sherwood-Kelly personally led the 1st 'Skins' across in the face of stiff opposition. He then scouted out a domineering bluff, held by the Germans, where he could see that his left flank had been pinned down by strong wire entanglements. On observing this, Sherwood-Kelly made his way over to the trapped Inniskillings with a Lewis Gun section and maintained covering fire until they were able to progress. As the Inniskillings' advance continued, Lieutenant-Colonel Sherwood-Kelly led them against a number of entrenchments and pits, successfully capturing five German machine-guns and forty-six of the enemy. The battalion struggled up towards the incline, although it was defended by numerous machine-gun units behind strong defences. The Inniskilling companies moved over the difficult ground, using dash and dive tactics, patiently cut their way through the wire and successfully assaulted the enemy. For his inspirational personal leadership that day, Lieutenant-Colonel Sherwood-Kelly, a South African, was awarded the Victoria Cross.[34]

At Croiselles, near Bullecourt, the first two German lines were quickly over-run by the Irish Division sent to capture a 3,000 yard frontage known as 'Tunnel Trench' and 'Tunnel Support'. It was comprised of four cement strong-points, each of which bristled with machine-guns. Tunnel Trench also had a subterranean structure deep underground and had originally been a support trench (with electric lighting and living quarters) which ran directly to the Hindenberg Line. The 6th Connaughts, 7th Leinsters and 1st Munsters quickly gained a foothold in the enemy front by using bombs and bayonets. Resistance, according to most accounts, was short-lived. Some 635 prisoners were taken by the Division and it was believed that 330 Germans had been killed. In his report on operations for 30th November to 47th Brigade, Lieutenant-Colonel Fielding stressed how hard the 6th Connaughts had fought at Tunnel Trench and 'Jove' strong-point, especially when the Germans counter-attacked in force. Here, Private White repeatedly caught the stick-grenades thrown at the Connaught position and actually tossed them back at the enemy, whilst another Connaught was found dead '…locked in a grip with a dead German'.[35] Yet, the initial assault was by no means universally swift. The 2nd Royal Irish secured its objective but it had met with serious opposition; indeed, 16th Divisional battalions had mixed success in the battle. The 10th and 1st Dublin Fusiliers gained their objectives with astonishing swiftness and yet others, such as the 7/8th Royal Irish Fusiliers, were stopped in their tracks. Under fire, the 7th South Irish Horse undertook a seemingly straightforward operation to dig a communication sap to connect 'Lump Road' to 'Tunnel Trench'. As British artillery and SIH machine-guns laid down covering fire, a small group of forty men led by Lieutenant H. Brocklebank, went over the top and began feverish work in digging this vital artery. The result was apparently 'excellent' but not without cost. Such routine duties were often dangerous and casualties were to be expected. However, in this case, as Brocklebank's men dug, they accidentally struck and damaged a submerged gas shell. The subsequent leak affected some twenty-two of these forty-one men, including Lieutenant Brocklebank. Despite this, the construction of the communication trench assisted the remaining companies of the South Irish Horse to hold their front line when the Germans launched ultimately unsuccessful counter-attacks to the right.[36]

By the end of the first phase of Cambrai, three German lines were occupied and only an incomplete enemy trench line stood in the way of open countryside. An opportunity to deliver the elusive 'breakthrough' was truly in sight but the tanks had become bogged down, or broken down, and their crews and attendant infantry were exhausted. Indeed, with typical irony, it was not even known at the time that a gap was there to be exploited. There were not enough infantry and the cavalry, whose job this was traditionally, were deemed to be too susceptible to machine-gun fire to be of assistance. Despite this, the 5th Irish Lancers played a significant part during the grim battle. On 23 November, sudden orders were received to 'saddle-up' and ride to the designated concentration point; from there they were held in readiness to capitalise on any potential breakthrough. The next day, they were subsequently ordered, as part of their brigade, to take part in a mounted operation to recapture Bourlon Wood. However, on the morning of 25 November, it was realised that any kind of mounted action was deemed 'impossible' and, instead, the dismounted battalion, led by Captain Batten-Pooll MC, was sent 'up the line'. Two days later, this unit was manning the trench-line at Bourlon Wood, witnessing low altitude flights by German aircraft and under sustained enemy bombardment. It was noted that, due to the fine construction of the trenches in the wood, casualties were slight and the shellfire made little impact. Soon after, the engagement intensified and the German attempts to soften up the positions on the wood became ferocious. It was during this bombardment that one of the Lancer stretcher-bearers, Private George Clare, from Chatteris in Cambridgeshire, was posthumously awarded the Victoria Cross for tending to the wounded whilst under fierce shelling and machine-gun fire.[37]

With the battle of Bourlon Wood raging nearby, the 36th Division went into action again on 23 November to secure the Canal du Nord lines right up to the Hindenburg Support, whilst the 15th, 8th and 12th Irish Rifles went along with the 9th Irish Fusiliers. These troops were heavily engaged but could not gain a foothold. The next two day's fighting was similarly gruelling and, without necessary tank support, pointless. The Germans were not inactive either. When a unit of sixty Germans emerged down the Hindenburg Line, it was promptly wiped out by the sustained Lewis Gun fire of the North Belfast 15th Irish Rifles. On 30 November, Ludendorff launched a full counter-attack which, in many areas, pushed the British back to their original lines. As part of this struggle, the British needed to recapture the dominating Guislain Ridge (with its associated ravines known as Pigeon, Targelle and Quail), which had become a dangerous enemy-held salient, right in the centre of the Bourlon

Wood—St Quentin Line. On 1 December 1917, the 6th Inniskilling Dragoons and 2nd Indian Lancers (Gardner's Horse) attempted a sudden fully-deployed cavalry charge against the German defences at the sugar beet factory of Villers-Guislain. The British counter-assault was to be supported by tanks but these, perhaps true to form and luck, failed to appear in time. The resultant charge was tragically predictable. Against the Indian and Ulster cavalrymen were German machine-gun nests on the dominating slope but the men managed to secure and occupy the enemy trench and held it against counter-attacks until ordered to retire at dusk. By this time, the Inniskilling Dragoons had suffered 169 casualties and lost 187 horses in the attack. One of these, Captain Clement Joseph Bentley Bridgewater, led the forward squadron in its charge against the position and was killed along with many of his men; as the unit's war diary bluntly stated, none '...returned of the leading squadron'.[38] Despite this, the Allies had inched ever closer to the open countryside with fresh hopes for victory tempered by their own inability to successfully exploit their advantages.

The Last Christmas of the War

On 6 December, the 14th Irish Rifles and 9th Inniskillings launched an attack at La Vacquerie to recapture ground lost in the recent German counter-attacks and, as they swept onwards, the enemy melted away. The instinct to push forward was too great and platoons from both units were isolated and then duly ambushed by fresh German troops. During this engagement, 2nd-Lieutenant James Samuel Emerson, a 9th Inniskilling subaltern from Collon (Co. Louth), led an attack that secured some 400 yards of trench. However, in the immediate German counter-attack, his hand was smashed by a bullet whilst another round ripped through the top of his helmet. Nevertheless, 2nd-Lieutenant Emerson gathered eight 'Tyrones' and clambered from the trench not only to meet—but eventually to repel—the enemy with grenades and bayonets. By this time, Emerson was the only officer left in his company and he refused to leave his men despite his own wounds. Indeed, he organised their defence for a further three hours before he was fatally injured leading yet another attack against the enemy. He was posthumously awarded the VC.[39]

   With Christmas approaching and the Ulster Division still in line, worn out by both battle and the cold, Captain Cyril Falls commented that they had coped far better than any 'authority' that had kept them there had a '... right to expect'. Consequently, Major-General Nugent formally asked that the

Division be sent to rest quarters for the Christmas period. It was backed by medical services and relief was granted. By mid-December, the South Irish Horse Battalion was relieved by the 7/8th 'Skins' and had returned to billets at St Emilie, only for these to be subsequently shelled by the Germans on 12 December. The blasts ripped the billets apart, killing twenty-eight men and wounding forty, forcing the 7th (SIH) Royal Irish into emergency accommodation. Over the next few days they were to be employed in work building shelters and other construction duties under the guidance of the 'Hants Pioneers'. As December wore on, the weather became distinctly wintry with flurries of snow and periods of very bad visibility. Some men of the 16th (Irish) sent home divisional 'Christmas 1917' cards, with the green shamrock proudly displayed above the battle honours of Hulluch, Loos, Guillemont and Ginchy. At the top, the divisional motto simply stated 'Everywhere and Always Faithful'. On Christmas Day, the Irish regiments maintained the spirit as well as circumstances allowed. The 7th Leinsters celebrated '...Yuletide in the traditional manner...', but the 6th Royal Irish held a Divine Service followed by Christmas dinner; the 10th Inniskillings, the 'Derrys', did likewise, with their dinner being served to the men by their officers and NCOs. On the same day, the men of the South Irish Horse were back in the front-line at Lempire, replacing the 6th Connaughts and enduring a less than festive spell of heavy shelling that morning. Unbeknown to any of these weary survivors of 1917, it was to be the last Christmas of the war.[40]

CHAPTER NINE

'To put an end to Turkish rule...'[1]

Macedonia, Mesopotamia, Egypt and Palestine, 1915–1918

As fighting at the Western Front had rumbled on, other campaign theatres sprang up in attempts to outflank the deadlock there. Following on from the Dardanelles, the array of enemy nations faced by the Irish regiments grew to include the Bulgarians, the Austro-Hungarians and, of course, the varied troops of the Ottoman Empire. These campaigns, often dismissed as 'sideshows', perhaps give a far greater indication of the sprawling, encompassing nature of the First World War, from the grim fighting in Persia to the final push in Egypt and Palestine.

Arrival in Salonika (Salonica), 1915

In the regional powder-keg of the Balkans, Serbian forces had gruellingly managed to fight off the initial Austrian offensives of 1914 and had even taken to the offensive themselves. However, when Bulgaria entered the war on the side of Austria-Germany on 13 October 1914 and invaded from the south and east, Serbia's military options diminished considerably. Only two viable escape routes remained. The French Army was marching from the Greek port of Salonika in an effort to reinforce the Serbian Army at Monastir. When the Bulgarians blocked the route across the mountains, this vital lifeline was cut in a stroke. The Serbian Army was forced into exile and the 450,000-strong army crossed into Albania, constantly hampered and hindered by the severe cold weather, lack of food and the intense hostility of the locals. Eventually, a skeleton army reached the Adriatic where French, British and Italian ships evacuated them.

At this point, the British felt that the Allies should also disengage from Salonika although the French insisted that the Serbian front was still viable. After Gallipoli, Greece's official support for the Allies had dwindled considerably and it had declared a form of studied neutrality, although it did allow Allied use of Salonika as a transit base. The harbour town possessed three serviceable, but comparatively poor, railway lines that spread out to Monastir, Belgrade and Constantinople; in contrast, roads and routes into the interior were notoriously haphazard. The mountainous region of Macedonia was only a recent addition to Greek territory (as a result of the 1913 Balkan War) and comprised four main valleys: the Vistrista, Mesta, Vardar and Struma. With the mountain roads and passes frequently difficult to traverse, the river became the usual mode of transport and communication. Consequently, it was to the busy, dirty, cosmopolitan and politically baffling port of Salonika that the 10th (Irish) Division arrived in October 1915. The senior British commander in Greece was none other than Sir Bryan Mahon and he now had the opportunity to demonstrate his capabilities.[2]

The 10th Division had been regrouped on the island of Lemnos to prepare for service in Macedonia, with many battalions having been shattered by the Gallipoli experience. The near-constant attritional warfare on the peninsula had left the men exhausted and ill-equipped for the conditions ahead of them. By the time the 5th Inniskillings left Gallipoli, on 1 October, they had incurred a further 88 casualties, whilst the 7th Munsters arrived at Salonika with only 323 men. Consequently, recruits from two English regiments (the Oxfordshire and Buckinghamshire Light Infantry and Dorset Regiment) were used to fill the ranks of the 6th and 7th Munsters with an influx of 6 officers and 293 men and 10 officers and 498 men, respectively. Such fevered redeployment of reserves and recruits, intended for regiments elsewhere, was not untypical, nor was it particularly welcomed by most of those concerned.[3]

Equally, most of the Irish battalions arrived at the bustling port of Salonika woefully under-supplied for the harsh Balkan expedition. The 6th Munsters were not only under-strength but, upon arrival, immediately dogged by lack of suitable equipment and clothing for the Macedonian winter, namely greatcoats. Similarly, the 6th and 7th Royal Dublin Fusiliers arrived still wearing their cut-down khaki-drill uniforms. The incredibly arduous conditions were to lead to some of the highest instances of malaria and dysentery of the war and, as such, astonishing low points in morale. In the excruciatingly hot valleys or malarial-filled swamps and freezing passes of Macedonia, death from disease was to become commonplace. One early casualty was Dubliner, Joseph Byrne, 6th 'Skins', who was listed as one of the numerous men who 'died' during late October 1915. Consequently, logistical deficiencies and operational constraints became some of the most pressing challenges which General Mahon had to tackle. Additionally, he was only given War Office permission to co-operate with French General Serrail in late October, when 30th Brigade was moved northwards by train to Ghevgeli. By mid-November, the rest of the 10th Division, under Brigadier-General Lewis Lloyd Nicol, joined them.[4]

Retreat from Serbia and Defence of Kosturino Ridge

A few days later, the 10th Division took over a roughly ten-mile section of mountainous front line from the French near the border town of Kosturino, north of Lake Doiran. The roughly-cut trenches, where they existed, were at some 2–3,000 feet and, as November drew to a close, blizzards and snow-storms became commonplace. Temperatures plummeted in some parts of the line to a staggering minus thirty degrees and men simply froze to death from exposure. The 5th 'Skins' considered themselves relatively lucky as they had been recently issued with serge (woolen) uniforms but the majority of others were still in tropical drill, causing '… enormous cases of frostbite'. Then, on 4 December, the Bulgarian Army launched its bitter offensive with a massive artillery bombardment. Captain C.M.L. Becher and the 6th Irish Rifles watched as the shells cracked the rocky outcrops and exploded beyond their position but they had little real idea of what was going on. To their extreme north, a Coy of 7th Dublins and the 7th Munster Fusiliers held the Division's vulnerable left flank, secured to their right by the 5th Connaughts and 10th Hampshires. The centre was manned by the 5th and 6th Inniskillings but a projecting spur on the Division's central line, known as 'Rocky Peak', was held by the 5th Irish Fusiliers. Holding the right flank of the ridge were the 6th Irish Rifles, along with the 6th Leinsters. The remainder of the 7th Dublins, 6th Munsters, 6th Dublins and 5th Royal Irish were all, crucially, kept in reserve. To their front, a mere 1,000 yards ahead, was the 'Hill of Howth' and, beyond this, was the Bulgarian frontier.[5]

On 6 December, a general order to retreat was put into operation but, before it could be fully implemented, the Bulgarians (under General Teodoroff) struck against the junction between the French and British Armies.

In response, the 10th (Irish) Division found itself holding Kosturino Ridge to buy the French time to fall back upon the safety of the Vardar valley. At the same time, the Bulgarians launched a huge assault against the ridge, with some seven divisions smashing against the single Irish Division. They got within forty yards of the 5th Connaughts and were only driven back by determined volleys and flanking fire (including a sharp bayonet charge) from the 5th Royal Irish Fusiliers on 'Rocky Peak'. As the light failed, Bulgarian artillery furiously shelled the Irish lines and another sustained attack came, with the 6th Dublins rushed in to plug the gaps left by the wounded and dying amongst the Inniskillings at 'Rocky Peak'. In the lull, reassuring tin-urns of tea were brought up to the men as they worked at evacuating the injured from the ridge, all the while under an intermittent bombardment. For the 6th Leinsters, at least, it was noted how cheerful they remained, although one description of them being '... riotously happy ...' seems unlikely. Despite this, morale on the ridge seems to have been resilient. At dawn on 7 December, under the cover of a clawing early-morning fog, the Bulgarians clambered up 'Rocky Peak' and made a surprise attack on the 5th Irish Fusiliers trenches. In the mist, the other Irish units could hear the din of battle unfolding and then, worryingly, it went terrifyingly quiet. Although they had fought determinedly, the Fusiliers had been pushed off 'Rocky Peak' and the Bulgarians were now able to dominate the Irish trenches on either flank.[6]

The 5th Irish Fusiliers' withdrawal left the Connaughts particularly vulnerable to attack which, in the shrouding mist, duly came. They fought on all morning and each intensified Bulgarian assault on the northern flank trenches was repelled with bayonets and bullets. When the latter began to run out, volunteers ran back to Battalion HQ and gathered as much spare ammunition as they could to bring back to the firing line. It bought the Connaughts slightly more time but, as the Bulgarians made fiercer and more sustained attacks, the gaps in the Rangers' ranks began to tell. At around 2.30 pm, the final mass Bulgarian advance was renewed and, this time, the Connaughts had nothing left. In an act of distinctly raw Spartan courage, they clambered out of their trenches and attempted to hold the enemy with their bayonets. When the Connaughts finally pulled back from the ridge, 450 were dead, wounded or missing.[7]

On the left flank, the 7th Munsters fought off a determined Bulgarian assault and held their trenches until ordered to withdraw via 'Three Tree Hill' and Kajali Ravine. A second defence line had been rapidly established on a rise called Crete Simonet, and the battered battalions of the 10th wearily fell back towards it, digging in here on 8 December. Wary of the Bulgarians surging forward with their advantage, Brigadier-General Nicol ordered his division to hold this new line to the last. They were assisted by French infantry and a mountain battery but, again, Bulgarian numbers began to dictate the battle's flow. Eventually, Brigadier-General King-King's 31st Brigade, seemingly outflanked and in danger of being overwhelmed, was bolstered by the spirited 7th Munsters. They had just marched through the burning village ruins of Tartali and, being ravenous, had helped themselves to tins of bully beef from a stack of flaming supplies. By this time, Nicol decided that his entire position was in danger of being enveloped and reluctantly ordered a further fighting retreat through the Dedeli Pass, all the time liaising with the 156th French Divisional General, Bailloud. One of the last units to abandon Crete Simonet was the 7th Dublins who, seeing the Bulgarians swarming up its heights, delivered a final five rounds of rapid fire before they hastily scrambled down the other side.[8]

The stand along Kosturino Ridge, Rocky Peak and Crete Simonet was, perhaps, the most defining moment of the Salonika campaign for the 10th (Irish) Division. In three days of savage fighting, British official losses on the ridge amounted to 1,209 casualties, of which it was believed '…just over half…' were in the Hampshires and Connaughts. Yet, it is calculated that 10th Divisional losses totalled some 300 men killed, nearly 370 wounded and 384 missing (mostly captured wounded). Among the 7th Munster dead was twenty-six-year-old Harry Morgan, from Cardiff, whose mother lived at Barry Docks; another, Patrick Durnian, 6th Inniskillings, came from Coolcoghill, outside Brookeborough (Co. Fermanagh). He had been a general labourer before the war and left behind his deaf father, James, and his elder sister Annie, a lace worker. Similarly, John Barry, 7th Dublins, from Kilmore Quay, Wexford, had moved to Hereford and had enlisted in Maesteg. Alongside him was Francis McBrearty who had left his family home in Ballybofey (Co. Donegal) and had enlisted in the Inniskillings in Strabane before being sent to the 7th Dublins; his father was a pedlar and Francis had been a former telegraph boy. They were all killed on the freezing, bloody, slopes of Kosturino.

Yet, the heaviest losses were among the 5th Connaughts, with some ninety-seven lost on the splintered slopes of Kosturino, including Festus Joyce, aged thirty-three, from Clifden (Co. Galway), where his father was a boat-maker. He came from an Irish speaking and military family; his brother, Stephen had enlisted as a Regular in the Royal Artillery in Glasgow in 1903 whilst Festus had fought at Mons. It was possibly due to the actions at Kosturino, or the freezing winter, that during the following month a number of men from the 5th Connaughts smashed open crates of alcohol (possibly a form of the interestingly-termed *'koniak'*) and got roaring drunk.[9]

Mesopotamia—the Capture of Basra and Siege of Kut, April 1916

In the meantime, another campaign theatre was pressing. In November 1914, a small British force had captured the ancient port-town of Basra in the isolated Ottoman outpost of Mesopotamia. This exotic but largely desolate desert region was inhabited by nomadic tribes who were in a near-constant state of rebellion against their Turkish overlords. Roads were practically unheard of and any inhabited areas were generally confined to the scattered riverside settlements along the river Tigris. Despite its archaeological and biblical heritage, however, the territory appeared backward and unimportant. Yet, under its sands, was oil.

As such, the objective of the British Mesopotamian Expeditionary Force was to secure the vital oilfields of Abadan, run by the Anglo-Persian Oil Company. Indeed, General Sir Charles Townsend's British force advanced from Basra up the Tigris and captured Kut al Almara with relative ease. It was only when they were within a few miles of Baghdad that the Turks managed to regroup. They checked the British, firstly at Ctesiphon, and then pushed them back to Kut where they were promptly cut off and surrounded by forces commanded by Baron von der Goltz. This led to one of the most humiliating British episodes of the Great War. Townsend's strategic and tactical sense dissolved in a form of blind panic and personal deficiencies. He informed his army commander in Basra that his 'British' garrison (ignoring his Indian troops) had only enough food and water for a month; they actually had enough supplies to hold out for as long as four. Yet, this urgent appeal naturally prompted a relief expedition.[10]

In early January 1916, General Aylmer's relief force of 19,000 British and Indian Battalions was immediately thrown back at Shiek Sa'ad and the disastrous battle of Wadi. It was in the context of this that Lieutenant-Colonel Murray's 1st Connaught Rangers arrived at Basra on 10 January to fight in the harsh conditions of the Arabian Desert. Their first experience of the tragic Kut operations was on 21 January, during a cloudburst at Umm al Hanna, a defile between the Suwaikiya marshes and Tigris, where the Turks had encamped. The rainstorm was so violent that visibility was negligible when the Connaughts were ordered to support the troops to their front in an attack. As they advanced, they were slammed into by fleeing Indian troops and, having stumbled on, they were met by a hail of deadly Turkish musketry. In the subsequent confusion, Lieutenant-Colonel Murray was hit and casualties for the battalion amounted to over 280 men.[11]

The humiliating Siege of Kut was compounded by incompetent error upon error, with all attempts to break the Turkish grip on the town ending in miserable and agonising failure. With the garrison seemingly short of food, water and supplies, General Townsend surrendered on 29 April 1916. Thousands of British and Indian soldiers were taken prisoner and placed in appalling conditions, with many dying through malnutrition or violent beatings. Townsend, however, was whisked away from Kut to spend the rest of his war in a luxury villa by the Sea of Marmara.

At 'Thorny Nullah' the 1st Connaughts were part of a daring night attack in open order to re-capture the trench position near Abu Roman. However, in the dark, the Connaughts got lost and went past their objective. Instead, they rushed the main Turkish trenches at Abu Roman, securing them in a brisk bayonet battle. In the confusion, the Turks holding 'Thorny Nullah' soon disappeared and this position was occupied properly by the 1st Connaughts at first light. Whilst more than seventy Connaughts had been killed or wounded, they had taken some sixty Turkish prisoners and captured their initial objective. Among their losses was Michael Cloherty, aged twenty-two and a general labourer from Galway prior to enlistment; he came from an Irish speaking household and left a widowed mother behind. Also among the Ranger dead was former farm labourer, twenty-six-year-old Joseph Rogers from Banagher Co. Laois/King's County whose father worked in a distillery and whose mother was a housecleaner. As with the conditions in Macedonia, the mixture of heat, cold and disease also took an intolerable toll and many Connaughts died without a shot being fired. They spent the summer months in trenches and beset by a rampant malaria epidemic. In the face of this misery, General Alymer's force had already retired from Kut before its surrender but the campaign still went limping painfully on.[12]

Defence of Salonika and the Struma Valley, 1916–1917

Meanwhile, the 1st Royal Irish Regiment had sailed for Salonika at the end of 1915, accompanied by the 1st Leinsters and 2nd Irish Fusiliers, as part of the 27th Division. At the same time, Major-General J.R. Longley arrived to assume permanent command of the 10th (Irish) Division. They all arrived to find widespread construction work around the port with soldiers transformed into navvies, preparing defences (the 'Entrenched Camp') to the north of the city. So much barbed wire was used around Salonika, from the Vardar marshes to the Gulf of Orfano, that it was wryly referred to as the 'Birdcage'. In fact, British forces in the region were now five divisions strong but many troops were busy with shovels rather than rifles. The 1st Royal Irish slaved away on the Seres Road in the Struma Valley whilst the 6th Leinsters, 6th Irish Rifles and the pioneers of 5th Royal Irish were transported by ship to the Gulf of Rendina to work on defences there. They worked in the harsh wintry conditions for almost four months, in weather which was unimaginably cold. As one Inniskilling officer recalled, if a greatcoat was taken off, a soldier simply '... stood it up on the floor'.[13]

In contrast, when the weather improved, the intense heat of the day became a major problem and revision of the daily routine became paramount. As spring turned into summer, the malarial mosquito became a detested intruder and one that ripped once healthy platoons apart. Yet, in general, the Macedonian theatre was considered to be a quiet posting and one which, whilst frequently uncomfortable, seemed fairly free of warfare. Of all the divisions at Salonika, it was the 10th (Irish) which had the fiercest fighting reputation. Indeed, as a young Englishman, William Rule, noted when he was attached to 31st Field Ambulance, he looked forward to wearing its famous green stripes on his sleeves, as they had a '... bit of honour attached to them'. Certainly, the men of the field ambulances did their best as they attempted to help men afflicted by malaria, dysentery and heatstroke. During the difficult advance up the Struma Valley, in June 1916, CQMS John McIlwain of the 5th Connaughts noted that many men fainted due to the intense heat on the march. The next day, they were harangued by their officers with threats of disciplinary action. It is also worth noting that in May, Lieutenant-General Sir Bryan Mahon was promoted to command the 'Western Desert Force' in Egypt but was struck down with heat-stroke soon after he arrived and had to be invalided home.[14]

Although route-marching and road-working were to become part of the accepted routine, there were still brisk and bitter engagements with the enemy. In one incident, Corporal Robert Gibney, 5th Irish Fusiliers, from Banbrook Hill (Co. Armagh), was awarded the DCM when he held a trench all day with only six men and, although wounded, would not retreat until he was directly ordered to do so. Corporal Gibney was a Boer War and Gallipoli veteran who had been an instructor in the Armagh National Volunteers in

1914. Contrastingly, at Salonika base camp, men worked hard at fatigues but had ample chance for recreation. On 12 July, a group of Orangemen from Omagh and Dungannon planned a celebration for the battle of the Boyne, to be held by a chestnut tree outside the city. Fascinatingly, the event was widely attended by men of all persuasions within the 10th Division and Worshipful Brother Thomas Campbell particularly thanked Private P. McQuillan of Moneymore '… their esteemed Catholic comrade…' for arranging such wide support. This sentiment was reiterated when a 'Brother Currie' thanked all their Catholic friends for accepting the invitation to attend the Boyne commemoration adding that the '…good-fellowship would survive the great struggle now going on'. Sadly, Private Peter McQuillan, who had enlisted in the 5th Connaughts in Glasgow and was a recipient of the Military Medal, was killed on 10 October 1918 in France. Some gatherings were more raucous, such as the celebrations for St Patrick's Day 1917, when men 'drowned the Shamrock' with too much 'koniak' and it was noted that there were less than a dozen sober men in camp.[15]

From late May 1916, the Bulgarian pressure and invasion of Greece had failed (despite the Greek surrender of Rupel Fort, guarding the crucial pass), providing the Allies with an opportunity to start operations against them. The British, who did not wish to begin an active offensive in the height of summer, were content to assist the French offensive by maintaining the defence of the Struma Valley. Ivor Powell recollected that when the 6th Leinsters had to patrol the Doiran Railway near Yanash, there was always a sense of uneasiness with the threat of ambush as they '…never quite knew what might happen'.[16] As the 10th Division criss-crossed the arid terrain, frequently in temperatures above a hundred degrees, they were beset with logistical problems, from communication to transport. As the summer wore on, the malarial mosquito continued to wreak havoc amongst the men.

In the autumn, Karajakois was captured, swiftly followed by Yenikoi on 3–4 October. The 1st Royal Irish and 1st Leinsters were still employed on road-building duties whilst the 27th Division was involved in the Yanokoi operation, with the much-depleted 10th Division. Indeed, despite being under-strength from disease, the town was attacked and captured by the 7th Munsters and 6th Dublins, with the 6th Irish Rifles, 6th Munsters and 7th Dublins in support. Later, the 6th Inniskillings and 5th Irish Fusiliers crossed the Struma as reinforcements, whilst the 1st Leinsters and 1st Royal Irish (still held in reserve on the heights) cheered the men on below. Soon the Rupel

Pass was secured and the Irish regiments went back to the contrasting routine of back-breaking repair work mixed with the unique attractions of the port of Salonika. During the battles of Karajakois and Yenikoi, 189 officers and other ranks were killed outright; one of these was Thomas Cullen from Kilmainham, Dublin, who had won the DCM at Gallipoli only to die with the 6th Dublins the following year.[17]

The next month saw a number of structural changes as the fractured 10th (Irish) battalions were regrouped. On 3 November, the 7th Munsters were officially merged with their 6th Battalion; the 6th Irish Fusiliers were subsumed by the 5th 'Faughs' the day before and three Regular Irish battalions (1st Royal Irish, 2nd Irish Fusiliers and 1st Leinsters) were drafted to the 10th Division. For the following nine months, the Division's war service comprised of sudden marches, assaults and small-scale actions which were part of a broader offensive thrust. Accordingly, the war in Macedonia was fought in a very different manner to the one on the Western Front and, despite the brutal conditions, unexpected opportunities for humour were rife. One officer of the 1st Leinsters noted that his men frequently enjoyed a '...joke and to make one...' which may suggest that this particular English subaltern might have been on the receiving end of some Leinster witticisms. Indeed, Captain Verschoyle recounted one story which ably demonstrates the impish relationship between officers and men in the Irish regiments. His platoon sergeant had a '... wicked sense of fun...' and somehow managed to acquire a goat up in the Macedonian mountains, which he turned into an appetising meal. In preparation for the meal he had also found some raw chillies which he then proffered to Verschoyle, innocently adding that the officer should try them as they were very tasty. Captain Verschoyle had never had chillies before, eagerly ate them and '... nearly burnt my whole inside out'. Nearly fifty years later, Terrence Verschoyle still laughed about it and believed that such an inter-rank prank could only have happened in an Irish regiment. Equally, all ranks in the 6th Leinsters had immense fun at the eccentric behaviour of Lieutenant Pickup, who decided to amass an extensive butterfly and beetle collection that hardly left him any space to sleep in his tent.[18]

Yet, from the point of view of the wider campaign, the stagnation of the military situation in Macedonia changed in May 1917, largely as a result of the revolution against the Greek King and his anti-Allied policies. Indeed, by June, the new Greek Government entered the war against Germany and Bulgaria, freeing up British troops who could be released elsewhere. Consequently,

Major-General Longley and the 10th (Irish) found themselves with a new campaign in an old theatre of war.

Mesopotamia and the Fall of Baghdad, 1916–1917

Meanwhile, in August 1916, General Sir Stanley Maude had been appointed to take command of British forces in Mesopotamia and, whilst Kut remained their objective, his immediate concern was Turkish dominance of the region. The enemy now controlled a sprawling front, which included the Perisan Gulf, the Tigris and the Euphrates. In order to tackle this directly, he slowly built up his forces in the Tigris region, in an effort to thrust towards Baghdad, and waited for the cooler winter campaigning season. Basra was reinforced and its railway systems expanded considerably; proper hospitals and supply depots were established and, perhaps most importantly, inland water transportation was developed.

In December 1916, a renewed assault was made on Kut with concerted pressure from aerial bombardment and trench raids. On 24 February 1917, the Turks finally retreated and the town was captured by General Maude, followed by Baghdad on 11 March. The veteran Turks withdrew northwards, fighting every inch of the way and, by the end of April, the 1st Connaughts were at Feluja and Baghdad. Their duties here were mainly policing and garrison details with other battalions, including the securing of the seventy-mile-long Baghdad railway. The 1st Connaughts were also in the general advance northwards to the new front line near Tekrit, at Samarra (where the railway terminated). When the Turkish defenders withdrew once more, the area became subject to the whims of the ever-hostile local tribesmen.

Since their arrival, the 1st Connaughts had, in effect, spent two years wasting away in the searing and disease-ridden dust of Mesopotamia, for very little gain. It is thought that a significant number of the men posted to the battalion had suffered from the effects of sun-stroke, dysentery or cholera at some point during the campaign, but the final battalion death rates for the period were still a sobering 286 men. Of this number, perhaps two-thirds were as a result of enemy action, with Private John Breen from Stratford killed during the April advance of 1917, whilst Private James Cassidy from Armagh died of disease in early 1918. It must have been with considerable relief–and not a little exasperation–that they embarked on 2 April 1918 from Nahr Umar for further desert duty—this time in Egypt and Palestine.[19]

161

Egypt and Palestine, 1917–1918

With the hardships of Macedonia behind them, the 10th Division was sent to Egypt in September 1917, in preparation for the Palestinian campaign, under the command of the former Inniskilling Dragoon, General 'Bull' Allenby. Most Irish battalions found themselves at Alexandria for the second time in their war careers, where they entrained for the Suez Canal rest-camp in preparation for the great offensive at Gaza. Indeed, the fighting in the Holy Land was to be a 'fluid' style of warfare against the Turks, in equally difficult climatic conditions but with seemingly greater relevance. It was an ancient land, resonant with the weight of Biblical and military history but with only one metalled road (the Great North Road) which ran from Beersheba to Jerusalem and followed the crest of the Judean Hills. Consequently, transport of everything, from ammunition, water and wounded, was done by mule, donkey or camel. Indeed, transportation was usually done by camel, especially the evacuation of wounded which was excruciatingly painful. One 6th Leinster recalled being wounded by Turkish shrapnel and the painful journey to a field ambulance, strapped to a pannier on the side of a camel.[20]

In early November, the 6th Leinsters had a long arduous march across the Sinai desert, being '...very short of water'. In fact, wells became an essential objective, to secure the water supply for transport and any further advance. As part of the initial phases of the Third Battle of Gaza, the 10th Division was pivotal in the capture of the vital wells at Beersheba. November saw almost constant fighting, with assaults on the Turkish positions at the Sheria, Rushdi—and the most formidable—Hureira Redoubts during the final stages of the battle of Third Gaza. The attack was delivered on 6 November, across a two-mile-wide plain devoid of any cover; the advancing battalions traversed this in artillery formation until they reached the Turkish trenches. The 2nd and 5th Irish Fusiliers punched their way into the Turkish lines and the enemy retreated towards the stronger Hureira position. The capture of this Redoubt was left to the 10th (Irish) on 7 November and, although the 2nd Irish Fusiliers met fierce resistance, the 6th Inniskillings managed to outflank the Turkish line and drove them out.[21]

The push for Jerusalem was slow and measured, dictated by the need to keep the supply of water steady and constant. General Allenby hoped to keep any fighting out of the city and aimed to sever the Turks from their own lines of supply by strangling the Jerusalem–Nablus road. Some of the applied pressure came from the 29th Brigade, with 6th Leinsters, 2nd Irish

Fusiliers, 5th Connaughts and 6th Rifles, occupying the Beit Duqqu sector on the outskirts of the city. Due to the nature of the terrain, defences were rocky sangars built above ground, but these were still dominated by Turkish fire from the opposing heights. During one patrol, Lieutenant-Colonel John Craske, 6th Leinsters, was scouting machine-gun outposts when he decided to sit down and wait for the gunfire to subside, only to be hit in the arm by a Turkish sniper. Nevertheless, the pressure on the supply route succeeded and Jerusalem surrendered on 9 December, with the majority of its Turkish garrison withdrawing towards Nablus. It is of great credit to both its Turkish defenders and General Allenby that the inhabitants of the city did not have to endure the savagery of siege warfare. Indeed, the entry into Jerusalem had a profound effect, as Ivor Powell, 6th Leinsters, noted. The sense of religious history was all-pervasive, especially when they walked up the hill of Golgotha, where Christ '... walked on the way to his crucifixion'. Yet, the war in Palestine continued apace.[22]

However, some battalions from the 10th Division, such as the 5th Connaughts, were detached to work on repairing and maintaining the main road towards the British railhead depot at Ludd, with the obvious signs of their Irish presence being confirmed by the placenames 'Connaught Road' and 'Ranger Corner'. At Kereina Peak in the Judah Hills on 27 December, two stretcher-bearers from the 6th Inniskillings were attempting to bring in the wounded from the firing line when one of them was hit. The other, James Duffy from Letterkenny (Co. Donegal), dashed back to fetch another bearer who was soon also wounded. Accordingly, Duffy worked by himself, under vicious fire, to bring in both the wounded bearers and patch them up as best he could. For this act of selfless courage he was awarded the VC.[23]

Operations in the Jordan Valley and Battle of Tell'Asur, 1918

The British pursuit of the Turks continued into the New Year and, as part of General Allenby's operations in the Jordan Valley, Jericho fell and the 10th fought its last major action as an Irish Division at Tell'Asur. This action was, initially, an attempt to secure the prominent Kalrawani Ridge near to the Wadi-El-Jib where the Turks were putting up determined resistance in the surrounding hills. Objectives for 30th and 31st Brigades were the two villages of 'Atara and 'Ajul, which held the crossing points over the Wadi; 29th Brigade was to take the line from Deir-es-Sudan to Nabi Salih. The fighting, from

9–10 March, involved every Irish battalion and the attack was carried out with great swiftness. The 2nd Irish Fusiliers captured positions at Sheir Kalrawani, weakening Turkish defences at 'Ajul. Meanwhile, the 5th Irish Fusiliers fought their way into 'Atara and the 1st Leinsters and 6th Irish Rifles swept into the trenches at Deir-es-Sudan and Deir-Nidham. The 5th Connaughts stormed the heights above Wadi-el-Jib, which were taken after approximately five hours of fighting. The next morning, the 1st Royal Irish set out at dawn and finally captured the key village of 'Ajul just after midday. Due to the gains made along the entire line on the first day, a composite attack by men from the 1st Royal Irish and 5th Royal Irish Fusiliers was sent against two enemy-held hills that overlooked the new positions. Again, at exactly 1.30 am, the leading two companies began their advance towards the hills but, finding the terrain almost impossible to navigate, they quickly telephoned Battalion HQ to warn them.

The advance was difficult and slow, as they had firstly to clamber down the irregular slopes of the Wadi which they had captured the day before and then climb up the steep sides of the Turkish-held hills. The 1st Royal Irish suffered 113 officers and men killed or wounded in the process, as the Turks bombed and fired down upon them from directly above. Captain Jeremiah O'Brien, aged twenty-six and from Cork, was killed leading 'D' Company in its precarious assault up the terraces where it was forced back upon itself, whereupon it regrouped with the survivors of 'B' Company. These few men again attempted to storm the crest at bayonet point but were beaten back by very steady and calm Turkish fire which claimed the lives of many men. Despite this, the position was duly taken in the early evening of 10 March, when the remnants of the 1st Royal Irish, supported by the 6th Dublins finally drove the Turks from the crest. The fallen from the battalion were buried on its summit and the position was renamed 'Clonmel Hill'—a fitting testimony to the 1st Royal Irish's participation in the battle of Tell'Asur.[24]

The Final Days in Palestine, April–October 1918

In April and May, the 10th (Irish) Division became 'Indianised', with the volunteer Irish battalions either disbanded or sent to France and Flanders. The resultant gaps in the Division were filled by units of the Indian Army, meaning that only three Irish battalions remained in the Division: the 1st Leinsters, the 1st Royal Irish and 2nd 'Faughs'. The experience of the 6th Irish Rifles Volunteer Battalion is perhaps typical. At the end of April, they made a successful attack on 'Sausage Hill', during the assault on Mezra. They were relieved by a Sikh regiment on 13 May and, finally, after many years of difficult campaigning, they were officially disbanded two days later at Deir en Nidham. By 15 April, another Irish battalion arrived for service in Palestine, with the 1st Connaughts landing at Suez from Mesopotamia. Throughout this period of structural change, the pursuit of the Turkish Army continued until the final dramatic offensive on Nablus.

In September, as the 29th and 31st Brigades eroded the Turkish hold over the surrounding environs, the 2nd Irish Fusiliers and 1st Leinsters fought to oust the Turks (assisted by German machine-gunners) from their trenches. During this fight, Private Michael Davis, aged thirty and from a farm in Cloontrask (Co. Roscommon), was killed; he was the only child of his widower father, Martin. Throughout the night of 19 September, the 1st Royal Irish had been on back-breaking road repair work at Wadi-el-Mutwy when they were ordered up to punch through the Nablus line. In the early hours of 21 September, they advanced across the southern plain and stormed Rajib, under direct fire from 29th Brigade's objective at Huwara. The engagement at this Turkish-held village was notably violent, with the Royal Irish capturing their objective in a ferocious bayonet-charge. This feat was all the more impressive given the fact that the men had virtually remained awake and active in duties, marching or fighting, for the previous forty-eight hours. In the associated assault on the Turkish HQ at Nazareth, the 1st Connaughts captured 'Fir Hill' from the enemy and, from here, were sent against the town of El Funduk, where the Turks had embedded an artillery column. This was captured in its entirety, which may also demonstrate that the general Turkish appetite for war had fairly dissolved. Within ten days, Damascus was taken and when the Armistice with Turkey finally came, on 31 October, the 1st Royal Irish was stationed at Burka, just outside Nablus. As the war ended in the Holy Land, an Armistice duly came into force in Mesopotamia on 1 November. By then, the 1st Connaughts were in Nazareth and the news of the Armistices coincided with a particularly fatal strain of malaria which swept the city and reduced their ranks still further.[25]

The war in Macedonia, Mesopotamia and Palestine had been achingly miserable and costly in lives. It had left a deep legacy on the men who served there, with relapses of ill-health or painful memories of the harsh conditions they had witnessed. Equally, it was all too apparent that the fighting on the Western Front was now undertaken in a nightmarish world. Other campaigns would drift from public consciousness and, as Irish Fusilier officer, Lieutenant Arthur Smith noted, many acts of courage ('… comrade giving life for comrade…') would be forgotten as the war rumbled to its awful conclusion.[26]

CHAPTER TEN

'The German offensive has begun...'[1]

The German Somme Offensive— 'Kaiserslacht', March 1918

B ack on the Western Front, by mid-December 1917, it was clear that there were major problems within Gough's Fifth Army. Since the end of Passchendaele, it had been placed in the reserve, in an attempt to reset and bolster its all-but exhausted units. By now, it had something of a whispered reputation for being a badly led graveyard for good soldiers. Even Field Marshal Haig had told Gough (the Senior Officer at the heart of the Curragh Incident and the disastrous assault on Langemarck) that Divisional Generals (and below) openly hoped they would not get transferred to Fifth Army.

Following the Russian Revolution, a mass of German manpower and resources, some fifty divisions, was about to descend upon the Western Front. Haig and the Allied High Command braced themselves for the inevitable onslaught and, again, it would fall upon the Somme. From the German perspective, 1918 was to be pivotal. The terrible slaughter at Passchendaele, referred to by General von Kuhl (Chief of Staff in Flanders) as the '... greatest martyrdom...' of the war, had a profound effect on the German military psyche. As such, German High Command reviewed its offensive capabilities at a conference held at Mons on 11 November 1917. There, General Erich Ludendorff decided that Germany could only muster one last great offensive against Britain before the United States' contribution took effect. Furthermore, he determined that any such offensive should take place by February or March

1918. This Spring Offensive would be launched mainly against the section of front held by the British Fifth Army under General Gough.[2]

The area chosen as the main thrust for the German offensive, St Quentin, included their formidable Hindenburg Line (securely positioned between Arras in the north and Chemin des Dames in the south), and this was clearly Britain's most exposed point. Indeed, Field Marshal Haig was aware that Gough's Fifth Army was not up to strength but seemed content that, should an attack come, Gough would be able to defend his line. Yet, for the Allies, any German pressure on the fragile link between the British Fifth and the French Sixth Armies, south of St Quentin, was a very real threat. If the British divisions holding this vital zone—including the 36th (Ulster) and 16th (Irish)—were forced back, then the French would be too. Should this happen, a gap would appear which led directly to Paris. Into this gap would stream Germany's new weapon—the mass use of specialist assault infantry, or stormtroopers, fighting in small, *hutier* (also termed 'infiltration') tactical units. Throughout the winter of 1917–1918, the finest of these German troops were formed into massed 'attack divisions' and trained incessantly.

Re-organisation on the Somme, January–March 1918

In January 1918, Fifth Army took over around forty-two miles of front line, with the 36th Division in XVIII Corps and the 16th Division in VII Corps. It was seen to be a quiet sector and, each day, casualties were relatively light. Yet, in early February, a bewildering series of divisional and regimental re-organisations occurred, largely due to the previous year's losses and lack of manpower. The axe seemed to fall particularly heavily upon the regiments of the 16th (Irish) Division. The official organisational order for the 16th Division said that, of the original battalions, only the 6th Connaughts, 7th (SIH) Royal Irish Regiment and 7/8th Inniskillings were to be retained. Battalion Commanders were informed which battalions were to absorb their units and it was their duty to reallocate personnel. It was stated, quite simply, that battalions had been chosen for '…certain territorial reasons…' and to protect the Regular or Yeomanry Regiments. The 16th (Irish) also lost Major-General Hickie at this time; he was replaced by Major-General Sir Amyatt Hull, who had no Irish connections, although he was considered a fine commander. With the atmosphere of battalion culls, Major-General Nugent was convinced that he too would be sent home, especially when he heard from Haig's Chief of Staff that divisional command was now to be given to '… younger men'.[3]

By 23 February, the gallant 7th Leinsters had been officially disbanded and most of its soldiers had been sent to the 2nd Battalion or, worse still, dispersed within the Labour Corps units of the '19th Entrenching Battalion'. The last entry in their war diary stated sadly that, with all their men dispersed and their stores and transport reallocated, they had '…ceased to exist…' and that their '…account is accordingly brought to a close'. Although the original volunteers of the Dublin Fusiliers continued to exist for a short while within 48th Brigade as the 8/9th Dublins, by February they too had been completely broken up and their strength had been equally distributed between the 1st and 2nd Dublins; similarly, the men of the 10th Dublin 'Commercial Pals' were struck off the Army List and redistributed. Like many other battalions, the 7/8th Irish Fusiliers were simply sent to where the need was greatest. The 6th Connaughts were perhaps lucky to survive the February cull but, already pathetically understrength, they were in no state to meet the oncoming German storm. Their fellow battalion in 47th Brigade, the 6th Royal Irish, was disbanded on 9 February at Saulcourt. Its men were distributed between the 2nd Royal Irish and the 7th (South Irish Horse) Royal Irish Battalion. Accordingly, a large contingent of over 300 men from the 6th Royal Irish arrived at Villers-Faucon the following day to join the 7th South Irish Horse.[4]

Equally, the Ulster Division saw painful reorganisation too. Many of the old units of Ulster Volunteers who had fought so well on 1 July were abruptly dissolved. The 8/9th Irish Rifles (East and West Belfast UVF) had been amalgamated after Langemarck and, in February, they were disbanded. Similarly, the 11th and 13th Rifles ('1st County Downs' and 'South Antrims') had been merged in late 1917 but they did not survive the February reorganisation. Neither did the men of the 10th (South Belfast) or the 14th (YCV) Irish Rifles; all of these men were redistributed amongst the remaining, or newly arrived, units of the Division. The 10th and 11th Royal Inniskillings ('Derrys' and 'Donegals') had already been disbanded in January and many volunteers were transferred to the 2nd 'Skins' with Colonel Lord Farnham, previous CO of the 'Derrys', appointed to command the new battalion. The 1st Inniskillings were finally sent to 109th Brigade and eventually reunited with the 2nd Inniskillings, which was also transferred to the same Brigade. Equally, the 1st Irish Rifles spent most of the war with the 25th Brigade of the 8th Division, until reorganisation transferred them to 107th Brigade in the Ulster Division. Even the 2nd Irish Rifles, frequently noted for its Nationalist sympathies, was sent to join the strongly Unionist 36th Division (which raised some eyebrows, according to John Lucy) and 108th Brigade, before being reallocated to 107th Brigade.[5]

In early 1918, the 1st Regiment North Irish Horse was mostly employed in fatigue work or military police duties but, whilst at Barly, on 18 February, the regiment was officially informed that it was to become the North Irish Cyclist Regiment. Over the next few days, the obviously painful process of sending the horses to their new homes began. By mid-March, all the regiment's horses had been distributed to the Transport Section, Base Remount Section or Veterinary Hospital. The men of the old Squadrons, North Irish Horse, must have been heartbroken to see their mounts dispersed so matter-of-factly and even more dejected when they arrived at Bapaume and were force-marched to Villers-au-Flos only to be remounted again—this time on bicycles.[6]

For the original Volunteers of the 16th and 36th Divisions, it was a deeply unsettling experience as new recruits, drafted from any available recruitment centre, filled up the ranks left by dead or wounded comrades. The fabled divisional ethos of both formations was certainly diluted if not actually dissipated. However, this reorganisation of battalions and squadrons was widespread. On 8 February 1918, the 2nd Irish Guards Battalion transferred to the 4th Guards Brigade, as part of the 31st (Yorkshire and Lancashire) Division. This Division had already had its 94th Brigade broken up and this had been temporarily replaced by the 4th Guards Brigade. That month also saw the disbandment of three Tyneside Irish battalions of the Northumberland Fusiliers, effectively removing the Tyneside 'Irish Brigade' from the Army List. Only one original battalion remained—the 2nd Tyneside Irish—which was duly moved to 116th Brigade of the 39th Division. In the same month, the 5th Indian Cavalry Division was disbanded and its brigades and regiments were scattered. As a result, the 8th King's Royal Irish Hussars were finally transferred to the 9th Cavalry (Hussar) Brigade of the 1st Cavalry Division (along with the 15th and 19th Hussars) for the remainder of the war.[7]

Preparations against the 'Kaiser's Battle', January–March 1918

A complete 'root and branch' reorganisation of the British defence system to absorb any German offensive action was also underway. As the British had discovered to their cost the previous year, Germany used the practice of 'elastic defence'; instead of defending their front to the last man, they garrisoned an 'outpost' line of small, supported, concrete forts, beyond their 'real' trench lines. Their function was to bluntly absorb an assault and inflict maximum casualties on the attacker. All efforts were focused on halting an enemy breakthrough before it had time to begin, rather than doggedly defending a section of front. Consequently, British High Command followed suit with the 'defence-in-depth' principle, adapting it accordingly.

By March 1918, the British system was effectively a 'three zone defence'; this was in response to a theory which had been put together, hastily in terms of its physical manifestation, but which was virtually untried. Defence of the British line relied on the 'zones' of 'Forward', 'Battle' and 'Rear', each with their own specific strategic role to play. Those advanced battalions in the Redoubts of the 'Forward Zone' were to keep an enemy attack at bay long enough for Reserves and support troops to man the 'Battle Zone' positions (Red, Yellow and Brown Lines). This was the real zone of defence, where everything at the disposal of the troops would be brought to bear upon the enemy and would, theoretically, push them back or crush them. For this to work successfully, however, it was vital that the troops holding the Forward Zone areas knew that their position was 'fluid' and that, when pressured, they would release ground and regroup in the Red Line.

Neither had it been envisaged that these forward units would be suddenly overwhelmed or surrounded by the enemy—a situation which may clearly oblige them to fight to the death or surrender. Yet, as Gough later admitted, these forward units were considered expendable and would be expected to hold onto the Forward Zones with their lives. With what was, perhaps, typical military amateurism, or optimism, what had taken the Germans years to construct was cobbled together by the British in a matter of months. Indeed, by March, the relevant defences were only partially constructed (or not even begun). When the 2nd Leinsters were ordered to keep one Coy in the front and pull everyone else back to the mid-Battle Zone (Yellow Line), they politely informed their superiors that such a line did not, at present, exist.[8]

The 'Kaiserslacht' *(Michael* Offensive) Begins, 21 March

In the early hours of 21 March, at 3.30 am, the Germans opened their offensive with a blistering bombardment. The shelling, including High Explosive and chlorine, mustard and tear gas, lasted for five hours. It was so severe that communications and telephone wires were snuffed out and, despite attempts at a counter-bombardment, British artillery batteries were effectively silenced. Even veterans of the First Somme or Passchendaele found this experience distinctly unnerving. The hurried order to 'man battle stations' flew down the through the British lines. To their front, under this maelstrom of shell and gas, the German trench mortars flattened the entanglements and barbed wire.

Then, in the early morning fog at 8.30 am, seventy-six crack German 'assault divisions' emerged from their lines and dashed towards the British Third and Fifth Armies. Along the ridge of Ronssoy, Lempire and Epehy, the 16th (Irish) Division defended a 2,000 yard frontage and the 2nd and 7th (SIH) Royal Irish, with two companies each from the 1st and 2nd Dublins and 2nd Munsters, manned the Forward Zone. Similarly, two companies from these regiments defended the Battle Zone behind, along with the 7/8th Inniskillings. The 6th Connaughts, 2nd Leinsters and 1st Munsters were with 47th Brigade in the reserve. The Forward Zone at St Quentin was held by the 36th (Ulster), with the 12th and 15th Irish Rifles and 2nd Inniskillings holding 'Jeanne d'Arc', 'Racecourse' and 'Boadicea' Redoubts. Behind them, the Battle Zone was garrisoned by 1st Irish Fusiliers, 1st Irish Rifles and 1st Inniskillings, with the associated 'Station', 'Quarry' and 'Ricardo' Redoubts. Waiting in the reserve, the 9th Irish Fusiliers, 2nd Irish Rifles and 9th Inniskillings seemed very far from the front line. As the morning broke across the lines of the 36th and 16th Divisions, visibility, due to the thick fog in front of their trenches, was almost impossible; the 2nd Royal Irish discovered that they had difficulty seeing their own wire.[9] Under the cover of this smothering mist, the German stormtroopers launched their blistering assault, with every soldier aware how important the upcoming attack would be. In the words of Feldwebel Max Schulz, 46th (1st Lower Silesian) Infantry Regiment this, their final battle, '... would be decisive'.[10] The 16th (Irish) and 36th (Ulster) Divisions were at the forefront of this German offensive and, all along the British line, a series of desperate holding actions were fought at the Forward Zone Redoubts. As planned, the German stormtroopers simply surrounded these strong-points and moved on, leaving the defenders pinned to their positions. However, the contests at these forward Redoubts soon became self-contained battles of their own, with the British helpless to halt the advances on either side of them and with the Germans incapable of using their mortars to reduce the strong-points.

Death, Retreat or Surrender...

At Ronssoy, the forward companies of the 7th (SIH) Royal Irish were obliterated as the German stormtroopers smashed through them; in fact, the Germans reached Ronssoy village before any alarm could be raised and practically swamped the Battalion HQ and remaining two companies. The fight at Ronssoy was desperate and, perhaps predictably, doomed. The remnants of the battalion were ordered to withdraw but, with most men and all but one officer wounded, it became a dire question of scraping as many men together as possible. Similarly, the 7/8th Inniskillings found themselves utterly and suddenly overwhelmed. The Battalion HQ had only discovered it was under attack when the men inside were bewilderingly surrounded and had to fight their way out. Lieutenant-Colonel Walkey was wounded in the process and many more battalion officers were either killed, wounded or captured; one of these men was the newly promoted Major Parr. Indeed, the shock of the attack was palpable. Not one company officer was left standing and, as a result, it became '… impossible to form a connective narrative of what happened'.[11]

Elsewhere along the line, other Forward Zone strong-points were quickly surrounded and forced to fend off attack after attack. The 'Racecourse' was one of the first of the Redoubts held by the 36th Division to be assaulted; a company of the 15th Royal Irish Rifles (and its Battalion HQ) found itself quickly submerged by the enemy advance and severed from its Battle Zone. However, the 'Boadicea' Redoubt, manned by Colonel Lord Farnham and the 2nd Inniskillings, had been overlooked in the initial German barrage and, as a result, it was in a far better position to withstand a sustained German assault. The attacking stormtroopers of the 1st Battalion of the 463rd Infantry Regiment, a unit drawn mostly from Hamburg, swept past 'Boadicea', leaving its 2nd Battalion to take the Redoubt. They brought up trench mortars and a bloody slogging-match began. Similarly, the majority of the 2nd Royal Irish defended the crest of the 16th Division's line, at scattered trenches and outposts in Lempire. Consequently, the Battalion's strength was strung out and easily swallowed by the rapid and destructive German advance. By 10.30am much of Lempire had been taken by the enemy and an unhelpful British barrage only succeeded in adding further casualties. Yet, the Allied troops made an extremely gallant stand and attempted to hold onto small pockets of their position, without support (nor any hope of such), for many hours.[12]

By late morning, the 6th Connaughts were still in reserve at Villers-Faucon and had taken cover during the German shelling in the 'anti-air-bomb' trenches by their rest huts. These usually took the form of shallow slit-trenches but Lieutenant-Colonel Fielding had ordered them to be deepened as a precaution. Consequently, there were no casualties in the morning, though the Connaughts' cook was thrown into the air when a shell hit the limber of the field kitchen he was working on. He coolly picked himself up and continued cooking the men's breakfast. Although the 9th (NIH) Irish Fusiliers were also in reserve, the news of the German advance quickly spread and soon, as Private William Allen stated, it was '… all hands to the pumps…' Similarly, the 9th 'Tyrones', under Lieutenant-Colonel Peacocke, received a chaotic flurry of orders in these early hours of the offensive. They were initially ordered to defend Somme dugout, then re-ordered to take up positions on the high ground at Happencourt. When they arrived there, they received new orders to head back towards Grand Seraucourt, where they formed a defensive flank with the 1st and 9th Irish Fusiliers. The confusion mirrored Ulster Division's perhaps 'haphazard' response to the German offensive. At around noon, 'Jeanne d'Arc', garrisoned by the 12th Royal Irish Rifles, was the first 36th Divisional Redoubt to fall into enemy hands as the defence melted away before the German assault. However, 'C' Coy, 12th Irish Rifles stubbornly maintained their other position at Le Pontchu Quarry and gallantly held it under Captain L.J. Johnston. He led a bayoneting party into Foucard Trench where they killed a small party of Germans who had managed to infiltrate the line; this became a battle zone for some four hours. Each time the Germans attacked they were repulsed, with prisoners sent back to Le Pontchu. However, with each fresh attack, the pressure on 'C' Coy's flanks increased.[13]

Midday and Afternoon

By midday, British High Command could not fail to grasp the severity of the situation now facing them. Their Forward Zone had all but disintegrated and the Battle Zone was also in danger of collapsing under the weight of the onslaught. The 1st Irish Fusiliers had been manning this line with the Battalion HQ at 'Station' Redoubt when, at 12.25pm, they got word that the St Quentin Forward Zone had been overrun. A mere twenty-two minutes later, rifle fire was heard to their left and, soon afterwards, the stormtroopers fell upon their positions. By now, the 1st 'Faughs' believed that the neighbouring 41st Brigade on their right may have already fallen back under the German pressure. The British, it seemed, were in total disarray.[14]

Meanwhile, in the 16th Division's Rear Zone, the 6th Connaughts were busy eating their dinners when Lieutenant-Colonel Fielding received urgent news that Ronssoy had fallen and the men were immediately ordered to plug the gap at St Emilie. Having established themselves here, Lieutenant-Colonels Fielding and Kane, commanding 1st Munster Fusiliers, were ordered to counter-attack the enemy and, through a flank manoeuvre, recapture Ronssoy.

However, there was to be no timed coordination in their attack and it was to be done without hesitation. It was promised that two tanks would support the battalions in their efforts. When he returned to the Connaught's lines, Lieutenant-Colonel Fielding found them under accurate and heavy shellfire, with one of the Coy commanders, Captain Wickham, already badly injured. Nevertheless, plans were made for an immediate thrust against Ronssoy to halt the German stormtroopers' advance in its tracks. When the fog finally lifted at around 1pm, the 1st Irish Fusiliers discovered that the flanking 41st Brigade on their right flank had disappeared. Instead, Germans were determinedly advancing up the railway cutting onto their position; they were only held at bay by the dogged resistance of the 'Faugh's' Lewis gunners. An hour and a half later, the Germans had worked their way past the 1st Irish Fusiliers' position, deep into British territory, but still the 'Faughs' fought on.

At the battle for Le Pontchu, the 12th Irish Rifles were losing more and more men with both sides involved in acts of suicidal bravery; one German single-handedly bayonet charged the 12th Irish Rifles' position and was cut down. For several hours, the 12th Rifles grimly stood in the way of the German advance. At around 3pm, a full German company (bizarrely marching in formation) advanced towards them. Captain Johnston's hundred or so men waited until the enemy was within point-blank range and then opened fire, stopping them in their tracks. However, it was a final gesture of resistance as, by now, the Germans had Le Pontchu completely surrounded. By the late afternoon, the defenders of Le Pontchu, 'Boadicea' and 'Racecourse' all appear to have hoped that they could maintain their positions until dark, when they could try to pull back to the Battle Zone. However, by early afternoon it was painfully obvious that escape or retreat was no longer an option; death or surrender clearly was. The redoubt defenders were on borrowed time. At 3.45pm, the 6th Connaught Rangers moved forward towards Ronssoy, with two companies leading their attack. As they neared the sunken road by Ronssoy Wood, they thought they could see the 1st Munsters supporting them on the right. It was, in fact, the Germans manning the factory ridge to their front, with swarms of stormtroopers gathering to attack them in flank. The bloody engagement that followed was a desperate fight for survival. Captain Crofton was killed leading 'A' Coy's defence, as was Lieutenant Fenton Cummins, MC; indeed, by the time they were forced to withdraw, the 6th Connaughts' casualties had been crippling. In the end, the promised tanks had also mounted independent attacks on the enemy elsewhere and had been wiped out. At Le Pontchu, the fight was over; the 12th Irish Rifles eventually surrendered at

4 pm, but only after an entire German battalion was seen advancing to their front and an enemy tank began to pour enfilading fire upon their position.[15]

Evening—the 'Forward Zone' Dissolves

The 15th Irish Rifles found themselves under attack on all sides whilst defending 'Racecourse' Redoubt, as German stormtroopers flooded their position. For over seven hours, they repeatedly hit the Redoubt with a combined assault force using flame-throwers and mortars, supported by grenades and machine-guns. It was here, that 2nd Lieutenant Edmund de Wind, although twice wounded, defended his position alone, until supported by a number of Riflemen. The small group then continued the defence, with de Wind and two NCOs repeatedly leading forays to clear the Germans from the trench. He was mortally wounded whilst clambering onto the top of the parapet to continue this duty and was posthumously awarded the VC.[16]

At 'Boadicea', Colonel Lord Farnham (now joined by a little stray dog) directed the 2nd Inniskillings' frantic defence all day. During a lull in the fighting around 5pm, a group from the 463rd Regiment approached under a white flag of truce. Like many other unit commanders that day, Lord Farnham had a stark choice. He decided that the result was a foregone conclusion and, at around 5.30 pm, 'Boadicea' surrendered. Before it did, however, Farnham insisted (probably sensitive to the disgrace brought upon Lieutenant-Colonel Mainwaring at St Quentin in August 1914) that the Germans provide him with an official written despatch. This clearly stated that his battalion had put up considerable resistance before they capitulated and that regimental honour had been satisfied. Accordingly, 252 Inniskillings walked out of 'Boadicea' and into captivity, including Colonel Lord Farnham, who did so carrying the little dog under his arm. At almost exactly the same time as 'Boadicea' fell, Lieutenant-Colonel Cole-Hamilton was forced to surrender 'Racecourse'; by then, he had less than thirty unwounded men left. Just over 150 15th Royal Irish Riflemen had held off two German battalions.[17]

The 1st Inniskilling Fusiliers were holding 'Ricardo Redoubt' under the command of Lieutenant-Colonel J.N. Crawford and were to cover the withdrawal of the 36th Division. Although the Germans swept on past the British front line, the 1st 'Skins' held out until they too fell back, arguably in some disorder, many either surrendering or being taken prisoner. At around the same time, the 6th Connaughts were still holding their positions at the 'Brown Line' defences, but Lieutenant-Colonel Fielding had pulled his own Battalion

HQ back. When he finally got back to Brigade HQ, Lieutenant-Colonel Fielding was informed that the counter-attack at Ronssoy had been a mistake and that these orders had actually been cancelled—but not in time to halt the Connaughts' advance. The 1st Munsters had received the countermand and acted accordingly. Fighting their way back to St Emilie, the survivors of 7th (SIH) Royal Irish scrambled back to the defences here at just after 7pm, under Captain A.V. Bridge, Sergeant Maloney and Corporal Harrison but, by this stage, the entire band totalled no more than around forty men. The Germans, on the other hand, had secured the quarries and territory north-east of Grand Seraucourt, in a move which now threatened to completely encircle the 1st Irish Fusiliers at Essigny Plateau. They gallantly fought on until 8.45pm, when the brigade order to pull back to west of the St Quentin Canal finally came. The 1st 'Faughs' fought a classic rearguard action all the way back to the canal bridge at Grand Seraucourt, which they reached at noon the next day.[18]

Other Irish battalions had also fought furiously against the German waves of the Kaiserslacht. The London Irish were in trenches by Metz-en-Couture and their forward 'A' and 'B' Coys bore the brunt of the German assault. As runners were being killed or wounded trying to reach Battalion HQ with information from the Forward Zones, Lieutenant-Colonel G.H. Neely, DSO MC, went forward with a small party to find out more. Although they were halted by intense shelling, they met up with a battered remnant of 'A' Coy who informed Lieutenant-Colonel Neely that the Germans had established themselves in the Forward Zone. By nightfall on 21 March, the men of the London Irish managed to straggle back to the Battle Zone. Amongst their dead was Private Cecil J.L. White, from Kingston in Surrey, a Freeman of the City of London. In 1914, he had married his sweetheart, Daisy Collins, and had a promising career. Yet, the cultural and patriotic pressures on him must have weighed heavily as he enlisted on 29 November 1915 in the 2/5th Battalion of the County of London Rifle Brigade. Later still, he had been transferred to the 1/18th London Regiment—the famous London Irish Rifles. Hastily, but reverentially, the London Irish dead were buried at the sugar refinery at Metz-en-Couture. Their graves, however, were obliterated in the savage fighting that soon followed.[19]

As evening descended on 21 March, it was clear that the Germans had successfully sliced through an astonishing nineteen miles of forward trench-line and captured five hundred artillery guns. British losses, at this stage, were confused and, among many units, sketchy. The 1st Irish Fusiliers noted that reported losses were only ten men killed with fifty-six wounded, including an officer. However, the scale of the unfolding disaster was told by the numbers of missing: 9 officers and 275 men. Like many battalions, the 7/8th Inniskilling Fusiliers had fought a grim rearguard all the way back to the village of Hamel, where they made a determined stand, holding it against repeated Germans attacks. The cost to this battalion was staggering: at the end of 21 March, 18 officers and 733 other ranks were killed, wounded or missing. To all intents and purposes, in one masterstroke, the Germans seemed as if they were suddenly winning the war. Captain Cyril Falls, a Royal Inniskilling Fusilier and on General Staff of the 36th Division, bleakly commented that the situation which had, initially, been seen as '... menacing, was becoming suddenly desperate...'[20]

Stemming the Deluge, 22–27 March

For those battered units of 47th Brigade who were holding the Brown Line, the evening brought news of a possible fresh counter-attack the following morning by the 16th Division. The Acting Commander of the St Emilie defences, Lieutenant-Colonel Crockett, had suggested that a new assault be made. Consequently, the remnants of the 6th Connaughts, 1st Munsters, 7th (SIH) and 1st Hertfordshires were assembled under the direction of the acting Brigadier-General. Predictably, the German offensive continued early on 22 March, after an intense bombardment and, again, assisted by the morning fog. This time, however, it was contained by the battalions now defending the Brown Line. Throughout the day, determined garrisons were still somehow blocking the enemy advance in the new front line but, without support or reinforcement, the threat of envelopment became pressing. When parties of the 2nd Leinsters began to file through the Brigade HQ area, it revealed that the Germans had finally broken through at the fragile join between 66th and 16th Divisions along the St Emilie to Villers-Faucon road. The following hour, the broken remains of the 13th Royal Sussex Regiment filtered past the 6th Connaughts HQ and soon units were '...falling back freely...', albeit quite calmly and in a notably unhurried way. With considered calm, Major-General Hull ordered a general retreat back to the Green (rear) Zone, in line with Fifth Army. As on the previous day, many units fighting in the front did not receive these orders to fall back in time and were consequently surrounded by the enemy. On the night of 22 March, a thin line of troops from the 1st Munsters, 6th Connaughts and 2nd Leinsters covered the retreat of 49th Brigade to the Green Line Rear Zone.[21]

At Jussy, the 5th Irish Lancers were holding the canal crossing against repeated waves of attack. Eventually at dawn on 23 March, German stormtroopers secured a bridgehead on the northern bank under a shroud of covering fog and, applying pressure on the Lancer's flanks, forced them to retreat to the nearby railway embankment. The regiment regrouped in relatively good order and collected its horses, with Captain John Rice and his men successfully disengaging from the enemy and leading some seventy-five horses back to the British lines. The pioneers of the 16th Irish Rifles were put under the command of the 9th Irish Fusiliers who were thrown into the cauldron along the banks of the Somme Canal. At around 10am, as a result of the general retreat of troops holding Ham (a small town near Peronne) on the Ulster Division's left flank, a Coy of 9th Inniskillings was hastily thrown in to support the remaining defenders (21st Entrenching Battalion) but soon the Germans had pushed them back further. During the subsequent fighting at Aubigny, on the main road to Amiens, the village was captured and lost repeatedly by the 9th 'Tyrones' who, in their last struggle for its capture sustained many losses but were unable to retake the bridges. Eventually, they too were forced to withdraw, soon after midday. Among their dead was CSM Robert 'Bobby' Hamilton, from Dungiven (Co. Londonderry), a man widely considered to be the bravest in the Battalion. Bobby Hamilton had formerly been a member of the 10th 'Derrys' and had been awarded the MM in December 1916. His friend, Jim Donaghy, recollected that, on cold nights, CSM Hamilton would bring a large steaming Dixie of cocoa up on his back for his men in the line. He was killed at the battle of Aubigny and, five days after his death, CSM Hamilton was posthumously awarded the DCM.[22]

Roughly an hour later, the Irish Rifles were ordered to take up positions east of Cugny, next to the 14th Division and simply ordered to hold their ground. They arrived early that afternoon, by which time most of the 14th Division (except its rearguard) had already retreated. At one point, the 2nd Irish Rifles became dangerously 'up in the air' and elements of 'C' Coy infiltrated the enemy lines. Their officer, Lieutenant Richard Brereton Marriot-Watson MC, with an almost 'Boy's Own Magazine' sense of dash, had approached the enemy, speaking German to them until his men were close enough to drive home their attack. Then the 2nd Rifles, swiftly reinforced by what was left of the 1st Irish Rifles, 13th Entrenching Battalion and a unit of dismounted French Dragoons, held off attacks by Regiments of the Prussian 5th Guard Division. At dusk, they were still valiantly holding their lines when the 13th Entrenching Battalion finally buckled, after their Colonel was mortally wounded. Despite the resultant gap opening between the 1st and 2nd Rifles, they fought on until finally withdrawing from Cugny just after 10pm. During the battle, Lieutenant Richard Brereton Marriot-Watson was reported missing and then, inevitably posted as killed in action. He had formerly served with the UVF and the 13th Irish Rifles but also became posthumously known for his haunting war poem, *'Kismet'*.[23]

Meanwhile, the 1st Munsters, 6th Connaughts and 2nd Leinsters were in the midst of a dogged fighting retreat near Doingt, always in range of German long-range heavy machine-gun fire and artillery. Advance groups of enemy stormtroopers constantly infiltrated closer and closer to their hastily created lines and soon swept into positions only recently vacated. During their bitter fighting in defence of the Brown Line around Hattenfield, the 1st Royal Munster Fusiliers were pinned down by machine-gun fire from a barn in No Man's Land. Their recently promoted CSM, Martin Doyle from New Ross (who, in 1909, had enlisted in the Royal Irish Regiment), now gathered a section together and led a bayonet charge against the building. The bullets swept the attackers down and only Doyle reached the barn, bayoneting the gun's crew and single-handedly capturing the weapon. For this action he won the MM but was soon taken captive afterwards. It was only when the 1st Munsters retook the ground in a counter-attack that CSM Doyle regained his freedom. The Germans, however, were still pressing hard and, when the 6th Connaughts reached Péronne, the Royal Engineers were actively setting demolition charges on the bridges, with every river-crossing a potential battlefield.[24]

East of Amiens, Lieutenant-Colonel C.M. Mort's 8th King's Royal Irish Hussars had just crossed the Somme when an officer of the 10th Hussars rode up and told Major A. Currell that his men were urgently needed, as German cavalry had been seen approaching en masse. As they rode onwards, they were suddenly confronted by over thirty stampeding horses from the 19th Hussars. The 8th Irish Hussars deftly galloped off the road to let them pass and rode into a nearby chalk-pit; however, whilst they were halted here a shell burst above them, causing more horses to stampede. In the confusion, the bridges at both the villages of St Christ (where the 19th Hussars recovered) and Falvy (where the 8th Hussars regrouped) were found to be destroyed. By now, the regiment had dismounted and had initially planned to defend the village but, before this could happen, efforts had to be made to get the horses over the river to safety. At this stage, the horses were on the brink of being uncontrollable but some were still capable of being calmed enough that they could be led across. Others simply swam to the opposite bank. Yet, a steady withdrawal was ultimately hampered by severe and accurate German shelling which repeatedly targeted the bridge area, with more of the Irish Hussars having to be taken off repair work to lead the, by now, panicked horses through the river. With every explosion the task became more difficult, with many mounts hit, until finally the decision was made simply to get the men across and abandon the remaining horses.[25]

By 25 March, the 36th Division was slowly falling back onto Villeselve, although the order (once again) failed to reach the Irish Rifles both of whose units were now at company strength. In the early hours of the morning, both battalions of Rifles eventually repositioned themselves on the Villeselve–Cugny road at Montelimont where, under heavy shelling, they again found themselves alone and with the enemy threatening their rear. At 3.30pm the 1st Rifles were forced to pull back, having been virtually surrounded; they had received no message from the 2nd Rifles. By the time the survivors of the 1st Irish Rifles fell back on Villeselve, the 2nd Irish Rifles had been virtually extinguished. It was later discovered that, when their ammunition ran out, the 2nd Rifles had fixed bayonets and charged the enemy. Although some Riflemen escaped to re-form with the 1st Irish Rifles and other stragglers, some 150 were captured. British brigades had been reduced to battalions, their battalions to companies and their companies had ceased to function as military units at all. The 6th Connaughts re-formed into a two-company strong battalion and, by collecting together stragglers and all available support and transport personnel, their fighting strength was considered to be 7 officers and 180 men. As if to demonstrate the devastating level of casualties, the South Irish Horse was, by now, a 'company' in the ominously named '47th Brigade Battalion'. When Arras was evacuated, the 1st Irish Guards frantically dug a defence support line at Boisleux-St Marc but they too were caught in the flurry of confused orders—firstly to relieve the Coldstreams, then the Scots Guards and then the Coldstreams once more. In front of the Guards Division, the Germans fell upon the Boisleux-Ayette line like an '…encompassment of were-wolves'.[26]

The Ulster and Irish Divisions' 'Last Battles', 26–30 March

Throughout these fraught days, the North Irish Cyclist Regiment was on full alert to move off whenever the order came, although this is noted in their war diary rather euphemistically as being for 'tactical reasons'. In fact, the British were retreating westwards, whilst their French allies were withdrawing south-west and soon an obvious gap would appear. On 26 March, General Foch was appointed Overall Commander of Allied Forces and, on the same morning, the Germans smashed through the widening hole between the British and French Armies at Roye. In response, Major-General Nugent was quickly ordered to send what remained of the Ulster Division to hold a line north of the River Avre, from L'Echelle-St Aurin to the Amiens–Roye road. Here, at Andechy, the 1st Irish Fusiliers, 108th Brigade, had wearily reached the village at 11am, when they found it occupied by the enemy. Lieutenant-Colonel S.U.L. Clements' orders were to block the Germans here for at least twenty-four hours to allow the French time to arrive at Montdidier. A fierce battle quickly developed which lasted all day. The most extant trench line for the 36th (Ulster) remained on the Erches–Bouchoir road and it was soon garrisoned that afternoon by the few hundred men of 107th Brigade (survivors from the 1st, 2nd and 16th Irish Rifles, assisted by 121st Field Coy RE and 21st Entrenching Battalion). The 2nd Irish Rifles, now only fifty men strong and led by Captain P. Murphy, found the situation '… somewhat obscure…' with what remained of the 1st Rifles holding their left flank but no-one to their right. It was thought that French infantry and cavalry were holding ground to their front but this, it turned out, was actually the enemy advancing. Accordingly, the Germans mounted several full-frontal assaults against them and, at dusk, brought up artillery and began to shell Erches and its associated lines. They then attacked the next morning with overwhelming numbers on three sides and eventually clawed their way into Erches, capturing it. The Ulstermen fell back once more and were relieved by the French. In this confused advance, an Ulster divisional staff car was ambushed whilst coming back from a conference; all the passengers, Colonel Place, Lieutenant-Colonel Furnell, 1st Irish Fusiliers and Major John G. Brew, acting CO of the 9th Irish Fusiliers were taken captive after a stiff fight.[27]

At first light on 27 March, the French withdrew on the right flank and forced the units of 109th Brigade to retreat across the Avre, whereupon Guerbigny fell to the advancing Germans. At 9.30 am, the enemy had marched into Montdidier without any serious resistance. With this, the 1st 'Faughs' were finally cut off and with no apparent orders to withdraw (again, these had failed to reach Lieutenant-Colonel Clements in the mayhem), they effected a last stand. It was thought that the last Fusiliers held on until 11.20am; what is known is that only one officer and nineteen men made it back to the British lines. To the north of Erches, near Arvillers, a tiny force of 15th Irish Rifles under Captain Miller could not be dislodged and only retreated when their trenches were finally all destroyed. When they did so, they made contact with Lieutenant-Colonel McCarthy-O'Leary's combined 1st and 2nd Irish Rifles and the whole force, three officers and sixty men, fell back to Arvillers. The 36th Division was, by 28 March, pulled out of the fighting line to Sourdon, well in the rear and, effectively, put out of action.[28]

Meanwhile, the 16th (Irish) had been holding the northern crossings on the Somme between Rouvroy and Froissy but were soon redeployed in the upcoming defence of Amiens and battle of Rosières. At 7am on 27 March, the Germans launched a massive strike, with eleven divisions, towards Amiens. The division covering Proyart was eventually outflanked but escaped to Hamel by splitting into 'battlegroups' under Lieutenant-Colonel Weldon, Lieutenant-Colonel Kane and Lieutenant-Colonel Fielding. This latter force consisted of a mixed group of Connaughts and Munsters which stoutly blocked the Amiens road, fending off numerous attacks at Raincourt and Framerville until they were reinforced. It was whilst he was rushing forward with a Lewis gun that Lieutenant-Colonel Fielding was injured, falling over a hidden trip-wire and dislocating his elbow. On the night of the 27/28 March, the assorted 2nd Dublins, 2nd Munsters, Royal Irish and Inniskillings of 48th and 49th Brigades punched their way out of the German encirclement, through Cérisy and Sailly-Laurette, to regroup at Hamel. By morning, the 16th Division was bolstered by odds and ends of men all drawn together from every available unit to man the 'Amiens Defence Line'. They were mainly sappers, drivers and engineers (including 500 men of the 6th United States Army Railway Engineers) and training schools' staff, all thrown into what became known as 'Carey's Force'. During this hasty defence, RSM Knight, 2nd Leinsters, found himself in charge of a force of men from four different regiments and, surrounded by the enemy, he organised a defence line. Throughout the night, under heavy attack, RSM Knight continually kept morale intact through '… a spirit of cheerfulness and confidence…' before evacuating them as ordered the next morning, in the face of another determined German assault. Captain McCann, MC, who was seriously wounded during the battle, said later that he had never been so proud of '… being a Leinster'.[29]

By now, the 16th Division had been filtered towards the Bois de Vaire and Bois des Tailloux regions where they faced their last determined German offensive on 30 March. When the enemy established a toehold in the fragile British lines, the 16th Division was used as a form of 'counter-strike' force and the 2nd Munsters and 2nd Dublins were rushed to dislodge them. Like their first battalions at Gallipoli, the 2nd Munsters and Dublins acted virtually as one unit and ousted the Germans but only after a brutal hand-to-hand battle. The following morning the Irish regiments were regrouped at Augbigny but, by this time, the German assault on the Somme was almost equally spent and the fighting began to slacken off. As the Chief of the Imperial General Staff, Sir Henry Wilson suggested to Haig on 30 March, the tide was finally turning, but the fatigue, casualties and pressure '…on our poor divisions…' was increasingly demanding. Similarly, Luddendorf's last throw of the dice came on 2 April, when he ordered a German advance upon Hamelet which was driven off by the 47th Brigade composite battalion of Connaughts, Leinsters and Munsters. Two days later, the German Somme offensive was over.[30] Among the Munster dead were Private John Moloney from Kildysart (Co. Clare) and Captain Cecil Chandler, MC, who had actually ended up commanding the battalion on 23 March, following the death of Lieutenant-Colonel Herbert Ireland on 21 March and the capture of the Acting Commanding Officer, Major Marcus Hartigan, the next day. As an 'Eighth Munster', Captain Chandler had recently been transferred to the senior Munster Battalion along with many of his INV men and, as such, he died with them.[31]

Counting the Cost

As a direct result of the 'Kaiserslacht', the vital towns of Bapaume, Albert and Peronne had fallen to the enemy and Amiens had been seriously threatened. The British had been pushed back almost to their starting point on the first day of the Somme, almost two years' previously. As if to demonstrate the confusion and chaos of the initial German assault, the 6th Connaughts lost their war diary in a direct hit on the Battalion HQ at 8.30am on the morning of 21 March. By 26 March, the Connaughts had suffered an unsustainable 22 officers and 618 other ranks in casualties. It was a similar story with the 9th Inniskillings who lost 23 officers and 464 men, whilst the 1st Irish Fusiliers claimed that losses for the entire month totalled 29 officers and 734 other ranks. Even the 5th Irish Lancers listed an appalling 130 casualties, with 36 missing and some 88 wounded, including Lieutenant-Colonel Cape. Those listed as killed in action included the redoubtable Captain John A.T. Rice, MC, who was severely wounded on 26 March, during heavy rearguard fighting. It later transpired that Captain Rice had been taken prisoner and died of his wounds on 14 April, whilst '… in German hands'. Two months later, he was posthumously awarded the Croix de Guerre.[32]

Whilst many battalions suffered heavy casualties during this period, for the 16th Division the whole episode had been a calamitous event. The official figures for both divisions suggest that 7,149 men were killed, wounded, missing or taken prisoner; the 36th Division officially lost 6,109 men. The vast majority of these men are simply listed as 'missing' but, according to Tom Johnstone, many of them were, in fact, wounded or dead, with calculations suggesting that the 16th Division sustained 4,340 killed or wounded and 2,095 missing. For the 36th Division, casualties mounted to 3,664, dead or wounded, with 2,445 missing. Whatever the statistics, however, in cold practical terms it meant that three divisions were to be removed out of line due to high losses: the 36th, 16th and 66th (East Lancashire). By 28 March, the 36th Division's 108th Brigade stood at just 14 officers and 321 troops—roughly a third of a full-strength battalion. On the same day, the 1st Royal Dublin Fusiliers could only muster forty-five men to arms.[33]

As the dust settled following the German breakthrough, the performance of a number of divisions, including the 16th and 36th, came under close scrutiny. Although it could be argued that many units from these divisions acted as a rearguard, effectively sacrificing themselves to allow the British line to 'correct and straighten itself', others may not have shown such exemplary conduct. Yet, every division, brigade, battalion and fractured unit in Fifth Army found itself fighting its own individual battles. Some fought to the death and others thought better of it. In the recriminations that followed, the 16th (Irish) were severely criticised for having low morale and 'fighting spirit'; the 36th (Ulster) escaped much of this denigration, although some believed they deserved it more. Haig's biting comment that the 16th Division had 'lost' Ronssoy may be more properly balanced with his additional perception that '...certain Irish units did very badly...' which seemed a very army-like 'no names, no pack-drill' form of ambiguous response. Unusually, it was also contrary to the view supplied to the War Cabinet by CIGS, the convinced Irish Unionist, General Wilson, who baldly informed them that the 16th Division, despite '... heavy losses was holding the ground well'. In fact, the German 18th and 50th Reserve Divisions had also recorded how difficult their advance was, given the resistance against them. If numbers of casualties alone could be equated with 'fighting spirit', then the 16th and 36th Divisions' reputations remain unimpeachable.[34]

On 28 March, Gough was relieved of command and replaced by General Sir Henry Rawlinson; Fifth Army was dissolved and renamed Fourth Army. The 36th Division was sent from Sourdon to the coast to regroup and the

16th was taken out of line (3 April), although its machine-gun companies and artillery stayed behind to assist the 14th Division. The surviving battalions were regrouped at Hallencourt and the remainder of the 16th Division formed into a composite brigade, to provide training for the newly arrived American Expeditionary Force. To many French observers, it seemed as if Gough's Fifth Army had been annihilated and that, militarily, it could neither be relied upon to fight, nor successfully reinforced to do so. It was also expected that Fifth Army's morale was irrecoverable and could contaminate other British formations. Yet, the general shock and confusion did not spread into a wider panic and, by and large, the British absorbed the German offensive. Indeed, largely due to the stubborn resistance in some areas, the momentum of the German advance slowed and, by 5 April, had reached its zenith. The considerable territorial gains made by the Germans came at such a high casualty rate that they too soon found themselves in crisis. When they did, the Irish regiments were in the vanguard of the Allied fight-back.

CHAPTER ELEVEN

'Each one of us must fight on to the end...'[1]

The Last Days on the Western Front

In March 1918, the Chief of the Imperial General Staff, Henry Wilson, maintained that a figure of 150,000 recruits could be forcibly conscripted from Ireland without any major disturbance—or certainly without disturbances which could not be handled. This was clearly not how others felt. A deep sense of division was also shown by the difference in opinion between the Inspector General of the RIC and the Commander-in-Chief of Irish Forces, Sir Bryan Mahon, regarding the implementation of conscription and recruitment in Ireland. Both felt major disturbances would break out; the former believed the RIC could not hold the line, the latter believed the army could step in.[2] Although Lloyd George's planned extension of conscription to Ireland was announced on 9 April 1918, it was never implemented. Indeed, its threat had brought swift reactions from all parts of Irish and Ulster society. There was one last-ditch appeal for recruits by the Lord Lieutenant and a quota system established but, even though a number of recruits were secured, it was obvious that manpower from Ireland was drying up and could not be relied upon to fill the gaps in the Irish regiments.

'Backs to the Wall'—Reorganisation, Defence and Disbandment, April–May 1918

The situation in the wake of the German breakthrough seemed very bad. By the start of April, the Ulster Division was extremely weak and a complete restructuring of the 36th's battalions at Gamaches was necessary to keep it in the field. It had quickly utilised entrenching unit personnel and its Reserve battalions were now filled largely by a number of young conscripts, mostly from Scotland and England. Against this thoroughly weakened British force, the Germans launched another offensive blow on 9 April with nine divisions smashing against eleven miles of front. With reports coming in that the Germans had punched through the 15th Scottish Division, the 4th Guards Brigade was swiftly dispatched to plug the gap at Vieux-Berquin, near Vierhoek at Hazebrouck on 10 April. Here, the 2nd Irish Guards delayed the German breakthrough in four days of intense fighting that cost the battalion dearly; 211 officers and men were killed or wounded, with 1 officer and 37 other ranks taken prisoner.[3]

The same day, the 12th Irish Rifles, 1st and 9th Irish Fusiliers were quickly 'sent and lent' to the 19th Division and flung into the defence south of Wytschaete. Again, previously hard-won ground fell to the enemy and men were cut down. Merville and Estaires were captured by the Germans and, when 'Hill 60' finally fell, the painful gain of Messines Ridge looked to be slipping away. Later that day, on 11 April, Field Marshal Haig issued the most eloquent and powerful Order of the Day of his entire career. He desperately urged his men to fight on to the last and, although they may be tired and with their 'backs to the wall', declared that there could be no retreat or surrender.[4] True to this order, when the Germans pushed against the 19th Division (who had not received their orders to retire), the ranks of the 12th Irish Rifles and 1st and 9th Irish Fusiliers fought on before being ordered to pull back upon Wulverghem. From 12–19 April, the 1st 'Faughs' were reorganised into a company and attached to the 9th (NIH) Irish Fusiliers for the subsequent battles around Hazebrouck, Bailleul and Mount Kemmel.

From 12–15 April, Acting CO of the 12th Irish Rifles, Major Holt Waring, the former Ulster Volunteer, North Irish Horseman and President of Waringstown Cricket Club, organised defences at Kemmel Hill. When the Germans attacked their front line, they were '… beaten off with rifle and Lewis Gun fire…' largely under Major Waring's direction. He then led the 12th Irish Rifles, with the 1st Irish Fusiliers, in a furious counter-attack to regain lost ground; over the next two days, the 12th Rifles repelled each attack until, finally, they were overwhelmed and had to retire. By 17 April, the survivors of 108 Brigade had been drawn together into a composite battalion of just 400 men, led by 1st Irish Fusilier's Lieutenant-Colonel Philip E. Kelly. They were sent to man reserve trenches on the slopes of Kemmel Hill. They came under constant shellfire and were only relieved on the night of 18 April, eventually marching back to the 36th (Ulster) Division at Poperinghe the next day. Although the Germans captured Mount Kemmel from the French troops holding it the next day, by the end of the month, it had been retaken along with Locre. When the 36th (Ulster) was eventually taken out of line and relieved by the Belgians, it had incurred a further 1,362 casualties in the Lys Offensive from 9–30 April. The men who had been lost could not be replaced and, consequently, the Ulster Division did not return to the front line until July.[5]

Similarly, April saw the 16th (Irish) Division dismembered, this time by the War Office. Mutinies (over army issues not political ones) within the 2nd and 7th Royal Irish Regiment and 7/8th Inniskillings had panicked High Command, concerned that their grievances were motivated by pro-Republican leanings. At Steenbecquel, the veterans of the SIH—now forming 'B' Company of the 47th Brigade Battalion—were undergoing their final period of reorganisation. Its personnel were split up throughout the army, with its remaining cavalrymen (106 and 1 officer) reposted to Cavalry Base to be reassigned to other mounted units; another 106 men were transferred to the 2nd Royal Irish Regiment. The pitiful remainder, some eight officers and fifty men, became instructors for the newly arrived United States Army, although they proudly retained the title of 7th (SIH) Royal Irish Regiment Training Staff. So named they also took over some 700 'Irish reinforcements' in the form of Dublin and Munster Fusiliers who were detached to help dig the GHQ line at Pecquer before they too were handed over to the 8th King's Royal Rifle Corps. The 2nd Royal Irish Regiment was itself transferred to the 63rd (Royal Naval) Division, with the battered 7/8th Inniskillings reduced to cadre strength and finally posted to the 34th Division.[6]

The 6th Connaught Rangers, meanwhile, were at Drionville when an order came through that a substantial part of the Battalion was to be transferred. The news came as a complete shock. They had been marching, so they thought, to another sector but, instead, some 281 men were to be drafted into the 2nd Leinsters and spread throughout its ranks. By 16 April, these Rangers had officially become men of the Leinster Regiment. It had been hoped that the disbandment of the 6th Connaughts had been carried out to bolster its parent Ranger battalions but, instead, the men were posted to other duties. It was an ignominious end for many of these proud men. By the end of April 1918, the 5th Royal Irish Lancers underwent a major reorganisation and received a new Commanding Officer in the form of Lieutenant-Colonel Robinson. A large draft of 9 officers and 138 men had also arrived from the Leicestershire Yeomanry, which may have had an impact on the unit's overall coherence as a group. However, given the Regiment's casualties the previous month, it was a very practical solution to the need to use available manpower to fill gaps in the ranks, wherever they may be. As if to prove the point further, Major-General Nugent's prediction regarding his own 'culling' came true when he was replaced as 36th Divisional Commander by Major-General Clifford Coffin VC on 6 May.[7]

Just as the 16th (Irish) Division was broken up and, with urgent developments elsewhere, the fate of the 10th (Irish) Division was likewise surely sealed. From April to May, the 10th Division was fully 'Indianised' with the original volunteer Irish battalions being transferred to the Western Front or disbanded. From April to May, the Irish regimental battalions received orders to embark for France and most, it seemed, were to fill the ranks of the 66th (2nd/East Lancashire) Division. As part of this process, the 5th Irish Fusiliers, 5th and 6th Inniskillings, 5th Connaught Rangers, 6th and 7th Dublins, 6th Leinsters and 6th Munsters all departed from Port Said for France. Yet, it would take weeks for these 'fresh' troops to arrive and, in the meantime, the pressures on the Western Front were mounting. By the summer, the Irish battalions were scattered among six 'non-Irish' divisions, although the 66th and 50th now included four Irish battalions each. Other distributions included the 2nd Leinsters and 1st Dublins (29th Division), 7th Royal Irish and 7/8th Inniskillings (30th Division), 2nd Royal Irish (63rd Naval Division) and 1st Munsters (57th Division). On 20 May, the 4th Guards Brigade and 2nd Irish Guards were posted as GHQ troops, where they remained until the end of the war. At Frencq, the instructors of the South Irish Horse training staff were teaching the men of the American 12th Machine-Gun Battalion and 4th Engineer Regiment in trench fighting, musketry bombing and Lewis Gun tactics. Ironically, it was just as those men of the South Irish Horse had initially been trained in September 1917 in the fighting ways of the infantryman.[8]

New Blood for the Western Front, June–August 1918

In June, many of the former 10th (Irish) volunteer battalions arrived in France. Whilst some of the 10th (Irish) veterans had arrived at the Western Front badly ill with malaria, most brought much needed fighting experience which could be used in other units. The 7th Dublins arrived on 1 June at Marseilles, where it was immediately reduced to training strength and its fighting troops allocated to its 2nd Battalion. By mid-June, the 7th Dublins were only at token operating strength and were posted to the 16th (Irish) Division at Samer, though they were actually returned to England just over a week later to be reposted. Whilst at Greatham, this small cadre of 7th Dublins was absorbed en masse by the newly raised 11th Royal Irish Fusiliers. Like the Dublins, the majority of troops in the 6th Munsters were subsumed by its 2nd Battalion, with the remainder a token unit which, as such, was eventually disbanded whilst attached to the 39th Division at the end of June.

Many other former 10th (Irish) battalions were similarly posted in an *ad hoc* manner. Of those initially sent to the 66th Division, the 5th Inniskillings were placed with 198th Brigade and the 6th Dublins were originally posted to 197th Brigade, before re-allocation to the 198th Brigade in September. Equally, the 5th Connaughts had been temporarily posted to the 14th Division but, on 22 July, were also transferred to the 66th Division, firstly to the 197th Brigade and then to the 199th Brigade. Other hard-fighting battalions seem to have been posted piecemeal throughout the army; the 6th Leinsters served briefly with the 14th and 34th Divisions before being sent to the 198th Brigade of the 66th, whilst the 5th Irish Fusiliers were only briefly attached to the 66th Division before being allocated to the 48th Brigade of the new 16th Division. Finally, the 6th Inniskillings, following a short period with various divisions, were finally posted to the 151st Brigade of the 50th (Northumbrian) Division. Indeed, the lack of any concerted attempt to keep these Irish battalions together only added to the general feeling of conspiracy in Ireland regarding the Irish Nationalist commitment to the British forces. By June, the 16th (Irish) Division had been redeployed to England, where it was officially to be brought up to combat strength. However, once in England, the dismemberment of the 16th Division as an Irish formation became almost inevitable. There were dark murmurings of political decisions at the War Office regarding its fate but the realities of attritional warfare were there for all to see. On paper, Ireland's recruitable population was still significant. In practice, the situation had changed beyond recognition since the heady wave of patriotism in August 1914. The implementation of Irish conscription once more became a pressing concern but, by summer 1918, it seemed as if Ireland (with the notable exception of Ulster and those with relatives who were still fighting) saw the war as increasingly irrelevant. Recruitment from Southern Ireland was now negligible, due to the powerful rise of Republicanism and its persuasive anti-recruitment campaigns. Additionally, Ulster's manpower resources had long since been used and, whilst a steady trickle of men continued to enlist, the numbers continued to dwindle. Despite the demand for men, the 1st Irish Rifles even sent two other ranks home to base for being 'underage'.[9]

Consequently, new recruits were found from elsewhere and the 16th Division which returned to France in July had effectively ceased to be an Irish formation, with one Welsh, two Scottish and five English battalions. Only one Irish battalion remained, the 5th Irish Fusiliers (from the 10th Division) along with the only original 16th Divisional Battalion—ironically, the Pioneers of the 11th Hampshires. Given the redistribution of Irish volunteer battalions into the 66th Division, observers found the diminishing 'Irishness' of the 16th Division hard to accept. It may have been that the men of the old 'Tenth' Division, as an 'apolitical' or 'unaligned' formation, were not considered appropriate 'like' replacements. However, as Stephen Gwynn stressed, they were all Irish battalions that could feasibly have been organised to form one united division. At battalion level, such operational restructuring was now commonplace; on 26 June, at Widdebroucq (north-east of Aire) reinforcements from the Royal Dublin and Munster Fusiliers, 500 and 250 respectively, along with 85 from the Royal Irish Regiment were handed over to the SIH Training Staff officially to become the 'new' 7th Royal Irish Regiment. Furthermore, the newly raised 11th Royal Irish Fusiliers continued their service with the 48th Brigade of the 16th Division, initially at Aldershot and then on the Western Front in July, before being totally subsumed by the 5th Irish Fusiliers at the end of August.[10]

Germany's 'Black Day', 8 August 1918

From May to July, the Germans launched three serious offensives against the French-held sectors, perhaps the most notorious being Chemin des Dames; this was a visceral blood-letting that ranked with Verdun in terms of perceived slaughter. In the aftermath of one of the most intense and unremitting bombardments of the war, by 6 June, German stormtroopers had secured the ridge and taken the bridges across the Aisne; in the push forward, they captured 50,000 prisoners and, when they halted at Chateau Thierry, they were a mere forty-five miles from Paris.

The subsequent battle of Matz (9–14 June) 'straightened' this attack line and gave Ludendorff a platform for the final offensive. Accordingly, on 15 July, the Germans thrust out at Rheims in an attempt to push on for Epernay and Chalon. However, on 18 July, they were again checked, this time when Foch successfully counter-attacked in the direction of Soissons. Whilst British troops were present in the Aisne and Marne sectors (five unlucky divisions that had been sent to Chemin des Dames as a supposed 'quiet' zone to recuperate), no Irish regiments were involved in these offensives. Indeed, at about the same time, the 36th (Ulster) had been sent back to the Messines sector, relieving a French division at Bailleul in conditions which were almost pastoral in comparison to their ordeals elsewhere. Whilst taking over reserve lines at St Jans Capel, a cow was presented to the rather bemused men of the 1st Irish Rifles by the Commandant of the 42nd French Infantry Regiment, whom they were relieving. Although it was undoubtedly a useful source of fresh milk, it is unrecorded who had the duty of looking after her.[11]

Meanwhile, the French counter-offensives in July ground the Germans back, although they gained sufficient time to consider renewing plans for an assault east of Montdiddier and in Flanders. Then, on 8 August, disaster struck them. The British were still maintaining pressure on the Somme and, at Amiens in a surprise attack, 450 tanks slammed into the German lines and overwhelmed them. The Germans fought desperately to halt the advance but all they could do was to slow it down. The tanks pushed from six to twelve miles into enemy territory and at last lived up to the Tank Corps' motto of 'From Mud, Through Blood, to the Green Fields Beyond'. Although this did not compare to the German's breakthrough in March, it rocked the enemy psychologically. Far from being moribund, the British had proved that they were still more than capable of offering offensive action. Ludendorff's horror and shock at the events at Amiens was expressed in his offer to resign command. He later described the 8 August as '…the Black Day of the German Army'. At the time both he and Kaiser Wilhelm were reputed to have admitted that Germany's resources were exhausted and that the war '…must be ended'.[12]

Yet, there were still vestiges of old thinking and failed imagination. As part of this operation, the 6th Inniskilling Dragoons, now serving with the 3rd Cavalry Division, were involved in another mounted charge around Mont Cremont Wood. The regiment was acting in support of the Canadian Cavalry Brigade and advancing up towards the Aubercourt–Ignacourt road, but they met with heavy resistance. As they moved against the dominating ridge along the Le Quesnel line in dismounted formation, they were still pinned down by flanking machine-gun fire from the German strongpoints, notably 'Point 78'. As this was holding up both the 'Skins' and Canadian assault, a bizarre order came directly from 7th Cavalry Brigade to effect a mounted sweep against the ensconced machine-guns. This task was allotted to the Inniskillings. As such, 2nd-Lieutenant Russi and his troop from 'C' Squadron drew their sabres and made a doomed mounted charge against well-prepared and defended machine-guns; he and his entire command became casualties. It was only when the attack was pushed home by the dismounted survivors of 'B' and 'C' Squadrons that the Germans were driven from their defences.[13]

Yet, the general momentum of advance continued and, at Messines, on 22 August, the Ulster Division was engaged in an action to strengthen its right flank. During this, the 15th Irish Rifles had startling success using Livens Projectors (used for gas attacks) to bombard the Germans. However, the 15th Rifles had replaced the gas with canisters which contained nothing more offensive than a similar stench. The Germans, quickly donning their respirators, evacuated their line as the 15th Irish Rifles calmly advanced into a virtually unchallenged area, capturing twenty-two prisoners, two machine-guns and—more surprisingly—a quarter of a mile on a half mile front. On 24 August, the 9th Irish Fusiliers, with the 1st 'Faughs' in support, crept their own line ever forward towards Bailleul though they were slowed by a determined German defence that resulted in over a hundred casualties. However, they still managed to capture sixty prisoners and some eleven machine-guns before the Germans gave up their ground under the cover of darkness.[14]

On 1 September, the Germans began a general withdrawal from the Bailleul sector and, although the 36th (Ulster) was due to pull out of the fighting line, instead it pushed forward. As 107th Brigade fought for Mont Noir, 108th Brigade eventually re-entered Bailleul. The next day, at Riencourt, the 1st Munsters were heavily pressed by a German attack and one Coy became disorganised when it became surrounded. Having lost all its Commanding Officers, CSM Doyle MM, took command and led a bayonet charge that broke the enemy's grip on their position and recaptured a number of Munsters. This included a wounded officer whom CSM Doyle then carried back to shelter. The Munsters were being bolstered by a tank and when Germans started to clamber over it, CSM Doyle led another attack and drove the enemy off, persisting even in the face of machine-gun fire. CSM Doyle duly assaulted the gun and crew, putting it out of action and capturing three of its gunners. The Munsters then repelled subsequent attacks on their position, all galvanised by the courage and leadership of Martin Doyle, the New Ross recruit who had enlisted for adventure in the Royal Irish Regiment in 1909, and who was awarded the Victoria Cross for his heroism that day.[15]

Advance on the Hindenburg Line

In late August, Lieutenant-Colonel J. Roche Kelly MC left the 7th Royal Irish and the battalion moved on west of Wulverghem where they were involved in heavy fighting from 1–2 September. Seventeen men were killed, including two officers, and fifty-five other ranks and three officers were wounded, with five other ranks listed as 'missing'. By 4 September, the Ulster Battalions of 109th Brigade had secured Ravelsberg Hill and were sent to support the 1st Munster Fusiliers and 29th Division's assault on Hill 63. This was eventually achieved the next day, despite the accustomed determination and heroism of the German machine-gunners. As this slow but dogged advance continued, the 6th Leinsters were eventually disbanded at Abancourt on 12 September, and the last 'volunteer' 10th 'Irish' battalion of the Leinster Regiment disappeared. Yet, by the end of the month, the push for the 'Hindenburg Line'—and victory—had begun.[16]

From 27 September to 5 October, the British wheeled past the Hindenburg Line and out into open country at last. With the breaking of the Wotan Position and the Drocourt–Quéant line, the next stage to capture Cambrai was something of an anti-climax given the precipitous withdrawal of the enemy; the opposition faced by the 63rd Naval Division in its assault there was far less significant than expected. In its ranks was the 2nd Royal Irish which was in the forefront of the attack (alongside Hawke Battalion) to capture the Hindenberg Support Line and Havrincourt. At the same time, in heavy fighting surrounding Cantaing, the 1st Munster Fusiliers were in action along the canal line and, after a prolonged battle, they captured 'Lock 5'. Indeed, as September drew to a close, the Marcoing Zone had been consolidated, securing territory from the Cambrai–Bapaume road to the banks of the Scheldt Canal. The 1st Munsters entered Proville to the south of Cambrai and the pressure on the German defenders increased. Yet, the stubbornly gallant defence of the German fronts existing along the Scheldt and Sensée canals and Canal du Nord, effectively stemmed British progress. By the time the commander of the 1st Munsters, Lieutenant-Colonel R.R.G. Kane was killed in action on 1 October, his battered unit had a mere 7 officers and 261 men remaining.[17]

As the Allied armies gathered for their last great offensive at Ypres under Marshal Foch, the rain hammered down incessantly. On 28 September, under the cover of a five-minute artillery barrage, the Allies attacked and, within hours, Zonnebeke had fallen to the Belgians. British II Corps similarly overwhelmed their opposition and made a grand advance. The 9th (Scottish) Division triumphantly conquered the Frezenberg Ridge and the famous 29th 'Iron' Division, lived up to its reputation and captured Ghelvelt. As part of this operation, some of the men of the 1st Dublin Fusiliers were hit by shellfire when they got too far ahead and were caught in the British creeping barrage.

However, the bombardment worked and the 1st Dublins rushed the enemy line and captured their objective with the loss of 126 wounded or dead. Meanwhile, the irrepressible 2nd Leinsters, advancing on either side of the infamous Menin Road towards the blasted remnants of Hooge, noted that the German shelling only really touched them as they neared 'Leinster Farm'. However, they knew the Germans real aim was to maintain the shelling of the Roulers zone with its attendant railway. Accordingly, they pushed onwards through a heavy mist and drizzle, behind the battalion's kilted pipers who, as they passed through 'Birr Crossroads', struck up the distinctive 'Brian Boru' march. With this, perhaps, spurring them on, the 2nd Leinsters made their way up towards the dominant ridgeline—through 'liquid mud' which came up to their knees in many places—and dug in.[18]

To support this advance, the 36th (Ulster) Division was quickly sent to take Terhand and plug the gap between the 9th (Scottish) and 29th Divisions. Consequently, 109th Brigade and the 2nd and 9th Inniskillings thundered forward, with the 1st 'Skins' in support, falling upon the lightly embedded German machine-gun nests at Terhand and Vijfwegen. By nightfall, both of these objectives had fallen to 2nd and 9th Inniskillings and they too dug in, waiting for 108th Brigade to pass through them and onto their next Ulster Division objective, the Menin–Roulers road. There was, as ever, a warning note, though. Both Inniskilling battalions had frequently taken out the enemy positions by sheer musketry skill, the bayonet and grenades, rather than artillery. The reason for this was simple. The swift British success was also nearly their undoing and the masses of necessary supply wagons and transport following in their wake became bogged down on the already congested and blocked Menin and Zonnebeke road system. As Captain Walker noted, the baggage and transport were struggling to catch up with their front-line Ulster battalions, with ammunition, rations and vital equipment all ploughing through the already churned-up landscape. In his words the '…surface and language were equally bad, and there was mud everywhere'. Under such conditions, rapid movement of all that was necessary to maintain the advance (artillery and ammunition) became increasingly problematic. The Zonnebeke Road fed both the 9th and 36th Divisions and their continued advance depended on the movement of their limbers, guns and divisional trains. Indeed, this was to have a direct impact on the next phase of their war; the assault on 'Hill 41' and the push for the river Lys.[19]

By now, most reinforcements in the Irish regiments were of Irish Unionist extraction or from Great Britain. One such new recruit was Frank Ernest

Parfitt, the son of a wholesale drapery salesman, who came from Stoke Newington and worked as a clerk for Harris & Dixon Ltd., Lloyd's brokers. He had enlisted in the London Regiment, but was soon transferred to make up losses in the 1st Irish Fusiliers. During the battle for the Wulverghem–Messines road, the 1st 'Faughs' were ordered to establish a position in the enemy trenches at White Gate ('Hill 63') and North Midland Farm. The attack began at 3am but, by 6.30am, the men had become pinned down by machine-guns at Neuve Eglise. There followed a severe British artillery bombardment of this stubbornly-held village, after which the 12th Irish Rifles led its assault and successfully captured it. Following the determined assault on Neuve Eglise, the combined losses were, again, stark. Among the attackers, the eighteen-year-old clerk from Stoke Newington, Frank Parfitt, lay dead.[20]

The Battle for 'Hill 41' and the Crossing the Lys

The Ulster Division's next objective rose sixty feet above the surrounding landscape and was topped by a series of three defended and concrete-fortified farmhouses—'Hill 41'. Consequently, 108th Brigade was sent to clear it, by the Menin–Roulers road, but these men were effectively unsupported as the artillery was still miles behind them, manhandling their guns along the muddy and shell-hole strewn road. With the 9th Irish Fusiliers moving up on the right, the 12th Irish Rifles on the left and the 1st Irish Rifles providing the Reserves, resistance was soon met. However, the 12th Rifles managed somehow to break through the Zuidhoek Copse to re-establish contact with soldiers from the 9th Division, whom they relieved at the Klaphoek Crossroads. Unfortunately, on the southern slopes of 'Hill 41', the 9th Irish Fusiliers were caught by merciless machine-gun fire that swept their flank as they advanced on the Gheluwe–Vijfwegen road. Whilst the 9th Royal Irish Fusiliers eventually made it through to the Menin–Roulers, no less than 6 officers and 130 men became casualties.[21]

The stubborn German defence of 'Hill 41' only cemented the notion that the war was not quite as near its finish as the High Command may have hoped. Without artillery to provide adequate barrage cover, three heavily defended hilltop farms on the crest of 'Hill 41' had effectively to be circumvented in order for the Brigade to reach its objective. For the next ten days, battalions surged back and forth against these farms in efforts to dislodge the Germans. On 1 October, after very bitter fighting, 'Twigg Farm', just below the crest, was captured by the 1st 'Faughs' but any further advance was halted by German machine-guns on the eastern slopes. This was also raking the men of the 9th Division who managed to capture Ledeghem from where the Lowland Brigade tried to assist the 'Ulsters' by outflanking 'Hill 41'. Again, the German machine-guns stopped any endeavours in their tracks. One last desperate attempt by the 1st 'Skins' also ended in failure but successfully—and accidentally—interrupted a mass German counter-attack on the 9th Division. Indeed, from their position at Manhattan Farm, Lieutenant-Colonel Smyth could see his King's Own Scottish Borderers potentially about to be overwhelmed when the 1st Inniskillings slammed against 'Hill 41' and drew the enemy towards them. To Lieutenant-Colonel Smyth, the timely intervention of the 1st Inniskillings had undoubtedly saved his men from a serious and potentially devastating German assault. The battle for the hill became one of intense hand-to-hand, close quarter, bayonet, rifle-butt or improvised trench weapon fighting.[22]

One of the last massed Irish regimental battles came on the Beaurevoir Sector of the Hindenburg Line, on 4 October, with the objectives of Prospect Hill, Gouy and Le Catelet. Three divisions of Rawlinson's Fourth Army were used (50th, 66th and 29th) with the 5th Royal Irish, 6th 'Skins', 2nd Munster and 2nd Dublin Fusiliers in the assaulting waves, with the 5th Inniskillings and 5th Connaught Rangers as battle Reserves. The 2nd Dublins assaulted lines west of Le Catelet, when suddenly five German battalions counter-attacked and captured the town itself; still the Dublins held their position. Meanwhile, the 6th Inniskillings advanced on Prospect Hill, but were caught in the flank by enemy fire coming from Gouy, so they promptly changed direction and engaged the Germans immediately instead. This allowed the supporting battalion (1st King's Own Yorkshire Light Infantry (KOYLI)) to successfully charge the hill and, after a gruelling combat, the KOYLI, Inniskillings and Royal Rifle Corps took the position. The following day, the assault continued in an attempt to capture Beaurevoir and, although this failed, the 2nd Munsters broke into Le Catelet. As they did so, two German machine-gun nests pinned them down and spread them out into dispersed cover. In an attempt to rally them, Lieutenant-Colonel Hubert Bernard Tonson-Rye pulled out his hunting horn and, after a few sharp blasts, Munster Fusiliers swarmed from every direction and the machine-guns were overrun.[23]

The next day, the British crossed the St Quentin Canal and, on 8 October, Beaurevoir finally fell as the second battle of Cambrai began. On 9 October, elements of the 1st Munsters slowly entered the outskirts of Cambrai to find it completely empty of the enemy, whilst at Serain, the 5th Connaughts captured not only the village but also eighteen artillery pieces. West of here, the 4th

Royal Irish Dragoon Guards were hit by artillery fire from Elincourt and their mounted progress was halted until the infantry cleared the way ahead. Although the Germans were still resolutely holding onto their ground, the nature of the warfare was now open with battalions advancing through streams and field systems, hedgerows and—for the first time since 1914—relatively undamaged villages. Although men were tired, the huge opportunities for victory were clearly beginning to be felt along with the feeling that '… at long last the decisive stage had been reached'.[24]

On 14 October, the artillery supporting the Ulster Division finally arrived in position from the Zonnebeke Road. With the ability now to provide a sufficient creeping barrage, the men of 107th Brigade attacked Moorseele and captured it, along with numerous prisoners, significant amounts of equipment and guns. Along the line, a remarkably similar story unfolded, as British and Belgian troops smashed the German front line backwards for a staggering four miles. By 16 October, the Allies were pressing close on Courtrai on the river Lys. Although the intended operation was to take the industrial town, in a last minute change of plan to avoid unnecessary civilian casualties, it was decided to force a river crossing instead. It is interesting to note that the spearhead for this operation was the 36th (Ulster) Division.

On the evening of 19 October, it seems that Major-General Clifford Coffin had decided that the Ulster Division had to cross the Lys without any further delay. Accordingly, the former Royal Engineer sent 109th Brigade to establish bridge-heads under cover of darkness. The assault was bitterly contested but ultimately a success. The men of 109th Brigade constructed makeshift bridges and soon the troops of 108th Brigade had also crossed the Lys. With the final victorious push against the Germans, the 1st Inniskillings were ordered to take four villages on the far side of the river Lys; they took Desselghem, Spriete and Straete but were held up and had to dig in at Dries, which was finally taken two days later. The 2nd Irish Rifles, at last, took the fortified hilltop village of Dries, which was held by a Prussian assault regiment and had been a considerable hindrance to the Division. The 1st Irish Rifles continued the advance only to be stopped once again by the interminable German machine-gun nests ahead. By 21 October, 107th and 108th Brigades were trying to move forwards but found themselves at the mercy of the stalled transport along the shattered roads behind them. At this point it was noted that much of the motor transport was continually breaking down. Equally, horse transport was in short supply due to the number of equine casualties from shellfire, casualties which were not—and could not be—quickly replaced.[25]

Three days later, the already battered 9th Irish Fusiliers sustained another 50 casualties in a grinding advance of only a further 1,000 yards and, by now, they could only muster 250 men. On 27 October, the Germans began a widespread and ordered withdrawal of their front line, still garrisoned by their elite stormtrooper divisions, which made the Ulster Division's tenacious pursuit a slow and painful business. Yet, by the evening, the 'Ulsters' were finally relieved by the 34th Division and ordered to march west to new billets at Mouscron. Indeed, it was to be the last time that these Ulster battalions were to be in the front line on the Western Front. Four days later, Turkey surrendered. The end of this truly Great War seemed tantalisingly near.

The Armistice, 10–11 November 1918

On 10 November, the 2nd Royal Irish were involved in their last ever battle, pursuing the Germans back across the very landscape they had fought over at the start of the war. In a full brigade assault, the 2nd Royal Irish Regiment pressed home their advance, although German artillery and machine-gunners doggedly attempted to impede their progress. By 8pm, the 2nd Royal Irish had taken their objectives and, as the Germans pulled back, they pushed forward. They reached the outskirts of St Symphorien at around midnight and found the town deserted. Finally, Lieutenant-Colonel M.C.C. Harrison's 2nd Royal Irish ended their long war at Spiennes just outside Mons. Ironically, their commander had been a junior officer in the battalion when they had made such a courageous stand here in the late summer of 1914. Among their recent dead was Lance Corporal James Darcy, from Kilkenny, who had originally joined the 6th Royal Irish in January 1915 before being transferred on its disbandment. James Darcy left everything he had in the world to his Aunt Mary, back in Kilkenny. One of his comrades, Alex Andrews from Cardiff (formerly Dublin Fusiliers) died of wounds the following day. Both men had come tormentingly close to surviving the war.[26]

Whilst many men felt the impending end was near, actual word of the Armistice flitted along the line during 10 November and the news was greeted with mixed responses. Some battalions made no reference to it at all, such as the 1st Inniskillings, 16th Irish Rifles and 9th Inniskillings; others greeted the news with disbelief, joy or a feeling of emptiness. The former Ulster Volunteers of the 'Tyrones', the 9th Inniskillings, found themselves billeted in the Belgian convent of St Annes, near Courtrai, where the nuns '...did all in their power...' to make them comfortable. In this they were helped by one nun who acted as interpreter as she had originally come from Kilkenny.[27] The 2nd Irish Guards celebrated the Armistice at Criel Plage, southwest of Le Treport, and the 1st Irish Guards concluded their war with fighting around Mauberge, three miles from Marlborough's famous 1709 battlefield of Malplaquet. They were informed of the Armistice whilst dispersed by companies near Assevant. One Irish Guardsman simply felt that hearing the news was like '…falling through into nothing…' and it was particularly hard for the men of the INV to take. When the war ended, its Volunteers were scattered throughout other battalions and regiments.

In the bright, clear, early afternoon of the 10 November, the 8th King's Royal Irish Hussars had reached their billets in Perunelz. Their horse lines were out in the open and the Hussars were busy preparing to continue their steady advance towards a rendezvous south east of Ath, where they were to meet up with the 1st Cavalry Brigade and support the 58th Division. However, at midnight on 11 November, their orders changed. Instead, they were ordered to rejoin the 9th Cavalry Brigade at Maffles, which they reached after a fast ride. The time was dead on eleven o' clock. Slightly bemused, the war diary noted that the Germans had '…only just left. Hostilities ceased at 11.00.' The Hussars duly occupied their designated outposts and awaited further orders. Rather than any mass celebration being recorded, the most memorable event appeared to be that it was a wet night.[28]

Meanwhile, the 16th Irish Rifles had been wearily working in the bitter cold on building pontoon bridges across the Scheldt. As they toiled, a number of them watched as numerous Very lights shot up into the skies at the front line and presumed that they were 'urgent prayers' for artillery support. Even when a number of soldiers heading back across the river told them that the '… war is over, boys', the sceptical Ulster pioneers apparently retorted, 'Aye, we know: over there…' The 2nd 'Skins' and 9th Irish Fusiliers noted this surreal experience as, around 8.00 pm, the sky above them was lit up in brilliant colours by '… searchlights and rockets…' and '…flares and rockets of all descriptions…' At the same time, rumours began to circulate that the Armistice had been signed. The 1st Irish Fusiliers, however, were very careful to state that it was, at this stage, only a rumour that Peace had arrived. In contrast to the muted response elsewhere, in the Ulster Division, the 2nd Inniskillings turned out to parade and '…celebrate the occasion!', whilst the 9th Irish Fusiliers, the remnants of 'Blacker's Boys', paraded behind their fife and drums and enthusiastically played in the streets of Mouscron.[29]

On 11 November, the 5th Irish Lancers were ordered to Mons, where they took up defensive positions around the heights at St Denis, reaching them at around 9am and bringing them into 'contact' with German patrols. However, just two hours later, the war was officially over. The 5th Lancers war diary simply states that 'Hostilities ceased at 11am' and matter-of-factly records that the advance squadron here remained in position until relieved that afternoon by Canadian infantry. It is perhaps fitting that the 5th Royal Irish Lancers were the last British regiment to leave the town of Mons in 1914 and the first British regiment to enter the town during the victorious advance of November 1918. Sadly, however, one of their last casualties was Private George Edwin Ellison, a Lancer who had served throughout the war. He was a thirty-year-old former coal miner who had been born in York, lived in Leeds and enlisted in Hull shortly before the outbreak of the war. Ironically, Private Ellison was killed in action during the 'contact' with the German patrols around the mine workings and pits surrounding Mons, just an hour and a half before the Armistice came into force.[30]

As the days ticked by towards War's End, although it was impossible for them to know it, the men of the 7th Royal Irish Regiment had continued their steady advance. Leaving Anseroeul for billets at Elleszelles, the battalion finally arrived there at 16.00 hours, on 11 November. It was here, when they arrived footsore and weary that they were informed of a divisional telegram stating that the war had officially ended some five hours previously. Perhaps unsurprisingly, the men greeted the news with 'very little excitement'. Indeed, the stunned, weary, silence that descended upon the men of the 7th Leinsters was shared by its Regular 2nd Battalion.[31] On the morning of 11 November, the 2nd Leinsters were marching along a muddy road to assemble at Arc-Ainières, when their Brigadier-General, on horse-back, galloped up to them wildly and shouted out that the war was over. The news dumbfounded them. If the Brigadier had expected wild cheering and exuberance, he was to be badly disappointed. The Leinsters greeted the news with almost sullen silence. The Brigadier, 'somewhat crestfallen', trotted back along the road presumably hoping that the next battalion would receive the information with a little more enthusiasm.

However, as they marched onwards, the men of the 2nd Leinsters began to discuss the possibilities of an Armistice animatedly and whether or not it was simply a German ruse. The discussion flew back and forth but, ultimately, they also wondered whether the news would herald a special 'rum issue', which they had not received for the previous four days. Then, the rumour slowly filtered through their ranks that officially the war was to end at eleven o'clock. When eleven o'clock came and went, the Leinster column, true to their reputation, did not cheer or make a sound. It was poignantly and poetically noted by Frank Hitchcock that the slight rustle of equipment, with steady tramp of feet, was the only noise they made. Like many of the Irish regiments themselves, the Leinster column marched on silently into history, to the rhythm of the soft rain, until '... even the sound of its footsteps died away'.[32]

CHAPTER TWELVE

'Out of the sight of men...'[1]

The Cost and Legacy, 1914-1918

As the minutes had ticked away to the Armistice, the warring nations still incurred numerous casualties. The dubious honour of being the last Irish regimental death is, obviously, a contentious one but, as has been noted, the last official soldier 'killed in action' was George Ellison, 5th Royal Irish Lancers. Yet, as Kevin Myers has revealed, his comrade Thomas Farrell, from Navan, was also fatally injured in the same incident and died of wounds on 12 November. It aptly illustrates that the complicated legacy of the war continued after the simple date of its cessation.

Indeed, a tragic list of those killed outright or who died, either from wounds or illness, can be compiled for this one simple, yet momentous, November day. It is thought that at least 32 Irishmen, or men from Irish regiments, seem to have shared this death date (out of 514) and a brief sample only confirms the eclectic nature of the war and its casualties. Captain Francis Montgomery Jennings, 8th Irish Hussars, formerly of Caius College, Cambridge, born in Cork in 1874 and schooled at St Mark's Windsor, died of wounds. As the 2nd Royal Irish ended their war at Spiennes, south of Mons, four of their number also died of wounds: two from Wales (Alexander Andrews from Deri in Glamorgan and John Stoneham from Llangeinor/Blaengarw, Glamorgan) and two from Ireland (Michael Kelly, a drummer from Waterford and John Joseph Murray from Granard). Similarly, four 6th Inniskillings appear to have died on Armistice Day, when the battalion was near Monceau: two from England (Robert Cork from Sutton and Peter Judge from Manchester), and two from Ulster (Lance Corporal Denis Doherty from Templemore and Joseph

Watterson from the Shankill, Belfast). Further afield, Liverpudlian Edward Fox, 1st Connaughts, died in a field hospital in Egypt, when the Rangers were stationed in Nazareth. Yet, perhaps most ominously, the former South Irish Horseman, Patrick O'Dea, died from influenza in the General Hospital at Rouen.[2]

By the closing months of 1918, Great Britain and Ireland had been decimated by death. Where warfare had already cut short the lives of millions of young men throughout the armies of the powers of the world, disease now came close on its heels. A virulent outbreak of 'Spanish' influenza swept across Europe in 1917 and left millions dead in its wake. It is estimated that twenty million people died during the pandemic and, when it reached Britain the following year, via the Western Front, some 200,000 men, women and children succumbed to its ravages.[3] In Ireland, to perhaps a lesser degree than in Great Britain, shortages in fuel, necessities and food were also biting at a populace increasingly dismissive of the war, even once victory for the Allies had been achieved.

Return to Arms, Ireland, 1918

After the Great War, of course, there came another war—this time in Ireland itself. It was a war which was to become noted for its bitterness, savagery and deep personal hatred. In this, it contrasted tragically with the vast number and awful anonymity of the casualties sustained in the mass slaughter of 1914–1918. In many ways, being so personal and immediate, its course and legacy overshadowed the First World War for many decades, especially in the Republic of Ireland. Yet, the creation of both Northern Ireland and the Irish Free State lay just as much in the trenches of Langemarck and the bluffs and beaches of Gallipoli, as the glens of Kilrush or the streets of Belfast or Dublin. In fact, the War of Independence/Anglo-Irish Conflict from 1919–1921, struck at the heart of Ireland's reasons for commitment to the First World War. Post-1918, there were serious, and heart-searching, redefinitions of what concepts of 'Britishness' actually meant. These were largely in response to the shared international trauma of the Great War but they were also due to the ordeal of a violent secession of part of the Union itself.[4] Both Unionists and Nationalists were determined, more than ever, that their recent commitment and sacrifices would not be in vain; ironically of course, this meant that both were destined to pull further apart. This perhaps gives considerable weight to the notion that the turbulent period from 1919–1921, originally known as

'The Troubles', may be more helpfully described as the transitional first phase of the Irish Civil War. The aftermath of Irish independence naturally skewed the political and cultural view of the impact of the First World War. To many in Britain and Ulster, their sacrifices had clearly been for King, Country and Empire, in the wider war for 'civilisation' and the '...liberties of Europe'.[5] This latter sentiment, branding the conflict as 'the European War' was certainly one which had been the defining rallying call to the Irish National Volunteers, to save Belgium from German imperialism and stand by Catholic France. However, attempts to make sense out of the years of loss from 1914–1918 only isolated Nationalist Irish veterans further.

Although this is not the place to account for the events of 1919–1921, one sadly relevant, but largely forgotten, incident may be worth mentioning. At College Park (Trinity College Dublin), a cricket match was held between the 'Gentlemen of Ireland' and the 'Military of Ireland' to raise money for the 'Warrior's Day Fund'. It echoed the very first cricket match played in Ireland, in August 1792, when the 'Garrison of Ireland' played an 'All Ireland' team at Phoenix Park. Incidentally, it was also where one Honourable Arthur Wesley, later Wellesley and First Duke of Wellington, appears to be credited among the 'All Ireland' side. Yet, the match on Friday 3 June 1921 was to be the last of its kind. It was a warm and bright summer's day in the city and, as the match continued, it turned into a fine Dublin evening. The players included many Irish regimental veterans but, in the afternoon sunshine, they could be forgiven that the horrors of the Great War were already slipping into history. Then at around 5.30 pm, two men cycled up Nassau Street and halted at the railings of College Park, where spectators had gathered to watch the match. Seven shots later, the mood had been shattered as the men emptied their revolvers into the crowd and made good their escape. The cricketers (and regimental bandsmen) dived to the ground (leading to false reports of a number of deaths) and civilian reactions ranged from 'mild concern' to a 'wild stampede'. Perhaps the gunmen were aiming for the 'soldier-cricketers'. Perhaps, they were simply aiming at anyone present. The painful reality was that one of their shots slammed into a twenty-one-year-old Trinity student, Kathleen (Kate) Wright, mortally wounding her. Although born in England, she was the daughter of an Irish clergyman, Reverend Ernest Alexanderson Wright, who had been the parish vicar of Cahir (Co. Kildare) and Seapatrick (Co. Down). Kate Wright was quickly taken to the St Patrick Dun's hospital by her fiancé, George Ardill (son of the Reverend Canon Ardill of Sligo) but was pronounced dead upon arrival. In the meantime, the cricket match resumed. Like a grotesque metaphor for 'The Troubles' itself, the game limped on, despite the act of self-harming violence. It was abandoned a mere fifteen minutes later on the orders of Trinity's Provost, Dr Bernard. Perhaps in accordance with the rules of fair play, in Dublin Castle's official statement, it was felt absolutely necessary to point out that the Military had been fielding at the time of the attack.[6]

Casualties amongst the Irish Regiments and the Personal Impact of Loss

Indeed, personal loss of life is the key to understanding the legacy of the First World War in Ireland. In 1968, Major Henry Harris famously estimated that the total number of Irishmen serving during the war was 494,000 men. This included men from not only the Irish regiments but also other British regiments and divisional and arms of service troops. It is a figure derived from the 'official' post-war calculation of 49,400 Irish War Dead with a presumption that there is a 'death ratio' of 1:10 to every serving soldier. As such, this may not seem unreasonable, although this figure does not take into account the strength of the recruitable population in the provinces. It is now thought that some 210,000 Irishmen fought in the army during the years of 1914–1918 (not including those who enlisted in units outside Ireland) but their impact was still phenomenal. Equally, the total number of Irish War Dead is now calculated at approximately 30–35,000, although an exact figure may never be truly ascertained. From an Irish regimental perspective, the death-rates for all battalions and squadrons total some 33,268 men and were drawn from throughout Ireland, Britain and the Empire. As might be expected, the regiment with the highest death-rate was the Royal Irish Rifles (6,920 deaths), followed by the Royal Inniskillings (5,772 deaths) and the Royal Dublin Fusiliers (4,778 deaths).[7]

Out of the thirty-two Irish counties, the five with the heaviest death total may at first seem surprising, but they aptly reflect the areas which recruited the most: Antrim, Dublin, Cork, Down and Londonderry. It is estimated that some 5,122 Antrim men died during the war, which not only included the massive recruitment pool of Belfast and its environs, but also the rural communities that enlisted so enthusiastically in the ranks of the Royal Irish Rifles. For Dubliners, their commitment to the war could also be adequately shown in their list of War Dead, with the city and county losing approximately 4,973 men. County Cork suffered the third highest total of War Dead, with some 2,226 Cork men lost, whilst Counties Down and Londonderry lost 2,056 and 1,343 men respectively. However, such sanitised statistics cannot adequately portray the true legacy of the personal loss. In Cloughjordan (Co. Tipperary), an uneasy tension was growing in the area and, in this context, one of its most famous military sons, Sergeant James Somers VC, finally succumbed to the consequence of his gassing in France. He died on 7 May 1918 and was buried, with full military honours, in the parish graveyard of Modreeny, where his father was still sexton.[8] Sergeant Somers' cortege was led by pipers and an Honour Guard from the Cameron Highlanders as his coffin, draped with the Union Flag, was finally laid to rest in the county that British soldiers had held so close to their hearts.

For some, the war provided them an opportunity to make soldiering a lifelong career. Captain the Honourable Harold Alexander served with great distinction with both the 1st and 2nd Irish Guards, becoming Lieutenant-Colonel of the 2nd Battalion until the end of the war. Famed as the 'last man' to leave the beaches at Dunkirk, he finally became Field Marshal Earl Alexander of Tunis. Similarly, Lieutenant-Colonel Adrian de Wiart (former 4th Royal Irish Dragoon Guards) VC, was perhaps one of the most gallant soldiers of his generation and, certainly, one of the most colourful. By the time he was awarded the VC (commanding the 8th Gloucestershire Regiment on the Somme from 2–3 July 1916) he had already lost an eye and a hand. Incredibly, during the First World War he was wounded no less than eight times and somehow survived to continue gallant service in the Second. Lieutenant-Colonel de Wiart died on 5 June 1963 and now lies in Kilnardish Churchyard (Co. Cork), a largely forgotten Irish hero of both world wars. Captain J. Batten-Pooll of the 5th Royal Irish Lancers, one of the 'Curragh Mutiny' officers who offered to resign his commission, survived the war and was awarded the DSO and MC for his wartime services. His brother, Captain Arthur Hugh Batten-Pooll had also served with the 5th Irish Lancers before transferring to the Munster Fusiliers, with whom he won a VC in a trench raid at Colonne in June 1916. For others, the opportunity to resume civilian life provided a thankful return to the ordinary. William McCreight Allen, 9th (NIH) Irish Fusiliers, was demobbed on 12 February 1919, returning home to Ulster by way of Dublin. When he got back to Belfast he found that the trams were all on strike so he had to walk home. He never regretted enlisting and felt that the war had left him neither a '… wiser nor sadder man'. He died at the ripe old age of ninety-nine, in 1995.[9]

Perhaps most interesting of all is the transformation of those who had served loyally in the British Army (and some of those with great distinction) to those who fought against their former comrades after the war. Tom Barry's or Emmet Dalton's experiences in the IRA are well-documented, but it is equally fascinating to note the role of the Royal Munster CSM Martin Doyle VC. On 31 January 1919, CSM Martin Doyle, 1st Munsters, was gazetted to the Victoria Cross, which he received from the King on 8 May. Two months later he was demobilised from the British Army but seems to have become an intelligence officer with the Mid-Clare Brigade of the IRA around this time. Indeed, whilst working at Ennis Barracks he appears to have passed information on the army over to the IRA, being posthumously awarded for this service by the Eire Government in 1940. By this time, Doyle had served with the new Irish Army throughout the civil war, retiring in 1937 with the same rank of CSM. Of interest is that, when Martin Doyle died, on 20 November 1940, he was buried in the British military cemetery of Grangegorman, beneath a regimental headstone. It simply stated 'Coy Sgt.-Major Martin Doyle, VC, MM, Royal Munster Fusiliers'. Similarly, James Duffy VC, 6th Inniskillings, was publicly proud of his British Army connections, which made him a target when he returned home to Letterkenny after the war. Indeed, he was duly kidnapped by the IRA, who also issued regular death threats to him from the 1920s onwards. However, he seems to have treated such intimidation with disdain, for Duffy continued to attend VC events, including the Centenary Review in London in 1956.[10]

The Peace Treaty and Regimental Disbandment, 1922

During this period, it can be argued that Britain no longer had any stomach to remain in Ireland for, in Mesopotamia, a larger war involving British regiments was spreading out of control. Indeed, in general, the war with Turkey had extended, or rather over-extended, the campaign theatres miserably. In 1919, the urgent need for more British regiments to garrison the unruly and ungovernable tribes of the Tigris Basin, seemed depressingly familiar. Given this, it is unsurprising that, in Ireland, by 1922, British political forces felt it may be easier to simply 'let go' and concentrate on other international matters.

The long and proud story of the southern Irish regiments came to an abrupt end with the Peace Treaty of 1922. Those regiments which had traditional recruiting grounds in the new Irish Free State were disbanded, leaving three Ulster regiments in the north. The cavalry was similarly treated, with the South Irish Horse disappearing from the Army List. Whilst the Royal Inniskilling Fusiliers, Royal Irish Fusiliers, Royal Ulster Rifles (with an initially unpopular name change), 5th (Royal Irish) Lancers, 4th (Royal Irish) Dragoon Guards, 8th (King's Royal Irish) Hussars and 6th (Inniskilling) Dragoons survived, decades of change and amalgamations awaited them.

Accordingly, on 12 June, six escort parties, five with associated Colours, marched into St George's Hall, Windsor Castle, where their standards were placed in the personal care of King George V and his descendants. It was reported that the King and the Colonels of the Prince of Wales' Leinster Regiment (Royal Canadians), Royal Dublin Fusiliers, Royal Munster Fusiliers, Royal Irish Regiment, Connaught Rangers and South Irish Horse wept openly at their symbolic act of disbandment. Indeed, King George's valedictory words to his southern Irish regiments were heartfelt and genuine. When he accepted their Colours into his protection, he promised that they would remain '... hallowed memorials of the glorious deeds of brave and loyal regiments'.[11] As such, they are still proudly displayed by the grand staircase at Windsor Castle.

Courage and Ignominy—Gallantry Awards and 'Shot at Dawn'

No work on the Irish regiments' contribution to the First World War would be complete without briefly considering those soldiers whose actions went above and beyond the call of duty and those whose deeds were perceived to have been found wanting. There is a remarkable similarity in the statistics, with 22 Irish regimental soldiers executed (out of 306) and approximately 29 Irish regimental soldiers awarded the Victoria Cross (out of approximately 415 army winners). Indeed, it is perhaps worth noting that, in the case of the Welsh regiments, some seventeen Victoria Crosses were won whilst thirteen members of Welsh regiments were shot at dawn. Furthermore, there is the impression that recommendations for gallantry awards were tighter within Irish regiments—and certainly the impulse to punish breaches in discipline were perhaps harsher—due to greater expectations of behaviour.

It is often noted that, in war, courage has to be witnessed as being exceptional for it to be officially recognised; of course, many acts of bravery go unnoticed and, indeed, bravery itself takes a multitude of forms. In the context of military recognition, a number of very specific requirements were necessary to propel a soldier towards the highest honour, and a good many received it posthumously. Some twenty-nine Victoria Crosses were won by the Irish regiments, with the highest numbers awarded to the Royal Inniskilling Fusiliers (eight) and the Leinster Regiment (four); the Irish Guards, Royal

Munster Fusiliers, Royal Dublin Fusiliers and Royal Irish Rifles each received three. The Connaught Rangers, Royal Irish Regiment and Royal Irish Lancers each won a single Victoria Cross. During the final weeks of the war, a flurry of VCs was won by Irish regimental soldiers: Lance Corporal Ernest Seaman (from Norfolk, 2nd Inniskillings, 29 Sept.), Martin Moffat (from Sligo, 2nd Leinsters, 14 Oct.), Lieutenant John O'Neill (from Lanarkshire, 2nd Leinsters, 14/20 Oct.), Sergeant Horace Curtis (from Cornwall, 2nd Dublins, 18 Oct.) and Norman Harvey (from Lancashire, 1st Inniskillings, 25 Oct.). Many soldiers were, possibly, inspired by such deeds and many more may simply have been content to survive war's experiences relatively unscathed. Yet, there was another group—those who were charged with actively attempting to avoid duty or abandon their comrades in the face of the enemy. For them, the ultimate penalty was death by firing squad.

Although the subject is an uncomfortable one, it also raises valid questions about the character and experience of the Irish regiments. Being subject to military law was the norm for Regular troops and the increased punishment for indiscipline in time of war was expected and understood by them; yet, for volunteers and conscripts, the harshness of army discipline could be intolerable. Thirty-six-year-old Private William McMullen from Belfast was a National Volunteer and joined the 6th Connaughts in Fermoy in early May 1915. Yet, less than a month later, he was noted as having been struck off strength for 'desertion'. Even in this short period he had been given eight days confined to barracks for being absent for nearly two days. Many new recruits found themselves 'on a charge' with reductions in pay, or a brief spell in the 'glasshouse' for minor infringements but, in disciplinary terms, it was the persistent offender that caused most concern. However, it was also sometimes convenient for High Command to blur the lines between this type of offender and those whose spirit had finally broken on the battlefield.[12]

To evaluate this properly, certain factors must be addressed, namely, whether or not the severe disciplinary record of the British Army from 1914–1918 was unique, or if other factors were at work. In this, the most obvious comparison is with the Imperial German Army, which strived to punish errant soldiers without the sustained use of the death penalty and seems only to have executed forty-three men in the course of the war. Similarly, French histories had always maintained a low number of executions in its ranks, amounting to 133 soldiers, even after the widespread mutinies and collapse in morale in 1917. This figure, however, has been recalculated with numbers rising to as many as 554.[13] Figures for British executions remain at 306 soldiers who were 'shot at dawn' for military crimes and, of these, 22 served with Irish regiments. A hundred years on, it is almost impossible to rationally assess the context to these men's executions. Some show clear-cut cases of disorientation, shell-shock or battle-fatigue, whilst others, undoubtedly, display aspects of 'bad character' and genuine attempts to desert their post. What can be said quite unequivocally though, is that the use of the death penalty by the British Army rose phenomenally from 1914–1918 and then subsided just as dramatically. It represents a strange peak in executions, unmatched before or since and was quite clearly associated with the specific problems faced by the British Army at the time.

The uncomfortable subject of eugenics and racial stereotyping may well have had an impact on the numbers within Irish regiments facing Field General Courts Martial. Whilst incomparable to the treatment of the Chinese or Indian Labour Corps, it would appear that there was a higher proportion of Irish regimental courts martial than those in English, Welsh or Scottish regiments. In 'non-Irish' units, many similar charges seem to have been directly settled by COs, without resorting to the court martial process. Yet, a distinct pattern of military crimes appear to be associated with Irish regiments, mainly relating to drunkenness, rank insubordination or even mutiny. In this last respect, Irish regiments indulged in 'mutiny', or perhaps simple disobedience, to a far greater extent than those from Great Britain. Even here, generalisation is dangerous as it would appear that each Irish battalion or squadron had its own unique disciplinary record. Perhaps most tellingly, however, is that where the death penalty was exacted amongst Irish units, it seems to have halted any further breaches in discipline.[14]

The comparison between how many men were sentenced to death by courts martial and how many were actually executed is also quite startling. Out of nearly 3,000 death sentences pronounced for military crimes, some 221 Irish soldiers were convicted, although most had their sentences commuted. Whilst many faced similar sentences and commutations, the hard fact remains that five Irish Riflemen, five Inniskillings, three Irish Guardsmen, three Leinsters, two Munsters, two Irish Fusiliers and two Dublin Fusiliers were subsequently tied to a stake and shot by their own side. Many soldiers at the time seem to have agreed in general with the verdicts carried out but their judgements were tempered with a certain amount of understanding. As Colonel Lambert Ward stated to his fellow MPs in the Parliamentary debates on the subject in 1919, many of these men had volunteered to serve their country and, in this, they simply '… tried and they failed'.[15]

'Guilt and Myth'—Making Sense of the First World War in Ireland

Following the carnage and losses of the war, it is entirely understandable that Britain and Ireland needed some way of laying the trauma of these years to rest. The most natural and emotional response was in acts of commemoration, through the erection of war memorials and compilations of Rolls of Honour. In political terms, the war was to usher in far-reaching changes regarding social attitudes to women and the class system; although, in Ireland, some of these trends were not nearly as pronounced as elsewhere. This was especially the case with regard to the commemoration and the treatment of Irish veterans. This issue struck deep at the country's political and constitutional heart and, equally sadly, was doomed to drive a wedge further between the divergent communities in Irish society. In the same way that Northern Ireland was founded upon the legacy of loss sustained during the Great War, so the Republic was forged by an intense feeling that the war had not been Ireland's fight after all.

Furthermore, there was distinct disquiet in some quarters that commemoration of Irish War Dead could be seen as a simple commemoration of pro-British Imperial loyalty. Of course, in Unionist circles, this link between commemorating the War Dead and a perceived sacrifice for the British cause was completely inseparable. Yet, sympathetic Nationalists found themselves in an increasingly difficult public position. Accordingly, the issue of how former soldiers were treated when they returned to Ireland is, unsurprisingly, complex and multi-layered. Despite the increasingly unreceptive atmosphere, attempts by the Redmondite and Unionist communities to parallel responses in Great Britain were maintained. As a result, the Irish War Memorial Trust was created with the sole purpose of raising funds to establish some form of permanent memorial for those who died in the Great War. To this effect, four years later they had completed and published the impressive eight-volume *Ireland's Memorial Records*. It must be stressed that this was at a perilous time; by 1923, Britain had disengaged from Ireland and the Irish Free State was racked by a brutal and savage civil war (into which many Irish ex-servicemen had been drawn). As such, the maintenance of this commemorative project was admirable.

The eight volumes of the Books of Remembrance contain the names of 49,400 War Dead: soldiers, sailors, airmen and nurses, who were Irish-born, had lived in Ireland at the time of their death, or had died serving in an

Irish regiment. Whilst it is now thought that 30–35,000 Irish died during the Great War, the enormous level of effort required to make sure that Ireland's contribution did not go unnoticed is obvious. The exquisite borders surrounding the sixteen or so names per page were designed and drawn in pen and ink by Harry Clarke. These marginal silhouette works of art are a striking hybrid style of Art Deco and Celtic symbolism. Clarke's illustrations echo the great Irish medieval tradition but also pair this savagely with the context of the Great War; the pages on the Books of Remembrance are filled with regimental badges, swirling flourishes, gallantry medals, gas-masked offensives, tanks, planes and, ultimately, Crosses of Sacrifice. The volumes were intended to be deposited in two pairs of book-rooms on either end of the Lawn (a courtyard-like space with a book-room at each of the four corners, representing the four provinces of Ireland).

However, as a consequence of the heightened tensions and associated hostility towards any form of perceived 'pro-British' memorialisation, the construction of a physical building in which the volumes could be kept had been seriously delayed. Despite the potential for controversy and discord, it was at the insistence of William T. Cosgrave, the first President of the Irish Free State, that the Islandbridge Memorial project was successfully completed. It is interesting to note that, despite the savage separation process between Great Britain and the majority of Ireland, the new Government still perceived the depth of loss felt by a huge number of its citizens. It was not until 1929 that an actual piece of ground was agreed upon and, in 1930, that the famous landscape architect Sir Edwin Lutyens was commissioned to design the War Memorial and Garden of Remembrance. The initial work eventually began in 1931 and construction of the Garden and Memorial was undertaken between 1933 and 1937. Indeed, perhaps most intriguing is that the workforce who built these impressive gardens, altar stone, book-rooms and Cross of Sacrifice was drawn from 50 per cent British Army ex-servicemen and 50 per cent Irish Army ex-servicemen. In the lean 1930s, such work was particularly welcome but there is something especially sad about ex-servicemen only being employable when building, effectively, a monument to their own demise and shattered potential. Poignantly, although completed in 1938, the Irish National War Memorial never had an official opening ceremony, as wrangling once more seemed to hold sway over the main purpose of commemoration.[16]

One of the first and most distinctive war memorials constructed was to the memory of the 36th (Ulster) Division—the Thiepval Tower on the Somme, unveiled by Field Marshal Sir Henry Wilson on 18 November 1921.

The memorial was, essentially, an exact replica of the 1861 'Helen's Tower', on the Clandeboye estate, which overlooked the strongly Unionist town of Newtownards. However, it was not simply chosen for its impressive Scots baronial style and all the nuanced messages it transmitted, for the men of the Division had trained for war under its shadow. For the 16th (Irish) Division, a memorial had already been erected to their memory in France by the time the Armistice was signed. Perhaps surprisingly, but certainly fittingly, this most poignant memorial to the Division was actually designed by Major-General Sir William Hickie, its Divisional Commander. He was determined that the 16th (Irish) should be remembered for their victory on the Somme so, in early 1917, he made drawings of a Celtic cross on a scrap of blotting paper and handed the design to his pioneer battalion. Ironically, the first—and arguably most apt—memorial to the Nationalist 'Irish Brigade' was made by the Englishmen of the 11th Hampshire Regiment. These pioneers took oak beams from the nearby derelict buildings and began to carve the impressive four-metre/thirteen-foot-tall wooden cross into the intricately traditional Celtic cross designed by Hickie. It was originally placed between the shattered villages of Guillemont and Ginchy where it remained until 1923 when the farmer who owned the land complained that it was interfering with his ploughing. Consequently, the bullet-hit wooden cross was removed to Ireland where it was eventually brought to one of the book-rooms at the Irish National War Memorial at Islandbridge in 1926. In that year, General Hickie also instigated the erection of three stone Celtic crosses at sites of deep connection to Irish forces. One was for the 10th (Irish) Division at Salonika, one was at Messines and the third was put up at Guillemont, where the original wooden cross to the 16th Division had once stood. On it, a memorial plaque simply reads, in Irish: 'To the glory of God and the honour of Ireland'. Below it, in English, follows:

> 'In commemoration of the victories of Guillemont and Ginchy, September 3rd and 9th 1916. In memory of those who fell therein and of all Irishmen who gave their lives in the Great War. R.I.P.'

The final 'butcher's bill' shows a phenomenal commitment from every part of society: the 10th (Irish) Division suffered over 9,000 casualties, the 16th (Irish) Division sustained over 28,000 casualties and the Ulster Division lost over 32,000 killed, wounded or missing during the Great War. Although these figures include 'non-Irish', there are also many Irish regimental soldiers omitted. Some, like CSM Michael Moran of the Irish Guards, famed for his 'what retreat?' utterance after Mons, are not included on these divisional memorials. Similarly, Private Thomas Woodcock VC, 2nd Irish Guards, was killed during the German breakthrough. Others, such as Cecil Barker, would never have been in the army under normal circumstances. Cecil had simply intended to pursue a career in the Church of Ireland but, instead, he died leading a section of 6th Irish Fusiliers against the slopes of the 'Pimple' at Gallipoli. Meanwhile, back near Ballina (Co. Mayo), at the home of tin smith Phillip Kennedy, a telegram arrived in late September informing him that his Connaught Ranger son, Stephen, was listed as missing. Two months later, another dreaded telegram came through. This time, it was the official notification that Private Kennedy had died '... from wounds received'. His small soldier's book and will were never forwarded home and his body, like so many thousands, was not recovered.[17]

Archaeology and the Irish Regiments

Archaeologists, however, are now frequently left with the task of identifying those individuals who are finally released from the soil of France, Flanders and further afield. Yet, the archaeological perspective, with its considerations of surviving landscapes, material culture and artifact evidence, is an aspect which can sometimes be overlooked within military histories. There has been significant archaeological research over the last twenty years or so, across the campaign theatres and covering the war in the air, sea and, of course, land. Whilst the subject is too large to be discussed in any detail here, a brief overview of sites and examples of work undertaken which is relevant to Irish regiments must suffice.[18]

Planned archaeological work, either non-invasive or excavation, has generally been undertaken at trench systems, burial sites, bunkers and dugouts. The geographical area for investigations is widespread, from France to the Dardanelles, Jordan to Flanders. Indeed, such is the wealth of archaeological material in the latter, from shrapnel, bullets and iron fragments alone, that there are sections of land which have an almost '... geological ferrous layer...' of their own.[19] First World War 'battlefield layers' tend to be distinctly prolific in their material, depending on the terrain and location of the battle-site. On the Western Front, the recovery of military paraphernalia from personal equipment such as buttons, cap badges and brass buckles, to shells, bullet casings, machine-gun parts, sniper shields, barbed wire and silent pickets is commonplace. Indeed, given the immense amount of material employed from 1914–1918, it is hardly surprising that so many artefacts, trench systems and, sadly, human remains, are regularly recovered by accident or through agricultural activity.

It is widely noted that the conditions of the ground in France and Flanders, and the quantity of discarded or deposited material, have often led to the '… excellent preservation…' of artifacts.[20] One such site, relevant to Irish troops, is at Auchonvillers ('Ocean Villas'), where the possibility of stray finds can be used to identify regimental movements across the landscape. The site has revealed artefacts of uniform and equipment, in particular, a cap badge from the Royal Irish Fusiliers. This was believed to have been lost at some point '… from July 1915 to early 1916'. However, the dateable loss of the cap badge and the unit it came from may be even more specific. According to the war diary and official history of the 1st Irish Fusiliers, 'B' Company was recorded as being present at Auchonvillers from October to November 1915. Whilst it does not necessarily follow that a member of 'B' Company lost his cap badge in those two weeks of 1915, it remains a distinct possibility.[21]

Equally, on the Somme in 2006, archaeologists from the 'No Man's Land' group (along with troops from the Royal Irish Regiment), excavated trenches at the Ulster Division's positions in Thiepval Wood. Initially, unexploded ordnance was recovered (shells and mills bombs) but many personal effects were found too, from shaving equipment to bully-beef tins. Subsequent work expanded into two important areas, including a front-line trench which was overlooked by the Schwaben Redoubt. Yet, some of the most recent public revelations regarding the Ulster Division's Somme sector site demonstrate the forgotten randomness of instant death and the accidental nature of the recovery of individuals. In 2013, a road-widening operation revealed human remains by the Ulster Tower (close to the site of the German first line). With them, was a clearly identifiable cap badge for the Royal Irish Rifles and it was believed that the individual had been caught by a mortar shell blast. Shortly afterwards, the remains of another soldier were unearthed on the opposite side of the road, near to Connaught Cemetery. Here, an 11th Royal Inniskilling Fusilier from the 1 July assault was finally recovered, with his bayonet still fixed to his rifle. Through archaeology and historical research, the Somme Association and Commonwealth War Grave Commission were finally able to identify him.[22]

However, it is not believed that there is currently any direct evidence to denote the presence of Irish regiments in the archaeological record at Gallipoli,

Jordan or Palestine. At Gallipoli, the Joint Historical and Archaeological Survey (part of a tri-nation scheme between New Zealand, Australia and Turkey), has investigated Anzac Cove, recording the extant trench systems before they are lost. This, as with work elsewhere, has been largely 'non-invasive', using Ground Penetrating Radar and mapping techniques, with several key locations investigated. These include Shrapnel Gully, Quinn's Post, Russell's Top/The Nek and an area near to the Lone Pine memorial. As such, this valuable work has relevance for the archaeology of the 10th (Irish) Division (specifically 5th Connaughts, 6th Royal Irish Rifles and 6th Leinsters) and has already revealed evidence for Turkish superiority in supply. Unsurprisingly, human remains are also regularly discovered, for example, during the road widening schemes in 2005 and 2008. Sometimes groups of individuals who died in the scrub are revealed and concur with reports in the war diaries, recollections and available photographic evidence. In 2001, human remains were uncovered behind Turkish lines at 'Kidney Hill', a site highly significant to Irish troops.[23]

Indeed, the landscape archaeology around many First World War sites is still a haunting environment with visible features directly attributable to the war. Such sites can be obvious, as at Guillemont on the Somme, where a substantial German dugout still survives with remains of German and Allied occupation debris inside. Equally, in Dublin, the pock-marked public buildings, with the important evidence at Moore Street, O'Connell's bullet-holed monument or the damage to 'Fusilier's Arch' in St Stephen's Green, are a fading legacy of the battle-scape of Easter 1916. Elsewhere in Ireland, other signs of the Great War also abound. There are training camps, from Ballykinler to Kilworth, once ignored and forgotten but now actively undergoing important investigation. There are the numerous and moving CWGC headstones, such as those to Private T. Knox, Connaught Rangers, who died of wounds on 29 November 1918 and is buried in St Multose's Church, Kinsale (Co. Cork), or forty-five-year-old Private T. Mulhall, 2nd Leinsters, who died on 19 January 1918 and was interred at Carlow Old Cemetery. Similarly, the substantial numbers of private memorials or graves in Ireland often go unnoticed, hidden quietly away in parish churches and graveyards, commemorating the fallen of the Great War.[24]

Legacy and Conclusion

Perhaps far too many narratives describe headless or limbless horrors from the carnage of the battlefield, frequently nameless and all of them heartbreaking. Lieutenant O'Sullivan's horrific 'jet of wet dust' from the blast before the assault at Guillemont *did* have a name, however; he was the former Belfast carman, Private Joseph Crowley, aged twenty-four. Perhaps luckily for his family they were 'regretfully' informed of his death in action in very vague terms, saying he had died at an unknown location on 3 September 1916. The men around him, however, were reduced to a '...state of utter delirium', broken by the horrifying sight they witnessed.[25]

On the other end of the scale, by mid-1915, 2nd Lieutenant The Honourable Captain Harry Harmsworth, Irish Guards, had been wounded twice, the last time so severely that he was 'blightied' home. Following his recovery, he was seconded to Lord French's staff in London, but he hated this 'cushy' posting and returned to his regiment in August 1917, just in time for the Cambrai offensive. On 27 November 1917, Captain Harmsworth was awarded the MC for his gallantry during the miserable operation around Bourlon Wood, where he again sustained serious injuries. By the time notice of his award arrived, Harry Harmsworth was in hospital, where he died of wounds a few weeks later on 12 February 1918.

For those who did not come back, many families were to receive a bronze memorial plaque—the 'Death Penny'—and an illuminated scroll, purporting to be from King George V. In many homes these items were preserved with almost religious sanctity; in some they took on the active appearance of reliquaries, in others they were carefully handed down from generation to generation. In our more cynical age, some find it easy to dismiss such gestures and hard to conceive that these items brought any solace to grieving next of kin. Yet, they became the tangible last abiding memento that their loved ones had ever existed in this world and that their exit from it had been, somehow, for a greater, nobler, reason. It is perhaps for exactly this reason that, within many Irish Nationalist homes, the death pennies, scrolls or medal groups were bitterly disregarded or sadly put away in drawers, not to be seen until many years later. However, the wording on the scroll conveys so much more about the losses of the Great War. When considered within the context of the men of the Irish regiments, and the eventual disbanding of the regiments themselves, perhaps some of its words take on a more poignant meaning. It tells the reader that those who died...

> ...left all that was dear to them, endured hardness, faced danger, and finally passed out of the sight of men by the path of duty and self-sacrifice, giving up their own lives that others might have freedom.[26]

The complicated, but compelling, story of the Irish regiments in the Great War gives us a fascinating insight into a military world which is now long gone. The men of the Irish regiments fought from 1914–1918 for complicated reasons. For some it was a professional way of life. Others saw the war as an 'escape-hatch' from rural or urban poverty. Yet others viewed it as a chance for adventure or excitement. However, for many volunteers, it was a simple and practical opportunity to demonstrate their patriotism, either for Ireland, for Britain or for both. It was an ideological, just as much as an idealistic, call. For those who came from Ireland's shores, their political and cultural motivation may, at times, have been almost paradoxical, sometimes counter-productive, but was always driven by a unique perception of their own patriotic identity. It is ironic, of course, that many Irishmen also saw their identity and patriotism in different ways, a fact which has only served to muddy the waters further. The tragic internecine blood-letting is perhaps best illustrated by the assassination of the redoubtable Field Marshal, Sir Henry Wilson (from Longford), by two IRA men. Wilson was returning from unveiling a war memorial at Liverpool Street Station when he was shot on the doorstep of his London home on 22 June 1922. He had attempted to draw his dress sword and defend himself against his attackers, Joseph O'Sullivan, a former Munster Fusilier from Bantry (Co. Cork), and Reggie Dunn a former Irish Guardsman from London. In the light of this, it is interesting that his death, like that of Major Willie Redmond, was observed in similar terms. One observer simply reflected that the Field Marshal had '... died for Ireland'. In a sense, of course, he had. They were all, in so many ways, to paraphrase Francis Ledwidge's haunting words, the helpless children of circumstance.[27]

Indeed, mirroring the opening words of Sun Tzu at the start of this book, these men were driven this way and that, first by their politicians, then by their generals and, finally, by events and history itself. The nature of this military symbiosis between Great Britain and Ireland, so often dismissed and sometimes denied, has frequently been a cause of fascination and, equally frequently, hostility. Yet, in the words of Nora Robinson, daughter of Sir Lawrence Parsons (the first Commander of the 16th (Irish) Division), Irish soldiers in the British Army held a mutual but '... unexpected affection and loyalty... which neither side can fully understand'.[28] Nora Robinson, writing many decades after the end of the Great War, saw this relationship as potentially both a contradiction and paradox. Yet, perhaps, the crux of this relationship lay in neither. Perhaps, these were simply men, drawn from throughout Britain and Ireland and serving in Irish regiments, doing what they best believed to be their duty.

219

Endnotes

AI–Audio Interview (Imperial War Museum, London)

Cen 1901/1911 – Census Returns (National Archives of Ireland, Dublin)

DeR – De Ruvigny's Roll of Honour 1914–24

IMR – Ireland's Memorial Records 1914–1918

ISW – Irish Soldiers' Wills (National Archives of Ireland, Dublin)

MIC – WWI Medal Index Cards, Army Medal Office, War Office

PRONI–Public Record Office of Northern Ireland

SD – Soldiers Died in the Great War

SDPC – Soldiers' Documents from Pension Claims (NA, Kew, WO364)

SSR – Soldiers' Service Records (NA, Kew, WO363)

WD – War Diary (NA, Kew, WO95)

Chapter One: From Ulster Crisis to Great War, 1912–1914

1 RIC Inspector General (PRONI, MIC/448/78).
2 Phoenix (1994), p.1.
3 Heslinga (New York, 1971); Robbins (1990); De Groot (1996); Jeffery (2000).
4 *Irish Independent*, 25 Nov. 1915; *Report of the Departmental Committee...* (London: HMSO, 1914), pp. 26–35.
5 *Irish Times*, 10 April 1912 and *Weekly Irish Times*, 17 Feb. 1912.
6 Fitzpatrick (1996), p.380.
7 James (1998).
8 *AI* : F.W.H. Holmes (*IWM* Catalogue No. 9147: 1985).
9 *SSR:* M. Devine.
10 In 1914, the 1st RDF was called the 'Blue Caps', whilst the 2nd RDF revelled in the name of the 'Old Toughs' (both from their days in India); the latter also referred to the whole regiment.
11 Elizabeth Meunger states that of the 5th Lancer officers (28) only 5 had Irish connections: Meunger (1991), p.18.
12 The Munsters were known as the 'Dirty Shirts' from their assault on Fort Bhurtpore in India (1805) when their shirts were seen by General Lake covered in black powder, sweat and blood after the battle.
13 In the Peninsula War, General Picton dubbed the 88th Connaught Rangers the Devil's Own; he also referred to them as the 'Connaught Footpads'.

14 *Cen* 1901 (NAI); Doherty and Truesdale (2000), p. 135; Dungan (1995), p.44; S. Kennedy, *SSR;* Lucy (1938), pp.13–14.

15 *AI* : T.T.H. Verschoyle, (IWM, Catalogue 8185: 1984).

16 'Britain's Roll of Honour 1914–1915' in *The Great War*, Pt. 95, Vol.VI (London: Amalgamated Press, June 10 1916) p. 395; Martin (2002), p.29; *WD*: Penrose (PRONI: D/3574/ E6/7). The Royal Irish Fusiliers were called the 'Faughs' after their motto: 'Faugh-A-Ballagh' or 'Clear the Way!'

17 Biggs-Davison and Chowdharry-Best (1984), p.308; Phoenix (1994), pp.27–30; William Redmond, *Irish News* 10 Feb. 1913; RIC Files (PRONI Mic/448/53).

18 Orr (1987), p.31.

19 Crozier (1940), p. 22; RIC Files (PRONI Mic/448/53); Yeates, (2012) p.17.

20 RIC Files (PRONI Mic/448/53).

21 Fergusson (1964); Stewart (1967 and 1981); Johnstone (1992); Beckett (1986); Harvey and Cape (1923); Byrne (2008), p.41; Jeffery (1985b), pp.10–11.

22 RIC Files (PRONI, MIC/448/78); Stewart (1967 and 1981); Buckland (1973); Haines (2009). Capt. Spender is widely credited as the UVF staff officer who organised the gun-running operation.

23 Captain George Berkeley Papers, Cork City and County Archives, IE CCCA/ PR12/56 /57 and Siggins (2005) p.53.

24 *Statement by Bulmer Hobson on Gun-Running at Howth and Kilcoole* (Irish Bureau of Military History, Dublin, 5 November 1947, W.S. 53), p.11 and hand-written note on p.16.

Chapter Two: Ireland's Regiments go to War

1 McClean (1991), p.14.

2 Fitzpatrick (1996), pp. 380–8; Jeffery (1985a), pp. 218–19; Callan (1987), p. 42.

3 *WD:* August 1914; 2nd Leinsters (WO95/1612); 2nd CR (WO95/1347); 2nd RIR (WO 95 /1415); 2nd RIRegt (WO95/1421); 2nd RDF (WO95/1481);1st RIF (WO 95 / 1482); 2nd RInnF (WO 95/1505); 2nd RMF (WO95/1279); 1st IG (NA, Kew, WO95/1342).

4 *WD:* 5th RIL (WO95:1134/2/1); *Derry Standard*, 3 August 1914; *Cork Constitution*, 6 August 1914; *Anglo-Celt*, 15 August 1914.

5 *Belfast Newsletter*, 20 August 1915; RIR (912) and RIF (988); see also Harris (1969), pp. 216–17; Doherty and Truesdale (2000), pp. 107–108.

6 *Irish Independent*, 7 August 1914; RIC Files (PRONI: Mic.448/53).

7 *Derry Standard*, 3 August 1914.

8 *Berkeley Papers*, 2 Sept 1914 (IE CCCA/PR12/56 /97); Gwynn (1919); Gwynn (1932); Bew (1996); Meleady (2014).

9 *The Great War*, pt. 93, Vol.VI, 27 May, 1916; Henry (2006) pp. 33–34.

10 Calvert (1996), p.8; J. Caffrey, *SD* Vol. 64, Pt. 69 CR; *Cen* 1901 (NAI); *IMR*, Vol. 1, p.335; M. Coulter, *SD,* Vol. 66; Pt. 73, RDF; *Cen* 1901 (NAI), *IMR*, Vol. 2, p.176; Inscription Aghada Old Churchyard, Cork; *Irish Independent*, 11 August 1914; *Belfast Newsletter*, 20 August 1915.

11   *AI*: T.T.H. Verschoyle, (IWM, Catalogue 8185: 1984); Laird (1925) p. 3; *Irish Independent*, 7 August 1914; Cooper (1994) pp. 15–17; *Irish Independent*, 10 Dec 1914.
12   *Longford Leader*, May 01, 1915.
13   T. S. Anderson, A. Allen, *SSR;* Hanna (1916), p.14 ff.
14   J. O'Dare, *MIC, SDPC*.
15   *Weekly Irish Times,* Sept 26 1914; *Belfast Newsletter*, 20 August 1915; *AI*: T.T.H. Verschoyle, (IWM, Catalogue 8185: 1984).
16   *Irish Independent*, 8 August 1914.
17   *Irish Independent*, 16 May 1914 and *Ulster Herald* 3 Oct. 1914; *The Derry People and Donegal News*, 15 August 1914; *Connaught Tribune*, 8 August 1914; *Irish Independent*, 31 Oct. 1914.
18   *Irish Independent*, 24 Sept 1914; B. Beggan, *MIC, SSR*.
19   RIC Files, (PRONI, MIC/448/78); *The Derry People and Donegal News*, 15 August 1914 and *Irish Independent*, 12 Dec 1914; Berkeley Papers (IE CCCA/PR12/44a); 'Obituaries', Mr G. Fitz-H. Berkeley; *The Times*, 21 November 1955.
20   Walker (1920), p. 4; Denman (1992); Hamblin (2014), p.50; Jeffery (2006), pp. 155–58.
21   *Irish Independent*, 30 November 1914.
22   *Irish News*, 20 November 1914; *Irish Independent*, 30 November 1914.
23   McConnell (1993) p.16; W. Gregg, *MIC, SSR*; McBride (2000), p.9.
24   Greenald (2002) p. 33; *Dublin Evening Mail,* 14 Sept. 1914.
25   Denman (1995) p. 85; *Irish Independent*, 12 Dec 1914.
26   Crozier (1940) p. 23.
27   'D Company, RIR Men from Kilkeel, Newry, Banbridge, Rathfriland Areas'; *North Irish Roots*, Vol. 14, No. 2 (2003), pp. 46–48; McGuicken (2004) p.26; J. Gregg, *SD*, Vol. 64, pt. 67, RIR; *Cens 1911, IMR,* Vol. 3, p.363.
28   *SD*: Vol.22 Pt.32 *RInnF; IMR*: W. Long, Vol. 5, p.131; V.M. Meyers, Vol. 6 p.138; F. Carter, Vol. 2, p.11; D. Griffith, Vol. 3, p. 371; *Employee's Roll of Honour,* Guinness Archives, St James' Gate, Dublin; *Irish Independent,* 26 Sept 1914.
29   Falls (1922) pp. 5–9; *Irish Independent*, 12 Dec 1914.
30   Bourke (1999), pp. 28–29.
31   Cowland (1930) pp.27–28.
32   *WD*: 1st CR (WO95/3923/1); 1st CR, Medical Officer (WO95/3923/2); *SD*: Vol. 64, pt. 69, CR.

Chapter Three: Mons to First Ypres, August 1914–December 1914

1   Lucy (1938), p.111.
2   George Curnock, *Daily Mail* 18 August 1914 and *Daily Mail* 11 August 1934.
3   *MIC, SD*: Vol.4, Pt.5 IG; *IMR*: R. Daughton, Vol.2, p.272; E. Daly, Vol.2, p.259; L. Farrell, Vol. 3, p.371; *WD*: 'A' Squadron, NIH (WO95:86); 'B' Squadron, SIH (NA Kew, WO95: 2380); *Irish Independent*, 31 Dec. 1915.

4   *WD:* E. McNeill Penrose (PRONI: D/ 3574/ E6/ 7); Horne, (1923) p.211 and p.382

5   *WD:* 4th RIDG, (WO95/1112/1 and WO95/1112/1/1); Gibb (1925), pp.2–5.

6   Lucy (1938), p.111.

7   *WD:* 2nd RIR (WO95/1415/1); 2nd CR (WO95/1347); Jourdain, (1924–1928), Vol.2 pp. 404–5; Holmes (1997), pp.100–6; Lucy (1938), pp. 112–14; *SD:* Vol.22 Pt.23 RIRegt. The 2nd RIRegt was effectively wiped out; a Celtic cross was erected east of Mons to commemorate them.

8   Lucy (1938), pp. 112–4.

9   *WD:* 1st IG (WO95/1342); Kipling (1923), p.32; 2nd CR (WO95/1347); Jourdain, (1924–1928), Vol.2, pp. 404–5.

10   *WD:* E. McNeill Penrose (PRONI: D/ 3574/ E6/ 7).

11   *WD:* E. McNeill Penrose (PRONI: D/ 3574/ E6/ 7); SQMS Clenshaw was subsequently awarded the DCM; Walker and Buckland (2007), p.114.

12   *WD:* 2nd RIRegt (WO95/1421/3).

13   *WD:* 2nd CR (WO95/13471).

14   *WD:* 2nd RMF (WO95/1279); Graves (1960), p.168.

15   Bridges (1938), p.87; Osburn (1932), p.83; see also Gibb (1925), Scott (1994).

16   *'Notes on the Retreat from Mons'*, M.J.W. O'Donovan (PRONI: D/3574/ E6/ 9); *Kildare Observer*, 1 January, 1916.

17   Kipling (1923), p.38.

18   Kipling (1923), p.41; *WD:* 1st IG (WO95/1342/4); 5th RIL (WO95:1134/2/1)

19   *WD:* 2nd CR (WO95/13471); 2nd RInnF (WO95/1505/2); 1st IG (WO95/1342/4); Jourdain, (1924–1928), Vol.2, pp. 426–47; Kipling (1923), p.42.

20   *WD:* 2nd Leinsters (WO95/1612/2); Whitton (1926), Vol. 2, p.29.

21   Whitton (1926), Vol.2, p.40.

22   *WD:* 1st RIF (WO 95/1482/1).

23   Hitchcock (1937) p.276; *WD:* 5th RIL (WO95:1134/2/1). Upon receiving Captain O'Brien Butler's personal effects, his family returned the gold watch to the Royal House of Hesse.

24   *WD:* 2nd RIR (WO95/1415/1); Falls (1925), pp.14–15.

25   Sergeant Jones was awarded the DCM and Captain Kentish was awarded the DSO for their actions. *London Gazette*, 11 Nov. 1914 and *Armagh Guardian* 20 Nov. 1914; *WD:* E. McNeill Penrose (PRONI: D/ 3574/ E6/ 7).

26   *WD:* 2nd RIRegt (WO95/1421/3); *SD:* Vol.22 Pt.23 RIRegt.

27   *WD:* 2nd Leinsters (WO95/1612/2); Walker and Buckland (2007) p.1255; Lucy (1938), pp.247–8.

28   *WD:* 2nd RInnF (WO95/1505/2); *SD:* Vol.22 Pt.32 RInnF, 1st IG (WO95/1342/4); *SD:* Vol.4, Pt.5 IG; *MIC, IMR:* R. Daughton, Vol.2, p.272; E. Daly, Vol.2, p.259; G. Griffith, Vol. 3, p.384; Kipling (1923), p.62.

29   *WD:* 1st CR (WO95/3923/1); 2nd CR (WO95/13471); 8th KRIH (WO95/1185/2); Jourdain, (1924–1928), Vol.2, pp. 450–51.

30   Falls (1925), p. 23; Johnstone (1992), p.63; Hitchcock (1938) p. 306; *Irish Times*, 30 Aug 1915.

Chapter Four: Ireland's Regiments at Stalemate—Western Front, 1915

1 *Londonderry Sentinel* – sadly, from Tuesday, 22 September 1914.

2 M. and E. Carbery, *Cen* 1911; *IMR:* Vol. 1 p.368, *Calendar of the Grants of Probate...* 1915; *Tuam Herald,* 26 December 1915.

3 *WD:* 6th ID (WO95/1176/3); 1 RDF (WO95/4310); *Cen* 1901; *MIC:* W. J. Finn.

4 F. Vere-Laurie (1921), pp.40–41.

5 Whitton, (1926), pp. 77–78; McClean, (1991), p.14; Burrowes (n/d), p.26; *Irish Independent* 11 Jan. 1915.

6 Kipling (1923), p.77; *IMR:* R .St. J. Blacker-Douglass, Vol.1, p.138; Private L. Farrell, Vol. 1, p.158; *SD:* Vol.4, pt.5 IG.

7 *WD:* 1st RIRegt, (WO95/2266/4); 1st Leinsters (WO95/2266/3); Walker and Buckland (2007), p.1253; Geohagan (London, 1927), p.76; *IMR:* R.M. Bowen-Colthurst, Vol.1, p.189.

8 *WD:* 1st RIR (WO95/1730/4); Taylor (2002), p.227; *MIC: Boston Evening Transcript*, May 4, 1915; Falls (1925) pp.29–30; Lucy (1938), pp.331–2; Vere-Laurie (1921), pp. 101–06; Greenald (2002) p. 32.

9 *WD:* 1st RIF (WO95/1482/1); E. McNeill Penrose (PRONI: D/3574/E6/7); Burrowes (n/d) p.30.

10 Davison (1985), p. 172; *WD:* 1st IG (WO95/1342/4); 1st RIRegt, (WO95/2266/4); *MIC: Boston Evening Transcript*, May 4, 1915..

11 *WD:* 1st RIF (WO95/1482); 2nd RDF (WO95/1481/4); E. McNeill Penrose (PRONI: D/3574/E6/7); Burrowes (n/d), p.30; Johnstone (1992), p75; Kerr (1916), p.115.

12 *WD:* 1st CR (WO95/3923/1); *SD:* Vol. 64, pt. 69; CR, J. Mynes; ,*MIC, IMR:* Vol.1, p.138.

13 *WD:* 2nd RMF (WO95/1279); *SD:* Vol. 66 pt.71, RMF; Jervis (1922), p.19.

14 *WD:* 2nd Northamptonshire Regiment (WO95/1722); 1st RIR (WO95/1730/4); Falls (1925), pp.31–33; *SD:* Vol. 64, pt. 67, RIR.

15 *WD:* 2nd Leinsters (WO95/1612/2); 2nd RInnF, (WO95/1350/); 1st IG (WO95/1342/4); *SD:* Vol. 66 Pt.71 Leinster Regt; *SD:* Vol.22 Pt.32 RInnF; *IMR:* P. Penders, Vol.7, p. 90; T. Quinn, vol. 7, p.168.

16 *WD:* 2nd RDF (WO95/1481/4) .

17 Hodges (2008), p.135; *WD:* 'D' Squadron, NIH (NA Kew, WO95:2854).

18 *Irish Independent*, 28 July 1915; *IMR:* J. Cole, Vol.2, p.89; *SD:* Vol.66 Pt.71 RMF; *MIC, WD:* 11th HLI (WO95/1775/2); J. Watson, *IMR*, Vol. 8, p.280; *SD:* Vol.60 Pt.63 HLI.

19 Hammerton (1933), pp. 399–400; McGill (1916), p.81; Johnstone (1992), pp.156–7.

20 *WD:* 2nd RMF (WO95/1279); Siggins (2005), p.52. (T) Capt. James Ryan, MC, served with the 1st King's (Liverpool) Regt. and was capped in 1912.

21 Kipling (1923b), p.25.

22 Crozier (1940), pp.57–58.

23   Falls (1922), p.25; Orr, (1987), p.105; Samuels and 'D.G.S.' (n/d), p. 13; *Irish Independent*, 28 Dec. 1915; *Belfast Newsletter*, 31 Dec 1915; Walker and Buckland (2007), p.1206.

24   Crozier (1940), p. 69; *Irish Independent*, 16 Dec. 1915; *WD:* 6th CR (WO95/1970/2); 'C' Squadron, NIH (NA Kew, WO95:1399); J. Crowley, SSR.

25   *WD:* 'A' Squadron, SIH (WO95: 2141); *Irish Independent*, 31 Dec. 1915; CSM J. Adams, *Papers*, (PRONI: D/3574/ E6/2/ 7).

26   S. Lemon, *IMR vol.*5, p.94, *SD* Vol. 64, pt. 67, RIR; *Belfast Newsletter* 31 Dec. 1915.

Chapter Five: The Gamble at Gallipoli, 1915

1   *Armstrong Papers* (WO 95/4296).
2   Wilkinson (1915); Aspinall-Oglander and Becke (1929/1932); Laffin (1980); Steel and Hart (1994); Haythornthwaite (1999); Steel (1999); Carlyon (2001).
3   *WD:* 1st RDF (WO95/4310); 1st RMF (WO95/4310); 1st RInnF (WO95/4311); C. Powell, ISW (NAI/ 2002/119).
4   Fox (1928), p.180, 'DeR' p.209, IMR, vol.4, p.285. Lieutenant-Colonel F.G. Jones died of wounds received at Krithia on 5 May 1915.
5   *AI* : R.B. Gillett (IWM Catalogue 19953 : 1965).
6   Kerr (1916), pp.138–9.
7   Wylly (1925), pp. 30–32; McDonagh (1916), p.62.
8   *WD:* 1st RDF (WO95/4310); Wylly (1925), pp. 30–32; McDonagh (1916), pp. 109–10; Crighton (1916), p. 67; Father Finn is buried in Joint grave F 4, V Beach Cemetery, Cape Helles; his original resting place was marked by a temporary cross made from an ammunition box.
9   *WD:* 1st RMF (WO95/4310); *AI:* W. Flynn, (IWM Catalogue 4103:1964); McCance (1927), pp. 47–9.
10   Wylly (1925), p.32–33; Walker and Buckland (2007), p.1268; *SD:* Vol.66, Pt. 73, RDF: *IMR:* F. Deegan, Vol. 2, p.291; W.T. Covill, Vol.2, p. 179; C. Powell, *IMR*, Vol. 7, p.129, *MIC, ISW*.
11   *AI* : R.B. Gillett (IWM Catalogue 19953 : 1965).
12   *AI:* W. Flynn, (IWM Catalogue 4103:1964); McCance (1927), pp 47–49; *AI:* R.B. Gillett (IWM Catalogue 19953:1965); Lieutenant Guy Nightingale in Dungan (1995), p.40; Walker and Buckland (2007), p.1263.
13   *AI:* R.B. Gillett (IWM Catalogue 19953 : 1965); Nevinson (1918), p. 98; *WD:* 1st RMF (WO95/4310, 1st RDF (WO95/4310).
14   McDonagh (1917), p.147.
15   Both Cosgrove and Doughty-Wylie won the VC. Walker and Buckland (2007), p.1268.
16   *WD:* 1st RInnF (WO95/4311); Fox (1928), p.185; *Nationalist* 28 Aug 1915.
17   *AI:* I. Powell (IWM Catalogue 16448: 1985–05-10).
18   *WD:* HQ, 29th Brigade, 10th (Irish) Division (WO 95/4296).
19   Cooper, *Tenth (Irish) Division*, p.54.
20   *WD:* 6th RIR (WO 95/4296).

21   *WD:* 6th Leinsters (WO95/4296); 10th Hampshire Regiment (WO95/4296); Cooper, *Tenth (Irish) Division*, p.58; *SD:* C.W. D'Arcy-Irvine, *IMR,* Vol. 2, p.270; *MIC: De Ruvigny's,* Vol.2, p.179; J.V.Y. Willington, *IMR,* Vol. 8, p.342, *MIC;* R. Pound, *The Lost Generation* (Constable, London: 1964) p.154; Morgan (2003), pp.101–35; Morgan (2009), pp. 1–10.

22   Lieutenant-Colonel F.A. Greer, *Papers* (PRONI, D/3574/E6/ 6b).

23   *WD:* 6th RInnF (WO 95/4835); *Belfast Newsletter,* 20 August 1915; *SD:* vol.22 Pt.32 RInnF.

24   *WD:* 7th RDF (WO95/4296); Hanna (1916), p.59; Laird (1925), p.25; *Belfast Newsletter,* 20 August 1915.

25   *AI :* T.T.H. Verschoyle, (IWM, Catalogue 8185: 1984).

26   *WD:* 6th RMF (WO95/4296); 7th RMF (WO95/4296), A. Joyce, *IMR,* Vol. 4, p. 294, *SD.*

27   *WD:* 5th RInnF (WO 95/4296), R. Coldwell, *IMR,* Vol. 2, p.88, *MIC; Belfast Newsletter,* 20 August 1915.

28   Walker and Buckland (2007), p.1259; The DCM was solely awarded to Private W. Bellamy.

29   *Belfast Newsletter,* 20 August 1915. His brother, Reverend E. Barker was a chaplain with the 36th Division.

30   *WD:* 6th RMF (WO95/4296); 7th RMF (WO95/4296); J.N. Jephson, *IMR,* Vol. 4, p. 263; K. E. O'Duffy, *IMR,* Vol. 6, p. 361.

31   J.R. Duggan, *IMR,* Vol. 3, p.40; *MIC:* CWGC, Cen *1911;* Walker and Buckland, (2007), p.435.

32   *WD:* 5th RIF (WO 95/4296).

33   *Nationalist* 28 Aug 1915

34   *WD:* 1st RInnF (WO95/4311).

35   *WD:* 5th CR (WO95/4296).

36   This issue is briefly addressed in Chapter Twelve.

37   Carlyon (2001), p. 607; *Meath Chronicle,* March 18 1916; J.O'Dare, *MIC,* SDPC.

Chapter Six: Emergency at Home— the Easter Rising, 1916

1   Popular reference to Dublin post-Easter Rising; see also Jeffery (2000), p.52.

2   Jeffery (2000), pp.44–47 Fitzpatrick (1996); Meunger (1997); Novick (2001).

3   *Irish Independent,* 9 July 1916, 18 Oct 1917. Interestingly, the *Soldiers' Rendezvous* was left unmolested during the Rising.

4   The following unit movements are from official histories, war diaries and Brigadier James (1998).

5   Hamblin (2014), p.86.

6   *Kildare Observer,* 4 December 1915.

7   Siggins (2005), p.53; Fitzpatrick (1996), p.382.

8   Garvin (1988), p. 46.

9   Papers, *Central Committee of Recruitment* (PRONI D/ 3809/1); NAI, DMP Files, Detective Department, 'Seditious Literature in Circulation'; *The Irish Volunteer*, 5 June 1915, p.4, Reel MFA/ 2/; *The Connacht Tribune*, 19 June 1915; *Belfast Newsletter*, 8 July 1915.

10   *Skibbereen Eagle*, 7 August 1915; NAI, DMP Files, Detective Department, 'Movement of Suspects', 16 August 1915, p.4 Reel MFA/ 2/; *Skibbereen Eagle*, November 13, 1915; *The Cornell Daily Sun*, 17 Nov 1915.

11   Plowman (2003), pp. 81–105.

12   *Belfast Newsletter*, 8 June 1915.

13   Allen (1999), p.11; *Irish Independent*, 25 May 1915.

14   *Kildare Observer*, 1 January 1916.

15   Roth (1995); Montgomery Hyde (1963), p.61; Flower (1917) p.1571; *Daily Telegraph* 17 May, 1916.

16   Street (1921), p.20; *Kerryman* 'Casualties in Dublin', 6 May 1916; Sheehy-Skeffington (1966), p.276.

17   Hally (1966), p.326; Martin (1967), p.131.

18   Falls (1925), p.88.

19   *The Times History of the War*, Vol.VIII (London, 1916), p.425; A. Allen, 10th RDF, *SSR.*.

20   Siggins (2005), *'Obituary, F.H. Browning' The Irish Times*, 2 May 1916; Warwick-Haller (1995), pp. 18–19; Caulfield (1965), pp.133–5.

21   T. Bowman (2003), p.193; Falls (1925) p.88.

22   Gwynn (1919), p.230; Leonard (1996), pp.263–5; Jeffery (200), p.52; Bowman (2003), pp.127–31; Captain J.C. Bowen-Colthurst, Report to CO, 3rd RIR, 9 May 1916 in HMSO *Irish Uprising* (2000) p. 139.

23   Lucy (1938), p. 45, p.319, pp. 351–2; Denman (1992), p. 143; Dallas and Gill (1985), p. 59; *WD*: 'D' Squadron, NIH, (WO95:2854).

24   *WD*: 8th RMF (WO95/1971/2); 7th Leinsters (WO95/1970/4); 9th RDF (WO95/1974/4); S. McCance (1927), vol. II, p. 197; Bowman (2003), p.129; F. Law (1985) p. 69; *The Incinerator*, June 1916, p.19.

25   Street (1921), p.39; F. Burke, *MIC*, SDPC, *IMR,* vol 1, p.288.

26   Burke (2011), pp. 205–6.

27   *Connacht Tribune* 6 May 1916; *Leitrim Observer*, 6 May 1916; *Connacht Tribune* 6 May 1916; Jeffery (2000) p.52; *Kerryman* 6 May 1916.

28   Ryan (1949), pp. 142–3; Gibbon (1968) pp.31–32; *Irish Times*, 17 June 1916; *Irish Independent*, 9 July 1916.

Chapter Seven: The Long Battle of the Somme, 1916

1   Crozier (1940), p.107.

2   This does not include the 1/8th (Irish) King's (Liverpool) Regiment, 1/18 and 2/18 London Regiment (London Irish Rifles) or 24th to 27th Northumberland Fusiliers (Tyneside Irish) battalions.

3   Falls (1922) p.29; T. Devlin, *IMR vol.* 2, p.315; *SD:* Vol. 64, Pt. 67, RIR; *WD:* 'E' Squadron, North Irish Horse (WO95:2445).

4   Walker and Buckland (2007), p.1212; *WD:* 'A' Squadron, SIH (WO95:2141); 'C' Squadron, NIH (WO95:1399); A. Devlin, *IMR* Vol. 2, p. 313; *SD:* Vol. 64, Pt. 67, RIR.

5   *WD:* 6th RIRegt. (WO95/1970); Johnstone (1992), p.209, p.212; Jeffery (2000) p.52; Walker (1920), pp. 34–35.

6   McDonagh (1917), pp.130–2; *WD:* 6th RIRegt. (WO95/1970); Walker, *The Book*, pp. 37–38; T. Cassidy, *IMR*, vol. 2, 26, *SD*, vol.22 pt.32 RInnF.

7   *Lyon Papers*, IWM, p.60; Denman (1992), p.69; *WD:* 6th RIRegt., (WO95/1970); 6th CR (WO95/1970); Walker and Buckland (2007), p.1225, p.1227.

8   *WD:* 14th RIR (WO95/2511).

9   Crozier (1940), p. 98; CWGC Martinsart British Military Cemetery, Plot 1, Row A, grave 1, T. Russell in Orr (1987), p.156; Gliddon (1994), p.315.

10 Crozier (1940), p. 101; *WD:* 14th RIR (WO95/2511/1).

11 Grand Orange Lodge of Ireland, notes regarding Lodge 862, Crozier (1940), p. 104.

12 Major-General Nugent, letter to Lieutenant-General Sir George Richardson in Samuels & 'D.G.S.' (n/d), p. 52.

13 Major Burke had already been mentioned in dispatches; twice from 1914–1916 and three times during the Boer War. He lost a son, Sergeant Fred Burke, 10th Dublins, in the Easter Rising. *Lisburn Standard*, 5 Jan 1917.

14 *WD:* 1st RIR (WO 95/1730); Falls (1925), pp. 66–67; C.C. MacNamara, *IMR*, Vol. 5, p.176.

15 *WD:* 12th RIR (WO95/2506/2); 14th RIR (WO95/2511/1); *London Gazette* 9 September 1916, Orr (1987), p.164; Gliddon (1994), p.14.

16 Samuels & 'D.G.S.' (n/d), p.60; *WD:* 9th RInnF (WO95/2510/3); 10th RInnF (WO95/2510/4); 11th RInnF (WO95/2510/5); W. Long, *IMR* Vol. 5, p. 131, *SD*, Vol.22 pt.32 RInn; F, McDonagh, *Irish on the Somme*, p.36.

17 *WD:* 11th RIR (WO95/2506/1); 12th RIR (WO95/2506/2); 13th RIR (WO95/2506/3); J. Davidson, *IMR*, Vol.2, p.274; *SD:* Vol. 64, pt. 67, RIR, *Cen* 1911 (NAI).

18 *Portadown News*, 25 November 1916; *WD:* 9th RIF (WO95/2505/2); 13th RIR (WO95/2506/3); 15th RIR (WO95/2505/5); 16th RIR (WO95/2498/2); W.H. Smyth, *IMR*, Vol.8, p.34; *SD:* Vol. 64, Pt. 67, RIR.

19 *WD:* 9th RIR (WO95/2503/2); 10th RIR (WO95/2503/3); *Starret Papers*, IWM, pp.64–66; McDonagh (1917), p.36; Middlebrook (1984), p.175; Belfast Citizens' Committee, *A Tribute to Ulster's Heroes* (Belfast: City Hall, 1919), p. 21; G. Gaffikin, *IMR* Vol.3, p.237; Siggins (2005), p.52. Major W. J. Peacocke was killed by the IRA on the doorstep of his Cork home, Skevenish House, Inishannon, 31 May/1 June 1921.

20 H. Macnaghten, *IMR*, Vol.5, p.176 (recorded as 1st Royal Highlanders); *SD:* Vol. 64, Pt. 67, RIR; R. Quigg and G. S. Cather, *London Gazette* 9 September 1916; Gliddon (1994), pp.3–5, pp. 18–22.

21 Falls (1922), p. 63.

22 *WD:* 2nd RIRegt. (WO95/1662/2); 2nd Regt. NIH, Appendix 'A', (NA Kew, WO95:874).

23 *WD:* 2nd RIRegt (WO95/1662/2); 2nd RIR (WO95/2247/1); 2nd RMF (WO95/1279); Falls (1925), p. 67.

24 *WD:* 2nd Regt. NIH (WO95:874).

25 *WD:* 1/8th King's Regiment (WO95/2887/1); J. Cameron, *IMR*, vol.2, p.274; *SD:* Vol. 12, Pt.13, 1/8th King's Regiment; *WD:* 2nd Leinsters, (WO95/2218/1); Whitton (1926), p.232; Hitchcock (1937) p.142.

26 Walker (1920), p. 60; Denman (1992), p.76; *WD:* 6th CR (WO95/1970/2).

27 McDonagh (1917), pp.141–2

28 *O'Sullivan Papers*, IWM, p.25; J. Crowley, *IMR* Vol.2, p.218; *SD:* Vol. 64 Pt. 69 *CR.*

29 *WD:* 6th CR (WO95/1970/2); 6th RIRegt (WO95/1970/3); 7th Leinsters (WO95/1970/4); *London Gazette,* 26 October 1916.

30 McDonagh (1917) pp.141–142; *WD:* 8th RMF (WO95/1971/2); 6th RIRegt (WO95/1970/3); 7th Leinsters (WO95/1970/4); J. Breen *IMR* Vol.1, p.222, *ISW* (NAI 2002/119).

31 McDonagh, p.145; *London Gazette,* 14 November 1916.

32 *WD:* 7th RIF (WO 95/ 1978/1); 8th RIF (WO 95/ 1978/2).

33 *WD:* 6th CR (WO95/1970/2); 8th RMF (WO95/1971/2); Fielding (1929), p.114.

34 *WD:* 6th RIRegt (WO95/1970/3); 7th Leinsters (WO95/1970/4); Whitton (1926), p.316.

35 Cooper (1994), p.36; Falls (1925), p. 74; *WD:* 7th RIR (WO95/1975/2); 7th RIF (WO 95/ 1978/1); 1st RMF (WO95/1975/3); 8th RDF (WO95/1974/3); 8th RInnF (WO95/1977/3).

36 *WD:* 7th RIR (WO95/1975/2); 7th RIF (WO 95/ 1978/1); 9th RDF (WO95/1974/4); 1st RMF (WO95/1975/3); McDonagh (1917), pp.162–3.

37 J. Corrigan *IMR* Vol.1, p.222, ISW (NAI 2002/119).

38 *WD:* 6th CR (WO95/1970/2); 7th Leinsters (WO95/1970/4).

39 Father Browne was wounded just ten days later; he was subsequently Mentioned in Despatches and awarded the Military Cross. Cobh Heritage Centre now has his medals. Reverend F.M. Browne, *MIC, WD,* 1st IG (WO95/1216/1); 2nd IG (WO95/1220/1); Kipling (1923a), p.159.

40 *London Gazette,* 20 October 1916; J. Dyra *IMR* Vol. 3, p. 66; *SD:* Vol.4, Pt.5, 'Foot Guards', *MIC;* he had previously served with the 1st IG as part of the original BEF. Walker and Buckland (2007), p.58 and p.60, Kipling (1923b), p.174.

41 *WD:* 1st RIF (WO95/1482/1); 2nd RDF (WO95/1481/4); Burrowes (n/d), pp.80–82; E.E. Hyde, *IMR,* Vol. 4, p.230, *SD* Vol. 64 Pt. 68 RIF; *London Gazette,* 25 November 1916.

42 Denman (1992), p.40; *WD:* 10th RDF (WO95/3118/4); W. O'Riordan, *IMR* Vol.7, p.34, ISW (NAI 2002/119).

43 *WD:* 2nd Regt. NIH, (WO95:874); Walker (1920), p. 82; Godley (1939), p.215.

Chapter Eight: Messines, Third Ypres and Cambrai, 1917

1   *WD*: 15th RIR (WO95/2505/5).

2   *WD*: 6th RIRegt. (WO95/1970/3); 2nd RIRegt. (WO95/1979/1); 2nd RIR (WO95/2247/1); E.W.V. Leach, *IMR* Vol.5 p.76; P.A.D. Jackson, *IMR* Vol. 4, p.249.

3   *WD*: 2nd IG (WO95/1220/1); Kipling (1923a), pp.113–14.

4   *WD*, 8th KRIH, (WO95/1164/2).

5   Falls (1922), p. 64; Fielding (1929), p.148; *WD*: 9th RInnF (WO95/2510/3); 7th Leinsters (WO95/1970/4).

6   *WD*: 7th Leinsters (WO95/1970/4); 6th CR, (WO95/1970/2); 7th RIR (WO95/1975/2); Fielding (1929), p.148, p.153, pp.155–8; *London Gazette*, 25 May 1917; *SD*: Vol. 64 Pt. 69 CR; *SD*: Vol. 66 Pt.71 Leinster Regiment; H.B. Mollman *IMR*, Vol. 4, p.144; W.R. Bradshaw, *IMR*, Vol. 1, p.211; G.A. Read, *IMR*, Vol. 1, p.335; Falls (1922), p.75.

7   Falls (1922), p. 66.

8   *WD*: 2nd Leinsters (WO95/2218/1); *The War Illustrated*, 30 June 1917; *London Gazette*, 8 June 1917; K. Phelan, *ISW* (NAI 2002/119).

9   *WD*: 10th RInnF (WO95/2510/4).

10   G. Sheffield (2002), p.200.

11   Fielding (1929), p.190.

12   Ryan (1917), p.64; *WD*: 7th Leinsters (WO95/1970/4); 6th CR (WO95/1970/2); 9th RIF (WO95/2505/2); *SD*: vol. 64, pt. 69, CR, vol. 64, pt. 68, RIF.

13   Geohegan (1927), p.116; Falls (1922), p. 92; Whitton (1926), p.410; *WD*: 7th Leinsters (WO95/1970/4); 14th RIR (WO95/2511/1); M. Cooper, *We Who Knew* (1994), p.65.

14   Lieutenant F.W.S. Jourdain in Steel and Hart (2000), p.54; Fielding (1929), p.189; *WD*: 7th Leinsters (WO95/1970/4); 14th RIR (WO95/2511/1); B. Grange in Doherty (1992), p.24.

15   *WD*: 15th RIR (WO95/2503/5); 9th RIR (WO95/2503/2) 7/8th RIF (WO95/1978/3); *SD*: vol. 64, pt. 68, RIF.

16   Falls (1922), p. 94; *WD*: 14th RIR (WO95/2511/1).

17   *WD*: 6th RIRegt. (WO95/1970/3); 2nd RIRegt. (WO95/1979/1); 7th Leinsters (WO95/1970/4); 1st RMF (WO95/1971/1); 1st Regt. NIH (WO95:816); Denman (1992), p.112.

18   Burke (2007), p.236–238; Denman (1995), pp.119–21; 'Roll of Honour: Major W. Redmond MP', *The War Illustrated*, 23 June 1917, No. 149.

19   *WD*: 8th KRIH, (WO95/1164/2); 5th RIL (WO95:1134/2/1); J. Black, C. Burnham, D. Cassells, P. Fitzpatrick, *SD* Vol.1 Pt.1 Cavalry of the Line.

20   Sheffield (2002), pp.204–5; Fielding (1929), p.190.

21   Kipling (1923), p.136.

22   *WD*: 1st RIR (WO 95/ 1730); 2nd Leinsters (WO95/2218/1); Falls (1925), p.102; Hitchcock (1937), p.290.

23   Dungan (1997), p.118; Myers (2014), pp.190–2; *WD:* 1st Regt. NIH (WO95:816); 2nd Regt. NIH (WO95:874).

24   *WD:* 2nd RIR (WO95/2247/1); O'Rahilly (1920), pp.535–6.

25   *WD:* 11th RIR (WO95/2506/1); 12th RIR (WO95/2506/2); 13th RIR (WO95/2506/3); 9th RIF (WO95/2505/2).

26   Falls (1925), pp.107–108; *WD:* 1st RIR (WO95/1730/4).

27   *WD:* 2nd RIRegt. (WO95/1979/1); 8th RInnF (WO 95/ 1977); 7/8th RIF (WO95/1978/3); 7th RInnF (WO 95/ 1977); 9th RDF (WO95/1974/4); 7th RIR (WO95/1975/2); Hamblin (2014), p.86; J.F. Eberli *IMR* Vol. 3, p.72; Falls (1925), p.109.

28   *Correspondence*, Major-General Sir Oliver Nugent, (PRONI D3835/E/2/502); Falls (1922), p.120; *WD:* 7th RInnF, (WO 95/1977); 8th RInnF (WO 95/1977); Gibbs (1920), p.389.

29   HMSO, *Quarterly Army Lists* (1920), p.709; W.J Doyle, *SD, IMR* Vol. 3, p.22, *DeR*, Vol.3, p.82.

30   *WD:* 2nd Regt. NIH (WO95:874); 7th (SIH) RIRegt. (WO95/1979/2). R. Hall, *SSR.*

31   *Portadown News,* 28 September 1917; Kipling (1923b), pp.145–7; *WD:* 2nd IG (WO95/1220/1).

32   *WD:* 1st RDF, (WO95/1974/1); 7th (SIH) RIRegt, (WO95: 1979/2); *London Gazette,* 8 November 1917.

33   *WD:* 2nd RMF, (WO95/1279); 2nd Leinsters (WO95/2218/1); Whitton (1926), vol.2, pp.373–4.

34   *WD:* 9th RInnF (WO95/2510/3); 10th RInnF (WO95/2510/4); 11th RInnF (WO95/2510/5); 1st RInnF (WO95/2305/2).

35   *Report to 47th Brigade,* Lieutenant-Colonel R. Fielding, 6th CR (WO95/1970/2).

36   *WD:* 7th (SIH) RIRegt., (WO95/1979/2).

37   *WD:* 5th RIL (WO95/1134/2/1).

38   *WD:* 6th ID, (WO95/1160); Hughes (2000), pp. 77–85.

39   *WD:* 14th RIR (WO95/2511/1); 9th RInnF (WO95/2510/3); Falls (1922), pp. 172–5; *London Gazette,* 13 Feb. 1918.

40   Falls (1922), pp. 176–7; *WD:* 7th Leinsters (WO95/1970/4); 6th RIRegt. (WO95/1970/3); 10th RInnF (WO95/2510/4); 6th CR (WO95/1970/2); 7th (SIH) RIRegt. (WO95/1979/2).

Chapter Nine: Macedonia, Mesopotamia, Egypt and Palestine, 1915–1918

1   *WD:* A.J. Smith, September 1918 (PRONI: D/3574/ E6/17A).

2   Robbins (1984), p. 44; Terraine (1997), p.86.

3   *WD:* 29th Brigade (WO95/4835); 30th Brigade (WO95/4296); McCance (1927), p.180, p.193.

4   *WD:* 6th RMF (WO95/4296); 6th RDF (WO95/4836); 7th RDF (WO95/4296); 6th RInnF (WO95/4838); J. Byrne, *IMR,* Vol. 1, p.323.

5   *WD:* 5th RInnF (WO95/4838); 6th RIR (WO95/4835); 7th RDF (WO95/4296); 7th RMF (WO95/4296); 5th CR (WO95/4835); *AI:* T.T.H. Verschoyle (IWM Catalogue 8185: 1984).

6   *WD:* 5th CR (WO95/4835); 6th RDF (WO95/4836; 5th RIF (WO95/4838); 6th Leinsters (WO95/4835); Whitton (1926), pp. 206–7.

7   *WD:* 5th CR (WO95/4835); Jourdain (1928), Vol. 3, p.120.

8   *WD:* 7th RDF (NA Kew, WO95/4296); 7th RMF (NA Kew, WO95/4296); McCance, Vol. 2, p.195.

9   *WD:* Johnston (1992), p.186; Falls (1933), p.82; *SD:* P. Durnian, *IMR* Vol. 3 p.62, Cen 1911 (NAI); H. Morgan, *IMR* Vol. 6, p.205, Cen 1911 (NAI); F. McBrearty, *IMR* Vol 5 p 267, Cen 1911 (NAI); J. Barry, *IMR* Vol. 1 p.97, Cen 1911 (NAI); F. Joyce, *IMR* Vol. 4, p.294, *MIC, SSR*, McIlwain Papers, 20 Jan. 1916 (IWM, 96/29/1).

10   See Townsend (2011) and Dixon (1994), p.101.

11   *WD:* 1 CR (WO95/5106).

12   Dixon (1994), p.243; *WD:* 1st CR (WO95/5106); Jourdain (1924), Vol. 1 p.508; M. Cloherty, *IMR*, Vol. 2, p.72; J. Rogers, *IMR*, Vol. 7 p. 265, *SD*, Cen 1911 (NAI).

13   *WD:* 1st RIRegt. (WO95/4836); 1st Leinsters (WO95/4834); 2nd RIF (WO95/4838); *AI:* T.T.H. Verschoyle (IWM Catalogue 8185: 1984.).

14   *Freeman's Journal*, 19 Feb. 1916; 'Letter, Private W. Rule, RAMC', McIlwain Papers, 5–6 June 1916 (IWM, 96/29/1).

15   Walker and Buckland (2007), p.1217; *Armagh Guardian* 23 June 1916; *Irish Examiner*, 22 August 1916; P. McQuillan, *IMR* vol. 6, p.110, Orr (2002), p.175.

16   *AI* : I. Powell (IWM Catalogue 16448: 1985–05–10).

17   *WD:* 1st RIRegt. (WO95/4836); 1st Leinsters (WO95/4834); 6th RInnF (WO95/4838); 6th RIR, (WO95/4835); 7th RDF (WO95/4296); 7th RMF (WO95/4296); 6th RMF (WO95/4296); 6th RDF (WO95/4836); 5th RIF (WO95/4838); Johnson (n/p, 1919), p.22; T. Cullen, *IMR* vol 2 p.224; *SD:* vol.66 Pt.71 RDF; Falls and Beck (1933), p.184.

18   Skilbeck-Smith (1930), pp.55–58; *AI:* T.T.H. Verschoyle (IWM Catalogue 8185: 1984); Whitton (1926), vol. 2, p. 215.

19   *WD:* 1st CR (WO95/5106); J. Breen, *IMR* vol.1, p.222; J. Cassidy, *IMR,* vol. 2, p.23, *MIC, SSR*.

20   *AI* : I. Powell (IWM Catalogue 16448, 1985–05–10).

21   *WD:* Nov. 1918; 2nd RIF (WO95/4838); 5th RIF (WO95/4838); 6th RInnF (WO95/4838); *AI:* I. Powell (IWM Catalogue 16448, 1985–05–10).

22   *WD:* 6th Leinsters (WO95/4835); 2nd RIF (WO95/4838); 6th RIR, (WO95/4835); 5th CR (WO95/4835); *AI:* I. Powell (IWM Catalogue 16448, 1985–05–10).

23   *London Gazette*, 28 Feb 1918.

24   *WD:* 2nd RIF (WO95/4838); 5th RIF (WO95/4838); 1st Leinsters (WO95/4834); 6th RIR, (WO95/4835); 5th CR (WO95/4835); 1st RIRegt. (WO95/4836); J. O'Brien, *SD,* Vol.22, Pt.23 RIRegt. Cen 1911 (NAI).

25   *WD:* 1st RIRegt. (WO95/4836); 1st Leinsters (WO95/4834); 2nd RIF (WO95/4838); 6th RIR (WO95/4835); 1st CR (WO95/4700).

26   *WD:* Lieutenant A.J. Smith (PRONI: D/3574/ E6/17A).

Chapter Ten: The German Somme Offensive— 'Kaiserslacht', March 1918

1   *WD:* 1st IG, (NA Kew, WO95/1216/1).
2   Blake (1953) p.279; Gilbert (1994) p.365.
3   *Operational Order,* 16th Division; Reorganisation of Infantry Brigades, Feb 1918 (WO95/1970); *Correspondence,* Nugent Papers (PRONI: D/3835/E/2/545).
4   *WD:* 7th Leinsters (WO95/1970/4); 8/9th RDF (WO95/1974/5); 10th RDF (WO95/1974/6); 7/8th RIF (WO95/1978/3); 6th RIRegt (WO95/1970/3); 7th (SIH) RIRegt (WO95:1979/2).
5   *WD:* 8/9th RIR (WO95/2503/3); 11th and 13th RIR (WO95/2506/4); 10th RIR (WO95/2503/4); 14th RIR (WO95/2511/1); 10th RInnF (WO95/2510/4); 11th RInnF (WO95/2510/5); 1st RInnF (WO95/2510/1); 2nd RInnF (WO95/2510/2); 1st RIR (WO95/2502/3); 2nd RIR (WO95/2502/4); 9th RInnF (WO95/2510/3).
6   *WD:* 1st Regt. NIH, (NA Kew, WO95/874).
7   *WD:* 2nd IG (WO95/1226/3); 8th KRIH (WO95/1115/1).
8   Gough (1931), p. 257; Whitton (1926), p.445.
9   *WD:* 2nd R.I.Regt. (WO95/1979/1); 7th (SIH) R.I.Regt (WO95:1979/2); 1st RDF (WO95/1974/1); 2nd RDF (WO95/1974/2); 2nd RMF (WO95/1975/4); 7/8th RInnF (WO95/1977/4); 6th CR (WO95/1970/2); 2nd Leinsters (WO95/2308/2); 1st RMF (WO95/1971/1); 1st RIF (WO95/2505/1); 1st RIR (WO95/2502/3); 1st RInnF (WO95/2510/1); 9th (NIH) RIF (WO95/2505/2); 2nd RIR (WO95/2502/4); 9th RInnF (WO95/2510/3); 12th RIR (WO95/2506/2); 15th RIR (WO95/2503/5); 16th RIR (WO95/2498/2); Geohegan (1922), p119.
10   Middlebrook (1983), p122.
11   *WD:* 7th (SIH) R.I.Regt (WO95:1979/2); 7/8th RInnF (WO95/1977/4).
12   *WD:* 15th RIR (WO95/2503/5); 2nd RInnF (WO95/2510/2); 2nd RIRegt. (WO95/1979/1); Falls, (1922), pp.193–203.
13   *WD:* 6th CR (WO95/1970/2); W. M. Allen (1999) p.12; 9th (NIH) RIF (WO95/2505/2); 9th RInnF (WO95/2510/3); 12th RIR (WO95/2506/2); Falls (1922), p.196.
14   *WD:* 1st RIF, (WO95/2505/1); Burrowes (n/d), p.110.
15   *WD:* 6th CR (WO95/1970/2); 1st RIF (WO95/2505/1); 12th RIR (WO95/2506/2); F.K. Cummins, MC *IMR,* Vol. 2, p.232; Falls (1922), p.197.
16   *WD:* 15th RIR (NA Kew, WO95/2503/5); *London Gazette,* 15 May 1919.
17   *WD:* 2nd RInnF (WO95/2510/2); 15th RIR (WO95/2503/5); Lieutenant-Colonel C. G. Cole-Hamilton in *Newton and Anderson Papers* (PRONI D961/8); Falls (1922), pp.193–203.

18 *WD:* 1st RInnF (WO95/2510/1); 6th CR (WO95/1970/2); 1st RMF (WO95/1971/1); 7th (SIH); R.I.Regt (WO95/1979/2); 1st RIF (WO95/2505/1).

19 Hamblin (2014), p.296.

20 *WD:* 1st RIF (WO95/2505/1); 7/8th RInnF (WO95/1977/4); Falls, (1922), p.200.

21 *WD:* 6th CR (WO95/1970/2); 2nd Leinsters (WO95/2308/2); 1st RMF (WO95/1971/1).

22 *WD:* 5th RIL (WO95/1134); 9th RInnF (WO95/2510/3); 16th RIR (WO95/2498/2); 9th (NIH) RIF (WO95/2505/2); Falls, (1922), pp.211–212; J. Donaghy in Mitchell (1991), p.151; *London Gazette,* 28 March 1918.

23 *WD:* 2nd RIR (WO95/2502/4); 1st RIR (WO95/2502/3); Falls, (1922), pp.211–212; 'Kismet', *Observer* 21 April 1918; R.B. Marriot-Watson *IMR,* Vol. 5, p.220.

24 *WD:* 1st RMF (WO95/1971/1); 6th CR (WO95/1970/2); Doherty and Truesdale (2000), p. 135.

25 *WD:* 8th KRIH, (WO95:1115/1).

26 *WD:* 1st RIR (WO95/2502/3); 2nd RIR (WO95/2502/4); Falls, (1922), p.216; 6th CR (WO95/1970/2); 7th (SIH) R.I.Regt (WO95:1979/2).

27 *WD:* North Irish Cyclist Regt.[1st Regt. NIH] (WO95:874); 1st RIF (WO95/2505/1); Burrowes (n/d), p.113; 1st RIR (WO95/2502/3); 16th RIR (WO95/2498/2); 2nd RIR (WO95/2502/4); 1st IG (WO95/1216/1); Falls (1922), p.223; Kipling (1923a), p.235.

28 *WD:* 1st RIF (WO95/2505/1); Burrowes (n/d), p.113; 15th RIR (WO95/2503/5); 1st RIR (WO95/2502/3); 2nd RIR (WO95/2502/4).

29 *WD:* 6th CR (WO95/1970/2); 1st RMF (WO95/1971/1); 2nd Leinsters (WO95/2308/2); 2nd RDF (WO95/1974/2); 2nd RMF (WO95/1975/4); 7th (SIH) RIRegt (WO95:1979/2); 7/8th RInnF (WO95/1977/4); Walker and Buckland (2007), p.1254; Whitton (1926), pp.455–6.

30 *WD:* 6th CR (WO95/1970/2); 1st RMF (WO95/1971/1); 2nd Leinsters (WO95/2308/2); Jeffery (1985), p. 33.

31 Hamblin (2014), p.50; J. Moloney, *SD,* Vol.66, pt.72, RMF; C.W. Chandler, *MIC IMR,* Vol. 2, p.35.

32 *WD:* 6th CR (WO95/1970/2); 9th RInnF (WO95/2510/3); 1st RIF (WO95/2505/1); 5th RIL (WO95:1134/2/1); J.A.T. Rice, MIC.

33 Edmonds (1937) p. 458; Johnstone (1992), p. 389; Denman (1992), p. 168; *WD:* 1st RDF (WO95/1974/1).

34 Blake (1953) p.296; *War Cabinet Meeting Papers,* No. 374, 27 March 1918 (CAB/23/5); Farrah-Hockley (1975), p. 290.

Chapter Eleven: The Last Days on the Western Front

1 D. Haig, 11 April 1918, *Order of the Day.*

2 *War Cabinet Meeting Papers,* No. 374, 27 March 1918 (CAB/23/5).

3 Hutchinson, (PRONI, D3804), p.24; *WD:* 2nd IG, (WO95/1226/3); Kipling (1923b), pp. 172–7.

4   D. Haig, 11 April, *Order of the Day;* Reid (2009), p.442.

5   *WD*: 12th RIR (WO95/2506/2); 1st RIF (WO95/2505/1); Falls (1922), p.237; Siggins (2005), p.52.

6   *WD*: 2nd RIRegt. (WO95/3111/3); 7th (SIH) R.I.Regt. (WO95:1979); 7/8th RInnF (WO95/2336/1); Bowman (2003), p. 206.

7   *WD*: 6th CR (WO95/1970/2); 2nd Leinsters (WO95/2308/2); 5th RIL (WO95:1134/2/1); Falls, (1922), pp.244–5, p.305.

8   *WD:* 5th RIF (WO95/1975/1); 5th RInnF (WO95/3140/1); 6th RInnF (WO95/2843/2); 6th RDF (WO95/4583); 7th RDF (WO95/4583); 6th RMF (WO95/4583); 7th (SIH) RIRegt. (WO95:1979).

9   *WD*: 1st RIR (WO95/2502/3).

10   Lavery (1920), p.182; *WD*: 7th (SIH) RIRegt. (WO95:2330).

11   *WD*: 1st RIR (WO95/2502/3).

12   Liddell Hart (1970), p.541–3.

13   *WD*: 6th ID (WO 95/ 1160).

14   *WD:* 15th RIR (WO95/2503/5); 9th (NIH) RIF (WO95/2505/2); 1st RIF (WO95/2505/1); Falls (1922) pp.250–1.

15   *WD:* 9th (NIH) RIF (WO95/2505/2); 1st RIF (WO95/2505/1); 1st RMF (WO95/1971/1); *London Gazette,* 31 January 1918; Doherty and Truesdale (2000), pp. 135–6.

16   *WD:* 7th (SIH) RIRegt. (WO95:2330); 1st RMF (WO95/1971/1); 6th Leinsters (WO95/3140/5).

17   *WD:* 1st RMF (WO95/1971/1).

18   *WD:* 1st RDF (WO95/2301/2); 2nd Leinsters, (WO95/2308/2); Wylly (1925), pp. 119–20; Hitchcock (1938), pp.286–8; *SD:*Vol.66 Pt.71 RDF.

19   *WD:* 2nd RInnF (WO95/2510/2); 9th RInnF (WO95/2510/3); 1st RInnF (WO95/2510/1); Falls, (1922), p. 269.

21   *WD:* 1st RIF (WO95/2505/1); 12th RIR (WO95/2506/2); Hamblin (2014), p.225; F.E. Parfitt *IMR*, vol. 7, p.62.

22   *WD*: 9th RIF (WO95/2505/2); 12th RIR (WO95/2506/2); 1st RIR (WO95/2502/3).

23   Ewing (1921), p.371; *WD*: 9th RIF (WO95/2505/2); 12th RIR (WO95/2506/2); 1st RIR (WO95/2502/3).

24   Jervis (1922), pp.51–52; *WD:* 2nd Munsters (WO95/2837/1).

25   Gibb (1925), pp.57–58; Jervis (1922), p.54; *WD:* 4th RIDG (WO95/1112/5).

26   *WD:* 1st RInnF (WO95/2510/1); 2nd RIR (WO95/2502/4); 1st RIR (WO95/2502/3).

27   *WD:* 11 Nov. 1918, 2nd RInnF (NA Kew, WO95/2510/2); 9th RInnF (NA Kew, WO95/2510/3).

28   *WD*: 8th KRIH (WO95/1115/1).

29   White (1996), pp.252–3. *WD*: 2nd RInnF (WO95/2510): 9th RIF (WO95/2505): 1st RIF (WO 95/2505).

30   *WD*: 5th RIL (WO95:1134/2/1).

31   *WD*: 7th (SIH) RIRegt. (WO95:2330). Whitton (1926), p. 479.

32   Hitchcock, *Stand To*, p. 306.

Chapter Twelve: The Cost and Legacy, 1914–1918

1   *Commemorative Scroll of Service*, Major J.G. Brew, RIF, KIA 6 April 1918 (PRONI: D/ 3574/ E6).

2   Myers (2014), p.19, p.187, p.208, *SD* (Irish Regiments only) and *IMR*.

3   G. de Groot (1996), pp. 247–8.

4   Morton (1933); Matless (1992), pp. 464–80.

5   Lawson, (2008), p. 98.

6   *Freeman's Journal*, 4 June 1921; *Irish Examiner*, 6 June 1921; *Freeman's Journal*, 7 June 1921; *Skibbereen Eagle*, 7 June 1921; *Fermanagh Herald*, 11 June 1921; *Donegal News*, 11 June 1921; Siggins (2005) p.55.

7   Fitzpatrick (1996), pp. 386–8; Callan (1987), p. 42; Casey (1997), p. 195; Harris, (1968) pp. 26–32.

8   Doherty and Truesdale (2000), p.113.

9   *WD*: 5th RIL (WO95:1134/2/2); W.M. Allen (1999) p.12.

10   Doherty and Truesdale (2000), p.136, pp.130–131.

11   *The Times*, 12 June 1922.

12   W. McMullen, *SSR*.

13   Pedroncini (1967), pp.3–9; Hynes (1990) p.214; Evans (1996) p. 482.

14   Oram (1998), pp.60–73; Corns and Hughes-Wilson (2001), pp.394–5; Denman (1991), p.360; Hickman (1995); p.54, Bowman (2003), p.203.

15   Corns and Hughes-Wilson (2001), p.463.

16   Denman (1992), p.94; Harris (1968), p.210.

17   S. Kennedy, *SSR*.

18   Pollard and Banks (2007), pp. iii–xvi; Brown (2005), pp. 25–33; Price (2006); Atherton and Morgan (2011), pp.289–304; Morrissey (2006), pp. 98–113; Pollard, Barton and Banks (2007); Doyle, Barton and Vandewalle (2005), pp.45–66; Fraser and Brown (2007), pp.147–172.

19   Pollard and Banks (2007), p. viii.

20   Osgood (2005), pp.212–13.

21   Fraser (2003), pp.10–11; *WD*: 1st RIF (WO95/1482/1); Burrowes (n/d), p. 54.

22   Robertshaw and Kenyon (2008), pp.22–24; *Belfast Telegraph* 29 November 2013 and 4 August 2014. My thanks go to Mr Matt Gamble, the Somme Association, for his helpful assistance.

23   My thanks to John Winterburn (Arab Revolt Project) University of Bristol and Dr Ian McGibbon (Ministry of Culture and Heritage), Govt. of New Zealand for helpful information in this area.

24   T. Knox, *SD*, Vol. 64, Pt. 69, CR, CWGC; St Multose's Parish Cemetery, Kinsale; T.Mulhall, *SD* Vol.66 Pt.71, Leinster Regiment, CWGC; Carlow Old Cemetery. Dowse brothers, *IMR* Vol.3 p. 9.

25   O'Sullivan Papers, IWM, Documents.7155, p.25; J. Crowley, *IMR* Vol.2, p.218, SSR.

26   *Commemorative Scroll of Service*, Major J.G. Brew, RIF, KIA 6 April 1918 (PRONI: D/ 3574/ E6).

27   Hart (1991), p.150; Jeffery, (2008), p.245; Ledwidge (1919), p.260, 'Soliloquy'.

28   Robertson (1960) p. 55.

Irish Regimental Order of Battle, 1914–1918

[Includes original regimental depot, unit type and main service location: from Brigadier E.A. James, *British Regiments 1914–1918, Parts I and II, British Infantry Regiments in the Great War; War Diaries and Official Histories*, see Sources and Bibliography]

4th (Royal Irish) Dragoon Guards (Regimental Depot: Newport, Monmouthshire)
[Regular] France and Flanders

5th (Royal Irish) Lancers (Regimental Depot: Woolwich)
[Regular] France and Flanders; regiment disbanded in 1922

6th Inniskilling Dragoons (Regimental Depot: Newport, Monmouthshire)
[Regular] France and Flanders

6th (Service Squadron) Inniskilling Dragoons (Regimental Depot: Enniskillen)
[New Army Volunteers] France and Flanders; squadron disbanded summer 1917 and absorbed by 9th Royal Irish Fusiliers in 1917

8th King's Royal Irish Hussars (Regimental Depot: Dublin)
[Regular] France and Flanders

North Irish Horse (Regimental HQ: Belfast)
[Special Reservists] France and Flanders; eventually subsumed by 9th Royal Irish Fusiliers to become 9th (North Irish Horse) Royal Irish Fusiliers

South Irish Horse (Regimental HQ: Beggar's Bush, Dublin)
[Special Reservists] France and Flanders; regiment eventually merged into the 7th Royal Irish Regiment to become the 7th (South Irish Horse) Royal Irish Regiment in 1917

Irish Guards—3 Battalions (Regimental Depot: Caterham)

1st	*[Regular]* France and Flanders
2nd	*[Regular]* France and Flanders
3rd	*[Reserve]* Draft-finding battalion

Royal Irish Regiment—9 Battalions (Regimental Depot: Clonmel)

1st	*[Regular]* France and Flanders, Salonika, Egypt and Palestine
2nd	*[Regular]* France and Flanders
3rd	*[North Tipperary Militia–Reserve]* Dublin, Templemore and Larkhill
4th	*[Kilkenny Militia–Reserve]* Queenstown, Gosport, Fermoy and Larkhill.
5th	*[New Army Volunteers]* Gallipoli, Salonika, Egypt and Palestine, France and Flanders
6th	*[New Army Volunteers]* France and Flanders
7th	*[New Army Volunteers]* France and Flanders, formed during the war to become (South Irish Horse) Royal Irish Regiment
8th	*[2nd Garrison Guard]* 'Home Service' unit in Dublin, France and Flanders, becoming a 'Service' battalion there in June 1918
1st	*[Garrison]* Gallipoli and Egypt.

Royal Inniskilling Fusiliers—13 Battalions (Regimental Depot: Enniskillen)

1st	*[Regular]* Gallipoli, Egypt, France and Flanders
2nd	*[Regular]* France and Flanders
3rd	*[Royal Tyrone Militia–Reserve]* Lough Swilly, Londonderry and Oswestry
4th	*[Fermanagh Militia–Reserve]* Buncrana and Clonmany
5th	*[New Army Volunteers]* Gallipoli, Salonika, Egypt and Palestine, France and Flanders
6th	*[New Army Volunteers]* Gallipoli, Salonika, Egypt and Palestine, France and Flanders
7th	*[New Army Volunteers–'The Fighting Seventh']* France and Flanders
8th	*[New Army Volunteers]* France and Flanders
9th	*[New Army Volunteers–'The Tyrones']* France and Flanders
10th	*[New Army Volunteers–'The Derrys']* France and Flanders
11th	*[New Army Volunteers]* France and Flanders
12th	*[Reserve]* Draft-finding battalion; reformed at Oswestry
13th	*[Garrison]* became a 'Service' battalion in June 1918, France and Flanders

Royal Irish Rifles—21 Battalions (Regimental Depot: Belfast)

1st	*[Regular]* France and Flanders
2nd	*[Regular]* France and Flanders
3rd	*[Royal Antrim Militia–Reserve]* Raised in Antrim

4th	*[Royal North Down Militia–Reserve]*	Raised in Newtownards
5th	*[Royal South Down Militia–Reserve]*	Raised in Downpatrick
6th	*[New Army Volunteers]*	Gallipoli, Salonika, Egypt and Palestine
7th	*[New Army Volunteers]*	France and Flanders
8th	*[New Army Volunteers–'Ballymacarrett's Own']*	France and Flanders
9th	*[New Army Volunteers–'The Shankhill Boys']*	France and Flanders
10th	*[New Army Volunteers]*	France and Flanders
11th	*[New Army Volunteers]*	France and Flanders
12th	*[New Army Volunteers]*	France and Flanders
13th	*[New Army Volunteers–'The County Downs']*	France and Flanders
14th	*[New Army Volunteers–'Young Citizen Volunteers']*	France and Flanders
15th	*[New Army Volunteers]*	France and Flanders
16th	*[New Army Volunteers–'The Pioneers']*	France and Flanders
17th	*[Reserve]*	Home Service
18th	*[Reserve]*	Home Service
19th	*[Reserve]*	Home Service
20th	*[Reserve]*	Home Service
1st	*[Garrison]*	India

Royal Irish Fusiliers—14 Battalions (Regimental Depot: Armagh)

1st	*[Regular]*	France and Flanders
2nd	*[Regular]*	France and Flanders, Salonika, Egypt and Palestine
3rd	*[Armagh Militia–Reserve]*	Armagh, coastal defence Ireland
4th	*[Cavan Militia–Reserve]*	Cavan, coastal defence Ireland
5th	*[New Army Volunteers]*	Gallipoli, Salonika, Egypt and Palestine
6th	*[New Army Volunteers]*	Gallipoli, Salonika, Egypt and Palestine
7th	*[New Army Volunteers]*	France and Flanders
8th	*[New Army Volunteers]*	France and Flanders
9th	*[New Army Volunteers–'Blacker's Boys']*	France and Flanders
10th	*[Reserve]*	Home Service
11th	*[Reserve]*	France and Flanders
1st	*[Garrison]*	India and Burma
2nd	*[Garrison]*	Home Service, Salonika
3rd	*[Garrison]*	Home Service, Bantry, Seaton Carew and Greatham

Connaught Rangers—6 Battalions (Regimental Depot: Galway)

1st	*[Regular]* France and Flanders, Mesopotamia, Palestine
2nd	*[Regular]* France and Flanders, absorbed by 1st battalion
3rd	*[Galway Militia–Reserve]* Crosshaven, Cork, Kinsale, Newcastle-Upon-Tyne and Dover
4th	*[Roscommon Militia–Reserve]* Queenstown, Bere Island, Crosshaven, Nigg (in Perthshire) and Fort George
5th	*[New Army Volunteers]* Gallipoli, Salonika, Egypt and Palestine
6th	*[New Army Volunteers]* France and Flanders

Prince of Wales's Leinster Regiment (Royal Canadians)—
7 Battalions (Regimental Depot: Birr)

1st	*[Regular]* France and Flanders, Salonika, Egypt and Palestine
2nd	*[Regular]* France and Flanders
3rd	*[King's County Militia–Reserve]* Cork, Portsmouth
4th	*[Queen's County Militia–Reserve]* Devonport, Dover and Portsmouth
5th	*[Royal Meath County Militia–Reserve]* Plymouth, Cork, Laytown, Glencourse and Portsmouth
6th	*[New Army Volunteers]* Gallipoli, Salonika, Egypt and Palestine, France and Flanders
7th	*[New Army Volunteers]* France and Flanders

Royal Munster Fusiliers—11 Battalions (Regimental Depot: Tralee)

1st	*[Regular]* Gallipoli, Egypt, France and Flanders
2nd	*[Regular]* France and Flanders
3rd	*[Kerry Militia–Reserve]* Bantry Bay, Cork, Ballincollig, Devonport and Plymouth
4th	*[South Cork Militia–Reserve]* Queenstown, Cork, Bere Island, South Shields, Scotland and Plymouth
5th	*[Royal Limerick Militia–Reserve]* Queenstown, Cork, Bere Island, North Shields, Scotland and Plymouth
6th	*[New Army Volunteers]* Gallipoli, Salonika, Egypt and Palestine, France and Flanders
7th	*[New Army Volunteers]* Gallipoli, Salonika
8th	*[New Army Volunteers]* France and Flanders
9th	*[New Army Volunteers]* France and Flanders

1st   *[Garrison]* Raised in Cork from 1st (Garrison) Durham Light Infantry; sent to Italy

2nd   *[Home Service]* Allocated to Portsmouth Garrison

Royal Dublin Fusiliers—11 Battalions (Regimental Depot: Naas)

1st   *[Regular]* Gallipoli, Egypt, France and Flanders

2nd   *[Regular]* France and Flanders

3rd   *[Kildare Militia–Reserve]* Cork, Pembroke, Gateshead and 'Humber Garrison', Grimsby

4th   *[Royal Dublin City Militia–Reserve]* Sittingbourne, Templemore and Grimsby

5th   *[Dublin County Militia–Reserve]* Sittingbourne, Curragh, Glencourse and Grimsby

6th   *[New Army Volunteers]* Gallipoli, Salonika, Egypt and Palestine, France and Flanders

7th   *[New Army Volunteers]* Gallipoli, Salonika, Egypt and Palestine, France and Flanders

8th   *[New Army Volunteers]* France and Flanders

9th   *[New Army Volunteers–'The Scholar's Battalion']* France and Flanders

10th   *[New Army Volunteers–'The Commercial Pals']* France and Flanders

11th   *[Reserve]* Aldershot

APPENDIX II

Estimated Deaths Incurred by Irish Regiments in Order of Loss

Figures are estimated from official sources (*'Soldiers/ Officers Died'*, *Commonwealth War Graves' Commission*, *Ireland's Memorial Records*, *War Diaries*) and refer solely to individual regimental death-rates; they are approximate and do not correspond to Irish-born fatalities.

Royal Irish Rifles:	6,920–7010 officers & other ranks
Royal Inniskilling Fusiliers:	5,772–5890 officers & other ranks
Royal Dublin Fusiliers:	4,778–4780 officers & other ranks
Royal Irish Fusiliers:	3,330–3,375 officers & other ranks
Royal Munster Fusiliers:	2,835–3070 officers & other ranks
Royal Irish Regiment:	2,603–2780 officers & other ranks
Irish Guards:	2,190 officers & other ranks
Leinster Regiment:	1,980–2,065 officers & other ranks
Connaught Rangers:	1,998–2050 officers & other ranks
4th Royal Irish Dragoon Guards:	189 officers & other ranks
6th Inniskilling Dragoons:	185 officers & other ranks
5th Royal Irish Lancers:	158 officers & other ranks
8th King's Royal Irish Hussars:	103 officers & other ranks
North Irish Horse:	48 officers & other ranks
South Irish Horse:	49 officers & other ranks

Sources and
Select Bibliography

Archives

National Archives, Kew (London)

War Diaries:

North Irish Horse:
A Sqdn: WO95/86 August 1914 – Dec. 1915, WO95/2914/1 Jan. 1916 – May 1916
B Sqdn: WO95/2380/1 August 1914 – May 1916
C Sqdn: WO95/1399/2 Oct. 1915 – June 1916
D Sqdn: WO95/2854/1 May 1915 – April 1916
E Sqdn: WO95/2445/1 Jan. 1916 – April 1916
F Sqdn: WO95/2413/1 Nov. 1915 – May 1916; WO95/816 Jan. 1917 – July 1917

South Irish Horse:
A Sqdn: WO95/2141/1 Sept. 1915 – May 1916
A & B Sqdns: WO95/930 May 1916 – August 1917
C Sqdn: WO95/1962/1 Dec. 1915 – May 1916
E Sqdn: WO95/2574/1 March 1916 – April 1916
S Sqdn: WO95/1324/2 May 1915 – Feb. 1916
HQ, A, B, F, S Sqdn: WO95/623 August 1916 – August 1917

4th Royal Irish Dragoon Guards:
    WO95/1112 August 1914 – March 1919, WO95/1112/1 August 1914 – May 1915,
    WO95/1112/2 June 1915 – April 1916, WO95/1112/3 May 1916 – Dec. 1916,
    (Dismounted Coy), WO95/1189/34 Jan. 1916 – Feb. 1916, WO95/1112/4 Jan. 1917
    – Oct. 1917, WO95/1112/5 Nov. 1917 – March 1919

5th Royal Irish Lancers:
    WO95/1134 August 1914 – Feb. 1919

6th Inniskilling Dragoons:
>WO95/1176/3 Oct. 1914 – Dec. 1916, WO95/1160/4 Jan.1917 – Feb. 1918,
>WO95/1155/4 March 1918 – March 1919, WO95/1166/4 April 1919 – Feb. 1920

6th (Service) Inniskilling Dragoons:
>WO95/2496/1 Oct. 1915 – May 1916

Corps Cavalry (North Irish Horse and Inniskilling Dragoons):
>WO95/874 June 1916 – March1918

8th King's Royal Irish Hussars:
>WO95/1185/2 August 1914 – Dec. 1916, WO95/1164/2 Jan. 1917 – Feb. 1918,
>WO95/1115/1 March 1918 – Feb. 1919

Irish Guards:
1st: WO95/1342/4 August 1914 – July 1915, WO95/1216/1 August 1915 – Jan. 1919
2nd: WO95/1220/1 July 1915 – Jan. 1918, WO95/1226/3 Feb. 1918 – Oct. 1918,
        WO95/1220/2 Nov. 1918 – Jan. 1919

Royal Irish Regiment:
1st: WO95/2266/4 Nov. 1914 – Nov. 1915, WO95/4894 Dec. 1915 – Oct. 1916,
        WO95/4836 Nov. 1916 – August 1917, WO95/4583 Sept. 1917 – June 1919
2nd: WO95/1421/3 August 1914 – February 1915, WO95/1497/2 March 1915 –
        May 1916, WO95/1662/2 June 1916 – Sept. 1916, WO95/1979/1 Oct. 1916
        – April 1918, WO95/3111/3 May 1918 – May 1919
5th: WO95/4575 July 1915 – Sept. 1915, WO95/4832 Oct. 1915 – August 1917,
        WO95/4575 Sept. 1917 – March 1918, WO95/2823/1 April 1918 – Feb. 1919,
        WO95/1335/2 March 1919 – October 1919
6th: WO95/1970/3 Dec. 1915 – Feb. 1918
7th: WO95/1979/2 Sept. 1917 – May 1918, WO95/2330/3 June 1919 – Oct. 1919
8th: WO95/2615/3 May 1918 – April 1919
1st (Garrison): WO95/4444 Feb. 1916 – March 1918, WO95/4456 April 1918 – June 1918

Royal Inniskilling Fusiliers:
1st: WO95/4311 Jan.1915–28 Feb. 1916, WO95/2305/2 March 1916 – Jan. 1918,
        WO95/2510/1 Feb. 1918 – March 1919
2nd: WO95/1505/2 August 1914 – Dec. 1914, WO95/1350/1 1915, WO95/2397/1
        Jan. 1916 – Jan. 1918, WO95/2510/2 Feb. 1918 – April 1919
5th: WO95/4296 August 1915 – Sept. 1915, WO95/4838 Oct. 1915 – August 1917,
        WO95/4585 Sept. 1917– May 1918, WO95/3140/1 June 1918 – May 1919
6th: WO95/4296 July 1915 – Sept. 1915, WO95/4838 Oct. 1915 – August 1917,
        WO95/4585 Sept. 1917 – May 1918, WO95/2843/2 June 1918 – May 1919

7th:	WO95/1977/2 Feb. 1916 – August 1917
8th:	WO95/1977/3 Feb. 1916 – August 1917; 7/8th: WO95/1977/4 Sept. 1917 – May 1918, WO95/2336/1 June 1918 – Sept. 1919
9th:	WO95/2510/3 Oct. 1915 – April 1919
10th:	WO95/2510/4 Oct. 1915 – Jan. 1918
11th:	WO95/2510/5 Oct. 1915 – Feb. 1918
13th:	WO95/2606/1 June 1918 – April 1919

Royal Irish Rifles:

1st:	WO95/1730/4 August 1914 – Jan. 1918, WO95/2502/3 Feb.1918 – May 1919
2nd:	WO95/1415/1 August 1914 – Oct. 1915, WO95/2247/1 Nov. 1915 – Oct. 1917, WO95/2502/4 Nov. 1917 – March 1919
6th:	WO95/4296 July 1915 – August 1915, WO95/4835 Oct. 1915 – August 1917, WO95/4580 Sept. 1917 – May 1918
7th:	WO95/1975/2 Dec. 1915 – Nov. 1917
8th:	WO95/2503/1 Oct.1915 – August 1917
8/9th:	WO95/2503/3 Sept. 1917 – Jan. 1918
9th:	WO95/2503/2 Oct. 1915 –August 1917
10th:	WO95/2503/4 Oct. 1915 – Dec. 1917
11th:	WO95/2506/1 Oct. 1915 – Oct. 1917
13th:	WO95/2506/4 Nov. 1917 – Jan. 1918
12th:	WO95/2506/2 Oct. 1915 – March 1919
13th:	WO95/2506/3 Oct. 1915 – Oct. 1917
14th:	WO95/2511/1 Oct. 1915 – Feb. 1918
15th:	WO95/2503/5 Oct. 1915 – May 1919
16th:	WO95/2498/2 Oct. 1915 – April 1919

Royal Irish Fusiliers:

1st:	WO95/1482/1 August 1914 – July 1917, WO95/2502/2 August 1917 – Dec. 1917, WO95/2505/1 Feb. 1918 – Feb. 1919
2nd:	WO95/4895 Nov. 1915 – Oct. 1916, WO95/4838 Nov. 1916 – August 1917, WO95/4585 Sept. 1917 – June 1919
5th:	WO95/4296 June 1915 – Sept. 1915, WO95/4838 Oct. 1915 – August 1917, WO95/4585 Sept. 1917 – April 1918, WO95/1975/1 June 1918 – June 1919
6th:	WO95/4296 July 1915 – Sept. 1915, WO95/4838 Oct. 1915 – Oct. 1916
7th:	WO95/1978/1 Feb.1916 – Oct. 1916
8th:	WO95/1978/2 Feb.1916 – Oct. 1916
7/8th:	WO95/1978/3 Nov.1916 – Feb.1918
9th:	WO95/2505/2 Oct. 1915 – March 1919
11th:	WO95/1978/4 July 1918 – August 1918
2nd (Garrison):	WO95/4923 Jan. 1917 – July 1917
2nd (Garrison):	WO95/4803 August 1917 –April 1919

Connaught Rangers:
1st: WO95/3923/1 Aug. 1914 – Nov. 1915, (Medical Officer) WO95/3923/2 Aug. 1914 – Nov. 1915, (Medical Officer), WO95/5106 Jan. 1916, WO95/5106 Jan. 1916 – March 1918, WO95/4700 April 1918 – June 1919
2nd: WO95/13471 Aug. 1914 – Nov. 1914, WO95/3144/1 Feb. 1919 – April 1919, WO95/153 May 1921 – April 1922
5th: WO95/4296 July 1915 – Sept. 1915, WO95/4835 Oct. 1915 – Aug. 1917, WO95/4579 Sept. 1917 – May 1918, WO95/3144/2 June 1918 – Jan. 1919
6th: WO95/1970/2 Dec. 1915 – July 1918

Leinster Regiment:
1st: WO95/2266/3 Dec. 1914 – Oct. 1915, WO95/4895 Nov. 1915 – Oct. 1916, WO95/4834 Nov. 1916 – August 1917
2nd: WO95/1612/2 August 1914 – Oct.1915, WO95/2218/1 Nov. 1915 – Jan. 1918, WO95/2308/2 Feb. 1918 – June 1919
6th: WO95/4296 July 1915 – Sept. 1915, WO95/4835 Oct.1915 – August 1917, WO95/4579 Sept. 1917 – May 1918, WO95/3140/5 June 1918 – Sept. 1918
7th: WO95/1970/4 Dec. 1915 – Feb. 1918

Royal Munster Fusiliers:
1st: WO95/4310 Jan. 1915 – Feb. 1916, WO95/1975/3 March 1916 – Oct. 1916, WO95/1971/1 Nov. 1916 – April 1918, WO95/2985/1 May 1918 – May 1919
2nd: WO95/1279 August 1914 – Jan.1918, WO95/1975/4 Feb. 1918 – May 1918, WO95/2837/1 May 1918 – May 1919, WO95/1279/1 August 1914 – Dec. 1915, WO95/1279/2 1915–1916
6th: WO95/4296 August 1915 – Sept. 1915, WO95/4837 Jan. 1916 – August 1917, WO95/4583 Sept. 1917 – April 1918
7th: WO95/4296 July 1915 – Sept. 1915, WO95/4837 Oct.1915 – Oct. 1916
8th: WO95/1971/2 Dec. 1915 – Nov. 1916
9th: WO95/1975/5 Dec. 1915 – May 1916

Royal Dublin Fusiliers:
1st: WO95/4310 Jan.1915 – March 1916, WO95/2301 March 1916 – Sept. 1917, WO95/1974/1 Oct. 1917 – April 1918, WO95/2301/2 May 1918 – May 1919
2nd: WO95/1481/4 August 1914 – Nov. 1916, WO95/1974/2 Nov. 1916 – April 1918, June 1918– April 1918
6th: WO95/4296 July 1915 – Sept. 1915, WO95/4836 Oct. 1915 – August 1917, WO95/4583 Sept. 1917 – June 1918, WO95/3140/2 July 1918 – April 1919
7th: WO95/4296 July 1915 – Sept. 1915, WO95/4583 Sept. 1917 – May 1918,
8th: WO95/1974/3 Dec. 1915 – Oct. 1917
9th: WO95/1974/4 Dec. 1915 – Oct. 1917
8/9th: WO95/1974/5 Nov. 1917 – Feb. 1918

10th: WO95/3118/4 August 1916 – June 1917
10th: WO95/1974/6 July 1917 – Feb. 1918

Misc. Regiments/Documents:
2nd Northamptonshire Regiment: (WO95/1722)
11th Highland Light Infantry: (WO95/1775/2)
10th Hampshire Regiment: (WO95/4296)
D. Haig, *Order of the Day,* 11 April 1918

Soldiers' Service Records, 1914–1918 (WO363)
Soldiers' Documents from Pension Claims (WO364)
War Cabinet Meeting Papers, No. 374, 27 March 1918 (CAB/23/5)

Imperial War Museum

Dept. of Documents:
W. Lyon Papers, Documents. 4790
McIlwain Papers, Documents. 96/29/1
J.F.B. O'Sullivan Papers, Documents. 7155
D. Starret Papers, Documents. 6659

Sound Archive:
W. Flynn (IWM Catalogue 4103:1964)
R.B. Gillett (IWM Catalogue 19953 : 1965)
F.W.H. Holmes (IWM Catalogue No. 9147: 1985)
I. Powell (IWM Catalogue 16448: 1985–05–10)
T.T.H. Verschoyle (IWM Catalogue 8185: 1984)

Public Record Office of Northern Ireland, Belfast
Adams Papers (PRONI: D/3574/E6/2/7).
Carrothers Papers (PRONI: D/1973)
Central Committee for the Organisation of recruitment in Ireland Papers (PRONI D/ 3809/ 1)
J. Hutchinson, *Early Reminiscences of a Royal Irish Rifleman, 1917–1919* (PRONI, D3804)
McCrory Journals (PRONI D1868)
Newton and Anderson Papers (PRONI D961/8)
North Irish Horse Papers (PRONI D1482)
Nugent Papers (PRONI: D/3835/E/2/545)
O'Donovan Papers (PRONI D/ 3574/ E6/ 9)
Penrose Papers (PRONI D/3574/E6/7/23)
Pollock Papers (PRONI D1581)
RIC Files (PRONI, MIC/448/53/78), (PRONI MICc/448/53)

National Archive of Ireland, Dublin

Dublin Metropolitan Police Files (Reels MFA/ 1/, MFA/ 2/ MFA/ 3)
Irish Solders' Wills 1914–1915 (NAI/ 2002/119)
Census Returns 1901
Census Returns 1911

Other Archive Material

Employee's Roll of Honour, Guinness Archives, St James' Gate, Dublin.

Captain George Berkeley Papers (Cork City and County Archives, IE CCA/PR12/56 /57).

Statement by Bulmer Hobson on Gun-Running at Howth and Kilcoole (Irish Bureau of Military History, Dublin, 5 November 1947, W.S. 53).

Committee of the Irish National War Memorial: *Ireland's Memorial Records 1914–1918,* 8 Vols. (Dublin: Maunsell, 1923).

Commonwealth War Graves Commission: *The War Graves of the British Empire, Twelve Tree Copse Cemetery Helles, Gallipoli.* (London, 1925; rep., Maidenhead, 1979).

De Ruvigny's Roll of Honour 1914–24 (CD-ROM, United Kingdom: Navy & Military Press Ltd.).

HMSO, Army Medal Office, *Medal Index Cards 1914–1918.*

HMSO, *Calendar of the Grants of Probate and Letters of Administration made in the Probate Registries of the High Court of Justice in England* 1915 (Principal Probate Registry 26 December 1915.

HMSO, *The Irish Uprising, 1914–1921 Papers of the Parliamentary Archive* (London: The Stationary Office, 2000).

HMSO, *Report of the Departmental Committee …to Inquire into the Housing Conditions of the Working Classes in the City of Dublin* (London: HMSO, 1914), pp. 1–53.

HMSO, War Office, *Officers/Soldiers Died in the Great War,* (Hayward, Suffolk: HMSO, 1989).

Household Cavalry & Cavalry of the Line, Vol.1 Pt.1; *Foot Guards (inc. Guards Machine Gun Regt)* Vol.4 Pt.5; *Royal Irish Regiment,* Vol.22 Pt.23; *Royal Inniskilling Fusiliers,* Vol.22 Pt.32; *Duke of Cornwall's Light Infantry,* Vol.35 Pt.37; *Hampshire Regiment,* Vol.38 Pt.41; *Black Watch (Royal Highlanders),* Vol.43 Pt.46; *Highland Light Infantry,* Vol.60 Pt.63; *Seaforth Highlanders (Ross-shire Buffs, the Duke of Albany's),* Vol.61 Pt.64; *Queen's Own (Cameron) Highlanders,* Vol.63 Pt.66; *Royal Irish Rifles,* Vol. 64, Pt. 67; *Princess Victoria's (Royal Irish Fusiliers),* Vol. 64, Pt. 68; *Connaught Rangers,* Vol. 64, Pt. 69; *Princess Louis's Argyll & Sutherland Highlanders,* Vol.65 Pt.70; *Prince of Wales's Leinster Regiment (Royal Canadians),* Vol.66 Pt.71, *Royal Munster Fusiliers,* Vol.66 Pt.72; *Royal Dublin Fusiliers,* Vol.66 Pt.73; *Labour Corps,* Vol.72 Pt.80.

Contemporary Newspapers and Periodicals

Anglo-Celt, Armagh Guardian, Belfast Newsletter, Boston Evening Transcript, Connaught Tribune, Cork Constitution, Daily Mail, Derry People and Donegal News, Derry Standard, Dublin Evening Mail, Kildare Observer, Irish Examiner, Irish Independent, Irish Times, London

Gazette, Londonderry Sentinel, Longford Leader, The Cornell Daily Sun, The Great War, The Irish Volunteer, The Times History of the War, The War Illustrated, Tuam Herald, Skibbereen Eagle, Ulster Herald, Weekly Irish Times

Publications and Articles

Allen, W.M. 'A Veteran Recalls' in B. Irvine, *Battle Lines*, No.16 (Journal of the Somme Association, 1999).

Aspinall–Oglander C.F. and Becke, A.F., *Military Operations: Gallipoli*, 2 Vols. (London: Heinemann, 1929–1932).

Atherton, I. and Morgan, K., 'The battlefield war memorial: commemoration and the battlefield site from the Middle Ages to the modern era', *Journal of War and Culture Studies*, Vol.4, No.3 (2011).

Bartlett, T. and Jeffery, K. (eds), *A Military History of Ireland* (Cambridge: Cambridge University Press, 1996).

Beckett I.F.W. and Simpson, K., *A Nation in Arms: a social study of the British Army in the First World War* (Manchester: Manchester University Press, 1985).

Beckett, I.F.W., *The Army and the Curragh Incident, 1914* (London: Army Records Society, 1986).

Bew P., *John Redmond* (Dundalk: Dundalgan Press, 1996).

Biggs-Davison J. and Chowdharry-Best, G.C. *The Cross of St Patrick: The Catholic Unionist Tradition in Ireland* (London: Kensal Press, 1984).

Blake R., *The Private Papers of Douglas Haig* (London: Eyre and Spottiswoode, 1953).

Bourke, J. (ed.), *The Misfit Soldier: Edward Casey's War Story 1914–1918*, (Cork: Cork University Press, 1999).

Bowman, T., *Irish Regiments in the Great War, Discipline and Morale* (Manchester: Manchester University Press, 2003).

Bridges, G.T.M., *Alarms and Excursions: Reminiscences of a Soldier* (Longmans, Green and Co., London, 1938)

Brown, M., 'Journey Back to Hell: Excavations at Serre on the Somme', *Current World Archaeology*, 10 (2005)

Buckland, P., *Irish Unionism 2: Ulster Unionism and the Origins of Northern Ireland, 1886–1922* (Dublin: Gill & Macmillan, 1973).

Burke, T., 'Fancy the Royal Irish captured Moore Street', *Irish Sword*, Vol. XXVIII, No. 1129 (Summer 2011).

Burrowes, A.R., *The 1st Battalion, The Faugh-A-Ballaghs in the Great War* (Aldershot: Gale and Polden, n/d).

Byrne, C., *The Harp and Crown: The History of the 5th (Royal Irish) Lancers, 1901–1922* (Lulu Books, 2008).

Callan, P., 'Recruiting for the British Army in Ireland during the First World War', *The Irish Sword*, XVII, 66 (1987).

Calvert, W., 'A Veteran Recalls' in B. Irvine, *Battle Lines*, No. 12 (Journal of the Somme Association, 1996).

Carlyon, L., *Gallipoli* (London: Random House, 2001).

Casey, P., 'Irish Casualties in the First World War', *The Irish Sword*, Vol. XX, No. 81 (1997).

Caulfield, M., *The Easter Rebellion* (London: Four Square Books, 1965).

Cecil, H. and Liddle, P. (eds), *Facing Armageddon: The First World War Experienced* (London: Leo Cooper, 1996).

Cooper, B., *The Tenth Irish Division in Gallipoli* (London: Herbert Jenkins, 1918).

Cooper, M., *We Who Knew* (Sussex: Book Guild, 1994).

Corns, C. and Hughes-Wilson, J., *Blindfolded and Alone, British Military Executions in the Great War* (London: Cassell, 2001).

Cowland, W.S., *10th and 11th Battalions the Hampshire Regiment* (Winchester: Warren, 1930).

Crozier, F.P., *A Brass Hat in No Man's Land* (London: Everyman, 1940).

Dallas, G. and Gill, D., *The Unknown Army: Mutinies in the British Army in World War 1* (London: Verso, 1985).

Davison, C., (ed.) *The Burgoyne Diaries* (London: Thomas Harmsworth Publishing, 1985).

De Groot, G.J., *Blighty – British society in the era of the Great War* (Essex: Longman, 1996).

De Montmorency, H., *Sword & Stirrup*, (London: Bell and Sons, 1936).

Denman, T., 'The Catholic Irish Soldier in the First World War: The "Racial Environment"', *Irish Historical Studies*, XXVII, 108 (1991).

Denman, T., *Ireland's Forgotten Soldiers* (Blackrock: Irish Academic Press, 1992).

Denman, T., *A Lonely Grave* (Blackrock: Irish Academic Press, 1995).

Dixon, N., *On the Psychology of Military Incompetence* (London: Pimlico, 1994).

Doherty R. and Truesdale, D., *Irish Winners of the Victoria Cross* (Dublin: Four Courts Press, 2000).

Doyle, P., Barton, P. and Vandewalle, J., 'Archaeology of a Great War dugout: Beecham Farm, Passchedaele, Belgium', *Journal of Conflict Archaeology*, 1 (2005).

Dungan, M., *Irish Voices from the Great War* (Blackrock: Irish Academic Press, 1995).

Dungan, M., *They Shall Not Grow Old* (Dublin: Four Courts Press, 1997).

Edmonds, J. *Military Operations: France and Belgium, 1918*, Vol 2, (London: Macmillan, 1937).

Evans, R., *Rituals of Retribution* (Oxford: Oxford University Press, 1996).

Ewing, J., *History of the 9th (Scottish) Division* (London: John Murray, 1921).

Falls, C., *The History of the 36th (Ulster) Division* (Belfast: McCaw, Stevenson & Orr, 1922).

Falls, C., *The History of the First Seven battalions, Royal Irish Rifles, in the Great War* (Aldershot: Gale and Polden Ltd, 1925).

Falls, C and Beck, A.F., *The History of the Great War: Military Operations, Macedonia*, Vol. 1 (London: HMSO, 1933).

Farrah-Hockley, A., *Goughie* (London: Granada, 1975).

Feilding, R., *War Letters to a Wife: France and Flanders 1915–1919* (London: The Medici Society, 1929).

Fergusson, J., *The Curragh Incident* (London: Faber and Faber, 1964).

Fitzpatrick, D., 'Militarism in Ireland' in T. Bartlett and K. Jeffery (eds.), *A Military History of Ireland* (Cambridge: Cambridge University Press, 1996).

Flower, N. (ed.), *History of the Great War,* 9 Vols. (London: Waverley Press, 1917).

Fox, F., *History of the Royal Inniskilling Fusiliers in the Great War* (London: Constable, 1928).

Fraser, A., 'The "Ocean Villas" Project –Update: World War One Battlefield Archaeology on the Somme', *Battlefields Review*, No. 28 (2003).

Fraser, A., and Brown, M., 'Mud, Blood and Missing Men: excavations at Serre, Somme, France', *Journal of Conflict Archaeology*, 3 (2007).

Garvin, T., *Nationalist Revolutionaries in Ireland* (Oxford: Oxford University Press, 1988).

Geohagan, S., *The Campaigns and History of the Royal Irish Regiment*, Vol. II (London: Blackwood & Sons, 1927).

Gibb, H., *Record of the 4th Royal Irish Dragoon Guards in the Great War 1914–1918* (Canterbury, 1925).

Gibbon, M., *Inglorious Soldier* (London: Hutchinson, 1968).

Gilbert, M., *The First World War* (London: BCA, 1994).

Gough, H., *The Fifth Army* (London: Hodder and Stoughton, 1931).

Graves, R., *Goodbye to All That* (London: Penguin, 1960).

Greenald, J., 'In the forefront of duty: Orangeism in World War One' in D. Hume (ed.), *Battles Beyond the Boyne – Orangeism in the Ranks, 1786–2000* (Belfast, 2002).

Gregory, A. and Paseta, S., *Ireland and the Great War – A war to unite us all?* (Manchester: Manchester University Press, 2002).

Gwynn, D., *The Life of John Redmond* (London: Harrap, 1932).

Gwynn, S., *John Redmond's Last Years* (London: Edward Arnold, 1919).

Haines, K., *Fred Crawford – Carson's Gunrunner* (Donaghadee: Ballyhay Books, 2009).

Hally, P.J., 'The Easter 1916 Rising in Dublin: the Military Aspects, Pt.1', *Irish Sword,* vii, (29) (1966).

Hamblin, J., *We Remember Those Who Lost Their Lives in the First World War* (London: Lloyds, 2014).

Hammerton, J.A., *A Popular History of the Great War*, Vol. II (London: Amalgamated Press, 1933).

Hanna, H., *The Pals at Suvla Bay* (Dublin: Ponsonby, 1916).

Harris, H.E.D., *Irish Regiments in the First World War* (Cork: Mercier Press, 1969).

Hart, P., 'Michael Collins and the assignation of Sir Henry Wilson', *Irish Historical Studies*, Vol.28, No.110 (Nov. 1992).

Harvey, J.R. and Cape H.A., *History of the 5th (Royal Irish) Regiment of Dragoons from 1689–1799, Afterwards the 5th (Royal Irish) Lancers from 1858–1921* (Aldershot: Gale & Polden, 1923).

Haythornthwaite, P., *Gallipoli 1915*, Campaign Series, 8 (London: Osprey, 1999).

Henry, W., *Galway and the Great War* (Cork: Mercier Press, 2006).

Heslinga, M.W., *The Irish Border as a Cultural Divide: A contribution to the Study of Regionalism in the British Isles* (New York: Assen, 1971).

Hickman, M., *Religion, Class and Identity* (Aldershot: Avebury, 1995).

Hitchcock, F.C., *Stand To: a Diary of the Trenches* (London: Hurst and Blackett, 1937).

Hodges, P., '"They don't like it up "em!": Bayonet fetishisation in the British Army during the First World War', *Journal of War and Culture Studies*, 1, 2, (2008).

Holmes, R., *War Walks* (London: BBC Books, 1997).

Horne, C.F., (ed.), *Source Records of the Great War,* Vol. II (New York: National Alumni, 1923).

Horne, J. (Ed.), *Our War: Ireland and the Great War* (Dublin: Royal Irish Academy, 2008).

Horne, J. and Madigan, E. (Eds), *Towards Commemoration: Ireland in War and Revolution, 1912–1923* (Dublin: Royal Irish Academy, 2013).

Hume, D., (ed.), *Battles Beyond the Boyne – Orangeism in the Ranks, 1786–2000* (Belfast, 2002).

Hynes, S., *A War Imagined* (London: Pimlico, 1990).

James, E.A., *British Regiments 1914–1918* (East Sussex: Naval & Military Press, 1998).

Jeffery, K., 'The Post-war army' in I.F.W. Beckett and K. Simpson, *A Nation in Arms: a social study of the British Army in the First World War* (Manchester: Manchester University Press, 1985a).

Jeffery, K., *The Military Correspondence of Field Marshal Sir Henry Wilson, 1918–1922* (Army Records Society, 1985b).

Jeffery, K., *Ireland and the Great War* (Cambridge: Cambridge University Press, 2000).

Jeffery, K., *Field Marshal Sir Henry Wilson: a political solider* (Oxford: Oxford University Press, 2006).

Jeffery, K., 'The road to Asia and the Grafton Hotel, Dublin: Ireland in the British world', *Irish Historical Studies*, Vol.36, No. 142 (November 2008).

Jervis, H.S., *The 2nd Munsters in France* (Aldershot: Gale and Polden, 1922).

Johnson, F.W.E., *A Short Record of the Services and Experiences of the 5th Battalion, Royal Irish Fusiliers in the Great War* (n/p, 1919).

Johnstone, T., *Orange, Green and Khaki* (Dublin: Gill & McMillan, 1992).

Jourdain, H.F.N., *History of the Connaught Rangers,* 3 Vols. (London: Royal United Services Institution, 1924–1928).

Kerr, S.P., *What the Irish Regiments Have Done* (London: Unwin, 1916).

Kipling, R., *The Irish Guards in the Great War – 1st Battalion,* (Staplehurst: Spellmount, 1997, rep. 1923a).

Kipling, R., *The Irish Guards in the Great War – 2nd Battalion,* (Staplehurst: Spellmount, 1997, rep. 1923b).

Laffin, J., *Damn the Dardanelles* (London: Osprey, 1980).

Laird, F., *Personal Experiences of the Great War* (Dublin: Eason & Son, 1925).

Laurie, G.B., *History of the Royal Irish Rifles* (Aldershot: Gale and Polden Ltd, 1914).

Lavery, F., *Great Irishmen in War and Politics* (Dublin: A. Melrose Ltd, 1920).

Law, F., *Man at Arms* (London: HarperCollins, 1985).

Lawson, T., '"The Free-Masonry of Sorrow"? English National Identities and the Memorialization of the Great War in Britain, 1919–1931', *History and Memory*, Vol. 20, No. 1 (2008).

Ledwidge, F., 'Soliloquy', *The Complete Poems of Francis Ledwidge* (London: Brentano's, 1919).

Leonard, J., 'The Reactions of Irish Officers in the British Army to the Easter Rising of 1916' in H. Cecil and P. Liddle (eds), *Facing Armageddon: The First World War Experienced* (London: Leo Cooper, 1996).

Liddell Hart, B.H., *A History of the Great War* (London: BCA, 1970).

Lucy, J.F., *There's a Devil in the Drum* (London: Faber and Faber, 1938).

Martin, P., 'Dulce et Decorum: Irish nobles and the Great War, 1914–1918' in A. Gregory and S. Pašata, *Ireland and the Great War – A war to unite us all?* (Manchester: Manchester University Press, 2002) pp.28–48.

Martin, F.X., 'The 1916 Rising – a Coup d'etat or a "bloody protest"?' *Studia Hiberncia*, vii (1967), p.131.

Matless, D., 'Regional Surveys and Local Knowledges: The Geographical Imagination in Britain, 1918–39', *Transactions of the Institute of British Geographers,* No. 17 (1992).

McBride, G., 'A Veteran Recalls', B. Irvine, *Battle Lines*, No.17 (Journal of the Somme Association, 2000).

McCance, S., *The History of the Royal Munster Fusiliers,* Vol. 2 (Aldershot: Gale and Polden, 1927).

McClean, C., 'A Veteran Recalls' in B. McKeen, *Battle Lines*, No.3 (Journal of the Somme Association, 1991).

McConnell, W., 'A Veteran Recalls', B. Irvine, *Battle Lines*, No.8 (Journal of the Somme Association, 1993).

McGill, P., *The Great Push* (London: Jenkins, 1916).

McGuicken, C., 'The 13th Battalion (1st County Down Volunteers) The Royal Irish Rifles in the First World War' in *County Down at War* (Down Survey, 2004).

McHugh, R., *Dublin 1916* (London: Arlington Books, 1966).

Meleady, D., *John Redmond: The National Leader* (Sallins: Merrion, 2014).

Meunger, E., *The British Military Dilemma in Ireland: Occupational Politics 1864–1914* (Dublin: Gill & Macmillan, 1991).

Middlebrook, M., *The Kaiser's Battle* (London: BCA, 1983).

Middlebrook, M., *The First Day on the Somme* (London: Penguin, 1984).

Mitchell, G.S., *Three Cheers for the Derrys!* (Londonderry: Yes Publications, 1991).

Montgomery Hyde, H., *Famous Trials: Roger Casement* (London: Penguin, 1963).

Morgan, G., 'The Dublin Pals' in S. Alyn Stacey (ed.), *Essays on Heroism in Sport in Ireland and France* (Lewiston, Queenston and Lampeter: The Edwin Mellen Press, 2003).

Morgan, G., *University of Dublin, Trinity College, War Dead: Dardanelles/ Gallipoli 1915* (n/p, 2009).

Morrissey, J., 'Ireland's Great War: Representation, Public Space and the Place of Dissonant Heritages', *Journal of the Galway Archaeological and Historical Society*, 58, (2006).

Morton, H.V., *In Search of England* (London: Methuen, 1933).

Myers, K., *Ireland's Great War* (Dublin: Lilliput Press, 2014).

Nevinson, H.W., *The Dardanelles Campaign,* (London: Nesbitt, 1918).

Novick, B., *Conceiving revolution: Irish nationalist propaganda during the First World War* (Dublin: Four Courts, 2001).

Oram, G., *Worthless Men, Race, eugenics and the death penalty in the British Army during the First World War* (London: Francis Boutie Publishers, 1998).

Orr, P., *The Road to the Somme* (Belfast: Blackstaff Press, 1987).

Orr, P., 'The road to Belgrade: the experiences of the 10th (Irish) Division in the Balkans' in A. Gregory and S. Pašeta, *Ireland and the Great War, 'A War to Unite Us All?'* (Manchester: Manchester University Press, 2002).

Osburn, A., *Unwilling Passenger* (London: Faber and Faber, 1932).

Osgood, R., *The Unknown Warrior – The archaeology of the common soldier* (Stroud: Sutton, 2005).

Pedroncini, G., *Les Mutineries de 1917* (Paris : Presses Universitaires de France, 1967), pp.3–9.

Perry, N., 'Nationality in the Irish Infantry Regiments in the First World War', *War and Society*, 12, 1, (May 1994).

Phoenix, E. *Northern Nationalism: Nationalist Politics, Partition and the Catholic Minority in Northern Ireland, 1890–1940* (Belfast: Ulster Historical Foundation, 1994).

Plowman, M., 'Irish Republicans and the Indo-German Conspiracy of World War I', *New Hibernia Review* 7, 3, (2003).

Pollard, T., and Banks, I., 'Not so quiet on the Western Front: progress and prospect in the archaeology of the First World War', *Journal of Conflict Archaeology*, Vol. 3 (2007).

Pollard, T., Barton, P. and Banks, I., *The investigation of possible mass graves at Pheasant Wood, Fromelles* (GUARD Report, 120005, 2007).

Pound, R., *The Lost Generation* (London: Constable, 1964).

Price, J., 'The Ocean Villas Project: Archaeology in the service of remembrance' in N. Saunders, (ed.) *Matters of Conflict: Material culture, memory and the First World War,* (London: Routledge, 2004).

Price, J., 'Orphan Heritage: Issues in managing the heritage of the Great War in northern France and Belgium', *Journal of Conflict Archaeology*, Vol. 1 (2006).

Reid, W., *Architect of Victory – Douglas Haig* (Edinburgh: Birlinn, 2009).

Robbins, K., *The First World War* (Oxford: Oxford University Press, 1984).

Robbins, K., *Cultural Traditions in Northern Ireland: Varieties of Britishness* (Belfast: Inst. Of Irish Studies, Queen's University, 1990).

Robertshaw, A., and Kenyon, D., *Digging the Trenches: The Archaeology of the Western Front* (Barnhurst: Pen and Sword, 2008).

Robertson, N., *The Crowned Harp* (Dublin: A. Figgis, 1960).

Roth, A., '"The German Soldier is not Tactful": Sir Roger Casement and the Irish Brigade' in 'Germany during the First World War', *Irish Sword*, XIX, No. 78 (1995).

Ryan, D., *The Rising* (Dublin, 1949).

Samuels A.P.I. and 'D.G.S.', *With the Ulster Division in France* (Belfast: W. Mullan & Son, n/d).

Saunders, N., (ed.) *Matters of Conflict: material culture, memory and the First World War* (London: Routledge, 2004).

Scott, P.T., *'Dishonoured': The 'Colonel's Surrender' at St Quentin, The Retreat from Mons, August 1914* (London: Tom Donovan Publishing, 1994).

Sheehy-Skeffington, H., 'A Pacifist Dies' in R. McHugh, *Dublin 1916* (London: Arlington Books, 1966).

Siggins, G. *Green Days: Cricket in Ireland, 1792–2005* (Stroud: History Press, 2005).

Skilbeck-Smith, R., *A Subaltern in Macedonia and Palestine* (London: Mitre Press, 1930).

Stanley, J., *Ireland's Forgotten Tenth; a brief history of the 10th (Irish) Division 1914–1918, Turkey, Macedonia and Palestine* (Newtownards: Somme Association, 2003).

Steel, N., and Hart, P., *Defeat at Gallipoli* (London: Macmillan, 1994).

Steel, N., *Gallipoli* (Barnsley: Leo Cooper, 1999).

Stewart, A.T.Q., *The Ulster Crisis* (London: Faber & Faber, 1967).

Stewart, A.T.Q., *Carson* (Dublin: Gill & Macmillan, 1981).

Street, C.J.C. ('I.O.'), *The Administration of Ireland, 1920* (London: Philip Allan & Co., 1921).

Taylor, J., *The 1st Royal Irish Rifles in the Great War* (Dublin: Four Courts Press, 2002).

Terraine, J., *The Great War* (Ware: Wordsworth Editions Ltd., 1997).

Townsend, C., *Desert Hell – The British Invasion of Mesopotamia* (Harvard: Harvard University Press, 2011).

Vere-Laurie, F., (ed.), *Letters of Lt.-Col. George Brenton Laurie, 1st Royal Irish Rifles* (Aldershot: Gale and Polden, 1921).

Walker, R.W. and Buckland, C. (eds), *Citations of the Distinguished Conduct Medal, 1914–1920* (East Sussex: Naval and Military Press, 2007).

Walker, G.A.C., *The Book of the 7th Inniskilling Fusiliers* (Dublin: Brindley, 1920).

Warwick-Haller, A. and S. (eds), *Letters from Dublin, Easter 1916: Alfred Fannin's Diary of the Rising* (Dublin: Irish Academic Press, 1995).

White, S., *The Terrors – 16th (Pioneers) Royal Irish Rifles* (Belfast: Somme Association, 1996).

Whitton, F.E., *The History of the Prince of Wales's Leinster Regiment* Vol.2 (Aldershot: Gale & Polden, 1926).

Wilkinson, N., *The Dardanelles* (London: Longmans, 1915).

Wylly, H.C., *Crown and Company: the Historical Records of the Second Battalion, Royal Dublin Fusiliers*, Vol. 3 (Aldershot: Gale and Polden, 1922).

Wylly, H.C., *Neill's Blue Caps: the History of the First Battalion, Royal Dublin Fusiliers*, Vol. 2 (Aldershot: Gale and Polden, 1925).

Yeates, P., *A City in Wartime: Dublin 1914–1918* (Dublin: Gill & Macmillan, 2012).

Index